THE

ENGLISH IN AMERICA

THE MIDDLE COLONIES

THE ENGLISH IN AMERICA

THE MIDDLE COLONIES

BY

J. A. Doyle

HERITAGE BOOKS
2009

HERITAGE BOOKS
AN IMPRINT OF HERITAGE BOOKS, INC.

Books, CDs, and more—Worldwide

For our listing of thousands of titles see our website
at
www.HeritageBooks.com

A Facsimile Reprint
Published 2009 by
HERITAGE BOOKS, INC.
Publishing Division
100 Railroad Ave. #104
Westminster, Maryland 21157

*From the edition of 1907
London*

— Publisher's Notice —
In reprints such as this, it is often not possible to remove blemishes from the original. We feel the contents of this book warrant its reissue despite these blemishes and hope you will agree and read it with pleasure.

International Standard Book Numbers
Paperbound: 978-0-7884-1008-6
Clothbound: 978-0-7884-8286-1

PREFACE.

This volume is the fourth of the series, three of which appeared some time ago, under the title of 'The English in America.'[1] It brings the history of the Middle Colonies down to the point where I left that of the Northern and Southern, *i.e.* the accession of the House of Hanover.

A fifth volume, 'The Colonies under the House of Hanover,' which is published at the same time as this, deals collectively with the whole body of colonies from that date down to the beginning of those disputes which ended in separation from the Mother Country.

JON. A. DOYLE.

ALL SOULS' COLLEGE, OXFORD:
    October 1906.

---

[1] *Virginia, Maryland, and the Carolinas,* 1882; *The Puritan Colonies,* 2 vols. 1886.

CONTENTS.

CHAPTER I.

FOUNDATION OF NEW NETHERLANDS.

	PAGE
Dutch as colonists	1
The early Dutch voyagers	4
Henry Hudson	7
The Dutch in the Hudson River	8
The Northern Company	9
Treaty at Tawasentha	10
The Dutch West India Company	11
Colonial progress of the Company	14
The patroons	16
Small proprietors	17
Increase of population	18
Position of the Governor	19
Peter Minuit	20
Wouter Van Twiller	20
Van Twiller and De Vries	21
Encroachments from New England	22
William Kieft	22
The Twelve and the Indian War	24
The Twelve and Kieft	25
Troubles with the Indians	26
Attacks on Kieft	27
The Council of Eight	28
End of the Indian war	29
Want of constitutional machinery	31
Report of the 'Rekenkammer'	32
Peter Stuyvesant	33
Representative government introduced	34
Municipal institutions	36
New Amsterdam becomes a city	38
Action of the town council	40
Stuyvesant's reform	42
Conference of delegates	43

CONTENTS.

	PAGE
Second conference	45
English influence	45
The greater burghership	47
Inefficiency of the Company	50
Increase of population	51
Religious condition of the colony	52
Independent congregations	53
Quakers in New Netherlands	55
Education	59
Industrial life	61
Dealings with Indians	63
Outbreak of war, 1655	64
Troubles with Indians in 1658	66
Dealings with the Five Nations	67
The Swedish colony	68
William Usselinx	69
Usselinx and Gustavus Adolphus	71
The Swedes at Swanendael	72
Formation of a Swedish Company	73
The Swedes on the Schuylkill	74
Growth of the Swedish colony	76
Hostility between Dutch and Swedes	78
Policy of Stuyvesant towards the Swedes	80
Further efforts by Sweden	81
Overthrow of the Swedish colony by Stuyvesant	83
Foundation of New Amstel	85
Difficulties besetting New Amstel	88
Proposed migration from New Haven	91
The Mennonites	92
Outward appearance of New Amsterdam	94
Education in New Netherlands	96

CHAPTER II.

THE ENGLISH CONQUEST.

New Netherlands gradually Anglicized	98
Treaty of Hartford	99
English settlers in New Netherlands	100
Stuyvesant favours the English	103
Disputes between Dutch and English	104
English territorial claims	106
Disputes between the Dutch and Maryland	107
Changed policy of England	110
Disputes between the Dutch and Connecticut	110
John Scott	112

CONTENTS.

	PAGE
Carteret and Berkeley	114
Calumnies against New Netherlands	115
Duke of York's patent	116
Moral aspect of the conquest	117
Grant to Carteret and Berkeley	118
Arrangements for enforcing the Duke's claim	119
Richard Nicolls	120
Defenceless condition of New Netherlands	121
Nicolls opens negotiations	125
Convention at Gravesend	128
Conquest at New Amsterdam	129
Submission of the rest of the colony	132
Carr on the Delaware	134
Nicolls's policy	135
System of legislation	136
Convention at Heemstede	137
Influence of New England	140
The Duke's laws	141
Ecclesiastical system	142
Penal system	143
Nicolls's treatment of the Dutch	144
Affairs at Albany	145
New York to be a check on New England	147
No disaffection among the Dutch	148
Treaty of Breda	149
Altered relations of the English colonies to France	150
Dealings with the Five Nations	151
The French and the Indians	152
Effect of the grant to Carteret and Berkeley	158
The New Jersey concessions	159
Settlement of New Jersey	160
Career and character of Nicolls	162

CHAPTER III.

THE DUTCH RECONQUEST.

Francis Lovelace	164
Disaffection on Long Island	164
General policy of the Proprietor	167
Affairs of New Jersey	169
Insurrection on the Delaware	169
Attack from Maryland	170
Outbreak of war with Holland	172
Dutch fleet threatens New York	173
Capture of New York	174

CONTENTS.

	PAGE
Action of the Dutch commanders	175
The colony under Colve	177
Disaffection among the English inhabitants	178
Motives of the Dutch for retaining the colony	181
Final cession of the colony by the Dutch	182

CHAPTER IV.

NEW YORK UNDER ANDROS AND DONGAN.

Altered position of New York	183
Position of Carteret and Berkeley	185
Fresh grant to Carteret	185
Andros appointed Governor	187
He reaches New York	188
Negotiations with Colve	188
Court martial on Manning	189
Demand for representative institutions	190
Dealings of Andros with New England	193
Ecclesiastical matters	195
Grievances of the colonists against Andros	197
Dispute about customs	198
Further demand for representation	199
Probable influence of Penn with the Duke	201
Dongan becomes Governor	202
His instructions	204
First Assembly summoned	205
Composition of the Assembly	206
The 'Charter of Liberties'	207
Revenue Act	208
Growth of English feeling and influence	209
Proposed incorporation of New York	210
Disputes with New Jersey	210
Disputes with Connecticut	211
The Proprietor becomes King	212
Incorporation of New York and Albany	212
Fresh land patents	213
Representative system annulled	214
James II.'s policy of consolidation	216
Dongan's anti-Canadian policy	216
The French and the Five Nations	217
Policy of Frontenac	219
French missions among the Five Nations	221
Frontenac replaced by De la Barre	222
Dongan's dealings with the French and the Indians	223
Policy of the Iroquois	225

CONTENTS. xi

	PAGE
Denonville succeeds De la Barre	226
Treaty of Whitehall	228
Policy of Dongan	229
He is supported by the King	231
James II.'s projects of colonial union	232

CHAPTER V.

THE REVOLUTION IN NEW YORK.

Constitution of the new province	236
Andros appointed Governor	238
French scheme of invasion	239
Mohawks invade Canada	239
News of the Revolution reaches New York	240
Nicholson's dispute with Leisler	241
Disaffection on Long Island	242
Malcontents seize the fort	243
Progress of the Revolution	244
Assumption of authority by Leisler	246
The New York convention	246
Anti-Papal panic	248
Elections held under Leisler	250
Position of Albany	251
The Albany convention	251
Preparations against French invasion	252
Albany makes itself independent of Leisler	253
Further encroachments by Leisler	255
Proceedings of the Home Government	255
Leisler usurps the governorship	256
An anti-Leislerite party	259
Dealings with the Five Nations	260
French scheme of invasion	261
Destruction of Schenectady	262
Violent conduct of Leisler	263
He calls an Assembly	264
Proposes a colonial convention	265
Failure of the campaign	266
John Schuyler's raid	267
The Assembly meet	267
Decline of Leisler's influence	268
Apathy of the English Government	269
Col. Sloughter appointed Governor	270
His arrival delayed	271
Defiant attitude of Leisler	272
He fires on the troops	274

xii CONTENTS.

	PAGE
Arrival of Sloughter	275
Submission of Leisler	276
His trial	276
Sentence on Leisler	278
An Assembly summoned	279
Discussion as to Leisler's execution	280
Leisler and Millbore executed	282

CHAPTER VI.

NEW YORK AFTER THE REVOLUTION.

Effect of Leisler's rebellion	283
Attempts to define the constitution	285
Bill of Rights	285
Death of Sloughter	287
Appointment of Fletcher	287
His instructions	288
Dispute about Church endowments	289
John Nelson and his Indian policy	290
Brooke's and Nicolls's memorial	292
Fletcher advocates consolidation	292
Difficulties with the Five Nations	295
French invasion in 1692	297
Expedition under Peter Schuyler	298
Difficulties of the situation	299
Fletcher and the Mohawks	300
French negotiations with the Mohawks	301
Conference at Albany, 1694	302
Indian envoys at Quebec	303
Mohawk prisoner tortured by the French	304
Frontenac restores Fort Cataracouy	305
Frontenac's progress through the Mohawk country	306
Raid against Albany	307
Fletcher's corrupt dealings	308
His alliance with the Assembly	310
Bellomont succeeds Fletcher	311
The election of 1699	313
Changes in the Council and Assembly	315
The French and the Five Nations	316
Bellomont's Indian and anti-French policy	318
Lack of missionary enterprise	320
Livingstone's policy	320
Cornbury becomes Governor	322
An interregnum	324
Revival of the Leislerite party	325
Trial of Bayard	328

CONTENTS.

	PAGE
Cornbury's policy	329
His financial misdeeds	333
His dealings with the Assembly	334
Ecclesiastical dispute	336
Trial of M'Kemie	337
Cornbury's disputes with the Assembly	340
Cornbury recalled	342
Appointment and death of Lovelace	343
Unsuccessful expedition against Canada, 1709	345
Peter Schuyler brings Mohawk chiefs to England	346
Character of Hunter	348
He visits Albany	349
Lewis Morris	350
Dispute about salaries and fees	351
Treaty of Utrecht	354
Dispute with the French about Fort Frontenac	355
Hunter's land policy	356
The negro plot	356
The Palatines	360
General effect of Hunter's policy	361

CHAPTER VII.

SETTLEMENT OF NEW JERSEY.

Quakerism as a power in colonial history	363
New Jersey the earliest Quaker colony	366
The first settlement of New Jersey	367
Dealings of the Proprietors with the existing settlers	368
First General Assembly	370
Difficulties with Proprietors and settlers	372
Rebellion headed by James Carteret	373
The Dutch reconquest	375
Recovery of the colony by the Proprietors	377
Transfer to Penn and his partners	378
Fenwick's proceedings	379
Andros's dealings with Fenwick	380
Division of the province	381
Policy of Penn and his associates	383
Articles of the constitution	384
Foundation of Burlington	386
Fresh disputes between Andros and Fenwick	386
Position of Penn and his partners	387
Dispute with Andros about customs	388
Penn's remonstrance	389
Settlement of the dispute	391
Andros attempts to levy customs in East Jersey	392

CONTENTS.

	PAGE
Andros arrests Philip Carteret and summons an Assembly	394
Further disputes between Carteret and the settlers	396
Working of the proprietary system	399
Transfer of Carteret's proprietorship	400
Penn and some Scotchmen purchase East Jersey	402
Barclay appointed Governor	404
Assembly called; its proceedings	405
The Fundamental Constitutions	406
They are modified	410
Material condition of the colony	411
Effect of the change of Proprietors	412
Further emigration from Scotland	413
New York jealous of New Jersey	416
Dongan's dealings with New Jersey	417
Contest for Staten Island	417
State of West Jersey	420
Fenwick's settlement incorporated	422
New Jersey forms part of Andros's province	423
Surrender by the Proprietors	425
Daniel Cox	426
Dealings of Andros with New Jersey	427
The Revolution of 1688 in New Jersey	427
Formation of a new proprietary	429
Hamilton Governor of both provinces	430
Bass succeeds him	431
Difficulty with New York about customs	431
The case of the *Hester*	432
Disunited state of New Jersey	434
Morris and Bass	435
Disputes about the governorship	437
Surrender of the colony by the Proprietors	439

CHAPTER VIII.

NEW JERSEY A CROWN COLONY.

General condition of the colony	444
Want of money	445
Dealings with Indians	445
State of education	446
Religious condition of the colony	447
Cornbury appointed Governor	448
His instructions	449
Difficulties of his position	453
Cornbury and the Quakers	454
His quarrel with the Assembly	454
Assembly elected	454

CONTENTS. xv

	PAGE
Its proceedings	455
Action of the English Government	460
Assembly of 1707	461
Its dispute with Cornbury	462
Assembly of 1708	464
Lovelace's instructions	466
Importance of the dispute between Cornbury and the Assembly	467
Interregnum between Lovelace and Hunter	469
Hunter appointed Governor	471
His attitude towards parties	471
Sandford expelled from the Assembly	473
Disputes between the Council and the Representatives	474
Triumph of Hunter's party	475

CHAPTER IX.

THE FOUNDATION OF PENNSYLVANIA.

Absence of biographical interest in American history	479
Character of Penn	480
His scheme of colonization	484
His grant of territory	485
His charter	487
His intentions as a colonizer	489
His 'concessions'	490
His policy towards the natives	490
The first emigration	491
Constitutional arrangements	491
Frame of government	491
Further grant of territory from the Duke of York	497
Welsh settlers	498
Incorporation of Newcastle	499
The first Assembly	500
'The Great Body of Laws'	501
Foundation of Philadelphia	502
Penn's treaty with the Indians	503
The second Assembly	505
The new charter	506
Penn's account of the colony	507
His descriptions of the natives	508
Penn accused of Popery	510
Difficulty about the Indian trade	511
Establishment of a small Privy Council	512
Lack of activity in public life	513
Legislative measures	513
Growth of the colony	514
Alarm from the Indians	515

CONTENTS.

	PAGE
Penn's instructions to his deputy	516
George Keith	517
Dispute between the province and the territories	520
Pennsylvania included in Fletcher's commission	522
Penn's remonstrance	523
Fletcher at Philadelphia	524
His disputes with the Assembly	525
Restoration of Penn	529
Act of Settlement	530
Penn's protest against smuggling	531
Penn revisits the colony	532
His proprietorship in danger	533
His territorial dispute with the settlers	533
Demand of Delaware for separation	535
The new constitution	536
Charter granted to Philadelphia	537
Penn finally departs	537
His dispute with Quarry	537
Hamilton becomes Governor	538
Succeeded by Evans	539
Evans falls out with the Assembly	539
The Assembly attack Logan	542
Further disputes	544
French intrigues with Indians	544
Gookin becomes Governor	545
Disputes in the colony	546
Penn's difficulties	547
Further disputes in the colony	549
Question about oaths	550
APPENDIX I. Peter Heyn's Memorial	553
APPENDICES II AND III.	554
APPENDIX IV. Middletown and Shrewsbury	554
APPENDIX V. Value of Land in Pennsylvania	555
INDEX	557

Errata.

Page 8, line 14 : *for* till at Albany *read* till at what was afterwards the site of Albany
Page 100, line 5 from foot : *for* Dock *read* Donck
Page 194 : *dele* marginal note 'Andros recalled '
Page 220, last line } *for* Caratacouy *read* Cataracouy
Page 239, last line but one
Page 292, line 13 : *for* Conestagawa *read* Conestago
Page 311, lines 13, 22, and 30, *for* Lancy *read* Lancey. The name is occasionally spelt without the *e*, but the spelling which I have adopted seems to be the correct one
Page 336, line 8 from foot : *for* twelve miles from Long Island *read* twelve miles from the southern point of Long Island
Page 378, line 22 : *dele* as we have seen
Page 444, note 3 : *for* Thorne *read* Thomas

THE MIDDLE COLONIES.

CHAPTER I.

FOUNDATION OF NEW NETHERLANDS.[1]

IN estimating the fitness of the Dutch for the task of colonization we must not mislead ourselves by picturing the Holland of the sixteenth after the Holland of the nineteenth century. The Holland that threw off the Spanish yoke was made up of city oligarchies, full of burgess pride and

_{The Dutch as colonists.}

---

[1] The loss of the records of the Dutch West Indian Company has most unhappily curtailed our sources of knowledge as to the establishment of the colony of New Netherlands. We have, however, a most valuable magazine of information in the *Collection of Documents* (fifteen volumes) by Mr. Brodhead, Mr. O'Callaghan and Mr. Fernow on the history of New Netherlands and New York. They consist of transcripts from Dutch, English, French and Swedish archives, carefully arranged, extending down to 1776. A somewhat similar collection, but much inferior in extent, arrangement, and value, is Mr. O'Callaghan's *Documentary History of New York*.

The *Minutes* of the City Council of New Amsterdam from 1653 to 1674. They have been translated from Dutch into English, partly by Mr. O'Callaghan, partly by Mr. Fernow, and published in six volumes. In addition to the above records the first volume includes the ordinances of the Director-General and his Council from 1647 to 1653. I refer to them as *Court Minutes*.

These ordinances have also been collected and edited by Mr. O'Callaghan in a separate volume, published in 1868.

Mr. Brodhead's *History of New York* (two volumes), extending from the foundation of the colony down to the suppression of Leisler's Rebellion in 1692, is a work of inestimable value. It is monotonous in style, and the writer too often hampers himself by a strict adherence to chronological arrangement. But its fulness, sobriety and impartiality, and the writer's

B

burgess luxury, yet self-denying and pitiless in their public spirit. That pomp, that material well-being which made Holland the wonder of foreign lands, brought with it no languor: a craving for wealth made the Dutchman a voyager and a discoverer: inborn energy and a spirit trained in strife made the struggle as welcome as the prize. The Hollander had indeed more than we readily see in common with his oppressor. Likeness of temper with unlikeness of principle, causes acting as surely with nations as with persons, severed the insurgent provinces from Spain. So, too, what the Moor had done for Spain, the Spaniard was doing for Holland. Tyranny successfully resisted, acting on the temper of an oligarchy, moulded a race of men ready to hold their own against the world, with a spirit of defiance which made the struggle in no wise distasteful. There were indeed wide differences between the Spanish and the Dutch discoverer. The Spaniard was on his best side a crusader, on his worst—and that was often uppermost—a self-seeking adventurer. A steady regard for corporate aims and commercial results underlay all that was done by Dutch explorers.

clear perception of the political influences at work are beyond praise. Mr. Brodhead uses a great number of documents which are still in manuscript in the New York State Records. I felt that to investigate these, when the subject in hand was no more than an outlying province of my main work, would be superfluous labour, and I have, therefore, trusted largely to Mr. Brodhead's guidance. His references and quotations are, indeed, so full that his work may almost be regarded as a collection of documents. There is useful material to be found in the *Collections of the New York Historical Society*, as also in Mr. Fernow's *History of the City of New York*, and Mr. Tuckerman's *Life of Stuyvesant*. For the history of the Swedish settlement much useful material is to be found in the Pennsylvanian Archives. Several documents of importance are published in Hazard's *Register of Pennsylvania*, vol. iv. Acrelius's *History of New Sweden* was originally published in 1759, and republished by the Pennsylvania Historical Society in 1874. The writer was the pastor of the Swedish Church at Christiania, and as such had access to written archives and was in a position to collect oral tradition. Ferris's *History of the Original Settlements on the Delaware* is a book of sound historical authority.

HOLLAND AND COLONIZATION

Yet the dealings of Kieft with the natives of the Hudson Valley were a faint copy of Spanish brutality, and the fate of Towerson and his comrades at Amboyna recalls the tragedy which swept away the French colony from Florida. There was a yet stronger point of likeness. Spain and Holland alike fell into the snare which England alone of colonizing nations wholly avoided. With both the era of colonization set in before the full tide of discovery, with its romance and its eager passions, had begun to slacken. Those who had the control of New Netherlands never learnt to regard the settlement as a detached, self-sufficing community. To them it was primarily a trading station. A state might grow up as best it could under the shadow of the factory.

In other respects Holland was ill-fitted for the task of colonization. She had no rural communities with those institutions and instincts of self-government which enabled the English village to reproduce itself so effectually on the shores of Boston Bay and on the banks of the Connecticut. She had no gentry to play the part of Winthrop, men whose tastes and associations were of the country, but who yet had a share in all that was best and strongest in the national life. It was certain that in any Dutch colony the interests of the farmer would give way to the interests of the merchant. Nor had even the urban and mercantile part of Holland that training in self-government needful for colonists. The whole political life of Holland existed in oligarchies ; each city was ruled by a close, self-electing order ; and so far as it formed part of the province, and through the province of the whole Federation, was solely represented by these oligarchies. The unflinching patriotism with which they had sustained the struggle with Spain gave them a hold on the national sympathy, which made full amends for their lack of any representative character. But to say that is only to urge the defence often put forward on behalf of a benevolent despotism. They who use that plea forget that it is not enough that a system should have secured good administration when the ruler and the ruled are at one; it must contain in itself some guarantee that it will work well under less favourable conditions. Study the early history of New Netherlands; compare its life with that of the English colonies on its north-eastern frontier. At every turn we are reminded that the Dutch settlers succumbed to difficulties which the English escaped, because the latter easily, almost spontaneously, adopted machinery which enabled the popular voice to make itself heard, while the Dutch in like circumstances were feeling for such machinery helplessly and blindly.

Up to a certain period Holland and England ran almost identical courses, not in colonization, but in those preliminary stages of discovery which introduce colonization. With the early Dutch explorers, as with their English rivals, the prospects of colonization counted for little. Far more important in their eyes was the discovery of new routes for trade. The Dutch entered on the field of Arctic discovery just at the time when it seemed to be abandoned by the English. In 1594 voyagers were sent out both from Amsterdam and Enchuysen in quest of a north-east passage to Cathay.[1] All that accrued was a fuller knowledge of the northern seas, of the coast of Nova Zembla and Spitzbergen, and of the sea of Kara. Then comes a lull of ten years. Meanwhile another motive was at work identical with that which had impelled the great English voyagers of the Elizabethan age. It was manifest to Englishman and Dutch

The early Dutch voyagers.

[1] Mr. Asper gives a full account of these voyages, but most unfortunately does not give his authority, or authorities, for them.

man alike that the American empire of Spain might be the vulnerable point in her armour. It would seem indeed to have been an English sea-captain (Beets or Bates) who, in 1581, first definitely put the idea in shape and laid it as a practical scheme before the rulers of the revolted provinces. That policy was followed up a few years later by one who might be called the Dutch Gilbert, William Usselinx.[1] The two men were no doubt severed by wide differences—difference of character, training, and circumstances. Gilbert was an English gentleman, anchored to high and unselfish purposes and to public duty, alike by hereditary tradition and those conceptions of chivalry which formed the better side of the English Renaissance. Usselinx was a citizen of the world, an adventurer, who had seen the ways and cities of men. He had been a merchant in the Azores, he had travelled in Spain and Portugal, possibly even in Brazil and the West Indies. Yet with all these differences there were between the two men points of likeness in temper, and even more in policy.

Each was sanguine and impetuous, aiming at great schemes full-blown, not content to lay unpretending foundations and leave time to do its work. Each, too, strove for a combination of objects which events showed to be irreconcilable, for a scheme which should be at once colonial, commercial, and warlike. To neither Gilbert nor Usselinx was it granted to have any share in such success as their projects achieved. There was nothing in Usselinx's career as strikingly tragic as Gilbert's end. Yet Gilbert, swept away as he sailed back from that enterprise which was heroic even in its failure, is not so sad a figure as Usselinx, branded as an

[1] All that is to be known about Usselinx is brought together in a monograph by Mr. Franklin Jameson in the second volume of the Papers of the American Historical Association.

unsuccessful and disappointed dreamer, hawking his schemes and his services at a foreign court, ready at last to be the rival of his countrymen who had first neglected and then imitated him. Usselinx, willing to work for Sweden when his own country would have none of him, willing when Sweden hung back to build up a company taken from among the various nations of Europe, was a type of that cosmopolitanism which was fatal to the colonial career of Holland. It was that spirit which made New Netherlands, with its eighteen languages,[1] a mart for men of every race who chose to seek it, not, like the English colonies, a community striving to reproduce the social and political life of the parent state.

If the schemes of Dutch projectors and the exploits of Dutch seamen suggest an English parallel, the likeness may be carried a stage further. The hindrances which fought against Usselinx were closely akin to those which fought against Gilbert's successors. James I., dreading lest Virginian colonization should excite the wrathful jealousy of Spain, has his counterpart in the Dutch Arminians anxious to avoid any measure which might drive the enemy to extremities. Yet theirs was something better than the timid servility which sacrificed Raleigh, and all those ends which Raleigh held most dear, to the hopes of the Spanish Marriage. The motive of Barneveldt and his followers was patriotic, though their patriotism may have been somewhat narrow and short-sighted. They looked on the question as Hollanders, just as Usselinx looked on it as a Belgian. They had no wish to see continued hostility with Spain, since such hostility if successful meant the return to Belgium of those exiles who had just furnished a new element of industry and enterprise to the population of

Dutch colonization hindered by political considerations.

[1] See p. 19.

Holland. To keep the Belgians was, in the judgment of the peace party, more gainful to Holland than to form part of a liberated and united Netherlands.

The course of Dutch discovery, interrupted for more than ten years, was renewed by one of the most brilliant of those great seamen of whom the sixteenth century was so fruitful, Henry Hudson. Although Hudson achieved his greatest exploits in the service of a foreign nation, yet England can claim him as hers not only by birth but by training. He was a pupil in that school of seamanship, as we may call it, founded by Cabot—the Muscovy company. That which has given Hudson's name an abiding place in colonial history—the exploration of the river now called after him—was a chance incident in a voyage undertaken with wholly different aims. In two successive years, in 1607 and 1608, Hudson had endeavoured to solve that problem which so many of his countrymen had set before them to no purpose, and to make his way to Cathay by the north-east. Baffled each time, in 1609 he renewed the effort.[1] He was then acting on behalf of the Dutch East India Company, with a crew half Dutch, half English. Some discord crept in; it may be that there were faults of temper and character in Hudson which led to trouble here, as they did to the tragedy of his last voyage. Throughout the voyage he was hampered in his exploration by the backwardness of his men, and by breaches of discipline which perpetually threatened to embroil them with the savages. This time he attempted a passage in a new direction. He was acquainted with John Smith, and had learnt from him the existence of a river, north of Virginia, which

---

[1] Mr. Asper publishes the original accounts of these voyages. That of the first is written by Hudson to one of his crew, of the second wholly by Hudson, of the third by his mate, Robert Juet of Limehouse, probably an Englishman.

Smith believed would lead to the Pacific. Hudson accordingly abandoned his scheme of finding a passage to the north, and coasted along the shore of Virginia. From the mouth of 'the King's river in Virginia where our Englishmen are' he turned north, and then, hoping in all likelihood that he had found the passage suggested by Smith, he sailed up the river which now bears his name. Relations with the natives opened badly, and in a midnight skirmish an Englishman was killed.

Hudson then unwisely captured some of the natives, and, as so often, a petty act of pilfering by a savage led to further violence. However, no serious obstacle was offered to the progress of the discoverers up the river till at Albany the exploring party which he had sent on in a boat reported the stream too shallow for further navigation. With Hudson's departure from the river his connexion with American colonization ends. The report which he brought home of the river, and his description of the Chesapeake Bay, disclosed a country which might amply repay its occupants. The sailors had 'caught great store of very good fish,' the natives had been, in the main, friendly. The country appeared fertile and rich in timber, and on the banks of the river Hudson had marked 'a very pleasant place to build a town.' The inducement most likely of all to operate with the Dutch was the abundance of furs, and the readiness of the natives to exchange them for knives and hatchets.

Cautiously and gradually Holland felt its way along the path which Hudson had opened. Trading voyages were sent out; young savages were brought home to Holland,[1] and the Dutch became familiar not only with the Hudson and Manhattan Island, but with Narragansett Bay[2] and the Connecticut. Holland claimed the river which Hudson

[1] Wassenaar in Callaghan, vol. iii. p. 25. [2] De Laet, vol. i. pp. 7, 8.

had discovered and made it her own in title, calling it after her young stadtholder, Mauritius. The highest point of the river which Hudson had touched was chosen as a permanent trading station, and received the name of Fort Nassau. There, in a moated and stockaded house, with thirteen cannon and a garrison of twelve men, a merchant clerk from Amsterdam trafficked with the natives for their beaver-skins.[1] On Manhattan Island a few huts were thrown up which served as winter shelter for a crew whose vessel had been burnt,[2] and though their exact site and character is unknown, there is ground for thinking that one or two more factory stations were in existence on the southern bank of the Hudson and in Delaware Bay.[3]

So far, however, nothing had been done towards the creation of a permanent and self-supporting settlement. That was only to come as the indirect result of an extended commerce. In 1614 that scheme for which Usselinx had failed to gain a hearing was revived. Early in that year a company was incorporated under a charter from the States-General, with the right of whale-fishing in the northern seas, and with the further object of discovering a north-east passage.[4] The success of the Dutch East India Company, formed in 1602, gave encouragement to such a scheme. The States-General, too, offered inducements to private explorers by promising that any discoverer of new lands should have a monopoly of trade there for four voyages.[5]

The Northern Company.

The principle of co-operation was soon carried further. In the autumn of 1614 some of those

[1] Brodhead, vol. i. p. 55.
[2] Ib. p. 48. Mr. Brodhead quotes original authorities.
[3] See the appendices to Asper's translation of Wassenaar.
[4] Brodhead, vol. i. p. 59. He refers to the Dutch archives.
[5] New York Documents, vol. i. p. 5.

merchants whose ships had been trading with the lands discovered by Hudson formed themselves into a company. The privileges which they received may be said to have called into existence the province of New Netherlands.[1] Their charter for the first time recognised and asserted on behalf of Holland a title to a tract of land on the American coast. It granted to the Company the exclusive right of trading with New Netherlands, and it defined that territory as lying between New France and Virginia, and extending from the fortieth to the forty-fifth degree of latitude. The name of the territory was beyond doubt an implied claim. Yet the document said nothing of adverse possession against the possible title of other nations, nor did it give any sort of territorial right nor any jurisdiction to the grantees. It did nothing but establish a commercial monopoly.

<small>The Amsterdam Company.</small>

Such rights as were granted to this body known as the Amsterdam Company were limited to four years. The scheme did not therefore profess to have in it any element of permanence. It could not possibly serve as a basis for colonization. Yet one of its proceedings had an abiding influence in colonial history. In 1617 it became clear that the settlement at Fort Nassau was unsafe against winter floods. The factory was moved to the western bank, near the mouth of a tributary stream, the Tawasentha.[2] In dealing with savages one cannot speak with strict propriety of territorial bounds. But the site of the settlement, if not in the lands of the Mohawks, was within their control, and an alliance with them was a needful condition for the safety of the foreign traders. Of the treaty ratified at the Tawasentha between the Dutch factors and the

<small>Treaty of Tawasentha.</small>

---

[1] The charter (translated) is among the New York Documents, vol. i. p. 11.

[2] Wassenaar, p. 9.

Mohawks nothing is known in detail.[1] But the alliance thus begun had an influence which cannot be overrated. The conquest of New Netherlands gave the English colonies a continuous sea-board. It gave them what was of even greater value in the coming struggle with France, the control of the Hudson and the friendship of the Five Nations.

The privileges of the Amsterdam Company came to an end in 1618. It soon had a successor with far wider aims and powers. The body incorporated as the Dutch West India Company was not endowed with any definite territorial grant.[2] Nor was it confined by its charter to America. It might extend its action not only to any portion of the American sea-board, but to the coast of Africa between the Tropic of Cancer and the Cape of Good Hope. Within these limits it was secured against any Dutch competitor. Within the same limits it might establish settlements over which it could exercise sovereign power, administering justice, making alliances and conducting wars, with no restraint beyond the obligation to report its doings to the States-General. Technically indeed a declaration of war must be approved by the States-General, but how could such a restraint act when barbarians many thousand miles away were the enemy? It is clear that there was not in this charter any special assertion of a territorial claim over New Netherlands. The document must be held to mean that all the territories referred to were *vacuum domicilium*, except where any other nation could urge some special claim of occupancy or possession. One great fault underlay

The Dutch West India Company.

---

[1] Mr. Brodhead (vol. i. p. 88) gives a full account of this treaty. The only specific authorities whom he quotes are Moulton and Schoolcraft. I cannot discover who Moulton is, and the reference to Schoolcraft is too vague to be of any service. I am, however, prepared to accept Mr. Brodhead's judgment as authority for the existence of the treaty.

[2] The charter is given both by Hazard and by O'Callaghan.

the constitution of the Company. Conforming too closely to that of the States-General themselves, it was a federation without an effective centre. The affairs were managed by five separate chambers of directors, representing Amsterdam, Zeeland, Dordrecht, and North Holland, with a fifth joint chamber for Friesland and Groningen. The business of these chambers was mainly financial. The capital of the Company was divided into nine shares; of these four were allotted to Amsterdam, two to Zeeland, and one to each of the other chambers. The directors were elected by the various chambers. Amsterdam had twenty, Zeeland twelve, each of the other chambers fourteen.

The executive was a board to which the Amsterdam chamber sent eight representatives, Zeeland four and each of the others two, while one attended on behalf of the States-General. Such a constitution was ill-fitted to give promptness or efficiency of action.

An elaborate federal constitution was not the only hindrance to the success of the Company. It belonged to a party rather than to the nation. It represented the views and gave effect to the schemes of the thorough-going war party, of those who were fain to force Spain to the last extremity, and thus it lost the support of the many wealthy merchants who favoured the policy of Barneveldt. Such hindrances told against the vitality of the Company, against its efficiency as an instrument for colonization. They did not abate its successful ambition, or check a stream of wealth which flowed from war rather than trade. Not our own East India Company in the days when it overturned thrones, and held the descendants of an emperor for its vassals, made more daring claims or furthered them with more high-handed gallantry. We read of the Company with its navy of a hundred ships and its army of fifteen thousand men, of Peter Heyn capturing the Spanish

The Company represents the war party.

treasure fleet, and returning with seventeen captive galleons bearing a treasure of twelve million dollars.[1] As we look on Heyn's stately memorial in Delft Church, and read how he, a second Jason, sailing to the colonies of the New World, tore from the King of Spain that Golden Fleece which had been a terror to other voyagers, and bore it home, not to Greece but to the United Provinces, we feel that the spirit of Drake and Hawkins had passed from the shores of Devon to the banks of the Texel.[2]

The directors of the Company, indeed, openly avowed that they had changed the purpose with which they had set out, that the career of a patriotic buccaneer was better than that of a merchant, and that it was cheaper for the States-General to entrust the war to a company who spent their winnings at home than to subsidize foreign mercenaries. Their object was not 'trifling trade with the Indians nor the tardy cultivation of uninhabited regions,' but 'acts of hostility against the ships and property of the King of Spain and his subjects.'[3] Thus, too, a shrewd and somewhat unfriendly critic notices that the Company having come into possession of Peter Heyn's booty bestowed not a thought upon their best trading port at Fort Orange.[4]

Such gains and such hopes were rendering the Company utterly unfit for the slow, dull task of colonization, with no immediate hopes of profit. At the very time that the Company was thus matching itself against the whole might of the Spanish Empire, and overawing the conquerors of Mexico and Peru, its settlers on the Hudson were hemmed into a ruinous village; that which should have been a fort, open on every side to the enemy,

[1] Brodhead (who quotes authorities), vol. i. p. 184.
[2] I give the text of the monumental inscription in an Appendix.
[3] Remonstrance of the West India Company against a peace with Spain, Brodhead, Documents, vol. i. p. 62.
[4] De Vries in N. Y. Docs. i .145.

the farms tenantless and unfenced, the site of its one warehouse hardly to be found, the only trace of prosperity in the estate of the resident director. Moreover the administration of New Netherlands was vested, not in the whole Company, but only in a section of it. That part of the corporate business was handed over to the Amsterdam chamber. Thus the Company as a whole had no direct control over the colony, and felt no responsibility for it. If any dispute arose between the chambers, or any lack of harmony in the working of the Company, New Netherlands as a dependency of Amsterdam would be looked on not merely with indifference, but with jealousy and ill-will.

All that the Company could claim to have done for colonization was to have set on foot a movement which had in it an element of vitality, a principle, though weak and torpid, of growth. In the history of New Netherlands there was nothing like that solid and effective progress with which New England stretched her robust grasp over the wilderness. Yet something was done. During the first seventeen years of the Company's corporate life settlements were established not only on the Hudson, but on Long Island and on Delaware Bay. A fresh post, called Fort Orange, was established on the west bank of the Hudson, to the north of Fort Nassau, which it superseded.[1] The name of Nassau was transferred to a fort near the union of the Schuylkill and the Delaware, founded in 1623, but deserted after three years' occupation.[2] By 1626 there were at Manhattan some thirty scattered houses.[3] In that year the place was regularly secured by a fortification and a battery.[4] Beside the farmers of Manhattan there was another agricultural settlement, that at

Marginal note: Colonial progress of the Company.

---

[1] *Journal of New Netherlands*, Holland Documents, vol. i. p. 181.
[2] *Ibid.* [3] *Ibid.* [4] Wassenaar, p. 37.

Waalboght on Long Island, formed by Walloons settled there in 1623.[1] Nassau was not the only settlement towards the south. Another called Swanendael was formed on Delaware Bay, at what is now Lewistown. That, however, was, as we shall see, but short-lived. The fur trade was the one means through which the colony seemed in any way likely to repay its founders. Its only other productive industry was ship-building. That for a while throve, though it was in all likelihood ostentation rather than reasonable enterprise which built and launched a vessel of at least six hundred tons.[2] Sawmills also were tried but did not answer. The Company, too, traded with New England, importing hither tobacco and live stock. That however was no benefit to New Netherlands, but rather to its prejudice, as giving the settlers competitors for the necessaries of life.

It is not a little to be regretted that the continuous records of the Company are no longer extant. Thus we have nothing like a clear history of the early economical life of the settlement, nor of the terms on which the first settlers occupied their holdings. It would seem, however, that not only the land, but the stock upon it, belonged to the Company. The so-called farmer was not so much a tenant as a servant paid by certain allowances in kind. The whole business of the Company, its land and its fur trade, was under the control of one official, the Director. He was assisted by a Council, and in conjunction with them had certain limited judicial powers. Below him were two other executive officers—the Koopman, that is, the bookkeeper and secretary, and the Schout, responsible for the observance of the criminal law. All these func-

[1] Brodhead, i. 155. He quotes the Albany Records.
[2] Letter from Mason, the proprietor of New Hampshire. N. Y. Docs. iii. 27.

tionaries were directly appointed by the Company, and seem to have been removable at pleasure.

It was plainly impossible that with this constitution the Company could extend its agricultural operations far. To supplement this, a scheme was introduced in 1629 for establishing a class of landed proprietors. Like a mediæval king, the Company allotted portions of its territory to individuals, on whom it conferred not only proprietary rights but also certain subordinate jurisdiction. These grantees— patroons as they were called—were tempted by an exceedingly restricted share in the Company's monopoly of trade. Each was to bring out fifty adult emigrants, and in return was to receive a tract of land reaching sixteen miles along the river, all on one bank or half on each, with no fixed limit of width.

[margin note: The patroons.]

The colonists whom the patroon took out were to be *ascripti glebæ*. The patroon himself was to hold manorial courts, from which there was a right of appeal to the Company. If he could found townships within his territory, he might himself appoint in them a staff of officials. A privilege of the Old World, too, was renewed for the benefit of the patroon. The tenant might grind corn nowhere but at his mill. On the patroons the Company cast a duty which they might themselves have fitly discharged, that of providing ministers and schoolmasters.[1]

The objections to these arrangements were many and obvious. It meant the introduction of a landed aristocracy among a people whose life in the Old World had done nothing to familiarize them with such a system. To leading members of the Company it offered opportunities for large and lucrative speculation in land. Thus we find one director, Kiliaen van Rensselaer, an

---

[1] The Charter of Patroons is in the *Collections of the New York Historical Society*, 2nd series, vol. i. p. 370.

Amsterdam jeweller, acquiring a territory on the upper Hudson so vast that as a concession to the general outcry he had to slice it up into five patroonships. It was a system, too, which went to make any effective central government impossible, alike for civil or military purposes. There was no cohesion between the patroonships, no interdependence : one might prosper without benefiting its neighbours. Moreover, the patroon was usually an absentee, and the conditions of a new country leave no margin for rent. The patroon often delegated his post to an agent; the land had, in modern phrase, to keep two gentlemen.

One indirect and remote gain the system brought. The inhabitants of each patroonship might appoint a deputy to confer upon its own affairs with the Director and Council of the Colony. It is a long step from that to a stable system of representative government. But in New Netherlands representative government was attained so slowly, and through so many incomplete experiments, that one may reckon even a faint and imperfect approach towards it as a step in advance.

Two attempts were made to modify the system, not wholly without success. In 1640 the patroonships were reduced in extent and a smaller class of proprietor was introduced, holding two hundred acres, and tilling it with five servants brought out at his own expense. Ten years later the Company tried the experiment of supplying tenants with stock. A tract of land was granted to a farmer. The ground was partly cleared, and there was on it a house and a barn. The tenant was to be supplied with implements and with live stock, four horses, as many cows, and a certain number of sheep and pigs. He was to pay a fixed rent, partly in money, partly in butter. For six years the stock were to remain on the tenant's hands at

Small proprietors.

the joint risk of himself and the Company. At the end of that time the Company is to receive back the stock or an equivalent.¹ But the system, however modified, had in it no element of success. The agricultural prosperity of New Netherlands did not begin till rural communities sprung up like those of New England, some actually formed by emigrants thence, others fashioned on that model.

In 1638 the Company granted to its subjects a strictly limited share in its own commercial advantages. *The Company modifies its monopoly of trade.* Private persons might import and export in the Company's ships, paying a duty of ten per cent. on goods brought into the colony, fifteen on exports. But inasmuch as it was at the same time enacted that each colonist was to pledge himself voluntarily to submit to the regulations and commands of the Company's officers, the scanty privileges rested on a precarious basis.²

Moreover, even if such a measure did something for the commercial prosperity of the colony, yet it failed to meet the chief need and to give life, strength, and cohesion to the several parts of the settlement. For a community which has yet to grow into civic life there is no little truth in the Greek theory, that it is against good order to have a crowd of traders coming and going.³

The change, however, did at least stimulate immigration. In eight years the number of farms had *Increase of population.* multiplied fourfold.⁴ But even this brought its drawbacks. It complicated the relations with the savages. The peace of the colony might at any time be imperilled by one unscrupulous trader. Commerce,

---

[1] These conditions are set forth in a pamphlet written by Tienhoven, the Secretary to the Colony, in 1650. O'Callaghan, vol. iv. p. 26.
[2] Brodhead, vol. i. p. 288.
[3] Aristotle's *Politics*, b. vii. ch. 6.   [4] Brodhead, vol. i. p. 290.

too, brought in a miscellaneous horde with no sense of corporate life, of a common origin, of common traditions. One is compelled to think that the statement of a Jesuit visitor in 1644 who found eighteen different tongues must have been coloured by a Frenchman's rhetoric.[1] But several of these tributary streams can be clearly identified. English there were, many no doubt, like Underhill, men whom the rigid ecclesiastical corporations of New England with their exacting tests excluded. Others, French Huguenots, Walloons, Scotch peddlers, Jews, have left the trace of their existence in the records of the community.

The result was a total absence of that unity which in New England was so intense. She with all her errors, and in a measure by those errors, created that 'cake of custom,' as a thoughtful writer has called it,[2] so needful to give firmness and cohesion where the conventional ties of old countries are absent, the want of which made the early political life of New Netherlands so weak and unstable.

Since the records of the Dutch West India Company have perished, nearly all the documentary evidence as *Importance of the Governors.* to its early proceedings that survives consists of controversial writings, attacks on officials and their defence. Indeed in the absence of records the whole subject becomes intensely personal : the characters and motives of the Governors assume a preponderating importance. To speak of the Governors at the outset by that name is almost misleading. It calls up associations of the full and vigorous political life of Massachusetts or Virginia. For some years the Gover nor, or, to give him his proper title, the Director of New Netherlands, was really but the manager of a large trading house.

[1] Father Jogues. His report is in O'Callaghan, vol. iv. p. 15.
[2] Bagehot, in *Physics and Politics*.

That is certainly true of the first Governor, Jacobsen May, and his successor William Verhulst. We can hardly say more of the third, Peter Minuit. Yet there was enough that was noteworthy and typical in Minuit's career and character to deserve notice. His course was not unlike that of Usselinx; each illustrates the fatal cosmopolitanism which marred the fortunes of New Netherlands. Sent out as Director-General in 1626, in 1631 he incurred the displeasure of the Company by favouring the patroons in their schemes for accumulating landed property.[1] Dismissed on this ground, like Usselinx he transferred his services to another country, and thus became one of the chief instruments in overthrowing the Dutch settlement. For while the Swedish colony itself fell easily before the energy of New Netherlands, the effort of that struggle left the conqueror in turn defenceless.

Peter Minuit.

Despite Minuit's lack of patriotism, his strenuous energy makes him stand out a vivid figure in annals which till then are void of biographical interest. His successor, Van Twiller, is saved from nonentity by strange incongruity of character and position. There is nothing to show him unfit to have carried on the affairs of the Company in ordinary times. In the mere head of a factory, his hard drinking, his bluster and his cowardice might have been atoned for by his tradesmanlike shrewdness. By the irony of fate he was placed at the head of affairs just as the colony was emerging from the purely trading stage, just as it was first entangled in conflicts which heralded the transfer of European battles to the New World. Full justice, too, was done to his grotesque failure by a shrewd and unfriendly observer. During his term of office the colony was revisited by David de Vries, that resolute and enterprising man, the leading partner in

Wouter Van Twiller.

[1] Brodhead, vol. i. p. 213.

the abortive attempt to form a settlement at Swanendael. With views that took in more than trade, he explored the Hudson, the Delaware, and the shores of Chesapeake Bay, planning the establishment of a whale fishery, making friends with the savages, and opening intercourse with the English in Virginia. We learn from his writings how, during his stay at Fort Amsterdam, an English ship sailed into the Hudson. Her captain, Eelkens, was a discharged servant of the Company. Like Minuit, he did not scruple to turn his local experience against his former employers. The voyage was more than an unauthorised intrusion on Dutch trade. It was accompanied by a claim on the part of Eelkens and his employers to equal rights with the Dutch on the river discovered by the Englishman, Hudson. De Vries tells us how Eelkens demanded a pass from Van Twiller; how, after a week's delay, no pass came, and how, thereupon, Eelkens sailed under the guns of Fort Amsterdam with the English flag flying, while the Director on the quay stood before an open cask of wine, drinking with his friends the health of the Prince of Orange, and appealing to them to protect him against violence. The Director's underlings did something to supply his own lack of courage. By judicious and persistent interference they withheld the Indians from trade with the new-comer.

The dealings of the Director with De Vries himself were marked by the same spirit of ineffective bluster. His dealings with De Vries. The Director demanded that De Vries's ship should be inspected before she sailed. De Vries refused; twelve musketeers were sent down to enforce the order; in quiet defiance of the threat De Vries rowed from the shore and bade his crew weigh anchor.

Two years later Van Twiller had thankfully to accept the services of the man who defied him. Fort Nassau, the Dutch station on the Delaware, was now deserted, and a small party from Maryland seized on the vacant site. One of them, a deserter whose motives are nowhere explained, brought news to New Amsterdam of the encroachment. Van Twiller at once sent De Vries to deal with the matter. A second party of twenty men was just ready to assist the new settlement. But the assailants arrived before the relieving force could sail, and the intruders were peacefully removed and transported back to Maryland.[1]

Like encroachments were being attempted with more success to the north by the New England settlers in the valley of the Connecticut. With no better resources, his employers supine about everything but the beaver trade, his colony a number of scattered outposts, with no actual organisation and no corporate life, one may doubt if Van Twiller could have done anything to check the strenuous advance of English Puritanism. Yet one may well believe that his known incapacity encouraged that defiant policy against which his more energetic successors were powerless.

<small>Encroachments from New England.</small>

Van Twiller's successor, William Kieft, was a man of widely different character. He had no lack of energy. If good government lay in the contriving of administrative machinery, he would have been a good governor. Within the little sphere of his province he aimed at ubiquitous despotism. His very first step was to reduce the Council to a nullity by nominating only one councillor and reserving to himself a double vote. Since the Council was the one judicial body, this practically made Kieft supreme and

<small>William Kieft.</small>

---

[1] For all these transactions De Vries himself is our authority. I cannot find any explicit statement to the effect that the Dutch reoccupied Fort Nassau. But that they did so is clear from what follows (*inf.* p. 73).

irresponsible in civil and criminal cases. He may not have been personally corrupt, though, even there, his character was not beyond suspicion. But he had no scruple about acting through corrupt instruments. In his secretary, Van Tienhoven, he had a subordinate who saw clearly that a minute and pervading despotism such as Kieft aimed at left room for plenty of official corruption. Thus, for instance, Kieft ordered that no deposition or other document should be valid as evidence unless written by the Secretary. Here the Secretary's greed and the Governor's love of official interference worked together. Kieft, too, was manifestly one of those who think that a community can be drilled into prosperity and morality. He fenced in trade with severe edicts. Many of his orders were in themselves reasonable. His error lay in forcing them simultaneously and with ostentatious severity on a community used only to lax authority. No officials were to trade in furs, and the right of exportation, lately granted to private persons, was withdrawn. To sell guns or powder to the Indians was made a capital crime. Kieft was plainly a man of austere private life. New Amsterdam, with its mixed population of sailors and traders, left plenty of scope for an earnest moral reformer. The Governor exercised the right of licensing vintners at his own discretion; hours were fixed for work. A proclamation was issued with a list of prohibited vices, including lewdness and calumny, and ending with the comprehensive form, 'all other immoralities.' Sailors, who no doubt contributed their full share to the catalogue, were to be on land only in the daytime.[1]

A man of winning tact or of commanding dignity and restrained temper might possibly have carried out such a policy. Kieft, it is plain, was neither. His

[1] For Kieft's regulation see Brodhead, vol. i. pp. 277-8.

only positive influence was that indirect one by which despotism works its own cure. His harsh and ill-judged interference woke in the settlers a spirit of resistance which under mere neglect and bad administration might have slumbered. Thus it came that under the most despotic of its early rulers the colony took its first steps, slight indeed, but yet containing the seeds of better things, towards representative government. As usual, external danger gave the opening for resistance. In 1641 a settler was murdered by an Indian in fulfilment of an ancient blood feud. Fifteen years before, a chief of the same tribe bringing furs to sell at Manhattan was robbed and murdered by three servants of Minuit. With the victim was his nephew, a young lad. He escaped and grew to manhood with a fixed purpose of revenge for the deed which he had beheld. His vengeance, however, fell on one who seems to have been in no way connected with the original outrage. One Claus Smit, a wheelwright, had settled in an isolated hut, north-east of Manhattan. The Indian visited him on the pretext of trade and, getting behind him, treacherously drove his tomahawk into Smit's head. Kieft was not the man to pass over such a matter. Yet he might well feel that it was a hopeless task to retaliate with an exasperated population at his back, and with no materials better than these at hand he might well refuse to be personally responsible for the security of the colony. His first need was popular support. Kieft at once called a general meeting of householders and laid the case before them, suggesting a demand for the surrender of the murderer; if that were refused, retaliation. The meet-

[marginal note: The Council of Twelve and the Indian war.[1]]

---

[1] Our knowledge of these proceedings is partly due to De Vries, partly to a letter or pamphlet in the N. Y. Docs. vol. i. p. 179. It is calendared by Mr. Brodhead by the title of *Journal of New Netherlands*. I refer to it by that title.

ing at once appointed twelve representatives under the presidency of De Vries to act for them. It is clear that Kieft had little intention of submitting his own judgment to that of the colonists or their delegates: he wanted support, not advice. Kieft's own policy was one of merciless retaliation and intimidation. The consent of the Twelve was reluctantly given. A troop of eighty soldiers was sent out to obtain redress; ignorance of the country, and one may well believe the backwardness of the settlers, brought the expedition to nothing. But though they returned to New Amsterdam without striking a blow, yet the attempt was enough to terrify the offending tribe. Peace was made, with a promise, never fulfilled, to give up the murderer.

Meanwhile the Twelve were availing themselves of the position which they had gained to make certain demands on behalf of the settlers. In the Fatherland, they said, every small village had its five or seven schepens. Yet the citizens of New Netherlands were allowed no share in the control of their own affairs. Even such a slight check on the Governor as was imposed by the existence of the Council was frustrated since places in that body were allowed to remain vacant. Let the Council be filled up and let the freemen elect four members of it. Let the elected Twelve representatives have a right of veto upon any taxes imposed. Let there be an annual muster under arms. These indeed would be the best security for popular rights. A people capable of bearing arms surrounded by enemies could with due perseverance make their own terms against a governor unsupported by mercenary troops.

Demands of the Twelve.[1]

Kieft, strong in his own despotic temper and in the anticipated support of the Company, hardly yielded an inch of ground. The muster might be held, but the

[1] For these demands and Kieft's answer, see Brodhead, vol. i. pp. 326–8.

Company could not afford to give powder. No control over taxation can be granted to the popular representatives. The Council Kieft admits is small. He is hoping for the arrival of some persons of rank. Then he will fill it up. The freemen may appoint four Councillors, two to retire each year. He winds up with the conventional plea for an arbitrary system : ' of what practical injury can the settlers complain ? '

Kieft's answer.

The only point on which Kieft gave way was in connexion with certain questions of trade. The Twelve had petitioned for trade with foreign vessels. This was granted with certain restrictions necessary for good order. The Twelve also treated the importation of English cattle as a grievance to the farmer. Accordingly it was provided that such importation should be limited to bulls and he-goats. There had been certain attempts to regulate arbitrarily the value of money. This had led to the exportation of specie. Kieft promised that it should be discontinued. With these bare instalments of reform the Twelve were dismissed.

It was not long before the troubles with the Indians were renewed. A native, who had been made drunk and cheated by a Dutchman, took the law into his own hands and murdered the offender. His tribesmen were required to give up the murderer. They offered a large store of wampum as compensation, but were unable or unwilling to arrest the criminal. There was reason to fear that this was not an isolated outrage. Rumours of an impending massacre ran through the scattered Dutch plantations.

Further troubles with the Indians.

Meanwhile their Indian enemies were themselves threatened on the other side by the Mohicans, and were fleeing from their villages to the coast. Two lines of policy presented themselves to the settlers. Some, headed by De Vries, saw in the danger of these Indians an opportunity for winning their gratitude. The houseless fugitives might be sheltered and abide in safety till the tide of Mohawk invasion flowed back. Others saw in the weakness of the enemy an opportunity for exacting retribution and striking terror. Kieft, having by his own act dismissed the Twelve, could not with any show of reason throw himself on their advice or require them to share his responsibility. Nevertheless when three members of that body petitioned him to declare war, he at once accepted their policy and justified himself by pleading popular approval. The result was a hideous and undiscriminating massacre, well nigh as black a chapter as any in the history of civilized men and barbarians. Nor was Kieft alone in his folly. A wanton raid by the Long Island settlers on the granaries of the friendly Indians brought another attack upon the settlers. On every side the colony was hemmed in with enemies of its own making. From a multitude of tribes owning no common allegiance it was impossible to obtain a secure peace. Terms indeed were made with the Long Island savages, but with little confidence or good will on either side. Later on in the summer news came that the savages about Fort Orange were up in arms, and that fifteen of the Dutch had perished. The settlers could only cower together within the fortifications of New Amsterdam, leaving behind a wilderness of wasted fields and burning houses.

In like trials the people of New England had ever been borne up by a strong sense of corporate unity and Attacks on Kieft. an unshaken confidence in rulers of their own choice. The unhappy New Netherlanders had no such stay in their distress. Hints at the expediency of deposing the Governor were heard. He who had ever turned a deaf ear to all popular remonstrance or demand now tried to shift the blame of his failure on his advisers. The plea roused the fury of one who had been at once the partner and the victim of Kieft's misdeeds. One of the three who had counselled war, Adriaensen, had seen his own plantation in flames and desolate. Kieft's attempt to shield himself was practically giving up Adriaensen to popular fury. The injured man broke in on Kieft, charged him with calumny, and then, supported by two of his followers, attempted the Governor's life.[1]

In these straits, beset by savages without and disaffected subjects within, Kieft as before sought to shift his responsibility on to the people. He again called a meeting of householders and asked for a committee. The settlers might well feel that it was useless to co-operate with one so arbitrary and so untrustworthy, one who thus evaded responsibility and defied control. They demanded that the Governor should nominate the board, leaving the householders a veto. At length after some wrangling the householders accepted Kieft's proposal and chose a board of eight.[2]

The Council of Eight.

They at once took an important step. Hitherto the colony had no relations with the mother-country save through the Company. The Eight now sent a letter to the Company setting forth their woes and their dangers. But at the same time they made a direct appeal to the States-General. Though it was not formally and avowedly an attack on the Company, yet every line of it told of the Company's neglect. There was, they said, no effective resistance. The garrison was insufficient and had no powder, while, thanks to the contraband trade, the enemy was abundantly supplied. Aid might have been got from New England, but the colony had no means of paying.

The Eight appeal to the States-General.[3]

[1] Brodhead, vol. i. p. 357.   [2] *Ib.* p. 365.
[3] Mr. Brodhead gives the text of the appeal, vol. i. p. 371, &c.

Last came a prophetic warning, which, even though the Company were deaf to it, might touch patriotic statesmen. If the colonists were left unaided, they would have to desert their homes and join their neighbours to the east. The whole country, with its fertile soil, its harbours and its fur trade, would become English territory.

All through the next year the war dragged on. It was not as when the Pequods threatened Connecticut, or when the various tribes on the New England frontier were marshalled under the dominant will of Philip. Here the settlers were menaced in every quarter by enemies acting with little concert. This, while it saved the settlers from one overwhelming attack, increased the ever present sense of insecurity and the difficulty of making an abiding peace. Mercenaries were hired from New England, among them that strange Puritan soldier of fortune, John Underhill. The strategy which he had learned under Mason stood him in good stead. On a March night, with snow-covered ground, a force of a hundred and fifty men surrounded an Indian village near the Connecticut. The occupants were over five hundred. Mason with greater inequality of numbers had boldly forced the palisade, and only resorted to fire when his troops seemed in danger of being overwhelmed. Underhill's strategy was more cautious and more merciless. The place was surrounded and every Indian that tried to break through was shot. Then fire was used to complete the work.[1]

Underhill's unsparing blow was effective. It at once brought the savages on Long Island and the adjacent mainland to terms, leaving the colony only threatened on the south and west. There, however, things were little better. But the opportune arrival of a hundred

[1] Brodhead, vol. i. pp. 390-1.

and thirty soldiers, sent by the Governor of Curaçoa, brought with it some security. During the whole of 1644 the settlers were clamouring for vigorous measures. Indifferent as Kieft no doubt was to the real well-being of the colony, yet one may well believe that he felt sorely hampered by the disunion among the settlers, and by the total want of any vigorous corporate life. We have evidence that, at least in the case of the patroons, desire for gain had swept away all sense of public responsibility and common interest. In the very thick of the Indian trouble a ship sent out by Rensselaer reached Manhattan. Amongst her freight were shoes. These were urgently needed for the soldiers. The supercargo refused to sell them. A dispute followed which led to a complete search of the vessel, and the discovery of a supply of arms and ammunition. There was at that time an extensive fur trade at Rensselaerwyck, and we cannot doubt that the guns and powder would have soon been in the hands of the men before whom the colony was cowering.[1]

Had the savages been actuated by any well-defined common purpose, had they been under the guidance of a leader with a deliberate scheme for exterminating the intruders, the case of the Dutch settlement would in all likelihood have been hopeless. Happily for the colonists the anger of the savages was, like their friendship, fickle and wayward: resentment led them to harass and to plunder, it could not give them the steady patience to carry a long war to a successful issue. In the summer of 1645 peace was made first with the Indians on the upper Hudson, soon after with those about Manhattan. The principle of the latter treaty was to restrict as far as might be all private and unauthorized intercourse between the settlers and the natives. No armed Indian was to enter the Dutch

[1] Brodhead, vol. i. p. 390.

settlement : no Dutchman was to visit a native village unless under the escort of a native.[1] This was followed by a treaty with the Mohawks.[2]

Five years of war such as had been waged had shattered the commercial prosperity of the colony in every direction. Its export trade depended on the purchase of beaver skins from the savages, its internal prosperity on agriculture, and both were at a standstill. Nor was the material loss and suffering all. Seven years before Connecticut had gone through like trials. She had emerged from them strengthened, schooled in endurance and self-reliance, in military discipline and civil cohesion. For New Netherlands there was no such compensation. The best that could be said was that harsh schooling had brought home clearly to men's minds the faults of their political system.

We have seen how imperfect was the amount of representation granted to the people. The Twelve and the Eight were in truth nothing more than executive committees appointed for a special purpose. They had no permanent constitutional functions. Nor did they serve to bind together the different parts of the colony. As a part of the machinery of government they were worthless : their value was that they did something towards enabling the people to make their complaints heard. They did not secure the forms of responsible government, but they taught the Company that it was not safe to leave the voice of the settlers unheeded. The remonstrance already mentioned was followed up by another petition, repeating even more emphatically the tale of the colonists' sufferings. The Eight charged Kieft with having through wanton brutality changed the Indians

Want of constitutional machinery.

[1] Brodhead, vol. i. p. 407.
[2] *Ib.* vol. i. p. 408. The treaty is referred to in Van Der Donck's account of New Netherlands. *N. Y. Hist. Coll.*, 2nd series, vol. i. p. 161.

from friends to foes, with turning a deaf ear to the wishes of the people, and misleading the Company with false reports. They petitioned for his removal, and for a fresh governor with more emigrants, not to be scattered abroad in patroonships or scattered holdings, but grouped as in New England in townships, each with its own elected officials, who, all in combination, should make up the government of the colony. It is to be noticed, too, that while the Twelve only addressed Kieft, the Eight went a step further, and petitioned the Council.[1]

Supine as the Company had been in care for their colonists, they at least saw that it was useless to retain Kieft. The whole question was referred to the 'Rekenkammer,' a committee of the Company appointed, strictly speaking, for the control of finance, but allowed to go beyond that and deal with general questions of organisation. They produced a report, proposing certain administrative reforms. Kieft was to be superseded and called to account for his first attack on the Indians. Trade was to be thrown open to all permanent residents in the colony, but there was to be no sale of arms to the natives. New Amsterdam was to be fortified and garrisoned: every settler throughout the colony was to have a musket and side arms; their efficiency was to be tested by two annual inspections. Kieft's successor was to take out with him a body of colonists who were to be grouped in townships as in New England. Lastly, representative government was to be instituted. The 'Freedoms,' the conditions that is by which the patroons held their estates, already provided that each township should appoint one or two delegates to represent it at Manhattan. This somewhat vague condition was now made definite by the proposal that deputies should meet every six months to confer

Report of the Rekenkammer.[2]

---

[1] Brodhead (vol. i. pp. 397-400) reproduces this memorial almost textually.   [2] N. Y. Docs. vol. i. p. 149.

with the Governor and Council on public affairs.¹ The reforms granted by the Company fell far short of these recommendations. They did not in fact amount to much more than a change of governor. But that change brought with it a change of system. Kieft's successor had in theory as little love for popular government as Kieft himself. But, unlike Kieft, he had an honest desire to govern the colony in the interests of the settlers, and practice showed that he could reach that end only through a concession of popular rights.

In 1645 Kieft was superseded and replaced by Peter Stuyvesant. The personal misconduct of Kieft and the selfish neglect of the Company had prepared the settlers to see an enemy in any governor. There was nothing in the personal character of Stuyvesant to efface such impressions. An austere Puritan in a community of lax morals, an educated gentleman with a strong dash of pedantry among tradesmen and boors, a martinet in a shifting crowd of varied origin with no fixed political institutions, Stuyvesant was at every step severed from his subjects by some barrier of principle or sentiment. Yet two things more than made amends. Stuyvesant had shown himself a good soldier: his loss of a leg, shot away by a Portuguese gunner before St. Martin's, impressed that side of his character on men's imaginations, and they soon had better reason for knowing that he could give the colony that security which was its first need. He had a still higher claim to honour. He, almost alone among all who controlled the destinies of New Netherlands, regarded the colony as a political society, not a trading station. His narrow and unsympathetic temper withheld him from entering fully into the life of the settlers. But if he did not

¹ N. Y. Docs. vol. i. p. 149.

trouble himself about their wishes, he was clear-sighted enough to understand their needs, and honest and public-spirited enough to struggle for them. He was in a sense the founder of the colony: he freed it from a commercial tyranny, from the dominion of traders and clerks; the colonists did the rest for themselves.

The new Governor took out instructions, embodying in some measure the reforms suggested by the Reken-kammer. The different townships were to send delegates to the Council. That, however, was a far less effectual guarantee for liberty than would have been a chamber of representatives sitting as a separate and independent body. A formal boundary was to be arranged with the Indians, and the settlers were to be organized as a militia. The colonists were to be persuaded to group themselves in townships 'as the English do.' Unluckily the Company forgot that these townships were only part and parcel of a system of self-government, and that they would never have existed but for the strong corporate feeling which actually called the community into existence before it had a local habitation.

<small>His instructions.[1]</small>

As I have said, Stuyvesant had no faith in popular government. On that subject his doctrines were as vigorous and as decided as those which Herodotus puts into the mouth of Megabyzus. Give the election of rulers to the commons, and every scoundrel will vote for his like. The thief, the drunkard and the cheat will each wish for a representative who shares his infamy.[2]

<small>Introduction of representative government.</small>

Stuyvesant, however, soon found that his trenchant theories must give way to practical necessities. The first thing to be done was to make the fortifications of New Amsterdam secure against attack. The Company could not or would not bear the whole cost:

[1] Brodhead, vol. i. p. 414.   [2] *Ib.* p. 574.

money had to be raised and the necessities of the ruler, according to regular historical precedent, made for the constitutional rights of the subject. A chamber of representatives was appointed by a process which divided the choice between the Governor and the freemen. The whole body of freemen from Manhattan and three adjacent districts were to nominate eighteen representatives. Of these, the Governor was to elect nine who were to form a second chamber, tribunes of the commons, as Stuyvesant with a characteristic touch of pedantry, called them.[1]

This was undoubtedly a step in advance of anything that had gone before. The Nine were more like constitutional representatives of the people than the Twelve or the Eight who had preceded them. Their functions were general: they were not called into existence by one special emergency. But if the change was a step towards representative government, there was yet a long distance to be traversed. The Nine were to deliberate with the Council on public affairs; three of them were to share the judicial functions of the Council, sitting in turn, one for a week. They had, however, no legislative powers: there was no provision for any exact division of powers between the Council and the Nine. Their undefined position was shown, too, by the fact that the qualifications of electors were not specified.

Indeed, it was hardly worth while to define the qualifications of the freemen since their function did not extend beyond the first election. After that the body was to become self-electing, with certain right of veto vested in the Governor. Every year six were to retire; before that retirement the Nine were to nominate twelve candidates for the vacancies, and of these half were to be chosen by the Governor.

[1] Brodhead, vol. i. p. 474; N. Y. Docs. vol. i. p. 309.

Another element was wanting. There was nothing of local representation in the system. The inhabitants of four districts elected, but they elected collectively, and there was nothing to hinder the whole nine from being residents in New Amsterdam.

Yet the system was a gain, not only as an earnest of better things, but in itself. Even if we regard it as only the appointment of a standing executive committee that was something. In such a community as New Netherlands it was something to spread power. Granted that the Nine were in theory an irresponsible body, yet public opinion could act upon them far more quickly and effectively than it could on the Governor and Council.

Popular rights in New Netherlands advanced on two distinct lines. The commonalty as a whole were slowly and imperfectly acquiring certain rights of self-government. Meanwhile the different sections of the community were acquiring like rights, locally, and in a restricted form. In New Netherlands the municipal freedom of the towns was acquired partly because circumstances made it a necessity, partly as the result of intercourse with New England. As early as 1645 Kieft granted a charter to a body of emigrants from Massachusetts. Their leader, Lady Deborah Moody, described by Winthrop as 'a wise and anciently [1] religious woman,' had been censured by the Church of Salem as an Anabaptist. She was apparently not banished, but withdrew peacefully of her own accord with a number of those who shared her religious views. They established themselves on Long Island at a place called by the Dutch Gravesand, a name which the new comers anglicised into Gravesend. In 1644 the settlement was attacked by the savages. Lady Moody, however, escaped the fate of her sister heretic, Anne

Municipal institutions.

---

[1] Anciently, *i.e.* formerly, with reference to her lapse into heresy.

Hutchinson. Her new home was well garrisoned with forty men, and after a stubborn resistance the assailants were beaten off. In the next year the freemen at Gravesend were incorporated as a township, with power to make such 'civil ordinances' as the majority should think good. They were to elect from among themselves three magistrates, approved by the Governor, who should act as a court.[1]

In the same year the like privileges were granted to the settlers at Breuckelen. In their case we have direct evidence that joint tenure was one of the incidents of their corporate existence, since the deprivation of a share on the common land was the penalty attached to disobedience to the elected magistrates.[2] The policy of creating municipalities with certain rights of self-government was carried further by Kieft's successor. Stuyvesant had, as we have seen, little liking for democratic institutions. But he had equally little liking for the independent jurisdiction of the patroons Just as a mediæval king built up extra-feudal communities with certain rights of self-government as a check on the nobles, so now Stuyvesant strengthened the townships as a check on the patroons. We have seen already how the independent patroonship of Rensselaerwyck became obnoxious to Kieft. Under Stuyvesant the struggle between the rights of the Company and the privileges of the patroons went on. The independent jurisdiction of the patroons was an obstacle to any common system of defence, and it also interfered with the commercial supremacy of the Company. Indeed, the trade with the natives in arms and ammunition was obnoxious in both of these ways. The principal offenders in these matters were the agents of Rensselaer, whose territory on the upper Hudson commanded the highway of the Indian fur trade. They

---

[1] *Doc. Hist.* vol. i. pp. 4-12.   [2] Brodhead, vol. i. p. 422.

refused to fulfil a stipulation specially inserted in the grant of territory binding the patroon to give an annual report of the condition of his settlement to the Company. Moreover they endeavoured to bind over their settlers not to appeal against any of their proceedings to the Governor and Council. One special act of insubordination brought matters to a head. Within the territory of Rensselaerwyck stood a little group of farmhouses forming the hamlet of Beverswyck. In March 1648 the Governor proclaimed a fast throughout the colony. The proclamation was posted in Beverswyck. Thereupon Van Slechtenhart, the agent for the settlement, declared that Stuyvesant had encroached on the rights of the patroon. A further dispute arose. Fort Orange actually stood within the territory of Rensselaerwyck. It was plainly needful that the authorities who were responsible for the safety of the fort should have some control over the land around. Stuyvesant with good reason forbade the erection of any houses within musket-shot of the fort. The agent defied this order, and was arrested and brought to New Amsterdam.

Under these circumstances it was natural that Stuyvesant should assert the direct authority of the Company over the settlers at Beverswyck, and it was natural too that he should purchase their loyalty by a grant of privileges. In April 1652 the Director on his own authority proclaimed Beverswyck a township independent of the patroon.[1]

New Amsterdam becomes a city. In the same year the privileges which had been granted to Breuckelen were extended to New Amsterdam. An order had been issued by the Company in 1650 that New Amsterdam should be made a municipal government with a Schout—that is to say, an official responsible for the administration of ordinary criminal justice, a Burgo-

[1] Brodhead, vol. i. pp. 491-4, 533-5.

master and Schepens, functionaries who may, by a convenient analogy, if not with scientific precision, be called a Mayor and Aldermen. Stuyvesant, as it would seem, considered that he might put this proposed constitution in force or not, as he pleased. It was not till two years after the issue of the order, till as we have seen the system of municipal government was establishing itself in other parts of the colony, that the privileges thus granted to New Amsterdam were actually enjoyed. One cannot doubt that the example of Breuckelen had a direct influence on her more important neighbour. As early as 1642 the Twelve in their remonstrance to the Company had pointed out that in the Fatherland every village had its five or seven Schepens. Now they saw a mere hamlet at their own doors enjoying like privileges. Were they to be withheld from the capital of the colony, with its five stone warehouses and its harbour, where twenty merchantmen might be seen riding at anchor? Stuyvesant can hardly be said to have yielded to the demand for popular government. Rather he stayed that demand by a partial and almost deceptive concession. New Amsterdam was to have two Burgomasters and five Schepens, but they were to be nominated by the Governor. Such a change did not in theory shift the basis of sovereignty. Yet, as was said before, in such a community as New Netherlands to delegate the exercise of power is an important change. Let the Governor choose his municipal staff with never so little regard to the wishes of the people, yet such a body must be in some measure amenable to public opinion.[1]

The value of the point gained was soon seen. Within six months of their appointment the new officials—the Town Council as one may for conveni-

[1] *Memorial History*, vol. i. p 278. The author, Mr. Fernow, refers to New York Documents.

ence call them—sent one of their number to Amsterdam to lay before the Company various grievances and complaints against the Governor.[1] Soon after they showed in another matter that though they might be Stuyvesant's nominees, they were not his obedient servants. The defences of the city were a subject of jealousy and dispute. The settlers were willing to spend money on palisading the city itself. They not unnaturally demanded that the Fort which existed mainly to secure the commerce of the Company should be fortified at the Company's expense. When the Town Council was called on to contribute to that end they refused.

Action of the Town Council.

In a New England township the town meeting would at once furnish a ready means for the expression of popular feeling. As it was, the Burgomasters and Schepens summoned certain leading citizens to devise means for meeting the public expenditure. Twenty-four townsmen attended the meeting. It was agreed to propose to Stuyvesant that the Excise be handed over to the Burgomasters and Schepens, to be applied to the payment of public expenses. This was submitted to Stuyvesant, but refused.

Two months later another meeting of town delegates chosen by the Burgomaster and Schepens was held. Their policy was a mere renewal of their past offer. But apparently the Burgomasters and Schepens only gave their consent to the arrangement on condition that the townsmen agreed to submit to such expenditure and such measures as should be enacted and adopted by them for the support of the city.

This second attempt was more successful than the first. Despotic as the government of New Netherlands was, yet leavened as her nationality was with alien elements, there was too much of the old Dutch temper,

[1] Brodhead, vol. i. p. 559.

of the spirit of the men who had defied Charles and Philip, to suffer the power of the purse wholly to pass out of their hands. According to what one may call the customary precedent of the Old World, external danger furnished the community with an effective weapon against its rulers. At the very time when the colonists were pressing their demands the New England confederation was only withheld from active hostility by the fortunate disloyalty of Massachusetts to its associates.[1] That danger was materially increased by the existence of settlements on Long Island, nominally under Dutch jurisdiction, but English in origin and sympathies. Obstinate Stuyvesant might be, but he was clear-sighted enough to see that, without some measure of popular support, his own position and that of the colony was desperate, and that he could only win that support by concessions on the lines suggested by the townsmen. On November 11 Stuyvesant announced that he was prepared to surrender a portion of the Excise to be administered by the Burgomasters and Schepens—the Town Council as we may for convenience call them. But the concession was fettered with conditions which went far to destroy its value. The Company must give their consent. The townsmen must maintain at their own cost a preacher and a schoolmaster.

These charges the townsmen at first said would swallow up the whole sum made over to them. Finally, however, after some demur they agreed to the terms.[2]

Later on in the year the Burgomasters and Schepens addressed a petition to the Company asking on behalf of the city fuller rights, modelled on those of Amsterdam. They asked that the burghers should choose their own Schout, that the Excise should be made over to them unconditionally, and that they

[1] See *New England*, vol. i. pp. 400-2.
[2] For all these negotiations see *Court Minutes*.

should have power to levy rates and expend the proceeds.¹

On January 24, before an answer could be received to these requests, the Burgomasters and Schepens again approached Stuyvesant. They proposed that the Council of the Colony should still be nominated by the Director, but from a list containing twice the number of names necessary, sent in by themselves. This Stuyvesant refused. As a minor concession he granted salaries to the officials, to the Burgomaster three hundred and fifty guilders a year, to the Schepens two hundred and fifty. This sounds like an attempt to bribe the recipients into an abandonment of popular rights.

In answer to the petition the Company made but a petty concession. The Schout was to be appointed as before by the Company, but was to be in some measure under the control of the Burgomasters and Schepens.²

The somewhat harsh and dictatorial temper of the new Director made almost impossible a task already difficult enough in itself. He was, like Dale, a resolute martinet, trained in military methods and determined to introduce discipline and something of austerity into the life of a lax and somewhat corrupt society. Attendance at Divine worship was made compulsory. The problem of enforcing sobriety and controlling taverns was dealt with in a manner which curiously anticipated the ideas of modern temperance reformers. Taverns were to close at nine in the evening. Inasmuch as brawling and fighting in taverns even on the Lord's day of rest was common, they were to be closed on Sunday till two in the afternoon, except for travellers, and for the sale of drink to be consumed in private houses.

Other ordinances imposed by Stuyvesant throw light on the life of the community. The danger of fire

<small>Stuyvesant as a reformer.</small>

¹ *Court Minutes*, vol. i. pp. 92–5. ² *Ib.* p. 157.

is shown by a regulation which enforced the sweeping of chimneys, and by a prohibition of any further building of wooden chimneys. By a later ordinance, thatched roofs and wooden chimneys are to be removed. An attempt is made to check the promiscuous influx of foreign traders by an ordinance permitting no one to engage in trade unless he has a house in the colony and resides for three years.

In conformity with the instruction of the Company an ordinance was issued urging the settlers to consolidate themselves into villages, but there is no trace of any attempt to enforce this. The mixture of urban and rural conditions which prevailed in New Amsterdam itself is shown by the prohibition of hayricks within the town, and of stray hogs, as unwholesome and unsightly, and likely to injure the fortification.[1]

The Excise was to be handed over to the Council and applied to the payment of salaries, and they might with the approval of the commons impose certain rates.[2] The disposition of the Excise soon gave rise to further disputes. The Town Council, it was alleged, expended the money exclusively on the city defences and neglected those of Fort Amsterdam. Accordingly the Governor, supported by his Council, resumed the Excise, and as before sold the right of levying it to the highest bidder.[3]

If, however, this portion of the popular demands appeared to have been lost almost as soon as gained, there were compensations elsewhere. Hitherto such assertions of popular rights as had been made had been limited to the capital of the colony. In November 1653 the agitation entered on a new phase. A conference of delegates met at New Amsterdam.[4] There were two from New Amsterdam itself, two each from Gravesend and Flushing, and

<small>Conference at New Amsterdam.</small>

---

[1] For all these regulations see *Court Minutes*, vol. i. p. 135.
[2] *Ib.* p. 218. [3] *Ib.* p. 341. [4] Brodhead, vol. i. p. 569.

two from a third English settlement on Long Island, incorporated by Stuyvesant in 1650, by the name of Middelburg. There were also two representatives of the Council of New Netherlands. It would not be easy to imagine a more curiously complicated situation. Stuyvesant throughout showed himself inclined to favour the settlements of English origin. Puritan rigidity appealed to him far more effectively than did the lax cosmopolitanism of New Netherlands. Between the Dutch settlers and the English immigrants there was little jealousy. Yet here were Stuyvesant's clients, one may almost call them, the English settlers, making common cause with their Dutch rivals.

The immediate object of the conference was one which did not directly touch the question of either popular rights or English encroachment. It was to take measures for protecting the colony against attacks by the Indians and by pirates.

No definite measures of defence were adopted, and the congress adjourned till the following month. But when once machinery is constructed which lends itself even incompletely to the assertion of popular rights, it is no easy matter to limit its action. The English representatives hinted that unless something was done for their protection the Long Island townships would have to form themselves into some kind of corporate association. Stuyvesant might look with undue favour on English claims. But an assertion of the rights of self-government, coupled with a scarcely veiled threat of secession, could not fail to move him. To balance the three English-speaking townships Stuyvesant announced his intention of incorporating three Dutch townships of Amersfort, Breuckelen and Midwout.[1]

---

[1] Breuckelen, it is scarcely needful to say, is the modern Brooklyn. Amersfort and Midwout are now Flatlands and Flatbush, at the south-east extremity of Long Island.

ENGLISH INFLUENCE.

Although these concessions were only promised and not formally granted, yet the inhabitants now ven-
<small>Convention of delegates.[1]</small> tured to act as a corporate body. Consequently when the convention reassembled in December its composition differed widely from what it had been a month before. Amersfort, Breuckelen and Midwout all sent representatives. So did the English settlement of Heemstede, which, though it had a share in summoning the first meeting, took no active part therein Amersfort for some reason was allowed three representatives. This brought the whole number up to seventeen, of whom nine were Dutch, eight English. We may fairly conjecture that Stuyvesant's object in incorporating the three townships was to ensure that neither party should preponderate, and also to grant no popular rights save such as were absolutely needful for the protection of the colony from invasion.

An historical paradox-monger, whom it would be flattery to call ingenious, has maintained the thesis that
<small>English influence.</small> North America owes everything that is wholesome in her political and intellectual life to Holland.[2] It would be nearer to the truth, though an exaggeration, to say that such political freedom as the Dutch colony enjoyed was won for it by the efforts of those English allies who came in the guise of invaders. We cannot doubt that the practical training in the arts of self-government which the English delegates brought with them from their earlier colonial home, the habit of readily translating the abstract doctrines of political freedom into concrete form, the comprehension of the value and limits of political machinery, made them now invaluable allies.

That view is confirmed by the fact that the drafting of a petition of rights and grievances was entrusted to

---

[1] Brodhead, vol. i. pp. 571-5.
[2] Mr. Campbell in *The Puritan in Holland, England and America.*

George Baxter. The document was in six heads. It complained of the arbitrary action of the Director both in making enactments and appointments, and granting lands to favoured individuals. Proclamations remained in force without the inhabitants being duly notified of their existence. There was no proper system of public defence. Settlements had been made on the strength of promised patents, and these had been delayed without reason.[1]

In no one specific instance did Stuyvesant acknowledge the justice of these complaints or offer a remedy of the alleged grievance. Yet we are not to suppose that the action of the delegates bore no fruit. We can distinctly trace in the subsequent policy of the Director a tendency to concession which we may fairly set down to the resolute attitude of the settlers.

Breuckelen already had two Schepens elected by the townsmen. In 1654 the number was raised to four, and they were allowed to elect a Schout. Privileges of the same kind were granted to Midwout and Amersfort, and the three villages were to unite into a district with an administrative council of elected delegates.[2]

The privileges of these outlying settlements formed in turn a standard to be arrived at by New Amsterdam. Thus in 1656 we find the Council complaining with good reason that, while almost every village in the colony had a municipal government of its own election, that of New Amsterdam was nominated by the Governor.[3]

After some dispute a compromise was reached which practically meant that the Burgomasters and Schepens should elect their successors, but that Stuyvesant should

---

[1] It was in answer to these representations that Stuyvesant delivered himself of his comprehensive condemnation of the system of popular election, *v.s.* p. 34.

[2] Brodhead, vol. i. p. 580.   [3] *Ib.* p. 613.

have a right of veto.¹ Two years later this was modified. An arrangement which had been before suggested was now adopted. The Town Council sent a list of names, twice as many as there were places, and Stuyvesant chose one half.²

The gradual and piecemeal growth of popular government in New Netherlands was strictly according to mediæval precedent. The parallel went a stage further. In the Old World the change from serfdom to municipal freedom was too often followed by a change from a democratic to an oligarchical municipality. New Netherlands did not escape the danger. From almost its earliest days the city had numbered among its population traders who had no fixed connection with the colony, and contributed nothing to its permanent stability and prosperity. In 1657 the Town Council sent an address to Stuyvesant calling attention to this, and petitioning that the right of trade should be restricted to burghers.

The greater burghership.

We learn incidentally from this petition that Scotch traders were a special object of jealousy and disapproval. 'They sail hither and thither to the best trading places, taking the bread as it were out of the mouths of the good burghers and resident inhabitants, without being subject in time of peace or war to any trouble or expense.' 'They carry away the profits in time of peace, and in time of war abandon the country and the inhabitants thereof.'³

The proposal of the Town Council fell in with Stuyvesant's love of rigid discipline and his oligarchical prejudices. He saw in it, too, an opportunity for increasing the revenue. Any trader might acquire the rights of burghership by paying a fee of twenty guilders.

¹ Brodhead, vol. i. p. 613.　　² *Ib.* p. 639.
³ The petition and Stuyvesant's answer to it are in the *Court Minutes*, vol. ii. pp. 286-7.

The same privileges were granted without payment to all who were born in the city or dwelt there for the oddly devised term of a year and six weeks, and to all who married the daughters of burghers.

This restriction was undoubtedly fair and expedient. Unfortunately it was made the occasion for a thoroughly unwise extension of the principle of oligarchy. Nor was this forced on by Stuyvesant; it was approved and in part suggested by the Town Council. The scheme created a class of great burghers as they were called, in distinction to the common or small burghers above described. This right was to be obtained by a payment of fifty guilders; those who enjoyed it were to be exempt from military service and from arrest, and they only were to be eligible for the city offices. This greater burghership was to be extended to the officers of the Company and to ministers of the Gospel, to those holding military commissions, and to all who had as yet served as Burgomaster and Schepens, and it was to be continued to all their male descendants. Since the Town Council was a self-creating and not an elective body, the system practically disfranchised for municipal purposes all but the richer citizens and the officials of the Company.[1]

Happily the mistake was soon seen and repaired. It is not unlikely that the purpose of the scheme was as much financial as political. Few took up the greater burghership; the scheme was unremunerative, and it inconveniently limited the choice of public officials. To meet this difficulty Stuyvesant at his own discretion nominated no persons to the greater burgher right, a proceeding approved of by the Burgomaster and Schepens.[2] This may perhaps be taken as an evidence

---

[1] On the ordinance creating the greater and smaller burghers see *Laws and Ordinances*, p. 301.

[2] *Court Minutes*, vol. ii. p. 315.

of the establishment of more friendly relations between the Director and those under him.¹

Eleven years after the convention of 1653, when the storm-cloud of invasion, soon to burst with over-whelming force, overhung the colony, another meeting of a like kind was called. Its proceedings will more fitly come before us as an incident in the struggle which made New Netherlands English territory. It is enough for the present to notice how imperfect an approach these conventions were to an effective system of representative government. They were called merely to meet an emergency; they had no defined functions or specified rights; they failed to give the citizens any certain or continuous training in self-government.

<small>The convention of 1664.</small>

Yet it would be a great mistake to set them down as useless. We fail to understand the constitutional history of New Netherlands unless we look at it as a struggle for popular rights against a body of commercial monopolists, fought not on any one battle-field, but here and there as occasion offered. There was not, as in the New England colonies, a comprehensive and systematic machinery of self-government under which the citizen had a double set of rights, the one as a townsman, the other as a freeman of the colony, while at the same time the relations of the municipality to the State were harmoniously adjusted. In New Netherlands we must cast aside all these ideas, and be content to study the measures by which at any time and in any fashion, whether as freemen of their town or citizens of New Netherlands, the settlers asserted and gained the right of managing their own affairs.

Looked at from one point of view, all these incidents

---

¹ Brodhead, vol. i. p. 271-2. He gives the text of the more important portions, and epitomizes the rest.

are stages in the political development of the colony. From another, they mark a continuous struggle against the narrow and selfish policy of the Company. Any care which they might have felt for the permanent advancement of the colony was dwarfed and thrust into the background by other interests, first by the struggle with Spain, then by the contest with the Portuguese for trade and territory in Brazil. When the Finance Board of the States-General urged the Company to a more liberal and public-spirited policy, the appeal was met with indifference and evasion. Certain definite reforms were proposed. The trade which supplied the Indians with guns and powder was to be abolished. The Amsterdam Chamber, speaking for the Company, simply answered by pointing out the immense price which the Indians were ready to pay. There should be more clergymen and schoolmasters: none were wanted. Stuyvesant should be recalled to report on the real state of the colony: his information was needless. Fifteen thousand guilders should be spent every year by the Company in exporting farmers and husbandmen: the Company could not meet such a charge.[1]

Inefficiency of the Company.

The colonists, too, could not appeal with any effect against the Company's officials. The Governor and the other servants could plead their instructions: the Company could plead that these instructions had been misunderstood or could disavow them altogether; between them the settlers looked in vain for redress or reform.

The colonists did indeed succeed in obtaining the recall of Kieft, but that was hardly from regard for the settlers; rather because his misgovernment was so manifestly making the colony a source of scandal and loss to the Company. The ineffectual struggle to get

[1] N. Y. Docs. vol. i. pp. 387-95.

rid of an obnoxious official, Cornelius Van Tienhoven, the hopelessness of any attempt to get a fair hearing against Stuyvesant, are sufficient illustrations of the mischief inherent in the Company's control. The charges of maladministration brought against Tienhoven may have been exaggerated. But it is clear enough that he was a man of notoriously disreputable life, that it was an open scandal to retain such an one in office. So too, in 1650, we find the Vice-Director writing pathetically to the Company that two letters of his protesting against the arbitrary proceedings of Stuyvesant had met with no answer. In a letter of the same date we find the select men of New Amsterdam complaining that while they were endeavouring to call the attention of the Company's Directors to the misconduct of Stuyvesant, members of that body were privately sending him messages of encouragement.[1]

The administrative failure of the Company was in part due to their system of choosing and promoting their servants. This is described by De Vries, who contrasts it with the method adopted by the Dutch East India Company. There every official passed through a regular gradation of service, learning his duties step by step. In the West India Company an untried man might be at once thrown into a position of dignity and responsibility without any preparation or training.[2]

The loss of the Company's Records leaves us without adequate data by which to gauge the progress of population during the years of the Company's control. By 1664 Stuyvesant estimated it at full ten thousand,[3] a number whose symmetry naturally excites suspicion. We have already seen how that

Increase of population.

[1] N. Y. Docs. vol. i. pp. 445-6.   [2] De Vries, p. 151.
[3] Brodhead, vol. i. p. 734. He quotes a letter of Stuyvesant's written June 10. 1664.

population was made up of miscellaneous nationalities. Diverse in origin, the settlers were not held together by that community of religion which was so terribly effective a bond of union for New England. Jogues was as much startled by the variety of sects as by that of races. Beside Presbyterian Calvinists, there were to be found Romanists, Lutherans, Anabaptists, and English Independents.

In this the colony only followed the example of the mother country. As there Calvinism was the recognised creed. The difficulties of the relations between Church and State were effectively illustrated on the small field of New Netherland history. The clergy were primarily responsible to the Classis of Amsterdam, the governing body, that is, of the Presbyterian Church in that city. At the same time they were paid by the Company, and were therefore in a certain sense its servants. Thus in 1638 a complaint was lodged with the Classis against Bogardus, the pastor at New Amsterdam. Bogardus wished to return and meet the charges, but was forbidden by Kieft.[1] Four years later the Classis licensed John of Mecklenburgh—or, to give him the name more familiar in New Netherland history, Johannes Megapolensis—as pastor of Rensselaerwyck. Thereupon the Company claimed the right to approve, and therefore by implication to veto, the appointment.[2]

Religious condition of the colony.

Church at Manhattan.

Till 1628 there seems to have been no ministry and no church at Manhattan. A congregation occasionally met and were ministered to by two functionaries of an inferior order, called *Krankbesoeckers*, visitors of the sick.[3] In that year an ordained clergyman sent out from Amsterdam ministered to a mixed

---

[1] Brodhead, vol. i. pp. 173, 278.   [2] *Ib.* p. 342.
[3] This is stated in the *Memorial History*, p. 189 (ch. v.). The editor, who is also the author of this chapter, gives the names of the two officials.

congregation formed of Dutch and Walloons.[1] Fourteen years later the outward fabric of the church was such as to call forth a remonstrance from De Vries. In New England, he told Kieft, the first thought after a settlement had fashioned its needful habitations was the church. The Dutch had lime, stone, and wood, why should they fall short?[2] Kieft, who to do him justice had some care for the dignity and good order of his settlement, answered to the appeal. His enemies tell, with grotesque indignation, how he took the opportunity of a great wedding feast to open a collection for the building of the church, how the guests responded with convivial enthusiasm, replaced next day by ineffectual repentance. It would be well for Kieft's reputation if that had been the weightiest charge brought against him.[3]

In 1652 a second pastor was appointed at New Amsterdam, and it is characteristically illustrative of the condition of the colony that he was chosen as able to preach in Dutch, French, and English.[4]

As early as 1643 Beverwyck had a church, and in 1654 a fourth was founded at Midwont, and before New Netherlands ceased to be Dutch territory there were churches at Breuckelen, and at Bergen in what is now the territory of New Jersey.

Other churches.[5]

The English emigrants, who had passed sometimes singly, sometimes in organized groups, into the Dutch territory, were for the most part men who had withdrawn voluntarily or under pressure from the too rigid ecclesiastical system of New England. It is therefore no matter for surprise that in New Netherlands we hear little of Independent churches, with a

Independent congregations.

---

[1] His name was Jonas Michaelius. A letter from him describing his position and the condition of his church is in the N. Y. Documents, vol. ii. p. 763. It is translated by Mr. H. C. Murphy.
[2] De Vries, p. 148. [3] Vertoogh in N. Y. Docs. vol. i. p. 299.
[4] Brodhead, vol. i. p. 537. [5] *Ib.* pp. 374, 581, 615, 692.

regular ministry. The nearest approach to such seems to have been at West Chester, where a party from New Haven had occupied the site where Mrs. Hutchinson met with her death, and at Middelburgh on Long Island. At neither place was there an established ministry nor an organized church, but Middelburgh had a preacher, and at West Chester we hear of certain collective religious exercises.[1]

It is probable that such congregations would have been more numerous but for an ordinance, passed by the Director and Council in 1656, prohibiting private conventicles.[2]

By 1654 the Lutherans at New Amsterdam had become numerous enough to demand a church of their
Lutherans. own. The petition was laid before Stuyvesant. State toleration was a principle as abhorrent to the Calvinist disciplinarian as it could be to Endicott or Dudley. The Presbyterian clergy of the colony supported the Governor, and the Company refused the request, accompanying their refusal with an instruction to Stuyvesant to do all in his power to draw over the Lutherans to the Calvinistic faith.[3]

New Netherlands had at least the compensating merits of her defects. If she had not the cohesion, the
Treatment of Nonconformists. constraining sense of corporate existence, which bound together New England, she at least escaped the hideous tragedies which deface the history of the Puritan colonies. Such persecution as there was in New Netherlands was no more than the petty and harassing interference which in the seventeenth century in every country almost inevitably followed any deviation from the accepted State creed. In 1656 Stuyvesant, moved by the complaints of the orthodox

---

[1] Letter from Megapolensis and Drusius to the Classis at Amsterdam. O'Callaghan, vol. iii. p. 69, &c.
[2] *Court Minutes,* vol. i. p. 20.   [3] Brodhead, vol. i. p. 582.

ministry, forbade all conventicles not called by established authority, and where doctrines were set forth not in harmony with the Calvinistic faith as defined by the Synod of Dort. Unlicensed preachers holding such conventicles and those attending them were to be punished by fine. The ordinance did not, however, apply to family worship.[1]

This proceeding brought upon Stuyvesant a sharp rebuke from his superiors.[2] Yet, when a Lutheran clergyman was sent out by the members of that Church in Amsterdam, Stuyvesant was permitted to silence him.[3] One concession only the Lutherans could obtain: to meet their views a slight modification was introduced into the Calvinistic liturgy.[4]

Quakers in New Netherlands. Quakerism, so appalling a portent to the New Englander with his rigid creed, his mechanical theology, and his precisely organized ecclesiastical system, was far less so to the Dutchman, whose land was already 'a staple of sects and mint of schism.'[6]

The sufferings of the Quakers in New Netherlands were light indeed compared with their fate in New England. Yet in the Dutch colony their attempts to figure as the unauthorized and self-appointed regenerators of society soon brought them into trouble. It was not till a year after the persecution of Fisher and Austin in Massachusetts that the Quakers made their first inroad upon New Netherlands. On the 1st of

[1] *Laws and Ordinances*, p. 211. [2] *Ib.* p. 618.
[3] Megapolensis as above. [4] Brodhead, vol. i. p. 642.
[5] The Quaker historians deal very scantily with the sufferings of the Friends in New Netherlands. I have, therefore, been compelled to rely mainly on Brodhead, and the authorities whom he quotes (vol. i. pp. 635-9, 689, 705-7). It would seem as if in the eyes of the Quakers the iniquities of New England had made so deep an impression that injustice perpetrated in other colonies was overlooked or forgotten. Besse, indeed (vol. ii. p. 182), attributes Stuyvesant's severity to the instigation of Willett.
[6] Marvell, ed. 1766, vol. iii. p. 290.

June, 1657, five of them landed at New Amsterdam. Their first reception by Stuyvesant was friendly, and they themselves ascribed the subsequent change to the influence of New Englanders. It is certain that conditions which will come before us again had forced Stuyvesant into an alliance with that section of his colony which had immigrated from New England, a section growing in numbers and importance. Yet the proceedings of the Quakers were in themselves so repellent to a man of Stuyvesant's temper that his action need not be assigned to foreign interference.

Of the five Quakers, three were women. Two of these—Mary Weatherhead and Dorothy Waugh—two days after landing began preaching in the streets of New Amsterdam. They were arrested and imprisoned, subjected not, as it would seem, to absolute cruelty but to much discomfort, and after eight days suffered to sail for Rhode Island.

In the meantime their three companions chose another field of ministration in Long Island. Two soon departed. The third, Robert Hodgson, was almost at once arrested. He contrived, however, to turn the magistrate's house where he was detained into a place for a religious meeting. The matter was reported to Stuyvesant; the Quakers and two of these who had befriended him were sent as prisoners to New Amsterdam, Hodgson himself brutally dragged for thirty miles over rough roads at the tail of a cart. The Council sat in judgment on him, and sentenced him to a fine of six hundred guilders. In default of payment he was to be flogged, and publicly worked in the streets for two years, chained to a wheelbarrow. With that craving for martyrdom which somewhat mars the heroism of the early Quakers, Hodgson refused the help of certain benevolent persons who would have paid his fine.

The sentence, however, was soon remitted. According to a Quaker tradition, not very probable in itself, Willett, of New England, who had been the instigator of Stuyvesant's cruelty, was now by popular clamour brought to repentance, or at least to a sense of shame. He interceded for the prisoner; his prayer was backed by Stuyvesant's sister, and within a month Hodgson was set free. Short as were Hodgson's missionary labours on Long Island, they seem to have borne fruit. In the very same month that he was suffering at New Amsterdam, his disciples had become numerous enough and in Stuyvesant's eyes formidable enough to make special measures needful. A proclamation was issued making it an offence punishable by a fine of fifty pounds to harbour a Quaker, while if a sea-captain landed any of the sect he was to forfeit his vessel.

The proclamation had unlooked-for political effects. The citizens of Flushing had already been excited by the punishment of one Henry Townshend, who had formerly lived in that town. For holding Quaker meetings in his house he had been fined. In default he was to be banished, and was to be flogged if he stayed in defiance of the order. When the proclamation was posted a number of the inhabitants drew up an address to Stuyvesant, declaring the injustice of his proceedings and distinctly refusing to obey his edict. Stuyvesant dealt with the recalcitrant town in a fashion for which mediæval history offers many precedents. Not only was the Schout who had been specially forward in befriending Quakers deposed and fined, the political rights granted by Kieft were withdrawn; the town was henceforth to be governed by a council of seven nominated from among its own inhabitants by the Governor. At New Amsterdam we hear no more of Quakerism. It continued to make its way among the half independent settlements on Long Island, harassed by fines and the dispersion of

Disturbances at Flushing.

meetings, but not, as in New England, the victim of any thoroughgoing attempt at extirpation.

To suppress a sect which had no organized ministry and no fixed places of worship was indeed a hopeless task unless the whole of the community were really in earnest in aiding the Government. Meetings were held in barns, in woods, and in fields. But in 1662, emboldened perhaps by impunity, the Quakers about Flushing established a regular meeting house in the abode of one John Bowne, a yeoman who had emigrated from Derbyshire.

Stuyvesant met this breach of law, as he deemed it, by a fresh proclamation. It was directed nominally at every deviation from the orthodox State creed. The conventicles of every other religion were declared illegal, and attendance at them was to be punished by fine. Seditious books were to be neither imported nor distributed, and all new comers were to report themselves to the Secretary.

At the same time Bowne was fined, and refusing to pay his fine was sent as a prisoner to Amsterdam. There by good fortune he contrived to get a hearing before the Directors of the Company. Stuyvesant's proclamation might well alarm them. In his eagerness to strike at Quakers he had asserted a doctrine which the rulers of the colony had never approved—the need of conformity as enforced by the State—a doctrine which must be fatal to a community composed as was New Netherlands. If the Directors were inclined to befriend the Quakers, the form in which Stuyvesant had made his attack gave them the very opportunity which they needed. They addressed a sharp admonition to Stuyvesant on the whole question of toleration, and of the proper method to be adopted towards sectaries. They laid down no theories of freedom of conscience. Apparently they held that the right to check heresy might be kept in reserve, a weapon to meet extreme cases. But in practice no man was to be molested as long as he created no civil disturbance. It would be better that there should be no sectaries: but if there were any let them be connived at, otherwise population, so needful to a youthful state, would be destroyed. Not a word was said of the Quakers, but the remonstrance of the Company gave them the protection which they needed. In that declaration we have the key to the policy which moulded the life of New Netherlands, the absolute opposite to the central principle of New England. The ideal of the one was a numerous and materially thriving population; religious diversity might be an evil, but, since the conditions of success required inclusiveness, such diversity must be permitted. The ideal of the other was rigid identity of thought, belief and purpose, running through all. If that could be won and material prosperity come with it, well and good. But the State must shrink from no exclusion which could bring that ideal one step nearer. May we not say that, even yet, in the character of the two states can be found some traces of the impress left on each by its founders?

On one point Stuyvesant and his subjects were agreed. We find each urging on the Company the *Education.* need for a fuller and more effective system of education. In their remonstrance, before referred to, sent home in 1649, the nine specify as one of the evils to be remedied the lack of continuous and systematic teaching. As early as 1633, indeed, a schoolmaster had come out to New Amsterdam, and the necessity of maintaining schools had been over and over again acknowledged by the Company. But there was no school-house, and no regular and certain provision for teaching. The school was opened at irregular intervals, at the uncertain choice or pleasure of individuals.[1]

---
[1] Vertoogh, N. Y. Docs. vol. i. p. 317.

In 1650 we find a schoolmaster appointed at New Amsterdam.[1] Two years later a higher class school was to have come into existence, held provisionally in the city tavern.[2] About the same time a school was established at Rensselaerwyck, at which the post of master was combined with that of clergyman.[3] In 1658 we find the Town Council of New Amsterdam making a petition to the Company, which at once illustrates the lack of education and the social and economical advance of the colony. They ask for a schoolmaster competent to teach Latin. At present all who wish for a classical education must seek it at Boston.[4] A community which has begun to feel a need for what one may call educational luxuries has emerged from that hard struggle for bare existence which is the first stage of colonial life.

The efforts of the settlers on behalf of education were seconded by Stuyvesant. A Latin schoolmaster, Alexander Curtius, was engaged. He was the joint servant of the Company and the municipality, receiving from the former five hundred, from the latter two hundred guilders, and eking out his salary by practice as a physician.[5]

The union of leech and teacher does not seem to have worked well. In 1662 Curtius returned to Holland. His place was filled by one Luyck, whom Stuyvesant had brought out as private tutor for his own household. Under him a high school arose, flourishing enough to attract pupils from Virginia.[6]

As it was in religion, so was it in social and industrial life. There was not in New Netherlands anything of that pressure of custom or of public opinion which in New England created uniformity in almost

---

[1] Brodhead, vol. i. p. 516.   [2] *Ib.* p. 537.   [3] *Ib.* p. 538.
[4] *Court Minutes*, vol. iii. p. 15.
[5] Brodhead, vol. i. p. 656.   [6] *Ib.* p. 634.

every department. In outward appearance, in productive industry, and in daily habits the settlements on Long Island can have differed but little from those of New England. On the Hudson and on the shores of Delaware Bay the traveller would have seen perhaps more likeness to Maryland or Virginia. Their tobacco plantations might be seen worked by negro slaves. The estates of the patroons were not unlike the great plantations of the southern colonies. There was, however, this difference. There was always a tendency, illustrated by Beverswyck, for villages to grow up within the patroonship, just as the English village or country town often grew up under the shadow of the manor. There were also another class of farmers, the tenants of the Company, already described, chiefly it would seem in the neighbourhood of Manhattan.

Industrial life.

One cause which undoubtedly depressed the free labourer, and prevented the growth of an industrial and territorial system like that of New England, was the presence of negro slavery. The slave, cheaply fed and slightly housed, is a formidable rival to the free labourer, and the large estate with its staff of servile labour crushes by its rivalry the small farm. The latter is incomparably better in its social results. It may be even a more efficient instrument of production, but of the product a larger portion is intercepted by the wants of the labourer himself, and a smaller margin left for mere return on capital.

Slavery.

There are no statistics of sufficient fulness to show at what rate the importation of negro slaves went on. We know that in the original instrument defining the privileges of the patroons the Company pledged itself to supply the settlers with negroes. That promise was repeatedly renewed in a manner which shows that it was a concession specially valued. It was also in a great measure by Dutch ships that Virginia was supplied with slaves from Africa. In practice the heavy duty imposed by the Company seems to have discouraged any large importation. As a natural consequence, too, most of those imported seem to have been in the employment of the Company. Thus we learn that the fort at New Amsterdam was mainly built by negro labour. The Company seems wisely to have made arrangements whereby its slaves should be gradually absorbed in the free population. In 1644 an ordinance was passed emancipating the slaves of the Company after a fixed period of service. They were still, however, to pay certain dues in kind, and their children were to remain slaves. By a like arrangement in 1663 certain of the Company's slaves were granted a qualified form of freedom, working alternate weeks, one for themselves, one for the Company.

One entry in the Records clearly shows that difference of climate and of economical conditions rather than any moral or religious motives excluded slavery from New England, since we find the settlers at Gravesend, in a petition addressed in 1651 to the Company, specially asking for an increased supply of negroes.[1]

The foreign trade of New Netherlands differed not only in its details, but in its whole principle, from that of New England. The system on which New England was organized left little place for non-resident merchants, or for any whose connexion with the colony was but temporary. At Boston the man who did not belong to a church must have felt himself one of a grade lower than his neighbours. Even a sea-captain and his crew we may be sure can have found Boston no pleasant port if they were wholly out of harmony with its population. Thus the trade of

Commerce.

---

[1] Letter from the townsmen of Gravesend to the Company referred to by Brodhead, vol. i. p. 526.

TRADE WITH THE INDIANS.

Massachusetts was mainly in the hands of residents; the capital that sustained it was largely supplied by the profits of the New England farmer. In New Netherlands it was otherwise. In the Fatherland there was little community between the burgesses or artisans of Amsterdam and the farmers and hinds of the adjacent country. So it was at Manhattan. The fact that trade was largely in the hands of a shifting crowd of divers nationalities went far to justify the rigid commercial policy of the Company.

There was another reason for that. The whole commercial prosperity of New Netherlands turned on that most perilous form of trade, trade with the Indians. On the part of the Dutch there was an unlimited demand for furs, and on the side of the savages an equally unlimited demand for guns, powder, and strong drink. Thus illicit trade was not only an offence against the revenue. It was far worse: the smuggler as an inevitable incident of his crime entangled the colony in the dangers of war, and supplied the enemy with munitions.

Trade with the Indians.

That the Company and those who administered its affairs in the colony should have steered the colony safely through these dangers atones for many of their shortcomings. The most important legacy which the Dutch rulers left to their English successors was the relations of the colony to the Indians, and it is to their high praise that these were relations of mutual trust and good will.

That in spite of Kieft's errors, a name perhaps too lenient, this should have been so was in no small measure due to the personal influence of Stuyvesant. Harsh, masterful, narrow in views and sympathy, yet he was essentially a just man. His self-reliance, his experience as a soldier, his stolid indifference to popular feeling, made him panic-

Stuyvesant's dealings with the natives.

proof. And no one can follow the relations between the European and the savage in every part of North America without seeing that justice far more than humanity was the key-stone of stable relations. The Indian might be treacherous himself, though his imputed treachery was often no more than the necessary consequence of negotiations in a language imperfectly understood. But he at least clearly knew whether those with whom he dealt were trustworthy or faithless. The unflinching devotion of the French missionary, the hearty good fellowship with which the French trapper threw himself into the life of the Indians, the worse compliance with which the rulers of New France made themselves accomplices in the atrocities wrought by their allies: all these were outweighed by isolated acts of treachery such as that by which Denonville and Champigny sent a band of Iroquois chiefs to the French galleys.[1]

The peace made in 1645 between the Dutch settlers and the natives held good for ten years. The breach Outbreak of war in 1655.[2] came, as so often, from an isolated outrage, harshly punished. A settler, lately one of the Company's officials, had his garden plundered by a native squaw. He brutally put her to death. In an instant an Indian force was ready to take the field. Early on a September morning sixty-four canoes carrying some five hundred armed savages appeared before New Amsterdam. The Indians landed and poured into the streets. Stuyvesant with the little army of the colony was away on service against the Swedes by the Delaware, and the enemy reckoned on finding a wholly defenceless town. But tidings of the danger reached the Governor, and he hurried part of his force back in

---

[1] An account of this, with references to the original French authorities, will be found in Parkman's *Frontenac*, pp. 140-2.

[2] Brodhead, vol. i. pp. 606-8.

time to meet the invader. For a while it seemed as if the savages might be brought to terms, but in the evening hostilities broke out. Van Dyck, the author of the act which had brought about the war, fell pierced by an Indian arrow. The savages were soon driven from the town. Taking to their canoes they turned to the south-west. Staten Island and the cultivated land on the south-west bank of the river were overrun, and in three days a hundred settlers were killed and a hundred and fifty more taken prisoners. From the settlements on Long Island and from the highlands of the Hudson fugitives, leaving their farms in terror, trooped for safety into New Amsterdam. Again the enemy seemed to threaten the capital. But before the blow fell Stuyvesant and the rest of his troop were back at Manhattan. In that crisis all his harshness, his arbitrary temper, his ungenial distrust must have been forgotten; the self-reliance and sobriety of the soldier and the ruler atoned for all. All straggling was forbidden; every available man, whether in the town or on the ships in the harbour, was put under arms. The wall of the town was hastily fortified, and parties were sent out to relieve and garrison the threatened villages.

The enemy at once fell back, terror-struck. Stuyvesant's moderation in using his victory was as conspicuous as his courage and promptitude in winning it. Van Tienhoven, trained in the school of Kieft, was for a war of retaliation. The Governor stood firm: he had shown the enemy that he did not and need not fear them. He now showed them that he only wanted safety, not vengeance. The captives were ransomed, save a certain number, detained among the tribes along the Hudson as pledges for peace.

Three years later trouble again seemed in store for the settlers on the upper Hudson. The natives, debauched by the traders who sold them brandy, were becoming at once familiar and vindictive; the Dutch dwelt in scattered settlements, open to attack, incapable of concentration or mutual support. The settlers in their fear called on Stuyvesant for aid. He not only sent the force asked for, but went in command. Not without difficulty he constrained the inhabitants to gather themselves into a compact settlement in a bend of the river, guarded on the landward side by a palisade.

Further troubles in 1658.[1]

He then held a conference with the Indians. In answer to his complaint of their outrages, they pleaded that such acts were the work of the young chiefs debauched by the drink sold to them by the white men, and that the one murder had been committed by an Indian from a distant tribe. Stuyvesant told them plainly that their excuses could not be entertained, that if they could they must apprehend the murderer, and make restitution for the damage they had wrought. If this was not done, speedy and severe retaliation would follow.

Peace made.

The Indians knew that, though Stuyvesant would not strike wantonly, he could strike heavily. A few days afterwards they returned. They had come, they said, to give a piece of land for the village, a present to the great Dutch sachem to reward him for his long and toilsome journey.

Stuyvesant's efforts to secure peace for his settlers on the upper Hudson were in part frustrated by their own imbecile brutality. A farmer near Esopus, for whom some Indians worked, foolishly gave them a cask of brandy. One of them in his cups let off his gun and caused an alarm. The officer in command of the garrison did his best to pre-

The Indians attack Esopus.

[1] Brodhead, vol. i. pp. 647-9. His account is apparently taken from the Albany Records.

vent a panic, but a party of settlers, defying his orders, rushed out and fired upon the savages.

The Indians were at once up in arms. But for Stuyvesant's forethought, in forcing the settlers to palisade their village, the whole settlement would in all likelihood have been cut off. As it was, a party sent to fetch help from New Amsterdam were intercepted and several of them burnt at the stake. One survivor made his way to New Amsterdam. There was sickness in the town, and it was with difficulty that a force was raised. At length two hundred men were despatched, but before they could reach the threatened settlement the besiegers had dispersed and were in the woods.

The one inestimable benefit which New York owed to its Dutch founders, a benefit shared by the whole body of English-speaking colonists, was the secure alliance of the Five Nations. They alone of the nations seem to have been capable of a continuous policy dictated by intelligent self-interest. Holding as they did the highway between French Canada and the middle colonies, they were both to French and English allies of supreme importance. The advances of French missionary-diplomatists had no lasting effect on that resolute, compact, and self-reliant polity. The foundations of peace with the Dutch were laid, as we have seen, at the Tawasentha, before the West India Company existed.

Dealings with the Five Nations.

The conditions under which the colony lived all tended to confirm the alliance. Between the Mohawks and the tribes along the Hudson, and the coast, there was continual ill-feeling. Over those tribes the Mohawks claimed a certain supremacy, and put it in force by a levy of tribute. The Dutch were compelled in self-defence to be chary in selling munitions of war to the Indians immediately about New Amsterdam. In the case of the Mohawks there was not the same need for caution, and Rensselaerwyck became a mart for guns and powder. Thus it was in a great measure through the Dutch alliance that the Mohawks could maintain their authority over the dependent tribes to the east. As we have seen, in 1645, just as the horrors of the long Indian war were abating, Kieft thought it well to confirm the friendship of the Mohawks by a fresh treaty.[1] Five years later an alarm, due probably in part to the mischief-making jealousy of the tribes on the Hudson, in part to that perpetual source of danger the unauthorized traders, made it needful for Stuyvesant to pacify the Mohawks with a subsidy.[2]

In 1660, when the neighbouring savages threatened the outlying settlement at Esopus with destruction, the Company were anxious that Stuyvesant should enter into an offensive alliance with the Mohawks. Stuyvesant at once pointed out the folly of a policy which would have taught the Mohawks to regard themselves as necessary to the Dutch.[3]

Nothing can illustrate more emphatically the difference between Dutch and English colonization than the early history of the Swedish colonies which grew up in the neighbourhood of the Dutch settlements, and in rivalry with them. We cannot imagine Gilbert and Smith, let them have been never so much baffled and neglected, taking service under France and helping to advance her colonial empire. But the two men who did most to establish the Swedish colony were Netherlanders, men who had urged and furthered Dutch colonial schemes, one a man who had actually borne a hand in the work of colonization. Yet it would be unfair to attribute this to a lack of patriotism in the Dutch character. Rather it shows how little the

The Swedish colony.

---

[1] P. 29. [2] Brodhead, vol. i. p. 523.
[3] *Ib.* p. 677. Mr. Brodhead quotes Stuyvesant's actual words, or at least a translation of them, from the Albany Records.

schemes of colonization concerned or represented the whole country. In helping another nation to encroach on the territory and thwart the policy of the West India Company, they were not interfering with a national enterprise, they were only hindering the schemes of a body of commercial monopolists.

Though Usselinx had no share in the successes, such as they were, of the Dutch West India Company, though he finally appeared as its rival and opponent, yet he might fairly claim to have done something towards calling it into being. It is scarcely possible to say how far the attitude of Usselinx towards Dutch colonization was dictated by patriotic, how far by selfish, motives. When the charter of the West India Company was under discussion he drafted a scheme differing in various important points from that actually adopted. The scheme proposed by Usselinx would have given the stockholders in the Company much fuller rights of representation. Each province was to have its own chamber in the Company. The directors in each chamber were not to be a fixed number, but were to vary in proportion to the amount of stock held by the members of the chamber, and were to be elected by these members.

William Usselinx.

There was moreover to be a dual system of government. Commerce was to be left to the Directors. But what one may call the political and diplomatic affairs of the Company were to be administered by a council elected by the whole body of stockholders. That council was to make regulations for the management of the Company, to appoint governors, and to control its alliances and its declarations of war. At the same time the actual task of legislating for the colony was to be vested in the colonists themselves.

Such a scheme might probably have stimulated the financial prosperity of the Company. By giving shareholders a more direct control over its affairs it would in all likelihood have increased their number, and made the undertaking more attractive. But there its advantages would have ended. Under such a system, as under that which existed, the permanent welfare of the settlers was almost certain to be sacrificed to the financial interests of the shareholders. Nor can it be thought that the system of dual government would have worked smoothly. It would have been impossible to define the spheres of business assigned to each body. That the board of Directors should have no voice in the appointment of a governor would have been practically fatal to harmony. Moreover in all dealings with the savages trade and defence were so inextricably mixed, that it would have been fatal to place each under a separate department.

The best side of Usselinx's proposal beyond doubt was that for giving certain legislative rights to the colonists themselves. That we may well believe would have made the colony more attractive to the better sort of emigrants. It might have gained a degree of stability and life which were denied it under the rule of the Company. On the other hand it would have multiplied administrative difficulties and possibilities of dispute. A conflict between the Company and the local legislature would have been inevitable. Selfish and negligent as the Company's rule was, we may well believe that New Netherlands would have fared worse, racked by the opposing interests of directors, shareholders and colonists.

Though Usselinx's scheme failed of acceptance he did not at once turn his back on the Company. He was willing to act as its agent, to do his best in collecting subscriptions on which he should secure a percentage, and to press its claims on the Government of the United Provinces. He had, in fact, so identified himself with American colonization, that he had learnt to regard his counsel and support as needful to any such scheme. To dispense with him was in his eyes at once a hopeless and an ungrateful attempt.

At length, in 1623, Usselinx found that he could not get what he asked from the Directors of the Company, and that the States-General showed no inclination to interfere. His own republic had failed him; he might fare better with a foreign kingdom, under a monarch of resolute will and far-reaching schemes. In 1624 Usselinx betook himself to Sweden and at once found a favourable hearing from Gustavus Adolphus. Usselinx laid before the King a scheme closely resembling that which he had drafted for the Dutch Company. A joint-stock company was to be created, its affairs managed in part by a board of directors elected by the shareholders, in part by a council nominated by the King. Colonization was not to be the sole or even the main object, and consequently the company was not to have any specified territory assigned to it. Rather it was to be a vast department, superintending all the European trade and all the colonization of the country. It does not appear whether it was to be granted a monopoly of foreign trade, or whether the promoters trusted to the resources of the company to drive all competitors out of the field.[1]

Usselinx and Gustavus Adolphus.

The difficulties which Usselinx encountered in Sweden were wholly different from those which had baffled him in his own country. There he was hampered by the eagerness of rival capitalists: in Sweden the difficulty was to awake zeal and to find capital. The resources of Sweden were wholly unequal to setting on foot such a scheme as Usselinx projected. The Thirty Years' War and the death of

Hindrances to Swedish colonization.

[1] A translation of the proposed Charter of the Company is published in the N. Y. Documents, vol. xii.

Gustavus were bars even to the achievement of any smaller project. It was not till five years after the death of Gustavus that a scheme was set on foot, due, no doubt, to the suggestive proposals and impetuous energy of Usselinx, but falling far short of his ideal. The Swedish colony in America was but a scanty and imperfect fulfilment of Usselinx's scheme; it held out no hopes of that personal reward which was a large element in all those schemes; he plays no part in its accomplishment, his connexion with it is but remote and indirect.

Such as the scheme of Swedish colonization was, it was largely due to the energy of Oxenstierna.

The settlement at Swanendael.[1] The influence of Usselinx had brought Swedes and Hollanders interested in American colonization into communication. In 1630 certain members of the Dutch West India Company had bought from the natives a tract of land on the banks of the Delaware. A settlement was formed at a spot named by the patentees Swanendael, now Lewiston in the State of Delaware. Isolated from the colony at Manhattan, the Swanendael settlement formed no integral member of New Netherlands. For a while it prospered, and in the second year of its existence one of its founders, De Vries, sailed from Holland intending to winter among the settlers. He touched at Manhattan and heard evil tidings. His settlement had been attacked and cut off by the Indians. He pursued his voyage, and we are reminded of that gloomy day when Grenville sailed in quest of Raleigh's settlers and found a row of desolate cabins. When De Vries landed he found the fort a ruin, nothing of its palisade left but charred remains, and the skeletons of his countrymen strewn among the bones of their slaughtered cattle. From an Indian he gleaned some account of the

[1] De Vries, p 32, &c.

tragedy. It had begun, as such feuds usually did, with a paltry theft by a savage. He had pulled down a tin plate bearing the arms of the Republic and melted it for tobacco pipes. The wrath of the Dutch commandant was such that the Indians to pacify him put to death the offender. The settlers saw the danger of this over-ready compliance and remonstrated, but too late. While the settlers were most of them working in the fields, the friends of the slain man attacked the fort. The commandant who chanced to be within was cut down with a tomahawk; the rest were surprised, and in the slaughter that followed not one escaped. The disheartened proprietors made no attempt to renew their settlement, and sold the territory to the West India Company.

When Oxenstierna definitely took up the scheme of American colonization, among those to whom he turned for advice and help was one of the Swanendael proprietors, Samuel Blomaert. That led to intercourse with the suspended Governor of New Netherlands, Peter Minuit. A scheme of colonization was set on foot which could hardly fail to bring its promoters into conflict with the Dutch West India Company, yet which was supported not only by Minuit and Blomaert, but by other shareholders from Amsterdam. Their subscriptions amounted to twelve thousand florins, half the estimated capital of the new company.

<small>Formation of a Swedish company.</small>

In 1637 a company was embodied by charter. Unlike that designed by Usselinx, it was distinctly a colonizing body; trade only followed so far as it was a necessary consequence. The company had a grant of land on the shores of Delaware Bay of undefined amount. The company was to appoint magistrates for the colony, from whom there was to be an appeal to the home government. There was to be civil equality between all Christian denominations. For ten years there were to be no duties, afterwards a tax of five per cent. on all imports and exports. All trade was restricted to Swedish ports and to vessels built in the colony itself. The second condition must for the first few years at least have been a dead letter.[1]

In the winter of 1637 Minuit was despatched with two ships to lay the foundation of the colony. In March he landed, and bought a tract of land from the natives near the mouth of the Schuylkill, where Wilmington now stands. As might have been expected the intrusion on Dutch territory did not pass unchallenged. Only three years before Fort Nassau had been rescued by the strong hand from English encroachment. If Minuit was allowed to carry out his scheme and thus to command the river, Fort Nassau might be rendered useless as a trading station. A protest was sent to Minuit;[2] it was met at first with subterfuges. No colony was intended, the ships were bound for the West Indies, and had only touched for wood and water.[3] The mask was soon thrown off. A fort was built and named Christina, after the Queen of Sweden.[4] It could hardly be called the foundation of a colony: it was rather the assertion of a territorial claim, and the establishment of a garrison under the shadow of which a colony might grow up.

Swedish settlement on the Schuylkill.

As a trading station the new venture was a success, and the Dutch trade in the Delaware was reported as 'wholly ruined.'[5] But such success left no time for agriculture, and the colony was dependent on the

[1] Acrelius in *N. Y. Hist. Coll.* 2nd series, vol. i. pp. 408-9.
[2] N. Y. Docs. vol. xii. p. 19.   [3] Vertoogh, p. 282.
[4] Report by Andrew Hudde; published in the *N. Y. Hist. Coll.* 2nd series, vol. ii. p. 429; cf. Acrelius, p. 409. This is also mentioned in a letter written from Jamestown to Secretary Windebank, May 8, 1638. Pennsylvania Archives, 2nd series, vol. v. p. 56.
[5] Brodhead, vol. i. p. 320.

mother country for supplies. There was neglect at home; through the winter of 1639 no food was sent out, and in the following spring the settlers were about to abandon their settlement. Their design was changed by succour as unlooked for as that which in such another crisis saved Virginia from desertion. In April 1640 a ship arrived with supplies, and brought a fresh body of emigrants.[1]

The colony, however, was not exclusively, probably not even in the main, composed of Swedes, since the opening clause of the charter gives permission to the intended settlers to depart from Holland. Sweden, however, was to have a monopoly of their export trade. The severe restrictions on popular rights under which the Dutch colonists lived must have been emphasized when contrasted with the privileges granted by the Swedish patent. That allowed the settlers to elect their own magistrates and officers. At the same time there was to be a governor appointed by the Crown, who might veto the orders of the local courts, and to whom appeals lay in judicial matters.

It was not only in civil matters that the Swedish colony enjoyed liberty denied to their neighbours. The two rival forms of Protestantism, the Augsburg Confession and 'the pretended reformed religion'—*i.e.* Calvinism and Lutheranism—were both to be admitted.

How curiously entwined were the colonial interests of Holland and Sweden, how little the Dutch regarded the matter with any national exclusiveness, was shown when in 1640 a settlement, modelled on the patroonships of New Netherlands, was established on the Delaware under a title granted by Queen Christina.[2]

Relations of Swedes and Dutch.

[1] Archives at Stockholm, quoted by Ferris, p. 52.
[2] Ferris (pp. 53-54) gives an account of this colony, quoting original documents; cf. Hazard, p. 66. The patent itself is in the Pennsylvania Archives, vol. v. p. 759.

One cause, no doubt, which made the Dutch tolerant of these intrusions was the presence of a common enemy. It might be impossible for the Dutch to check the tide of English encroachment on Long Island or on the banks of the Connecticut. But it was different with outlying stations for trade, such as the Newhaven merchants were striving to establish on the Delaware, and Kieft was glad to form an alliance whereby he secured the aid of the Swedes against these intruders.[1]

In the summer of 1642 the Swedish Company was enlarged. Fresh capital was subscribed, and a monopoly of the tobacco trade with Sweden and Finland was granted.[2] More settlers were sent out, among them a number of skilled woodcutters from Finland, and the colony was placed under the command of an experienced soldier, John Printz.[3]

Progress of the Swedish colony.

His instructions are interesting as showing the purpose and hopes of the Swedish Government. The necessity for armed resistance to the Dutch was contemplated, and provision made accordingly. It is clear that the colony was to be regarded as created for the commercial benefit of the mother country, not as a self-supporting community existing for itself. Printz is to encourage mining and the production of timber, wool, silk and tobacco. A monopoly of the last-named commodity was to be granted to the Company. The attitude of the Swedish Government towards this matter was not unlike that of James I. to the Virginia Company. Tobacco was an obnoxious luxury. But if men will use it, let the colonial company get the benefit of it. Unhappily there was another point of likeness between the Swedish colony and Virginia. In neither case did the founders see that a young colony will, at least at the outset, need all its labour to establish and

[1] Ferris, p. 59.   [2] N. Y. Docs. vol. xii. p. 21.
[3] Acrelius in *N. Y. Hist. Soc. Coll.* 2nd series, vol. i. p. 411.

THE SWEDISH COLONY.

support itself, and that all thought of exportation must be postponed till the primary needs of the settlers have been satisfied.[1]

Printz shifted the head-quarters of the Governor to Tinicum, some fifteen miles above Fort Christina and twelve below the site of Philadelphia. Log huts clustered round the fort forming the village of New Gottenburg. Another fort, called Elsenburg, was built and garrisoned on the eastern bank of the river, near what is now Salem in New Jersey.[2] By this policy the tables were completely turned upon the Dutch. Fort Nassau instead of being a check on the Swedish colony was cut off from the mouth of the river, and rendered little better than a useless encumbrance.

By 1645 the whole number of male emigrants amounted to ninety, beside women and children. There were also a few English who had been suffered to remain on submitting to the Swedish Governor. The little community had not reached the stage when there is any need for definite constitutional machinery. The Governor was, in theory, responsible only to the home authorities. In fact it can never have been a matter of any difficulty for the whole body of freemen to express their wishes and opinions.

The social life of the settlers seems to have resembled that of New England rather than New Netherlands. They were gathered together in the two villages of Christina and Gottenburg.[3] There were beside three detached tobacco plantations. The relations of the settlers to the Indians were friendly, and the worst calamities that befell the colony during its first ten years of existence were the neglect of the

Social and religious life of the colony.

---

[1] A translation of the Instructions is published in Hazard's *Register of Pennsylvania*, vol. iv. pp. 64–8.

[2] De Vries, p. 181. Hudde in *N. Y. Hist. Coll.* 2nd series, vol. i. pp. 428–9.

[3] There may have been a third village at Elsenburg.

home authorities to send adequate supplies, and the destruction of New Gottenburg by fire in the dead of winter. The Lutheran religion was publicly recognised. Religious service indeed was celebrated with a frequency and regularity which distinguished New Sweden alike from Dutch and English neighbours. Full service was said on Sundays and high days, there was preaching on Wednesdays and Fridays, and daily prayers were read, at New Gottenburg by an ordained clergyman, at the smaller settlements by lay readers especially appointed to that end. It is plain that this was a side of colonial life to which no small importance was attached by the authorities in Sweden. Thus we find Peter Brahe, the President of the Royal Council, in one of his despatches, admonishing Printz to let no leaven of Calvinistic faith or practice creep in from his Dutch or English neighbours. The established faith of the settlers in New Netherlands sat so lightly upon them, that this difference could do little to affect the relations between the two colonies. But it may have had some influence on a strenuous and narrow-minded Calvinist such as Stuyvesant.[1]

Indeed the whole character of that Governor made it certain that he would deal in a very different temper from that of his predecessors with any encroachment on Dutch territory or Dutch privileges. Moreover the disappearance of the common enemy, the English, from the disputed territory removed a guarantee, if not for friendship, at least for peace. During the early days of the Swedish settlement the Government of the United Provinces had done its best to prevent any collision. A Swedish vessel returning from America with a heavy cargo was arrested by the command of the East India Company. The

Hostility with New Netherlands.

[1] Brahe's letter (Anglicized) is quoted in Winsor's *Memorial History*, vol. iv. p. 459.

Swedish Ambassador at the Hague at once protested, and by an order of the States-General the vessel was set free.[1]

Gradually and inevitably causes for discord multiplied themselves. The position of Fort Nassau could not but give rise to trouble. Since the Swedes commanded each bank of the river the Dutch could only enjoy on sufferance any trade in the upper waters of the Delaware. In the summer of 1646 a sloop from New Amsterdam laden with goods for the Indian trade touched at Fort Nassau, and by the order of the commander there sailed into the Schuylkill. But Printz at once forbade the voyage in terms so determined and threatening that it was abandoned. So, too, when the Dutch arms were set up some twelve miles above Tinicum, on the western bank of the Delaware, they were insultingly pulled down by the order of Printz. An envoy sent by Hudde, the commander of Fort Nassau, to remonstrate was received by the Swedish Governor with scoffs and threats of violence.[2] The arrogance and self-confidence of Printz seems to have effectually awed Kieft and his underlings. In Kieft's successor the Swedish Governor had to deal with an opponent of his own metal. One of Stuyvesant's first acts was to send Printz a protest against his encroachments. Printz seems to have ignored this. There is no proof of any hostility between the Swedes and the Indians; if there had been such, it would almost certainly have been recorded. It is clear, however, that the savages looked with some suspicion on the Swedes as intruders, and sympathized with the Dutch in that rivalry which was now plainly manifest. The Dutch were occasional visitors, who brought brandy

---

[1] N. Y. Docs. vol. i. p. 116.

[2] Official Report in the New York Documents, vol. i. p. 537, &c. This was received in January 1656. It is entitled *Secret*. There is nothing to show who drafted it.

and guns and gunpowder, and did not threaten any territorial encroachment. The Swedes were necessarily more guarded in their dealings; the savage may have already suspected that his hunting grounds were doomed before the axe and plough of the white man. Invited by the Indians on the Schuylkill, Hudde built a wooden fort and, as it would seem, made preparations for a settlement. While the work was going on a party of twenty-four Swedes appeared, and, after ineffectually threatening Hudde, cut down all the trees around the fort, probably to enable troops to act more readily against it. Whatever may have been the object, it is clear from the way in which this is reported that the Dutch viewed it as an outrage. During the whole autumn the same style of warfare was waged: houses were built by Dutch settlers on the Schuylkill and pulled down by the Swedes.[1]

Stuyvesant plainly saw that nothing could be done by maintaining detached outposts against the enemy. If the Dutch were to keep their hold on the Delaware, it must be done by establishing a secure communication with Manhattan. To this end he abandoned and demolished Fort Nassau, and built in its place Fort Casimir, four miles below Fort Christina.[2] The sound strategy of this was obvious. Ships from Manhattan could now support the Dutch in the Delaware without having to run under the enemy's guns. The position was reversed, the Swedes were now cut off from the mouth of the river. As a further measure towards strengthening his position, Stuyvesant purchased from the Indians the frontage along the west bank of the river for about twenty-five miles below Fort Christina.[3]

Policy of Stuyvesant.

---

[1] Hudde (referred to on p. 77) gives a very full account of these transactions.

[2] Report, p. 590.   [3] *Ib.*

How well judged was Stuyvesant's policy was shown by its effect on the Swedish settlers. In 1653 we find Printz writing to his own Government that it was useless for him to attempt the expulsion of the Dutch from the river unless he was reinforced. Some of his settlers wished to withdraw and place themselves under the Government of New Netherlands; they were only withheld because Stuyvesant declined to take them without permission from his own Government.

Meanwhile the Swedish Government was doing little to strengthen or encourage its settlers. Such efforts as it did make were unfortunate. In 1649 a vessel, sent out with seventy emigrants and large supplies, was cast away near Porto Rico.

Further efforts on the part of Sweden.

In 1653 Printz's appeal for help became so urgent that the authorities at home saw the need for resolute action. The Company by its own voluntary act placed itself under the control of the Swedish Board of Trade. The conclusion of the Thirty Years' War had left Sweden encumbered with a number of unemployed soldiers. Those who directed her colonial policy decided to make use of these colonists on the Roman model; they were at once to till and to garrison the land. Three hundred emigrants were chosen, of whom fifty were to be of this class. At the head of the party the Board placed their own Secretary, John Rising, with a commission as Deputy-Governor under Printz. Two vessels were chartered for the voyage. They met with that persistent ill-fortune which followed Swedish emigrant ships. One vessel could not be got ready for sea in time and a number of the emigrants had to be left behind. In the meantime Printz, worn out by old age, and disheartened by the failure of the authorities at home to send succour, thinking too, as it would seem, that he could do more for the colony by a personal appeal than by

G

his despatches, had sailed for Sweden. Before doing so he had abandoned Fort Elsenburg. On May 21 the fleet under Rising touched at that point. Though it was no longer in military occupation, in all likelihood there were settlers in the neighbourhood, and from them the new comers would hear of Printz's departure. This left Rising in supreme command. His orders were to do his best to secure each side of the Delaware, and if he could to persuade the Dutch to abandon Fort Casimir, while he was himself to fortify nearer the mouth of the river. But all this was to be done by peaceable means. It was better, so his orders said, to leave the Dutch in possession than to run any risk of letting in the English. Such were Rising's written instructions.[1] But it is almost certain that there was a party in the Company who were for bolder measures,[2] and it is plain that Rising's own wishes went that way. Before landing or holding any communication with the upper settlements he bore down on Fort Casimir and summoned it to surrender. Defence was rendered impossible by want of ammunition. This was due, it was said, to the dishonesty of the commander, Gerrit Bikker, who had traded away his powder to the Indians.[3] No attempt was made to hold the place; Rising took possession, changed the name to Fort Trinity, and left a skilled engineer who had come with him to strengthen the defences. All these proceedings he reported in a despatch to Stuyvesant, mentioning at the same time that certain Dutch settlers whom he had found near Fort Christina had taken the oath of allegiance to Sweden.

Disputes with the English, which but for the

[1] A translation of these instructions is in the *Pennsylvania Register*, vol. iv. p. 143.

[2] Otherwise it would have been impossible for Printz and Rising to adopt the aggressive policy which they did.

[3] N. Y. Docs. vol. i. p. 605.

fortunate, but unscrupulous, policy of Massachusetts must have resulted in war, now fully occupied Stuyvesant, and for twelve months no attempt was made to recover Fort Casimir or to contest the possession of the Delaware. Stuyvesant however was not the man to sit down quietly under such an encroachment. It is clear too that his superiors in Holland, neglectful as they often were of the welfare of the colony, would resent anything which touched their own dignity and their own interests. In November 1654 the Governor received orders to 'avenge the infamous surrender' of Fort Casimir by driving the Swedes out of the country, and to arrest Bikker, the commander, who had so tamely surrendered the fort.[1]

Opposition of the Dutch.

Stuyvesant had somewhat strangely chosen this time for a voyage to the West Indies, and nothing could be done till his return.[2] His whole conduct towards Indians, English and Swedes showed that he was no lover of war, nor anxious for small advantages of little value, but that when he did strike he struck decisively. It was not till July 1655 that Stuyvesant returned. He at once resolved to carry out the policy suggested by the Company, though an attack of illness compelled him to depute some share in the task of preparing the expedition.[3]

By the first week in September a squadron of seven vessels was ready. Between six and seven hundred men were embarked, and Stuyvesant himself took the command. The fleet sailed up the Delaware and were suffered without opposition to land fifty men, who cut off Fort Casimir from the upper settlements. Schute, the commander of Fort Casimir, finding himself thus isolated, surrendered at the first summons.

Stuyvesant reduces the Swedish colony.

[1] N. Y. Docs. vol. xii. p. 85.   [2] *Ib.* p. 90.   [3] *Ib.* p. 91.

Thence Stuyvesant sailed on to Fort Christina. There again he was suffered to land and erect his batteries. The first summons to surrender was met with refusal. Stuyvesant did not open fire, but contented himself with investing the fort while his troops pillaged the surrounding country. In nine days symptoms of mutiny within the fort compelled Rising to surrender. The Swedish garrison marched out with the honours of war, and the Dutch flag floated over the fort.[1]

In spite of the bloodless nature of the conquest and the leniency shown to the Swedish settlers, certain measures of force were needed to secure the new territory. A Swedish vessel with a hundred and thirty emigrants on board was not allowed to touch within the Delaware, and certain Swedes who were found intriguing with the Indians were arrested and sent to New Amsterdam.

A population so motley as that of New Netherlands could easily absorb and assimilate a fresh element. It was too for the temporary peace of the colony to have converted a neighbour separated by no definite or easily kept boundary from a rival into a dependency. Yet if the lands on the Delaware could have become once more a mere hunting-ground for savages, New Netherlands would have been stronger and safer. On each side English colonies were closing in: a longer sea-board only made the Dutch colony an object of greater suspicion and jealousy. In case of an attack, too, the resources of the colony would be divided. There were now two points too far apart for mutual help, at which a maritime invader might strike.

Effects of the conquest.

In another way also the conquest of New Sweden was in the long run a danger to New Netherlands.

[1] The authorities for the Dutch conquest are to be found in the first and the twelfth volumes of the N. Y. Documents.

The complaints of the Swedish Government were unheeded at the Hague. The attitude of the Dutch was a practical declaration that title based on discovery—a form of title which gave scope for endless dispute and litigation—was to take precedence of title based on the plain and obvious fact of occupation. Stuyvesant and his employers set up a principle which only six years later was turned against them to their own destruction. Financially, too, the expedition against New Sweden was a heavy—events showed, a fatal—blow to the Company. The deficit created by the cost of the expedition had to be met by borrowing twenty-four thousand guilders from the city of Amsterdam. Thus the colony tied round its neck a load of debt, which crippled its military resources, and forced it to deal with its territory on commercial rather than military and political grounds, in the cheapest, not the most efficient, fashion.

The whole administrative history of the colony showed that its weakest point was lack of centralization. *The city of Amsterdam forms a colony.* The patroonships, the half independent municipalities founded by colonists from New England, were sources of discord and weakness. Yet in dealing with its newly acquired territory the Company brought in a further element of variance. The city of Amsterdam proposed to find a home for a number of Waldenses, the survivors of the 'slaughtered saints,' 'slain by the bloody Piedmontese.' In the Old World Holland was the one consecrated asylum for the victims of religious tyranny. Gradually a wider refuge beyond the Atlantic was being opened also; that process was beginning which, as it has been said, makes the history of American colonization the history of the persecutions of Europe. The conquest of New Sweden enabled the Government to find a refuge for these outcasts. By surrendering Fort Casimir and the territory for about twenty-five miles below it, on the south-west bank of the river,[1] the West India Company was able to liquidate its debt to the city of Amsterdam. This was the more necessary since the Company was embarrassed by recent losses in Guinea and Brazil. They acted, in fact, like a landlord who sells a portion of his estates to free the rest from encumbrances. Financially this was no doubt sound policy, but a government in dealing with its territory cannot limit its view to finance. The cession was a confession of administrative incapacity. The Company did not, however, wholly divest themselves of their tenantry on the Delaware. The Swedes had built a solid log fort on Tinicum Island, about twelve miles below the spot now occupied by the city of Philadelphia. This remained under the jurisdiction of the Company; so also did Fort Christina, of which the name was now changed to Altona.[2] Since there was to be a division it would have been far better if that had gone too, and if the responsibility of maintaining order on the Delaware, and of protecting the settlers against the Indians, and holding the territory against English encroachment had been laid undivided on the city government of Amsterdam.

The city at once took in hand the task of dealing with the newly acquired territory. The management of the colony was vested in a committee of six, chosen by the burgomasters from among themselves. Specific conditions were drawn up to attract emigrants. They were to be carried out without payment, the site for a house was to be given them, and they were to be clothed and fed for one year at the expense of the city.

[1] The south-east boundary was the now called Boomtjes (corrupted into Bombay) Hook. Mr. Keen in his map places this at the northern extremity of Boomtjes Hook Island. It does not appear to me quite clear that it may not have been at the southern end. In the latter case the territory would be about thirty miles.

[2] Brodhead, vol. i. p. 631.

Whether any labour on behalf of the colony in general was required in return does not appear. We may be sure, however, that the promoters of the colony did not intend it to be what, if these conditions had stood alone, it might become—a home for idle paupers. After the first year the colonists were to be supplied with the necessaries of life and with seeds out of a public magazine, at a rate not higher than that current in the mother country. For ten years the colony was to be free of taxes; after that the settlers were to be taxed at the minimum rate imposed on any inhabitants of New Netherlands. There was to be a municipal government modelled on that of Amsterdam itself. No regular clergy were appointed, but there was to be a schoolmaster who should conduct a simple religious service. In most of these conditions there is a certain vagueness, something which suggests an anxiety to frame attractive conditions, with no very definite ideas how they were to be fulfilled. The relations between the government of the new municipality and that of the West India Company were arranged with a laxity which could not fail to give rise to dispute. The city of Amsterdam was to have 'high, middle, and low jurisdiction,' while at the same time the sovereignty and supreme authority was to remain vested in the Company. More definite expression was given to this by the provision that the council of the new town should have final jurisdiction in small cases, but where the matter at issue exceeded one hundred guilders, there should be an appeal to the Director and Council of New Netherlands.[1]

The best part of the policy adopted by the city was their choice of a Governor, Jacob Alrichs. Portions of a despatch are extant from which we learn the condition

[1] There is a translation of these conditions in the *N. Y. Hist. Soc. Coll.* vol. i. p. 291. They are also in the Documents, vol. i. p. 630.

in which he found things on his arrival, and the policy which he adopted. Fort Casimir was occupied by a garrison. Round the fort were grouped about a dozen families, living under a system which was a combination of municipal government and martial law. Any disputes that arose were settled by the Commander in concert with two schepens and a secretary appointed by the Company.

Jacob Alrichs appointed Governor.

This government Alrichs suffered to remain in force for a while, pending a definite settlement, and in such a manner as to secure the rights of the existing inhabitants. Finally it was superseded, as it would seem peacefully, and with the approval of the settlers, by a Council of seven, from whom were chosen three schepens, a secretary, and a schout. The spiritual wants of the community were provided for by the appointment of two elders and two deacons.

The colony was laid out precisely on the model of a New England village. The land was apportioned as far as might be at the choice of the settlers themselves, and every man fenced his own lot. But this was not allowed to cause straggling. The settlers were grouped in a town of a hundred and ten houses, built round a square, with a public store-house and a barrack for the garrison. One may say in fact that Alrichs transformed a fort into a village.[1] In accordance with a principle accepted alike by Dutch, English, and Swedish settlers, the town was named, after a suburb of the parent city, New Amstel.

Foundation of New Amstel.

As might have been foreseen, the system of government soon gave rise to disputes. The authorities of the city of Amsterdam held that Alrichs and his settlers were responsible only to them. Stuyvesant appears to have contended that the city was

Hindrances to the colony.

[1] For these details see Alrichs's despatches in Hazard's Pennsylvania Archives, 2nd series, vol. v.

only in the position of a territorial proprietor, and that the jurisdiction of the Company was intact. Alrichs, he complained, did not, in the oath of allegiance which he administered to the settlers, make any mention of the Company, and the restrictions in trade were disregarded.[1]

Yet though Stuyvesant may have fallen short of the standard of moderation aimed at by Alrichs, he went far enough in that direction to earn the disapproval of his inferiors. We find the Council remonstrating with him for keeping Swedes in office, and also for a promise that in the event of any dispute between Holland and Sweden they might remain neutral.[2]

The fair hopes with which New Amstel began soon came to nought. Heavy sickness fell upon the colony,[3] and those who were well were too busy in building and fencing to till the land. Those in Holland who should have supplied provisions were negligent, and the colony had to depend for its food on Manhattan.[4]

Indifferent though the West India Company might have been as to the welfare of its settlers, the emigrants at New Amstel had no reason to congratulate themselves on being under different authority. Disheartened at the unprofitable aspect of their venture, the Town Council of Amsterdam with shameless and cruel indifference threw to the winds their agreement with their settlers. The colonists who went out had been promised a supply of provisions: that was now limited to those who had left Holland before December 1658. The exemption from taxes was to expire before the time originally named, and all goods exported were to be sent to Amsterdam. By the strenuous protest of their colonists, and by the more liberal example of the

[1] N. Y. Docs. vol. ii. p. 68.
[2] Penn. Archives, 2nd series, vol. vii. p. 555.
[3] N. Y. Docs. vol. xii. pp. 225, 227. [4] Ib. 236.

West India Company, the Council were shamed into abandoning the last measure.

To the other troubles of these unhappy settlers were added rumours of an attack from Maryland. We cannot wonder that men turned their backs on the colony. Alrichs made vain attempts to detain them, urging that they were bound for a fixed term by their covenants. In such a country it was a hopeless task to keep unwilling inhabitants. Some fled to Manhattan, others, including soldiers from the garrison, to Maryland and Virginia.[1] Alrichs himself died.[2] Yet even in its weakened condition the colony was capable of giving trouble to New Amsterdam. Alrichs' successor, Alexander D'Hinoyossa, was self-willed and turbulent. He practically claimed to be independent of the Company's authority, and to control the whole trade and navigation of the Delaware.[3] At the same time he showed no respect for the civic authority of Amsterdam which he was supposed to represent, and he was even charged with declaring that, unless he met with due support, he would follow in the steps of Minuit and transfer his services to a foreign Power.[4]

It is not surprising that the Town Council of Amsterdam should have wished to throw back their unhappy venture on the West India Company, nor more surprising that the latter would have nothing to say to the proposed transfer.

In 1661 the Government of Amsterdam resolved to make one further attempt for the success of their colony. A fresh agreement was drawn up by the West India

---

[1] Alrichs' despatches in N. Y. Docs. vol. ii. pp. 54, 64, 70.
[2] Letter from William Beckman, N. Y. Docs. vol. xii. p. 289. Beckman was appointed by Stuyvesant to represent him on the Delaware.
[3] Beckman to Stuyvesant, N. Y. Docs. vol. xii. pp. 363-5, 368.
[4] This charge was supported by several depositions, N. Y. Docs. vol. xii. p. 376. It was evidently believed by Beckman, who does not seem to have started with any prejudice against Hinoyossa.

Company and approved by the States-General, under which the colony was to be not so much replenished as New conditions for emigrants. settled afresh on a new footing. Emigrants were to be exempt from all dues to the Company; they were to have free rights of mining, fishing and trawling, and might even, if dissatisfied with the Director, choose his successor. It does not seem clear —perhaps those who drafted the document did not wish to make it clear—how far these conditions were to apply to the existing inhabitants.[1]

Such changes might do a little to lighten some of the burdens under which the colonists suffered; they might add something to the material prosperity of the colony. They could not in themselves do anything to cure what was probably the most deeply seated of her troubles, that exaggerated cosmopolitanism which had prevented the developement of any national life, and made civic unity well nigh impossible.

How far those who controlled the destinies of the colony were from understanding their needs and Proposed migration from New Haven. deficiencies was strikingly shown in the same year. The men of New Haven, the entertainers of the regicides, of all the New England colonies the narrowest and most exclusive in their ecclesiastical system, were beginning to dread what the Restoration might have in store for them, and what encroachments they might have to expect from their more compliant neighbours in Connecticut. Some of them already began to contemplate that policy of migration which a few years later bore such singular fruits, and a deputation of four leading men waited on Stuyvesant, proposing to avail themselves of the newly granted privileges. They asked for a grant of land, to which the Indian title should be extinguished by the Dutch Government. The townsmen were to elect their

[1] For the conditions see Brodhead, vol. i. p. 696.

own magistrates and officers, and to exclude and admit settlers at their own discretion. The township was to be, as in New England, identical with the Congregational Church. Lastly, there was to be a synod of all the English Churches in New Netherlands. Such an arrangement could have only one effect. It would consolidate the Englishry, as we call those of New Netherlands, into a well-defined and homogeneous body, and enormously increase the danger of English encroachment.

It was, however, only at rare intervals and under the pressure of some exceptional excitement that the rulers of New Netherlands awoke to a sense of that danger. Stuyvesant was prepared to grant all that the deputies from New Haven asked for, the right of self-government only excepted.

The States-General, however, were prepared to grant even that with certain restrictions. The Director and Council of New Netherlands were to have a veto in the election of officers. The local court might not pass sentence of death, except where the criminal confessed his guilt, and the penal code was not to apply to any Dutch who might settle within the township.

In the meantime, however, the applicants themselves seemed to have abandoned their scheme, and the concessions bore no fruit.[1]

Another attempt to form a small *imperium in imperio* was more successful. Among the strange ramifications of Protestantism to which the Reformation in Germany gave birth was the sect of the Mennonists. The members of the sect claimed for it a continuous descent from the primitive

The Mennonists.[2]

---

[1] For these negotiations with New Haven see Brodhead, vol. i. pp. 695, 708.

[2] For the Mennonist settlement see Brodhead, vol. i. p. 698. A good account of the sect, its origin and early history, is given in an Appendix to Proud's *History of Pennsylvania*.

Church and a share in that war of persecution which, at the opening of the thirteenth century, swept over the south of France and made itself felt, though less widely and less fiercely, in the Low Countries. It is impossible to say what currents may have been flowing below the surface during the centuries which separated Luther from Henry the Deacon. Practically we may look on the Mennonists as a religious society called into life about 1520 by Simon Menno. He appears to have been a Dutchman who migrated to Germany. Their repudiation of infant baptism caused them to be included in the comprehensive title of Anabaptists, but they seem never to have been even suspected of any share in the profligacy and lawlessness commonly associated with the name. Like the Quakers, they denied the lawfulness of oaths and of war, and dispensed with an ordained clergy. Isolated members of the sect, possibly small congregations, seem to have found their way into New Netherlands before 1640, since they are mentioned in Father Jogues' enumeration of the numerous sects and authorities to be seen at New Amsterdam.[1] They are also mentioned in 1657 in a formal report by two of the Dutch Calvinist ministers in the colony. But as they speak of 'Mennonites' at Gravesend, a settlement founded from New England, it is probable that they used the name vaguely as a synonym for Baptist.

At all events these were at most isolated and inorganic movements. But when the city of Amsterdam was casting in every direction for methods of reviving and replenishing the colony it entered into negotiations with a Mennonist community. They obtained a grant of land at the Hoarkill, near the mouth of the Delaware where Lewiston now stands. Thus they were effectually separated from the main body of

[1] See p. 19.

the colony at New Amsterdam, an arrangement probably acceptable to both parties. The community was to consist of married couples and single men not under twenty-four, and free from debt. There were to be simple religious exercises, but no clergy. The officials of the community were to be in the first instance nominated by the community; a further selection was to be made by the burgomasters of Amsterdam. There was to be a primary assembly of the whole body of settlers; a majority of two-thirds was required for legislative purposes, and their enactments had to be ratified at Amsterdam by the municipal government. A similar majority of two-thirds might expel any person of objectionable character. Property was at the outset to be held in common. But it is clear that the Mennonists, or at least this section of them, did not hold the Anabaptist tenets of community of goods, since at the end of five years there was to be a division of property.

Like the Plymouth pilgrims the Mennonists started their enterprise on borrowed capital. Twenty-five hundred guilders (a little over two hundred and sixty pounds in English money) was advanced by the city of Amsterdam, and the whole community of emigrants was liable for repayment.

The Mennonist settlement on the Delaware was virtually the expiring effort of Dutch colonization. Before we pass to the next phase in the history of New York, the English conquest, it may not be amiss to see what was the outward aspect of the territory which changed masters. The only portion of the colony outside the capital where a traveller would have found signs of continuous habitation was Long Island. There were to be seen agri-

Outward appearance of New Amsterdam.[1]

---

[1] For what follows I have relied to a considerable extent on Mr. Tuckerman.

cultural communities having their origin from New England, and closely resembling the villages of New England in outer aspect. Their history, however, and their relations to the government of the Dutch colony belong in reality to a later stage of our history, to the transformation of the Dutch colony of New Netherlands into the English dependency of New York, and will be more fittingly dealt with hereafter.

In the rest of the colony the settled parts formed detached bases in an unreclaimed wilderness. Along the Hudson were villages of two sorts. On the patroonships, the houses of the farmers and the cabins of the labourers were in all likelihood grouped together for defence against the Indian, somewhat like the type of mediæval town which had its origin in a manorial settlement. Elsewhere along the waterway of the Hudson and on the shores of the Delaware were fortified trading stations, with a wooden palisade and a few cannon, and grouped close to them for protection small farmsteads and the houses of the handicraftsmen, such as the smith and the carpenter, who were needed for the simple life of such a community.

The patroon was often a merchant as well, with a town house in New Amsterdam. In the city there is nothing to show the actual amount of trade done in the colony, or the number of ships touching there during the period of Dutch rule. But there is abundant evidence that a crowd of traders of divers nationalities continually came and went; as early as 1642 Kieft found it necessary to build an inn for their accommodation. Regulations were framed intended to confine the trade of the colony to *bona-fide* residents for six years; seemingly, however, traders in foreign vessels might land their cargoes and sell them. The prohibition of non-resident traders was in all likelihood to check those who made a temporary lodgment in the colony without any of the rights or responsibilities of citizenship.

The resources of the town make it impossible that there could be anything of grandeur in its outer aspect. The majority of the houses were of wood. In 1655 Stuyvesant passed an ordinance prohibiting the construction of wooden chimneys, and two years later he went yet further and ordered those which were in existence to be pulled down. Only a few of the streets were paved, and those only with cobble stones, and the only drainage was a gutter down their middle. Yet the old Dutch town must have had elements of beauty which its successor, with all its stateliness and regularity, has lost. Many of the houses stood surrounded by orchards and gardens. Trees along the sides of the streets must have recalled to the Dutch emigrant the towns of his native land. That likeness was increased by a canal filled in in 1676, and running where now is Broad Street. Another impressive feature of the old town has vanished. Where now are the Battery and the Bowling Green, hemmed in and dwarfed by colossal trading houses, there stood Fort Amsterdam, separated from the houses of the city by an open space of green sward.[1]

In many respects New York cosmopolitanism, lacking in corporate feeling and in any sense of civic dignity and responsibility, was ill-fitted to assimilate with those English colonies to which its geographical position specially attached it. But New Netherlands and New England had at least one point of likeness. Amid all their keen pursuit of material wealth, the rulers and citizens of New Netherlands had not wholly forgotten the claims of the mind.

Education in New Netherlands.

[1] This is proved by an ordinance of the Council, passed in 1648, which prohibited the pasturing of sheep and goats between Fort Amsterdam and the 'Fresh Water,' *i.e.* evidently the Hudson and the East River.

Before 1664 there were nine schools in existence in the colony, and amid all the difficulty and distress which beset the colony in 1659 time and money were found for the establishment of a High School with a Latin class. It would be interesting to know how after the English conquest the rival claims of the Dutch and English tongues in education were adjusted. But we may be sure that the existence of an educational system open to each nationality must have done not a little to obliterate distinctions and promote fusion.

In March 1663 a change was made which might well have come sooner. The Company made over to the city of Amsterdam the whole of their territory on the Delaware. The grantees were to have no power of alienation, and they were bound to garrison the country sufficiently and to send out four hundred emigrants each year. As a step towards fulfilling these promises a hundred and fifty emigrants were sent out during the summer.

Transfer of the Delaware territory to the city of Amsterdam.

CHAPTER II.

THE ENGLISH CONQUEST.[1]

AN important chapter in American history loses all its meaning if we look on the English conquest of New York New Netherlands gradually Anglicized. as an isolated event. An English King and his advisers decreed that New Netherlands should be part of the British Empire, and they carried through their purpose. Their action by itself could not have enabled the Dutch settlement to take its place in the English group of colonies; for that change a path had been prepared by the independent action of English citizens.

For nearly thirty years before the overthrow of the Dutch power on the Hudson two processes had been at work. There had been hostile and aggressive action on the frontier, a tendency to dispute the right of the Dutch to a particular boundary, and even to deny altogether their territorial title. Besides there was the process of peaceful incursion by which an English element introduced and established itself among the Dutch population.

The territorial struggle was practically limited to the north-east frontier. The debatable land was the valley of the Connecticut. The extension of the English settlements into that valley was indeed in two ways

---

[1] The authorities for this, and the following three chapters, are much the same. There are a few documents among the *English Colonial Papers* which bear on the history of New York, and which are not included either in Mr. Brodhead's or Mr. O'Callaghan's collections.

THE TREATY OF HARTFORD.

the origin of the contest. For one thing it so placed the Dutch and English settlers that disputes were sure to arise. Furthermore it was a necessary condition for the formation of the New England confederacy. Without Connecticut as a third party there could have been no union between the unequally balanced powers of Massachusetts and Plymouth. The creation of the confederacy concentrated the resources of New England, and gave it a machinery with which to contest its right.

Effect of the settlement of Connecticut.

The first ground of dispute was the settlement at Hartford. As early as 1639, in the governorship of Kieft, the Dutch had cause to complain of encroachment and molestation in that quarter. The charges were met not with denial, scarcely with justification, but with counter-charges complaining that the Dutch monopolized the trade of the Hudson and the Delaware, to the total exclusion of the English.

Disputes at Hartford.

Three years later the dispute was renewed. The English complained of isolated acts of violence by the Dutch and of the illegal detention of runaway servants.

In 1650 matters were temporarily arranged at an interview which Stuyvesant had with the Federal Commissioners at Hartford. A boundary line was drawn which was to hold good for Long Island and also for the mainland. This boundary was to be made more effective by a sort of neutral zone, as no permanent Dutch settlement was to be formed within six miles of the line. The question as to runaway servants was to be settled by accepting the same rule, that of extradition, which regulated the intercolonial dealings of the New England confederacy.

Treaty of Hartford.[1]

---

[1] The negotiations between Stuyvesant and the Commissioners and the agreement are in Hazard, vol. ii. pp. 154-70, and are copied in the *N. Y. Hist. Coll.* 1st series, vol. i.

H 2

The difficulty, however, went too deep to be thus removed. Matters were being complicated by the second process of which I have spoken, that by which an English element was being infused into the Dutch population. The earliest English-speaking community which formed politically a portion of New York was Greenwich, on Long Island. It was settled in 1640 by that Captain Patrick who had played so unsatisfactory and discreditable a part in the Pequod war. He and his associates acquired the land which they occupied by purchase from the Indians. The demand that they should submit to the Dutch Government was at first met with a vague declaration of neutrality. In 1642 they took the oath of allegiance to the States-General, with the understanding that the town was to enjoy the same rights as those granted to a patroonship.[1]

English settlement at Greenwich.

In the same year two more parties of emigrants, men whose religious opinions made New England an unsafe home for them, founded settlements on like terms at Newtown [2] and West Chester.[3] The founder of the first-named settlement was Francis Doughty, a clergyman expelled from New England for a somewhat obscure expression of unorthodoxy.[4] His daughter apparently soon after his arrival married Adrian Von der Dock, a leading Dutch colonist who held office under Kieft and Stuyvesant.[5]

Other English settlements on Long Island.

In the same year a more distinguished exile from New England, Anne Hutchinson, took refuge with her

---

[1] Records in Hazard in *N. Y. Hist. Coll.* as above; Brodhead, vol. i. p. 296.
[2] Vertoogh, pp. 301-3.
[3] Brodhead, vol. i. pp. 334-3; Winthrop.
[4] According to Mr. Brodhead (vol. i. p. 333) his offence was stating that Abraham's children should have been baptized.
[5] Brodhead speaks of them as married in 1646.

family near New Rochelle. She only escaped from her Christian persecutors to fall a victim to the savage. In 1643 a war party attacked Annie's Hook, as the settlement was called, and cut off every living soul save one young girl.[1] In 1644 another English settlement was formed at Heemstede,[2] and in 1645 two more at Flushing and Gravesend.[3] It is clear that at the latter place there were also Dutch settlers, and the relations between the two sections illustrate the dangers of this state of things. In 1653, when matters stood so that war might at any time break out, the English settlers at Gravesend changed their established mode of choosing magistrates, endeavouring, it is said, by an electioneering manœuvre, of which the nature is somewhat obscure, to secure a magistracy who should be on the side of the English.

The Records of these townships show to what an extent they had brought with them those traditions of self-government which were so essential a part of the life of New England. We see that Southampton elected annually three magistrates called Townsmen, nor is there anything to show that the consent of the Governor was required for such election. The town meeting also elected constables, it passed resolutions dealing not only with such local affairs as the fencing of the common field and the preservation of highways, but with a question of such general interest as the selling of drink and ammunition to the Indians.[4]

[1] Winthrop, vol. ii. p. 136; Brodhead, vol. i. p. 366.
[2] The grant by Kieft of territory at Heemstede to English settlers is quoted by Thompson, vol. ii. p. 3.
[3] *Ib.* vol. ii. pp. 68, 171.
[4] There is in O'Callaghan's *Documentary History*, vol. i. p. 457, a very valuable monograph by John Lyon Gardiner written in 1798, on the early history and constitution of the English townships on Long Island. See also Bishop's *History of Election in the United States*.

Besides these actual English settlements there was a large English element among the population of the colony, especially among the traders at Manhattan. At an early day we find Englishmen taking a share in the public life of the colony and directly infusing English ideas and establishing English influence.

Englishmen hold public offices in New Netherlands.

We see this tendency showing itself as early as the time of Kieft. In 1642 he appointed George Baxter as ' English Secretary '—a post which in all likelihood included that of interpreter, and which he retained under Stuyvesant.[1] It is easy to understand the selection of an Englishman for such a post. But there could be no such explanation of what happened a year later. When Kieft, under the pressure of popular discontent, permitted the election of a council of eight, two of those chosen, Isaac Allerton and Thomas Hall, were immigrants from New England.[2]

In 1650, when Stuyvesant was engaged in a dispute with the confederation of the New England colonies, he appointed two men of English name and blood to act on his behalf as arbitrators. One of them, Thomas Willett, had apparently been born and brought up at Leyden. But he had come to Plymouth in 1629, and there is nothing to show that he had any connexion with New Netherlands, except that in the course of a somewhat varied commercial career he had traded in the Hudson.[3]

His parents were in all likelihood among the original fugitives from England to Holland. During the early part of his career in America he was in charge of one

---

[1] Mr. Brodhead (vol. i. p. 337) calls Baxter ' one of the exiles from New England.' I do not find any mention of him either in Bradford or in Winthrop.

[2] Brodhead, vol. i. p. 365.

[3] All that is known about Willett is brought together in a monograph in the *American Historical Magazine*, vol. xxiii. p. 232.

of the Plymouth factories on the Kennebec. When the hostility of the French, and the dread of an Indian attack, put an end to that enterprise he returned to Plymouth, and we soon after find him trading both on the Delaware and on the Hudson. From 1651 to 1655 he held office as an assistant in Plymouth.

Yet only a year before Stuyvesant, in his dispute with New England, had selected Willett to act as an arbitrator on his behalf. This is all the more noteworthy because his other arbitrator was also an Englishman, that George Baxter already mentioned. He, however, would seem to have been a refugee from New England.

The personal prepossessions of Stuyvesant did much to increase the influence of this English element. To his temper the stern polity of New England, with its one accepted faith and its rigid moral discipline, was far more congenial than the lax cosmopolitanism of his own colony. Hence he was even reproached with sacrificing the interests of his own colony at the bidding of English advisers. Moreover, his strong sense of justice and his steady preference for peaceful counsels, a preference sometimes obscured by his unconciliatory and ungracious temper, inclined Stuyvesant in all dealings with the English to choose Englishmen settled within New Netherlands as his diplomatic agents. His choice may have made the personal relations between Stuyvesant and the English smoother. That was more than outweighed by the lack of confidence and the sense of irritation engendered in the Dutch. Thus the only props by which the autonomy of New Netherlands could possibly have been stayed up—independence, self-reliance, and exclusiveness—were being steadily undermined. How little the West India Company understood the danger, how the real condition of their colony was for them a

Stuyvesant favours the English.

sealed book, is illustrated by their conduct in 1661. By that time there was no room for doubt as to the danger of English rivalry and English encroachment. Yet the Company, anxious to populate the territory on the east bank of the Delaware, held out special inducements to emigrants, promising among other things that they should if they pleased be independent of the Governor of New Netherlands. This invitation was more expressly addressed to 'English Christians,' and was approved by the States-General.[1]

In 1653 a fresh dispute broke out between Stuyvesant and the Commissioners of the New England confederacy.

Dispute in 1653.
Of that dispute I have spoken elsewhere.[2] The principal feature of it was the attempt to accuse the Dutch of an alliance, or an understanding of some kind, with the Indians, to the prejudice of the English. So far as that charge rested on any evidence, it rested on the vague statement of Indian witnesses. What the New Englanders thought of the savage is plain. The Commissioners would have been indignant if told that any charge to their discredit could be established by such testimony. Yet Englishmen might be forgiven if the thought of Amboyna haunted their mind, and if the memory of Pequod outrages begat morbid and irrational suspicions.

With New England, jealous, apprehensive, and arrogant, hostilities always lay near the surface. In 1653 they seemed likely to be kindled by the action of the mother country. Holland and England were at war. The Protector sent orders to the New England colonies to be ready to act against New Netherlands. At the same time a fleet of four vessels was despatched to New England, with instructions to consult those in

[1] Brodhead, vol. i. p. 688.
[2] *English in America: New England*, vol. i.

power there. If it then seemed well, the fleet was to attack first Manhattan, and then the other Dutch settlements on the Hudson. The persistent refusal of Massachusetts to act with her confederates caused delay, and before that difficulty could be overcome England and Holland were at peace.

The conduct of the English within New Netherlands while war was impending was such as to open the eyes of Stuyvesant and the Company. Citizens of New Amsterdam were in correspondence with the rulers of New England. Newtown and Gravesend were openly disaffected. The latter town had taken the opportunity to claim municipal independence by electing a council of twelve independent of New Amsterdam. In November 1654 Stuyvesant himself visited the place, and removed two of the most conspicuous English partisans from the magistracy. In four months' time they were back in the town, declaring it to be subject to the English Commonwealth. This time they were imprisoned. Yet the English party there seem to have kept their ascendancy, and to have used it at the next election of magistrates with tyrannical contempt for the interests of their Dutch fellow-citizens.[2]

Disaffection of the English immigrants in New Netherlands.[1]

As we have seen, in 1654 another English settlement had been established at West Chester, near the site of Anne Hutchinson's ill-fated colony. In the spring of 1656 it was reported that the settlers there were sheltering criminals and carrying on treasonable correspondence with the natives. An armed force was sent against them. There was some slight resistance, which was soon suppressed. As in almost every other like case, Stuyvesant's policy was one of extreme, probably

[1] Brodhead, chap. xvii. He quotes local records.
[2] Brodhead, vol. i. pp. 596-8.

of erring, lenity. A few of the offenders were banished; the main body of the settlers submitted, demanding, and obtaining as the price of their submission, the same rights as the other rural municipalities of the colony.[1]

It is to be observed that each of these disaffected settlements was beyond dispute within the bounds of New Netherlands as fixed by the treaty of Hartford. Their resistance, therefore, had not strictly and technically anything to do with New England. The inhabitants were acting just as any disaffected Dutch colonists might in resisting the authority of the Company. Practically, however, it was impossible to sever the action of Englishmen in New Netherlands from that of Englishmen across the border. Moreover, these little English townships contained all that was most vigorous in the political life of the colony. A community thus honeycombed by English influence would to a certainty be powerless against English attack.

Meanwhile New Netherlands was threatened with territorial encroachment from another quarter. The peace of Hartford pledged the members of the New England confederacy to respect the frontier claimed and defined for the Dutch colony. But that treaty was binding only on those who made it. It did not affect the mother country, nor any of her colonies save New England.

English claims based on discovery.

If a claim of territorial sovereignty, asserted by a grant or patent, though not followed by occupation, be a title, then England beyond question had such a title to the valley of the Hudson. The original patents of the Northern Virginia Company extended to a point somewhat north of the Merrimac. The great patent of New England in 1620 had for its southern boundary a point fifty miles south of Manhattan. Lord Balti-

[1] Brodhead, vol. i. p. 628.

more's patent of 1632 was worded with distinct reference to the New England patent. His territory was to extend northward till it reached the southern boundary of New England.

It may be said these are trivial technicalities, that it was absurd to suffer the sovereign Powers of Europe, on the strength of vague, uncertain, and disputable claims of discovery, to parcel out the New World; to allow huge tracts to lie idle, unless those who needed them and could turn them to profit would consent to be denationalized. The New England colonies, who in such a matter might be regarded as morally if not legally representing England, had in a formal document acquiesced in the Dutch occupation. On the strength of that implied consent Dutch colonists had invested capital and labour, had given up their homes, and re-shaped their whole lives. But, pedantic as the view was under which they were dispossessed, it was the very view which the Dutch had themselves adopted in their dealings with the Swedes.

Retribution for once assumed a direct and appropriate form. Till the Dutch had shown a real deter-

<small>Maryland claims the Delaware.[1]</small> mination by the conquest of New Sweden and the foundation of New Amstel to make a settlement on Delaware Bay, the Maryland government had been content that so much of Baltimore's patent should be a dead letter. But in 1659, just as New Amstel was in the thick of its troubles, came an alarm that the Governor of Maryland was about to enforce his claim. Soon after an envoy, Colonel Utie, appeared at New Amstel. His instructions were to warn the

---

[1] The chief authorities for these disputes are: (1) a long extract from the Maryland Records, in the *N. Y. Hist. Soc. Coll.* 1st series, vol. iii. p. 368, and the report of Alrichs, the representative of Stuyvesant at New Amstel; this is quoted by Hazard, p. 260, &c.; and (2) Heerman's Journal in the N. Y. Docs. vol. ii. p. 88.

Dutch Governor to withdraw, and to endeavour to win over the settlers peacefully by fair promises. Utie was received by Alrichs and by Beckman. The latter was acting for the Company as their commissioner in charge of that portion of the land on the Delaware which they retained. Utie pleaded the Maryland patent; the Dutch authorities pleaded their own undisturbed possession; both parties stood their ground, and Utie returned to his own colony.

The matter was laid before Stuyvesant, and he decided to send two representatives to Maryland to protest against the threatened encroachment.

Dispute with Maryland. The Governor and Secretary of Maryland now showed a lack of diplomatic skill which has not been without its lasting results. Instead of confining themselves to the claim originally made by Utie, they pointed out that Baltimore's patent included the whole of the Dutch territory, not only on the Delaware but on the Hudson. They reminded the Dutch envoys that Baltimore was expressly empowered to extend his colony as far as the southern border of New England. 'Where,' then asked the Dutch representatives, 'is New Netherlands?' Calvert's answer, 'I do not know,' probably satisfied the speaker as an effective statement of an extreme view, but there was in it little practical wisdom. Even if the two claims rested legally on the same ground, every man of common sense would see that to hand over Delaware Bay to the English and to hand over Long Island and the Hudson to them were things widely different. Nor could it really be said that each claim rested on the same legal grounds. At the time when Baltimore's patent was drawn up, the banks of the Delaware were vacant territory. Manhattan had been for nine years a settled colony. The very words of the patent expressly limited Baltimore's rights to a country hitherto uncultivated.

This tactical error on the side of Maryland might well embolden the two Dutch envoys to propose that the boundary question should be referred to arbitration. Either a court of six commissioners, chosen, three by each side, or the two home Governments should decide. The Governor now tried to change his ground. He was only dealing, he said, with the question of Delaware Bay. But the false step was one which could hardly be retraced. It was clearly the interest of the Dutch to pin the Marylanders to their claim in its original and extreme form.

The Governor finally contented himself with a general denial of the validity of the Dutch title, and did not specify whether his denial was total or partial. The two Dutch envoys withdrew. One returned to New Netherlands; the other went on to Virginia in the hope of enlisting the sympathies of Berkeley and his Council against Maryland. The relations between the Dutch and the Virginians had always been friendly; the envoy was received with general expressions of goodwill, and certain arrangements were made for trade between the two colonies. But to meddle with any territorial question outside his own colony was, Berkeley said, wholly beyond his power and that of his Council.[1]

Nothing was done by Maryland, probably in part because the colony was too much weakened by internal dissensions for any effective action. The diplomatic victory secured by the Dutch envoys did little for the profit of New Netherlands. Yet it had an abiding influence. When, thirty-six years later, the claim of Maryland to the Delaware was urged against an English grantee, the negotiations of 1659 were held to have an important bearing on the case.

[1] Brodhead, vol. i. p. 684.

As yet the English Government had felt but little motive to press their alleged right to the territory of New Netherlands. For whenever that question had presented itself the practical issue had been not the claim of Maryland to the Delaware, but the claims of Connecticut to the territory on Long Island and on the opposite mainland. To strengthen the hands of Connecticut was assuredly a policy which would never have commended itself to Charles I. and his advisers. They were not likely to have discriminated between the tempers and characters of the New England colonies. To them the whole group were homes of disaffection and Nonconformity. The attitude of the Crown towards New England was based on a vague notion of repression; no definite and constructive principle of administration entered into it.

Changed policy of England after the Restoration.

But with the Restoration a new era began. The navigation laws were to be methodically and stringently administered, and thus the whole commercial resources of the plantations were to be organized for the good of the mother country. This alone furnished a strong motive for the annexation of New Netherlands. There could not be a uniform and effective system of customs as long as the Manhattan Bay and mouth of the Hudson were in the hands of a foreign Power.

Moreover the aggrandisement of Connecticut was a step of prime importance in the colonial policy of the English Government. That colony under a loyal and courtierlike governor, and propitiated by a charter which confirmed its existing territorial rights and conferred fresh ones, was to be a check on the Roundheads of Massachusetts. The charter granted to Connecticut in May 1662 described the frontiers of the colony with an obscurity which seemed almost designed to create litigation. It is scarcely possible to

Position of Connecticut.

arrive at any precise and satisfactory view of the boundaries, or to see where the south-west corner of the colony was. But plainly it was understood on all hands that Connecticut was to take in a part of Long Island and certain settlements on the mainland opposite which under existing arrangements belonged to New Netherlands. In fact the charter wholly overrode the treaty of Hartford.

The government of Connecticut lost no time in the attempt to enforce their newly acquired territorial rights. A commissioner was sent to the various townships hitherto under Dutch rule to notify the change of jurisdiction.[1] The effect of a gradual infusion of an English element now made itself felt. There was in all these settlements a Dutch and an English party. The dispute which followed resembled in many respects the contest between Connecticut and Newhaven. There was, however, this difference. The men of Newhaven were almost unanimous in their determination not to be absorbed into Connecticut. On the other hand it seems pretty clear that in this case the resistance came from the government of New Netherlands, while the greater part of the inhabitants desired annexation.

Territorial claims of Connecticut.

In October 1663 two Dutch representatives sent by Stuyvesant appeared at Hartford to protest against the proceedings of Connecticut. As in the case of New Haven, the very man who had obtained the instrument tried to modify the application of it. Winthrop declared that the patent was not meant to encroach in any way on New Netherlands. The three commissioners who acted for the Connecticut government replied with good sense that in such a matter the Governor could speak for himself only ;

Attempted negotiation in 1663.

[1] Brodhead, vol. i. p. 719.

they had merely to deal with plain questions of fact.¹

The negotiation ended much as that between New Netherlands and Maryland did. Each party stood its ground and insisted on the rights granted by charter. Connecticut, however, so far gave way as to propose a temporary compromise. They would for the present leave the settlements towards the south of Long Island unmolested, if the Dutch would in turn abstain from exercising any jurisdiction on the rest of the territory. This compromise, however, satisfied neither party, and Stuyvesant's envoys returned to New Netherlands.

Scarcely had they returned when Stuyvesant heard that certain members of the English party were striving to settle the question by force. In some of the disputed townships on Long Island they had proclaimed the King of England, changed the magistrates, and given English names to the towns. Stuyvesant thereupon wrote to the General Court of Connecticut offering to accept those terms of neutrality which his envoys had refused.

<small>The English townships on Long Island resist Dutch authority.²</small>

Soon after, matters were complicated by the appearance on the scene of that adventurer who played so disreputable a part in New England history, John Scott.³ In this instance he traded with shameless and successful audacity on the conflicting interests of different parties. From Connecticut he obtained authority to act as a commissioner for the

<small>John Scott on Long Island.</small>

---

¹ Brodhead, vol. i. p. 720. The Journal of the envoys is in the N. Y. Docs. vol. ii. p. 385. ² *Ib.*

³ I have spoken of John Scott in my earlier volume, *The English in America: Puritan Colonies*. Mr. Palfrey, in his *History of New England*, has brought together a number of facts about Scott's career (vol. ii. p. 564). In 1682 a certain Colonel John Scott killed a hackney coachman on Tower Hill. An advertisement for his apprehension appeared in the *London Intelligencer*. It describes his appearance, and states that he was 'a great vindicator of the Salamanca doctor.' It is not unlikely that this man was identical with the Captain John Scott of Long Island.

reduction of certain townships on the northern part of Long Island. At the same time he managed to win the favour of New Haven, then bitterly exasperated against Connecticut by threats of annexation, professing himself able and willing to secure for them the territory which they had long coveted on the Delaware.

Scott soon made it plain that he had not the slightest intention of using the authority which he had received from Connecticut for the good of that colony. Among the Long Island settlers there was a party favourable neither to Dutch rule nor to that of Connecticut. Many of them had fled from religious persecution in New England. There were Baptists, Quakers and Antinomians. At the same time Stuyvesant had taught such men that, though Dutch rule might be better than that of a Puritan settlement, it fell far short of an ideal of religious freedom. The existence of such a party was no doubt among the influences which brought about the easy conquest of New Netherlands.

Scott now with no little craft turned this to his own account. How far he was in the secret counsels of the King and his advisers does not appear. But he seems to have had some means of knowing what was not made public till six months later. Addressing men who were, as he knew, ready for a change of master, and yet adverse to the claims of Connecticut, he announced that Long Island had been granted to the Duke of York, and he seems to have persuaded the inhabitants that he was a fit person to act as President pending the establishment of a proprietary government.[1]

Out of all this anarchy and confusion there seemed no way save by the intervention of some power strong enough to override all the conflicting claims. Such intervention was at hand. A memorial in the State Papers shows that before the end of 1663 the English

[1] For Scott's proceedings see N. Y. Docs. ii. pp. 393-410.

Government was taking measures to ascertain in detail what were the military resources of New Netherlands, and what help in the work of subjugation might be looked for from the English colonies. To this end three Commissioners—Sir John Berkeley, Sir George Carteret and Sir William Coventry—were appointed. They report that they have discoursed with several persons well acquainted with the affairs of New England, including inhabitants of Long Island. Of the nineteen hundred settlers on the Island, two-thirds are Dutch, the rest English. From Connecticut and New Haven they could reckon on a force of thirteen or fourteen hundred men. The other New England colonies would send volunteers, and in all likelihood the Crown could hire an auxiliary body of Indians. Such a force, aided by three King's ships and three hundred regular soldiers, would be enough to reduce the Dutch colony.[1]

The English Government investigates the resources of New Netherlands.

One point connected with the memorial is worth noticing. Two of the Commissioners who were urging the King to annex New Netherlands had a distinct personal interest in the matter. Carteret and Berkeley were already colonial proprietors since, in 1663, they had, in conjunction with others, received the proprietary grant for Carolina.[2] The alacrity with which they secured for themselves a reversionary interest in the territory to be taken from the Dutch showed that they must by this time have measured the profit which might accrue from annexation, and taints their advice with some suspicion of a personal motive. They in fact represented the better side of a movement of which the meaner was represented by such men as Scott. After the Restoration the impulse which carried men to the New World reawakened with

Policy of Carteret and Berkeley

[1] *Calendar of Col. Papers*, 1664, Jan. 27.
[2] *Ib.* 1663, March 24.

marvellous force. The Civil War had unsettled men; it had cut short their civil careers, and deprived them of the training which fitted them for such careers. Home ties were broken; to some England had become a strange country, to many it was filled with recollections which called forth only sorrow or vindictiveness. Impulses were at work akin to those which urged Gilbert and Smith and Gorges, and a host of meaner men, towards the New World. The motives of the new generation were on a lower scale; the dreams of the crusader and the gold seeker were replaced by the designs of the land speculator and the placeman. We may be sure that, beside those councillors whose influence is recorded, there were many who felt that it was to their own personal interest to urge the Crown to a policy of annexation.

Another document in the State Papers dating from the same time shows us the kind of argument which was used to encourage and justify the annexation of New Netherlands. It is a letter, the writer and the recipient of which are neither of them named. One would fain hope that Scott was the author. It lies as inventively and unblushingly as his acknowledged writings, and one would wish that even in that corrupt age there were not two such on the outskirts of public life. It urges the plea of occupation, and gives a most astounding sketch of the history of English colonization. Troubles in Scotland had prevented the discoveries of Cabot being followed. But towards the end of the seventeenth century, Captain White and other Englishmen took up the task with such energy that five thousand of them lost their lives. Hudson's discoveries were not made for the Dutch, but in the employment of Sir John Popham and two English merchants.

Calumnies against New Netherlands.[1]

[1] *Cal. Colonial Papers,* 1664, p. 622.

Other arguments were adduced: isolated acts of wrong committed by the Dutch against English settlers, and against those Indian tribes who had befriended them. Even if the particular statements were true, they could only justify the English Government in demanding restitution. The annexation of a colony was strange amends to claim for the private wrongs of two dispossessed farmers. If indeed the case had been one where men's policy was likely to be decided by argument, such lies could have done nothing but harm. Any reasonable man would see that the case which could find no better argument must be indeed a weak one. Most of all might the Connecticut settlers who had real grievances, and who could bring forward arguments which might in some measure justify annexation, feel irritated at such a travesty of their case. In plain truth the policy of annexation was simply one of expediency, adopted by an unscrupulous Cabinet. The wrongs of the New England colonists, the plea of discovery were pretexts, meant to give a faint show of decency.

In March 1664 the purpose of annexation was definitely announced. A patent was granted to the Duke of York making over to him two tracts, one north of Massachusetts, the other Long Island and the whole territory between the Connecticut and the Delaware. Over these provinces the Duke was invested with sovereignty, with the usual reservation that his proceedings must not be contrary to the laws of England. Also the subjects were to have a right of appeal to the Crown. Nothing was said as to the conditions or limits of such appeal. With these reservations the Duke had full power to appoint judges and executive officers, and either to exercise in person

The Duke of York's patent.[1]

[1] The patent is printed in full in N. Y. Docs. vol. iii. p. 265, and in an Appendix by Brodhead, vol. ii.

the right of making laws and ordinances, or to delegate it as he thought fit.

In one important point the whole document had a transparent air of fiction. It spoke throughout as if the whole territory in question was vacant soil, now to be dealt with for the first time. Nothing was said of the necessity of conquest, nothing of the claims of the United Provinces or the West India Company, nothing of the status or the liberties of the existing settlers. Their civil rights, their property, their freedom of worship were placed at the mercy of an irresponsible ruler, with only the slight and shadowy protection of an appeal to what was virtually a foreign Power.

Nor was that all. The Duke's grant dealt as recklessly with the claims of Maryland and of Connecticut as it did with those of New Netherlands. It was a flat contradiction of Baltimore's original grant. The bounds of Connecticut were so vaguely defined by the charter that it is hard to say what did and what did not conflict with them. But at least the new instrument raised difficulties in that quarter which it made no attempt whatever to settle.

Nothing can be said in defence of such a measure. Yet, however much we may condemn the actors, there is little to be indignant at in the result. The transfer of New Netherlands only brought about at one blow what would otherwise in all likelihood have been done by a weary and wasteful process, culminating in war. The northern part of Long Island and the adjacent mainland was becoming more and more a debateable ground. Connecticut, now the most independent, if not the most influential, of the New England colonies, would have been constantly on the watch for advantages, able to support her partisans in each township, offering irresistible inducements to come under her dominion. New Netherlands, crushed by

Moral aspect of the conquest.

debt, and harassed by the claims of Maryland on the other side, could do nothing for the defence of her soil. Piecemeal annexation would have led at last to some open dispute, for to force on such a dispute would have been to the interests of Connecticut. New Netherlands would have passed into English hands, and the territory placed under the control of Andros in 1686 would have been substantially the same, though he would have held it by a different title.

Nor can one feel that any real wrong was done to the Dutch. The colony was not a national undertaking; it was not the nation which lost. The blow fell on the Company which had proved itself unworthy of its trust. The real loser was not Holland, but a third Power which looked on with folded hands, unconscious of the great stake which it had on the struggle. To the generation of Englishmen who conquered New Netherlands, the gain seemed no more than the completion of a continuous Atlantic sea-board. Its real value was that, by acquiring the control over the valley of the Hudson, England secured for herself ascendancy over the Mohawk country and the tribes that dwelt therein. Thus, and thus only, could England check her rival France in that policy which aimed at connecting the upper waters of the Hudson and those of the Ohio by a continuous line of outposts, and which would thus make impossible the extension of the English colonies towards the Pacific.

The first use which the Duke made of his new rights argued ill for his future policy as a colonial proprietor, and illustrated the motives of those who had advised him. By an instrument, dated June 1664, he conveyed to Berkeley and Carteret all that part of his province yet to be won,

The Duke's grant to Berkeley and Carteret.[1]

[1] The original grant does not appear to be among the *Colonial Papers* in the Record Office. It is printed in Leaming and Spicer's Collection,

which lay between the Hudson and the Delaware. There was a certain vagueness in the instrument. It was in form an ordinary conveyance of land. But since the Duke's territorial rights were combined with certain political rights, it was nearly certain that an attempt would be made to interpret the transfer as carrying with it political sovereignty. Berkeley and Carteret, already in the recognised colonial sense Proprietors of Carolina, were unlikely to accept in another part of America the position of ordinary landholders.

The ease with which the conquest was achieved may be held to have justified this prospective sale of the bear's hide. The attempt was to be combined with another and, as it proved, a decidedly more difficult undertaking. Four commissioners were appointed to reduce New Netherlands, and at the same time to visit the New England colonies and report upon their condition. This in itself showed that the reduction of New Netherlands was designed as part of a comprehensive scheme for dealing with the colonies. Of the New England scheme, and of the three Commissioners to whom that part of the work was mainly entrusted, I have already spoken.[1] Happily for the future of New Netherlands, their colleague was a man of widely different stamp. There is hardly a character in history which presents such a web of seemingly contradictory impulses and principles as that of James II. The part of a colonial administrator formed an important portion of his career, and there his inconsistencies are seen to the full. We see him always painstaking, at times

Arrangements for enforcing the Duke's claims.

---

not as a separate document but as cited in a later patent of the date of Queen Anne. L. and S. 3, &c. It is also printed in the New Jersey Archives with the heading 'From the New Jersey State Library.'

[1] *Puritan Colonies*, vol. ii.

generous in his policy, granting popular rights liberally and wisely, again withdrawing those rights as it would seem in arbitrary caprice, imperilling, at last overthrowing, his own position by wilfully refusing to understand the motives and sentiments of those whom he had to govern. But in one respect—in the choice of officials—his conduct towards his colonial subjects is throughout creditable. It would have been well if in this matter the house of Hanover had imitated the last Stuart King. Two of the governors whom he appointed, Nicolls and Dongan, were not merely men of high ability and character, men whose political principles towered far above the standard of their contemporaries; they were men who approached colonial questions with exceptional width of view and statesmanlike foresight, men able to deal with questions which could only be settled by a rare union of strong will and conciliatory patience. Nicholson fell short of them somewhat in intelligence, far more in moral character, and in elevation and steadiness of aim. Lovelace and Andros were men of a meaner stamp, yet it was distinctly in capacity rather than virtue that they were lacking. Andros, indeed, failed because being a second-rate man he was set to do work which needed a first-rate one. At his worst James never launched on the colonies any of those butcherly ruffians or those greedy and self-seeking adventurers of whom scores were to be found clamouring for such employment. In the attacks of New England pamphleteers, Andros—a man it is true of arbitrary temper and without a particle of administrative sagacity, but honest, religious, and in the main humane and courteous—figures as a bloodthirsty idolater. What would they have said had the colony fallen under the yoke of Kirke or Tyrconnel?

Richard Nicolls, who by the terms of the commission was invested with a certain supremacy over his three colleagues, and who practically enjoyed supreme control over the expedition against New Netherlands, was one of the few Cavaliers whose character and intelligence seem to have profited by his experience of the Civil War. An Oxford student of promise, he had been compelled at nineteen to 'leave the books in dust, And oil the unused armour's rust.' In the Civil War he commanded a troop of horse in the royal army. He shared the exile of the royal family, and acted as groom of the bedchamber to the Duke of York.[1] It is said that he was specially fitted for his task in America by a knowledge of the Dutch tongue.[2] His present instructions were plain. New York was not to be merely threatened, nor occupied as a temporary measure with a view to extracting any concessions. Dutch authority was to be overthrown, and the settlers were 'to be reduced to entire submission.' At the same time there was to be no interference with private property or with freedom of trade.

Four hundred and fifty soldiers, embarked on four ships, formed the attacking force.[3] In the middle of May they sailed from Portsmouth, and before the end of July Nicolls reached Boston.[4] Thence after a short stay the fleet went on to Long Island, where they were joined by a reinforcement from New Haven commanded by Scott.

[1] For Nicolls's antecedents see a note by Mr. C. D. O'Callaghan to Wooley's *Journal in New York*, being the second volume of Gowan's *Bibliotheca Americana*.

[2] This is stated by a writer in the *American Historical Magazine*, vol. xxi. p. 181, but no authority is given. It is not unlikely that a Royalist should have learnt Dutch during his exile.

[3] The number of ships is repeatedly stated by English and Dutch authorities.

[4] Maverick writes from Piscataway on July 20, and speaks of a voyage of nearly ten weeks. N. Y. Docs. vol. iii. p. 65.

Nothing could be more helpless than the condition of New Netherlands. For years the colony had been struggling on the edge of bankruptcy, and the expedition against New Sweden gave the final blow. So straitened was the colonial exchequer that in 1663 Stuyvesant had to raise the money needed for the ordinary purposes of government by borrowing on the security of his cannon.[1]

<small>Financial distress of New Netherlands.</small>

All attempts to rouse the home Government were useless. Charles and his advisers befooled the Dutch Ambassador, and Stuyvesant's cry for help was frustrated by persistent denials of any hostile intention. The Company vainly flattered themselves that the Puritans of New England would take no part in a policy which must strengthen the hold of the Crown over the colonies. The English envoy indeed, the apostate Puritan, George Downing, in some measure disclosed what was intended by a frank declaration, like that made by Calvert, that New Netherlands had no real legal existence.[2] But even if those who guided the counsels of the States-General suspected mischief, their jealousy of the West India Company kept them inactive. The colony was, in fact, overthrown by that narrow and short-sighted policy which had prevented it from being in any real sense a national undertaking.

<small>Apathy of the Dutch.</small>

Not indeed that, as things were now, a more strenuous policy on the part of the States-General or the Company could have availed much. The general body of the settlers, even so far as they were loyal to the Company, had no military organization, they had not even that civic cohesion which may serve as a rough and imperfect basis for

<small>Defenceless condition of the colony.</small>

[1] Brodhead, vol. i. p. 720.
[2] In a memorial addressed to the States-General, Downing had the audacity to use these words: 'As to the business of the New Netherlands this is very far from being a surprise or anything of that nature, it being notoriously known that that spot of land lies within the limits, and is part

such organization. Moreover the whole resources of the colony were centred in the capital. If an invader had seized Boston, his work would have been only half done. It would have been a heavy blow to the trade of Massachusetts, but much of her civil and economical life would have been left. She could still have harassed an enemy in a guerilla war, possibly have worn him out. In New Netherlands, when once the capital was gone, there was no material either for defence or even for retaliation.

Fort Amsterdam, the one citadel on which the security of the town, and therefore of the colony, was thus staked, was designed for defence only against the savages. It was simply valueless against a civilized enemy, with ordnance. Its walls were little more than earth mounds, barely ten feet high. Not only could they be battered from the sea, but even with the feeble cannon of that day shot could be dropped into the heart of the town from rising ground close to the walls on the western side. Private houses had been suffered to be built close to the walls, and it would have been necessary to destroy these as a preliminary to any scheme of defence, otherwise they might be seized and then utilized for purposes of attack. The fort had no proper supply of water. Moreover Stuyvesant avowed the Company had just landed four hundred negroes, and thereby created an exceptional strain on the resources of the colony.

When after all was over Stuyvesant pleaded these excuses, the Company met him with the answer that he might have procured powder from private traders, and that he had neglected to warn his employers of the deficiencies and dangers of his situation. They also

of the possession of his [the King's] subjects of New England, as appears most evidently by their charter, and that those few Dutch that have lived there merely upon tolerance and sufferance and not as having any rights thereunto.' N. Y. Docs. vol. ii. p. 302.

complained that he had listened to clergymen and other cowardly people, and that if private houses were in the way they should have been pulled down. In other words Stuyvesant was only to remember that he was a military commander, and to ignore his responsibilities as a civil governor. He was to hold the fort at any cost, quite regardless of what might happen to the inhabitants.

In June 1664 Stuyvesant, having been warned that the expedition had sailed from England, called the attention of the Burgomasters and schepens to the impending danger. All that he got in return was the singularly discouraging reply that they would exert themselves as much as they had done heretofore.[1] A little later, in response to a further appeal by Stuyvesant, they did make some show of activity. The inhabitants were impressed to work, one-third of them every day, at the fortifications; a civic guard was formed for the town; to increase the supply of food maltsters were forbidden to malt any grain, and at the request of the Town Council a certain quantity of arms and ammunition were transferred from the fort to the town.[2] The town itself on its landward side was guarded only by a decayed palisade which might possibly keep savages at bay, but was powerless against an enemy with firearms. To hold this, a defence of fully a mile in extent, there were available a hundred and fifty regular soldiers and some two hundred and fifty half-drilled volunteers. Even had the strategical frontier been stronger it would have been of little avail, since the whole stock of powder in the citadel was only six hundred pounds.[3] In addition to its own essential weakness of situation and

[1] *Court Minutes*, vol. v. p. 88.   [2] *Ib.* p. 105.
[3] For the state of the defences and the stock of powder, see Stuyvesant's explanation and a deposition of four inhabitants. N. Y. Docs. vol. ii. pp. 430, 475. For what follows I have relied mainly on Brodhead, whose account is largely based on manuscript authorities.

lack of resources, the town had no outlying forts to check an advancing enemy either by land or sea. Thus the land force advancing from New England obtained quiet possession of the whole of Long Island, while the fleet sailed unchallenged along the coast and anchored in what is now Jamaica Bay, some ten miles northeast of the mouth of the harbour. On the 19th of August Stuyvesant sent a message to Nicolls asking what was meant by his approach. The answer was sent up by Cartwright, one of the Assistant-Commissioners, accompanied by three of Nicolls's staff. It demanded a complete surrender of all territory held by the Dutch, but promised security of life and property to all private persons. The demand was met, as might have been expected, with a flat refusal from Stuyvesant; thereupon it was repeated, accompanied by the threat of an immediate attack.[1]

Nicolls however had the wisdom to see that in such a case success won at the point of the sword would go far to frustrate its own purpose. He had not only to conquer, but if it might be to conquer without alienating. That process by which the Dutch colony had been Anglicized now told its tale. The New England force in its march down Long Island must have had ample opportunities of learning how matters really stood within the walls of New Amsterdam. Nicolls must have known by this time that there was no real spirit or power of resistance, that if he were but patient the prize would fall into his hands. He took counsel with Winthrop. From him he learnt that the one thing which might provoke the Dutch to hold out was the dread of losing their trade with Holland. Let him only guarantee that, and there was no fear of resistance. Nicolls accepted Winthrop's view and authorized him to offer an assurance that there should

Nicolls conciliates the Dutch settlers.

[1] N. Y. Docs. vol. ii. pp. 410-14.

be no interference with the trade between the colony and Holland.[1] In promising a special dispensation from a statute Nicolls was undoubtedly going beyond his powers as an English officer; in making a stipulation of such importance without authority from his principal he was going beyond the special terms of his commission. The best excuse that can be urged is that he had to act in an emergency which compelled him to take upon himself responsibility, and that his anxiety to deal fairly and liberally by the Dutch made it certain that he would spare no exertion of his own to secure the fulfilment of his pledge.

With this authority from Nicolls, Winthrop wrote to Stuyvesant. He pointed out that resistance would only bring the whole force of the New England colonies down upon the Dutch, while surrender would involve no more than a nominal transfer of authority. There would be 'little alteration but submission to and acknowledgment of' the King's supremacy. In using the latter argument Winthrop showed a characteristic incapacity to see the real point at issue. It might be a very good reason why the colonists themselves should be willing to surrender: it could be no justification to Stuyvesant for abandoning the post entrusted to him by his employers.

Negotiations between the Dutch and English.

Bearing this letter, endorsed by Nicolls and his colleagues, Winthrop was rowed up in a wherry to Manhattan wharf. With him were five leading representatives of the New England confederation chosen from all three colonies. Stuyvesant and the Town Council received the embassy at a tavern; formal

[1] Brodhead (vol. ii. p. 28) quotes the actual text of Nicolls's letter to Winthrop. The freedom of trade stipulated for was granted for seven years. Three years later Stuyvesant reminded the English Government of this pledge. This may be taken as ample proof of the fact that such a pledge had been given.

expressions of courtesy were exchanged; then Winthrop handed in the letter and departed.

Immediately they had heard the letter, the Burgomasters demanded that a town meeting should be called and Winthrop's despatch made public. This Stuyvesant refused to do. Nor was that all; so determined was the Governor to keep the general body of citizens in the dark that he tore Winthrop's letter to pieces. Later tradition has represented this as an act of petulant wrath. Overbearing and arbitrary though Stuyvesant was, it is far more likely that his own version was true, and that he deliberately sought to prevent the citizens having any knowledge of the terms offered.[1] We must remember that throughout the aims of the citizens and those of the Governor were different. It was enough for them if they saved life, property, and commercial rights. As for political freedom, the Company had left them little ground for dreading any change. Stuyvesant, on the other hand, had to consider his duty as a servant of the Company, and his honour as a soldier. We need not believe that he was indifferent to bloodshed, or that he was prepared to expose the city to pillage and the garrison to destruction in a hopeless cause. That it was a hopeless cause he must have known well; yet he may have believed that to stimulate the citizens to some show of resistance was his best chance of securing honourable terms.

But even if such a policy were expedient, the time had gone by when it was practicable. It was plainly impossible to keep the general body of citizens in the dark when once the letter had become known to the Burgomasters. Stuyvesant's only hope now would have

Obstinacy of Stuyvesant.

---

[1] N. Y. Docs. vol. ii. p. 445. Stuyvesant here implies that the destruction of the letter was approved of, not suggested, by the whole Council. It seems odd that it should not have been burnt.

been to throw himself frankly on popular support, to make one last bid for that confidence which he had so fatally disregarded. Vague rumours of the promised concessions got abroad; the work of palisading the town ceased: a mob gathered round the council chamber and clamoured for a sight of Winthrop's letter. Stuyvesant's attempts to pacify, or rather to overawe, them failed; at length the Secretary Bayard recovered the fragments of the letter and handed a copy to the Burgomasters, to be disposed of as they pleased.

Meanwhile Stuyvesant, with calm defiance and impracticable obstinacy akin to his Calvinistic faith, sent Nicolls an elaborate protest, pointing out the soundness of the Dutch title, based as it was on discovery and purchase from the natives, and sanctioned by continuous possession. It had, moreover, as he pointed out, been recognised in the treaty of Hartford made in 1650 between the government of New Netherlands and the New England confederacy.[1]

Nicolls at once waived all such discussion. The question had been settled for him by the Government for which he acted, all he had to do was to carry out his orders; he would suspend operations for forty-eight hours, and thus give time for consideration. If the city was not then surrendered, he must attack.[2]

The delay was not merely humane and conciliatory; it was eminently politic. We may be sure that Winthrop and his colleagues were able to form some idea how matters stood within the fort. Time, they could see, was sure to fight for them. In another way Nicolls was able to turn the interval to good account. It was most important to him to isolate New Amsterdam, to emphasize as far as might be the submission of the outlying settlements, and to show what fair terms he was ready to grant. He summoned

The Convention at Gravesend.

[1] N. Y. Docs. vol. ii. p. 411. [2] Ib. p. 414.

all the settlers on Long Island to a general convention at Gravesend. Most of them attended. Some of the townships had already accepted the authority of Connecticut. Winthrop with characteristic compliance, and with equally characteristic readiness to substitute his own personal opinion for the authoritative voice of the colony, withdrew all claim to this territory. Nicolls's policy in dealing with it foreshadowed, perhaps designedly, his treatment of New Netherlands. He kept in power all the officials appointed by Connecticut, till a convention of deputies could be held to settle a scheme of government.

The townships within the Dutch border, encouraged as we may well believe by this, submitted at once. Volunteers from the newly acquired territory joined the New England troops, and the whole force advanced towards New Amsterdam and encamped at Brooklyn.[1]

The English land force was then put on shore at Gravesend and joined the troops at Brooklyn. Two of the ships were stationed at Governor's Island. The other two sailed up the Hudson past Fort Amsterdam. Thus the inhabitants were effectually cut off on all sides alike from succour and from escape.

The attack.

Stuyvesant had his guns mounted and ready. But at the last moment he was dissuaded from firing on the enemy. The English fleet lay off the fort and suffered discord within the city to fight for them. The conduct of the garrison soon showed how they looked on themselves as the servants of the Company, bound only to the defence of the fort, with no responsibility towards the town and its inhabitants. When Stuyvesant withdrew his troops from the fort to the town, ominous words were heard among the soldiers. There was wealth, they said, in the houses of the burgesses, and girls there

[1] Brodhead, vol. ii. p. 32.

K

who could afford to wear gold ornaments.[1] The citizens were between the upper and the nether millstone, and those who had heard of Nicolls's moderation might well feel that the enemy without was less to be feared than the defender within.

The main difficulty was to persuade Stuyvesant to yield. To the crowd that thronged about him with vague entreaties that he would surrender he only answered that he would sooner be carried out dead. But on the 5th, a formal remonstrance was handed to him signed by the Town Council and nearly ninety of the chief inhabitants, among them Stuyvesant's own son.[2] Unless Stuyvesant's intention on leaving the fort was to make one last appeal to the patriotism of the citizens, it is difficult to see his object. Within the fort the garrison might at least have died hard, or even won honourable terms. In the town, with no defence but a wretched wood paling, and cumbered by a defenceless and disloyal mob of civilians, their case was utterly hopeless. At length Stuyvesant was brought to see this and sent a message to Nicolls. A conference was agreed on and commissioners were appointed, six from each side, who met at Stuyvesant's house. The English were represented by the two Assistant-Commissioners, Carr and Cartwright, two representatives from Connecticut and two from Massachusetts.[3]

Stuyvesant gives way.

When Stuyvesant sent commissioners it was practically an admission of defeat. There was little difficulty

---

[1] Stuyvesant's report, mentioned above, p. 124. This threat was accompanied by another, which throws a curious and somewhat prophetic light on the social and economical life of the colony. 'We now hope to find an opportunity to pepper the devilish Chinese who have made us smart so much.' In all likelihood these Chinese were petty traders and money-lenders, who lived on the necessitous and extravagant.

[2] N. Y. Docs. vol. ii. p. 248.

[3] Brodhead, vol. ii. p. 35.

in settling the conditions of surrender. The garrison was to march out with the honours of war. The general principle of the surrender as applied to civil inhabitants was to leave everything unaltered. The new Proprietor stepped into the rights and the responsibilities of the Company. Dutch emigrants might come in as before, and there was to be free trade with Holland. The existing laws which controlled religious affairs and inheritances were to remain as before, and there was to be no change in the municipal constitution. If in spite of these concessions any Dutch settler wished to leave the colony, he should meet with no hindrance.[1]

The ease with which the transfer was effected is best shown by the fact that on the day after the surrender the Town Council[2] met as though there had been no interruption to their proceedings. Beyond doubt the conquest was an unrighteous outrage, but for the citizens it meant gaining masters who had shown themselves moderate, compliant, and sympathetic, in place of those whose coldness, greed, and neglect had well nigh brought the colony to ruin. Formal documents addressed to those in authority cannot be taken as speaking with absolute truth. But the memorial which the citizens within two months of the conquest presented to the Proprietor was in substance a fair expression of their views. It described Nicolls as 'gentle, wise, and intelligent,' and it looked forward to the time when the city, if not hampered by foolish restrictions on commerce, should count its inhabitants by thousands, and should carry on with the whole world a trade which should yield a vast revenue to its Proprietor and still leave its citizens wealthy.[3]

Effect of the conquest.

[1] The articles are in the N. Y. Docs. vol. ii. pp. 250–3.
[2] *Court Minutes*, vol. v. p. 107.   [3] *Ib.* p. 160.

Only one difficulty arose. Three weeks after the surrender Nicolls required from the settlers who chose to remain an oath binding them as long as they stayed within the English dominions to obey the King, the Proprietor, and their officers. The settlers thought seemingly that this was inconsistent with the terms of surrender. On this point they were reassured by Nicolls. He declared that the articles of surrender were not in the least broken, or intended to be broken, by the words of the said oath. Thereupon two hundred and fifty Dutch citizens took the oath, among them Stuyvesant himself. There was nothing in this which need create any difficulty if the States-General ever succeeded in reasserting their authority. For the oath only bound those who took it to obedience so long as they were in British dominions. They might fairly argue that New Netherlands was not so *de jure*, and that the obligation wholly fell through if it ceased to be so *de facto*. That may have reconciled Stuyvesant and members of the old official party to their position. No such motive for acquiescence was needed by the main body of citizens.[1]

The overthrow of the capital shattered at once what little power of resistance there was in the colony. The conquest of the rest followed as a matter of course, with equal ease and equal completeness. On the 29th of August Stuyvesant evacuated New Netherlands.[2] Nicolls at once divided his available forces. Part were sent to reduce the settlements up the valley of the Hudson, part to gain possession of the territory on the Delaware. The former expedition was placed under the command of Cartwright. He was preceded at Fort Orange by a member of Stuyvesant's official staff, De Decker, who

The rest of the colony submits.

---

[1] *Court Minutes*, vol. v. pp. 143–5; Brodhead, vol. ii. p. 47.
[2] Brodhead, vol. ii. p. 42.

had hurried thither in the hope of rallying his countrymen to resist. The attempt was useless. The settlers at Fort Orange and those at Esopus yielded as easily as the inhabitants of Long Island. All private rights were secured and no civil officers were dismissed. The only measure of force needed was the banishment of De Decker. As at New Netherlands, the new government at once stepped into all the position and the liabilities of its predecessor.[1]

This had one important effect. Certain Iroquois chiefs appeared at Fort Orange, and entered into friendship with the English. Cartwright granted the same rights of trade which the Indians had before enjoyed from the Dutch, and promised assistance if the Iroquois were attacked by the tribes on their eastern frontier. The Five Nations had already entered into friendly relations with the colonists in Massachusetts, but this was their first formal recognition as allies by any English colony.[2]

While Cartwright was thus completing the English conquests on the upper Hudson, Carr was despatched with two ships and a military force to the Delaware. In touching the Dutch colonists on the west bank Nicolls was clearly going beyond his commission. The territory of the Duke of York was definitely bounded by the Delaware river. At the same time if the plea of discovery, on which alone the conquest of New Netherlands could be justified, was good for Long Island, it was also good for the territory on the Delaware. On that theory the Dutch were intruders; the claims of Maryland might be dealt with hereafter. Accordingly Carr was to explain to such of the Maryland officials as he might meet that the Dutch were being evicted as intruders, but that the Duke of York laid no claim to the territory, that inquiry should be

[1] Brodhead, vol. ii. pp. 45–7.   [2] *Ib.*

made into the territorial rights of Maryland, and that in the meantime the land was to be held for the King.

Nicolls's instructions to Carr all made for moderation and forbearance. If the Swedes would make unqualified submission and take the oaths of allegiance and fidelity, they were to be unmolested in person and estate, to enjoy freedom of conscience and equal rights of trade with English subjects; magistrates then in office were to remain so for at least six months.[1] But on the 10th of October the English fleet anchored off New Amstel. There things took much the same turn that they had at New Amsterdam. The civil population at once accepted the English supremacy. But the commander of the fort, Hinoyossa, played the same part as Stuyvesant, and even carried it further. He refused to surrender. The ships opened a broadside, and a land force headed by Carr's son attacked the fort. One cannot blame the Dutch soldiers for failing to hold against a civilized enemy with firearms a wooden palisade only designed to stop savages. But their musketry must have been sadly at fault, since they lost thirteen men without a single casualty on the side of the assailants.[2]

Hinoyossa's resistance gave Carr a pretext for severity of which he was not slow to avail himself. *Carr's misconduct on the Delaware.* The Dutch garrison were sold as slaves into Virginia.[3] Not only was the public property belonging to the corporation of Amsterdam plundered, but private goods were not respected. Without regard for Nicolls's authority or for the Duke's proprietary rights, Carr appropriated the choicest pieces of reclaimed land for himself, his son, and one of his

---

[1] Pennsylvania Archives, vol. v. p. 547.

[2] Carr's report to Nicolls, N. Y. Docs. vol. iii. p. 83.

[3] Van Schweringen's account in N. Y. Docs. vol. iii. p. 342. Van Schweringen was the Dutch Schout at New Amstel.

chief followers.¹ Nor was the pillage confined to those who might by a strained construction be held as implicated in Hinoyossa's resistance. The unhappy community of Mennonites were cruelly plundered by a boat's crew sent thither by Carr to take possession.² The men of that age, familiar with the horrors of the Thirty Years' War, did not think as we do of such atrocities. The Civil War, too, had done something to demoralize Englishmen, and one should feel that Nicolls rose above the standard of his own day rather than that Carr fell below it. Happily for the settlers on the Delaware, matters were so far peacefully settled at New Amsterdam, that Nicolls was able to visit his new conquest in person, and in some measure to exact restitution from his subordinate. Had New Netherlands been a more united community, Carr would have done much to prevent a peaceful settlement. But constituted as the colony was, a blow which fell on the Swedes and Mennonites on the Delaware was of little concern to the Dutch at Amsterdam, of none at all to the half-English villages on Long Island.

This state of things did much to lighten Nicolls's task. The colony was in fact little more than a *tabula rasa* on which he could impress such political principles as he thought best. By giving the colony a government really capable of the task of administration and defence, by binding together the loose and imperfectly jointed members of the community into a coherent whole, it was possible for Nicolls to bring home to the colonists that the English conquest was the real beginning of their national life.

Nicolls's policy.

To this task Nicolls betook himself strenuously and soberly. One of his first steps was to make the colony

---

¹ Nicolls to Arlington, N. Y. Docs. vol. iii. p. 115.
² Van Schweringen as above.

English in outward appearance by a thorough change of names. The province itself and its capital, New Amsterdam, each became New York. New Amstel, though only taken from the Dutch and not yet claimed for the Proprietor, became Newcastle. Fort Orange and the adjacent hamlet of Esopus were named Albany. Two other local names were given in honour of the Proprietor. Long Island was called Yorkshire, and the whole territory between the Hudson and the Delaware, Albania, a title which was soon forgotten when that territory came to be settled under the grant to Berkeley and Carteret.[1]

The absence of any fixed representative system lightened Nicolls's labours, since it freed him from any necessity of sweeping away or even curtailing popular rights. He and his council stepped by a perfectly easy process into the place occupied by their Dutch predecessors. The supreme legislative power was vested in a newly created body. The magistrates of each township were to meet as a Court of Assize, which was to make laws for the colony. For judicial purposes there were to be intermediate courts composed of these same magistrates, and held triennially in each of the three divisions called ridings of Long Island. This Court was simply the Quarter Sessions of an English county. The magistrates were appointed by the Governor, and held office during his pleasure. Thus in theory the Court was a mere channel through which the sovereign power of the Proprietor was exercised. Practically, however, it was sure to be amenable to the opinions and wishes of those from whom the magistrates were chosen, and among whom they lived. To distribute the exercise of power, though that power be delegated, has in practice many of the same effects

System of legislation.

[1] For these changes of names see Nicolls to the Duke of York, N. Y. Docs. vol. iii. p. 105.

as extending power, and is a natural and appropriate step towards such extension.[1]

It is to be noticed that this system only took in Long Island. For it was a radical principle in Nicolls's policy to regard the colony as consisting of two distinct halves, the English and semi-English settlements on Long Island and the Dutch settlements along the Hudson. The Court of Assize was chosen only from the former; it had to deal with the latter only so far as in conjunction with the Governor and Council it was the supreme legislative body.

This distinction was more emphatically marked in Nicolls's legislative policy. He summoned a convention, which met in February 1665 at Heemstede, on Long Island. Each of the towns on Long Island sent two delegates, and two also attended from West Chester on the mainland. The Dutch settlements on the mainland were unrepresented. The convention was not in any way to form a fixed or permanent element in the constitutional machinery of the colony. It was the counterpart of the Landtag which had been summoned in the days of Stuyvesant at some special crisis in the history of the colony. Nor was its function to legislate, though it is plain that some of its members had gone there with that expectation. Nicolls clearly saw that the English half of the colony, as we may call it, required different legislation from the Dutch half. Formed as they largely were of immigrants from New England, he could not do better than give them a system modelled as far as might be on those which the New England colonies had framed for themselves. To this end he obtained copies of the codes in force in Massachusetts and New Haven. The code of Connecticut existed only in manuscript, and

Convention at Heemstede.[2]

---

[1] Brodhead, vol. ii. p. 64.   [2] *Ib.* p. 67.

though Nicolls asked for it, no copy could be made soon enough.

From these, aided by his council and certain leading men acting as magistrates, he fashioned a body of laws to be laid before the convention. Nicolls was no doubt a man in advance of his age, yet the whole proceeding may be looked upon as marking a definite change in the relations between the mother country and her colonies. Twenty-five years earlier such a proceeding would have been impossible. No functionary acting virtually as the servant of the Crown would have dared to admit that he could be indebted to a colonial legislature for any knowledge of the needs of the colonies or of the principles on which they ought to be governed, least of all to a legislature composed of disaffected Puritans. Nicolls's policy was an admission of the fundamental principle that the colonists themselves best understood their own wants and their own method of life. At the same time Nicolls clearly showed that he accepted that only as a guiding principle, and that he was not prepared to act on it without limitations, or to follow it wherever it might carry him. When the code drawn up by Nicolls and his advisers was laid before the convention, the delegates expressed themselves dissatisfied. They went back to the promise which Nicolls had given at the previous meeting at Gravesend, that the newly acquired province should enjoy 'equal if not greater freedom and immunities than any of his Majesty's colonies in New England.' This they interpreted as promising the introduction of a system of municipal self-government. The New England colonies, they urged, chose their own magistrates; if Nicolls's words meant anything, they themselves were entitled to the same privilege. One township indeed (Southold) claimed that peculiar and unsatisfactory right, the nomination of military officers

Proceedings of the convention.

by the townsmen. The same township, true to those political principles which had hitherto guided New England, and which a hundred years later were to be the creed of the whole body of colonies, demanded that all taxation should be imposed by a body of deputies, and that magistrates should be dependent for their salaries on the freemen.

These demands were met by Nicolls with that tact and judgment which marked all his proceedings. Certain amendments in detail Nicolls accepted. He further gave a general promise that if any township required a change in the laws, and demanded it at the General Assize through its own magistrate, the matter should be considered. That well illustrates the strength and the weakness of the system introduced by Nicolls. Its merits were in a measure personal. He might administer the system equitably and with a due regard for the interest of all. There was no guarantee that it would be so administered by his successor. Nor could a justice nominated by the Governor be regarded on any constitutional theory as the representative of the commonalty. Yet it was proved by events, as might have been foreseen, that magistrates chosen from the settlers among whom they lived were in practice exponents of popular feeling. That view underlay the answer which Nicolls made to the demands of the freemen. He frankly met their demands for self-government by telling them that, according to the letter of his instructions, the choice of magistrates was vested in the Governor. Beyond that he could not go. If they wanted more they must go to the King for it. But he reminded them they were no worse off than men in England, where all judicial authority emanated from the Crown.

Nicolls's dealings with the convention.

The implied *reductio ad absurdum* was not as effective for men living in 1665 as it would be to-day. But underlying it was the sound doctrine that, when power is widely diffused, it is sure to fall under the actual, though perhaps informal, control of public opinion. Whether that control is efficient will depend rather on the elements of which public opinion is made up, than on the machinery through which it finds expression.

Confidence in their capacity for resisting any abuse of arbitrary power, together with gratitude and good will towards Nicolls himself, led the settlers to accept a settlement which in theory fell far short of their demands. Another reconciling—or perhaps one should rather say restraining—influence was at work. The reduction of New Netherlands was but a part of the work entrusted to Nicolls by his commission. It also gave him almost unlimited administrative power in the New England colonies. The settlers on Long Island were connected by origin and interest with New England, and we may be sure that they were sufficiently influenced by those ties to feel the need for dealing in a spirit of conciliation with Nicolls and his colleagues. The Long Island settlers, too, looked for guidance to Connecticut, and that was the very colony which had most inducement to take a moderate and friendly attitude towards the Commissioners. One of Nicolls's measures after the conquest had been to settle the boundary with Connecticut. As we have seen, the southern portion of that colony was very loosely defined by its new patent. There can be no doubt that if Nicolls had rigidly insisted on the Duke's legal rights to all the territory to which the Dutch could plead a title, he might have very seriously embarrassed Connecticut. Nicolls wisely saw that the same policy which had granted Connecticut such favourable terms, detaching her from Massachusetts and annihilating New Haven, made it expedient now to deal liberally in the interpretation of those terms. He accordingly assented

Influence of New England.

to an arrangement by which five townships, lying strictly within the limits of the Duke's patent, were ceded to Connecticut.[1] It was at the same time arranged that a boundary line should be drawn running at a uniform distance of twenty miles from the Hudson. Either through incapable surveying or through deliberate fraud on the part of those who acted for Connecticut, the line was drawn some miles too far to the southeast, and thus a question was left open which gave rise to much future dispute and litigation.[2]

For the present, however, the point seemed to be settled on terms peculiarly favourable to Connecticut. In winning the good graces of that colony, Nicolls was doing much to put himself on a friendly footing with the English part of his own province, while the liberality of the Connecticut charter and the spirit in which it had been interpreted were an earnest of the good results of loyalty.

The Duke's laws, as the body of enactments drawn up by Nicolls and ratified by the convention was called, were a code, not a constitution. Yet in one or two matters it may be said to have defined constitutional relations. It did not create a complete system of self-governing townships such as existed in New England, but it did invest the townships with certain rights. Each town was to choose from its own freemen eight overseers. Of these, four were to retire each year. The eight were to choose a constable from among their own number. This body might act as a court for the trial of civil cases concerning sums under five pounds, and might pass by-laws for their towns. Each township, too, was to assess its own rates.

In New England the township carried with it a necessary incident, the church; we may almost say that

---
[1] Nicolls to the Duke of York, N. Y. Docs. vol. iii. p. 106.
[2] Brodhead, vol. ii. p. 556.

the township and the church were the same body looked at from different points of view. The Duke's laws followed this as closely as was possible in a community where the various religions of the settlers made any common ecclesiastical system impossible. There was to be in every township a church, the denomination of which should be settled by the majority of the householders. They were to elect a minister, but he could not be instituted unless he had received ordination in England or in some recognised Protestant country. Moreover ministers were so far to conform to the usages of the Church of England that they were to pray for the royal family, and to preach not only on Sundays and on the 5th of November, but on the anniversaries of the execution of Charles I. and of the Restoration. They were also required to baptize the children of all Christian parents, and to marry all persons who offered themselves, and who complied with the needful legal formalities. Each township was to maintain its church and pay its minister, and this responsibility was to be enforced by churchwardens, appointed by the overseers. Though the obligation of contributing fell upon all, yet no professing Christian was to suffer in any way for his religious opinions.

Ecclesiastical system.

Such a system would have been thoroughly odious in the eyes of such a one as Endicott or Dudley. It left the heretic at large; it required from the ministry an open acknowledgment that they were within certain limits the servants of the Crown. Above all it introduced that 'polypiety' which was abhorred by the Massachusetts Puritan. Nor did it only in theory make it possible. Composed as New York was, it was certain that the Calvinist, the Lutheran, and the Baptist would all be strong enough to form churches. Yet in real truth such practice came nearer the theory on which

New England started, that of independent religious societies, than the actual practice of Massachusetts, where each church was independent in name only, in fact was under the control of a vague public opinion.

The penal portion of the code showed something of the stringency of Puritan legislation. The clause protecting the Christian of whatever creed from persecution was in practice an ample guarantee for toleration. The theory of freedom of opinion was completely set at defiance by a clause which made it a capital crime to deny the true God. But the clause which granted toleration within the field of Christianity no doubt did all that was practically needed.

Penal system.

A clause which made it a capital crime to strike a parent showed plain traces of its Puritan origin. The laws contained certain restrictions on servitude; these, however, do not seem to contemplate the case of the negro, but of the hired labourer, or the indented servant, bound for a fixed time.

One restriction imposed on the first class was that they were bound to take their wages if their master pleases in merchantable corn. Indented servants might not trade on their own account, but might not be transferred from one service to another for more than a year without their own consent.

The code contemplated a somewhat parental attitude on the part of the government towards master and servant. The overseers were empowered if a master 'abused his servant tyrannically and cruelly' to admonish him, and on the second offence to interfere. If the injury amounted to maiming the servant became free. On the other hand, if a servant complained unreasonably he might be punished by the addition of three months to his term of service.

Trade with the Indians in arms, ammunition, and drink was not absolutely forbidden, but could only be carried on under a license from the Governor, and all purchases of land from them had to be formally entered in a public register.

On one important point the Duke's laws throw light on the social and economical condition of the colony. They clearly contemplate the existence of a common arable field, to be pastured by the different commoners after the corn harvest.[1]

Though the Governor refused to accept that part of the military system of New England by which each company elected its own officers, yet, as there, the inhabitants were organised into a militia, with divisions corresponding to the shire and the township. There were to be four trainings a year in each township, one joint one in each riding, and one every second year for the whole militia of the colony. All males over sixteen unless specially exempted were liable for duty. This obligation, however, did not bind them to serve outside the colony. For any external service, such as assisting the New England colonies against the Indians, a volunteer force might be raised.[2]

It is plain that this code was intended to apply at once and entirely only to the half-Anglicized colonies on Long Island. It is not altogether clear what was in the meantime the position of the Dutch.

The motives which withheld Nicolls from forcing the new code on the Dutch settlers made themselves *Nicolls's treatment of the Dutch settlers.* felt in his whole policy. It had been made a matter of reproach against Stuyvesant that in disputes between his own countrymen and the English he had shown a readiness to lean towards the latter, and to be guided by their counsels. The English settlers on Long Island might with some show of reason

---

[1] This is noticed in Mr. Elking's monograph 'The Dutch Village.'

[2] The Duke's laws are to be found in the *N. Y. Hist. Coll.* 1st series, vol. i.

have brought a like charge against Nicolls. His administrative policy was equitable towards all. But towards the Dutch it showed a special anxiety to smooth over difficulties. This was conspicuously illustrated in the matter of titles to land. The code decreed that all landholders must take out a patent in regular form from the new Proprietor. Under an unjust governor this might easily have been made the pretext for a wholesale process of spoliation. As it was, it involved the payment of a quit rent and a fee to an official. This demand was at first disregarded. The Court of Assize found it necessary to call attention to this at its first meeting in 1665, and again more stringently in 1666.[1] In Long Island and among the English settlements on the mainland it was strictly enforced. But in the city of New York, where the inhabitants held patents from the Dutch Company, the fees were lightened, and at Albany a certain amount of indulgence was shown in granting time for payment.[2]

The history of Albany during the years which immediately followed the conquest furnishes a good illustration of the tact and judgment which Nicolls brought to bear upon his task. From the outset the English troops there, removed like those at Delaware from under the eye of their commander, had been a source of annoyance to the Dutch population. The existing civil officers were all retained. The military authority of the conqueror and the civil authority of the conquered, face to face, could hardly fail to breed ill blood. We find Nicolls anxiously charging his chief commander in these parts, Brodhead, to restrain his soldiers from annoying the settlers in any way, to turn a deaf ear to all whispered slanders against

Affairs at Albany.

---

[1] *N. Y. Hist. Coll.* 1st series, vol. i. pp. 410-8.
[2] Brodhead, vol. ii. pp. 109-10.

the Dutch, not to become the head of a party, but to govern equitably in the interests of all.

Brodhead's conduct soon showed how Nicolls's admonitions were needed. In the winter of 1666 the settlers at Esopus, sixty-four miles below Albany, showed a disaffected spirit. When Brodhead went out in quest of recruits, men withheld their neighbours from joining. They might have to fight for their enemies against their own friends.

Brodhead showed no anxiety to profit by Nicolls's advice and example. He was fool enough to imprison a settler who insisted on keeping Christmas on the 25th of December according to the New Style, not yet adopted by England. He had an undignified quarrel with a person, throwing a dish at his opponent's head and then arresting him.

The Dutch civil magistrate insisted that the prisoner should be handed over to him. This Brodhead refused. Thereupon a mob of sixty villagers gathered together and attempted a rescue, and in the tumult which followed one was killed.[1]

As soon as the news reached New York, Nicolls sent three commissioners to hold an inquiry and to deal with the offenders. His choice of agents, one English and two Dutch, was significant. There was, however, little room for national partiality, since they were closely tied down by instructions from the Governor. They were to suspend Brodhead. He had neglected his instructions, and had broken the law in disregarding the application of the magistrates. The ringleaders were to be sent to New York for trial; the rest were to be pardoned, but in such a manner as to show that in future authority would be strictly enforced. The settlers were to learn that henceforth any man

[1] Brodhead, vol. ii. p. 122.

who should take up arms against the soldiers was a rebel.[1]

Four of the chief offenders were singled out and sent down as ordered to the capital. Nicolls's mode of dealing with them was characteristic. Their case came before the council. In theory Nicolls was no more than president, and had no superiority but that given by a casting vote. We may be sure, however, that the sentence to be passed depended very largely on his personal wishes. A rigorous sentence would have been probably unjust, certainly impolitic. Nicolls, however, saw that it was better for him individually to have a reputation for firmness than for clemency. He expressed his opinion that all four had been guilty of a capital crime. The council backed by the principal settlers interceded, and Nicolls commuted the sentence to banishment. The form of the sentence shows how completely and definitely the Dutch and English sections of the colony were treated as distinct. Heymans, the chief offender, was excluded from every part of the colony. The other three were only banished from Albany, with its suburb of Esopus, and from New York. The sentence was soon relaxed, and within two years we find Heymans holding a civil office.

It is not difficult to see the guiding principles which throughout underlay Nicolls's policy. His experience as a commissioner in Massachusetts must have shown him that self-governing townships of the New England pattern were not the material out of which to build a colony loyal to the Proprietor. On the other hand the alien colony might by wise policy be made an instrument for curbing the disaffection of Massachusetts. Nicolls's views on this point are

<small>New York to be a check on New England.</small>

---

[1] The names of the commissioners and their instructions are in the N. Y. Docs. vol. iii. p. 149.

[2] Brodhead, vol. ii. p. 143.

clearly set forth in a letter written to Arlington in the spring of 1666. He has begun 'to set up a school of better religion and obedience to God and the King than were to be found in New England.' With good administration New York will in time rival and ultimately overthrow the commercial prosperity of Boston. Nicolls had been willing to use the English settlers on Long Island and their kinsmen in New England as an instrument for the reduction of the Dutch colony. But a passage in the very same letter shows that he had no real faith in that alliance. He had seen, he says, that he cannot depend on Connecticut. For the defence of the colony he must rely on the troops whom he brought with him from England.[1]

The general principles set forth in this letter were the same which had led Nicolls a year before to buy from the savages a tract on the west bank of the river below Albany, and to issue invitations to emigrants calling their attention to this territory. It was his policy to build up on the foundation of the Dutch settlement in the valley of the Hudson a colony dissociated from New England, to serve as a stronghold of the royal power.

How little of real national feeling there was among the Dutch settlers was plainly shown by the history of the years 1666 and 1667. All through the first-named year the settlers must have known how things stood in Europe. Some tidings must have reached them of those terrible days in the summer of 1667, when news came to London that the Dutch fleet had broken the chain at Chatham and that the flower of the English navy were seized or burnt; when men at Greenwich or Wapping lay down each night believing that the morning would bring De Ruyter's ships in full sail before their eyes, and when

No disaffection among the Dutch.

[1] N. Y. Docs. vol. iii. pp. 113-5.

citizens were sending their hoards into the country to be buried in the ground. All the resources that Nicolls had at his command were the regular troops whom he had brought out with him, a force of four hundred and fifty men, weakened by the loss of the detachments drawn off to garrison Albany and Newcastle. At the same time Dutch privateers were threatening Virginia and making the American coast unsafe for English merchantmen. If the settlers in New York really felt the English yoke irksome, if they had any wish to return to their allegiance to Holland, can we doubt that they would at once have seized the opportunity and struck a blow? Yet while Nicolls was eagerly expecting news from Europe with a foreboding of some fearful calamity to England, and while he was apprehensive what the Dutch ships might do off the American coast, it is plain that a rising of the Dutch settlers never entered into his calculations. It is clear from his despatches that he is far more anxious for the arrival of stores from England than he is about the threats of the Dutch West India Company. How secure he felt on that head we can best judge from a letter of November 1667, where he reports that he is organizing a part of the colonial militia as horse and dragoons to guard the north-west frontier against the French.[1]

In the autumn of 1667 the treaty of Breda gave England secure possession of her new province. The principle of that treaty was that each country should retain all territory that it had captured during the present war. When an abortive negotiation was opened in 1665 the States protested that New Netherlands should not be included in any such compact. That, they averred, had been taken from them in peace and ought, therefore, to be given back without

Treaty of Breda.

---

[1] Nicolls to Arlington, N. Y. Docs. vol. iii. p. 167.

any equivalent.[1] They, however, now abandoned that claim. Surinam and Poleron in the Nutmeg group of islands had been taken by the Dutch arms and were retained. The whole policy of the Dutch taught them to value such possessions far more than the comparatively unprofitable tract on the American coast, with its contentious inhabitants, ever vexing the Government with appeals against the Company, ever liable to be embroiled with New England or the savage tribes. The protestations of the West India Company were of no effect. They in vain pointed out that the possession of New Netherlands by England meant her supremacy over Northern America. France never could hold Canada against such odds; England would thus gain an addition to her resources which could confirm her empire over the seas.[2]

One may doubt whether either of the negotiating parties could see the full force of such reasoning. In England public opinion was not altogether satisfied that the change was a gain. It was good hap, far more than any far-sighted wisdom, which at this juncture gave England what was really the keystone of her American Empire.

Yet even while negotiations were going on, events must have been forcing a perception of the truth on Nicolls; he must have begun to see that any dispute with Holland was only important as it bore upon that mighty struggle which was drawing near, and which his own success was doing so much to hasten. To the Dutch colony the Mohawk alliance had been a needful condition for safe trade, for security from invasion by savages, and by a civilized enemy as ruthless as the savages. To the English who

Altered relations towards France.

[1] Brodhead, vol. ii. p. 93.
[2] Memorial of the West India Company to the States-General March 25, 1667. N. Y. Docs. vol. ii. pp. 511-3.

replaced the Dutch it was all this and more. With the Mohawks hostile there must be perpetual dread of invasion not only for the dwellers on the Hudson, but for the whole body of the New England colonies. To detach the Mohawks from their old alliance would be the first step for France in that policy of aggression, which if it succeeded must be a lasting bar to the union of the English colonies. Henceforth the history of French Canada and the history of the British colonies are inseparably connected, and in all their relations New Netherlands is the chief meeting-point.

If the King of France and his advisers failed to understand the situation, it was not so with the French rulers of Canada; that can be seen from a despatch sent by Talon, an important official in the colony, to Colbert. Let the King, he says, arrange for the restitution of New Netherlands by the English, and then purchase it from the States-General. Thereby France would have two entrances into Canada, and would gain a monopoly of the Northern fur trade, the Five Nations would be at their mercy, and New England would be kept within bounds.[1] The whole situation could not be summed up more clearly and effectively.

The conquest of New Netherlands at once brought the English into direct relations with the Mohawks. Within a month of the time that Cartwright took the command at Albany, the chiefs of the Mohawks and the Senecas appeared there and confirmed by treaty that alliance which had hitherto bound them to the Dutch. There was to be peace and trade between the two nations, and the English were to aid the Mohawks if necessary against the tribes on the lower waters of the Hudson.[2]

Dealings with the Five Nations.

[1] N. Y. Docs. vol. ix. p. 57.
[2] The treaty, with *facsimiles* of the marks which were the equivalents for the Indian signatures, is in the N. Y. Docs. vol. iii. p. 67.

This alliance, however, was only binding on the Mohawks and the Senecas. There would seem at this time to have been a certain absence of unity in the action of the Iroquois confederacy. The occasion was a critical one. The transfer of the Hudson valley to the English was accompanied by a change in the administration of Canada. Hitherto the French colony had been virtually no more than a station for trade and missionary work. The relations with the savages had been mainly controlled by the Jesuit, the trapper, and the hunter. The executive had been perpetually hampered by disputes with the ecclesiastical authority. But in 1664 a governor was appointed of comprehensive views, and of resolute and aggressive temper, and he was furnished with military resources equal to carrying out a vigorous policy. Though the Marquis of Tracy was seventy, yet it is clear that age had done nothing to weaken his will or his mind. He had under his command a regiment of twelve hundred men, raised originally in Savoy. It had done good service in Eastern Europe, and bore the name of its original commander, the Prince of Carignan.[1]

Tracy's first military measure was to secure the connexion between the St. Lawrence and the Hudson. To this end three forts were built along the valley of the Richelieu, the stream connecting Lake Champlain with the great river of Canada. On the 30th of June Tracy landed at Quebec. By the end of July his engineers were at work upon the forts, and before the summer was out the work was complete. Next year the same policy was carried further, and an island on Lake Champlain was occupied and fortified.[2]

---

[1] For the Carignan regiment see N. Y. Docs. vol. ix. p. 32, with editor's note.

[2] 'Fort Anne, recently constructed by Sieur de la Mothe on an island in Lake Champlain.' Report in French Archives, translated, O'Callaghan, vol. i. p. 48.

The wisdom of this measure was at once seen. Through the autumn the Hurons, the allies of the French, took refuge under cover of the new forts from the attacks of the Iroquois. The Iroquois saw, too, that they could no longer count on their woods and streams for safety. Chiefs of the Oneidas and Onondagas came to Quebec and asked humbly for peace. Henceforth they were to be the vassals and allies of France. Such at least was the interpretation which the French put on the treaty, yet it must be remembered that in dealings between civilized men and savages a strict interpretation of language is hardly possible. But at least the savages promised in their own figurative language, as interpreted by the French, to clasp their new allies by the waist, not merely to hold them by their skirts. The Iroquois were to plant villages within the French territory, and the French were to send among them traders and missionaries.[1]

It is scarcely possible to estimate what might have been the effects of this treaty on the whole future of America had it been carried out fully and loyally. Though the Indian spokesmen were taken only from the Oneidas and Onondagas, yet they claimed to speak for the Senecas and Cayugas, or at least for a section of each tribe as well.[2] Of the Five Nations only the Mohawks held back. Their late dealings with the English had shown a certain disposition on their part for separate action. Unluckily for the French the Mohawks were in fighting power the backbone of the savage confederacy. Since they could not be won they must be intimidated.

In January 1666 one of Tracy's lieutenants, De Courcelles, was despatched into the Mohawk country at

---

[1] An English translation of the treaty is in the N. Y. Docs. vol. iii. p. 121, &c.

[2] I infer this from the language of the treaty.

the head of five hundred men. In the dead of winter a force of civilized men set forth on a march of nine hundred miles through the wilderness. In one way the season was favourable to the enterprise. When the forests were bare of leaves the savages had not the same opportunities for attacking from ambush. Moreover the treaty with the four tribes had secured the approaches to the Mohawk country. The Hurons, who were to have shown the French the way, shrank back and failed them. With no guide save the sun in the heavens, in snow-shoes, carrying their blankets and their food, the gallant little troop forced its way through the Mohawk country. Their scheme seems to have been to strike terror by devastating the Mohawk villages. It is hardly surprising that they should have failed to find their goal. They overshot the mark, and in less than three weeks after they left Quebec reached a point two miles from the Dutch settlement of Schenectady. Here for the first time they heard of a hostile Indian force in their neighbourhood. A detachment was sent against them ; a portion of them fell into an ambush, and the Mohawks appeared at Schenectady with the scalps of four of their victims. The surviving French were met by a deputation of three Dutch settlers protesting against the invasion of the dominion of the King of England. Courcelles replied that he had only come against the Mohawks, and added, whether truly or not one can hardly judge, that he had not heard of the English occupation. He knew, however, that France and Holland were now allied against England, and for a moment he thought of striking a blow at Albany. But he gave up the scheme

Tracy invades the Mohawk country.[1]

---

[1] Probably the best authority for this expedition is an unsigned report by an Englishman in O'Callaghan, vol. i. p. 50. This is preceded by a French report, apparently official. This is very bald, and is conveniently silent about the discomfiture by the Mohawks and the interview with the settlers from Albany.

when he learned that the place was garrisoned and had
artillery. The Dutch settlers, relieved from the fear of
invasion, received the strangers kindly ; food was supplied and quarters offered, but De Courcelles thought
that discipline might suffer if his men entered the village, and that the comforts of Dutch firesides might disincline them from the homeward march. Seven, however, of his wounded men were left to be cared for at
Albany. De Courcelles then turned towards the frontier.
The force reached Quebec some sixty short of its full
numbers, but most of the missing men had only
straggled, and save a few they reached home in safety.

Now that war was declared between England and
France the attitude of the savages assumed an importance which it had never had before. The Mohawk
alliance was what the Afghan alliance has been in later
days to England and Russia.

The English flattered themselves that the aggressive
policy of Tracy had failed, and that the Mohawks would
look on the French invasion as mere wild fire,
without substance or danger. The events of
the following summer showed that the calculation was too sanguine, and that the Mohawks
were wavering. Even more than before they saw themselves isolated and threatened. The Senecas sent an
embassy to Quebec to confirm the treaty made in their
name,[1] and the erection of the island fort on Lake
Champlain was a further source of terror. In June a
second force, this time of four hundred men, was made
ready to invade the Mohawk country.[2] But before it
started news came which seemed to make it needless. The English commander at Albany, hardly under-

*Negotia-
tions of
the Five
Nations
with the
French.*

[1] An account of this treaty, taken from the French Archives and translated into English, is in the N. Y. Docs. vol. iii. p. 125.

[2] Tracy to the commissaries at Albany, July 19, 1666, translated,
N. Y. Docs. vol. iii. p. 131.

standing what was at stake, advised the Mohawks to make terms with the French, and sent a despatch to Tracy telling what counsel he had given.[1] The letter was brought by the chiefs of the Oneidas. A representative of that tribe had joined in the treaty of 1665, but it seems doubtful whether the whole tribe regarded themselves as bound by his action. The letter from Albany was taken by Tracy as a guarantee for the peaceful intentions of the Mohawks, one may almost say as a formal surrender by the English of the alliance. Negotiations were at once opened; instead of an invading force envoys were sent to treat with the Mohawks at Albany; if they preferred it they might come in safety to Quebec.[2]

Just as the prize seemed won, an attack on a French hunting party by the Mohawks changed all. Some were captured, others killed. Among the latter was Tracy's nephew, De Chazy. The Governor at once recalled the envoys and reverted to his original scheme of an invasion. But when the invading force was on its march it was met by a Mohawk embassy. The conduct of the Mohawks makes one think that this was no more than a feint to secure time. The envoys went on to Quebec and began dealings for peace. Before long one of them, in an outbreak of passion, avowed himself the murderer of De Chazy. He was at once put to death, and his principal colleagues thrown into prison.[3] The death of that one savage counted for much in the future fortunes of England and France.

Failure of the negotiations.

Accordingly in the autumn of 1666 another expedition was arranged against the Mohawks. This time Tracy himself took the command with six hundred regulars and as many militia. The force penetrated about a hundred miles south of Lake Champlain, and

---

[1] Commissaries of Albany to Tracy. N. Y. Docs. vol. iii. p. 164.
[2] *Ib.* vol. ix. p. 44. [3] *Ib.* vol. iii. p. 135.

three Mohawk villages were destroyed with their granaries, containing a two years' store of corn. But nothing was done in the way of permanent occupation, and Tracy was content to trust to the terror inspired by the raid. Meanwhile Nicolls had become fully alive to the need of encouraging and supporting the Mohawks. His wish that the whole body of English colonies should give them active support was hindered by Connecticut. Unfortunately the Mohawks were at enmity with the Mohicans, who were, alone of the New England tribes, the constant allies of the English. Possibly in consequence of this, Nicolls somewhat modified the support given to the Mohawks. They were advised to seek a good peace with the French, but to seek it if needs were by a show of force. They should insist on the demolition of the newly built chain of forts, and should tell the French that the Mohawk country was within the dominions of the King of England, and that the inhabitants of it owed him allegiance.[1]

In spite of this advice the Mohawks sent an embassy to Quebec in 1667, asking that missionaries should be sent into their country, and making no stipulations, but offering to give hostages for good behaviour.[2] Immediately after this Tracy had been recalled, as his services were needed for the campaign in Europe. His successor (Courcelles) had direct instructions to make another raid into the Mohawk country and to intimidate—even as far as might be to annihilate—that stubborn tribe.[3] But the submissive attitude of the Mohawks seemed to make such policy unnecessary. Instead of an armed

[1] Brodhead, vol. ii. p. 120.
[2] Brodhead (vol. ii. p. 128) says that the Indian emissaries came just after Tracy's departure. But Tracy in a despatch, dated Quebec, April 30, 1667, says: 'I have granted conditions so reasonable to the Mohawks that I doubt not they will accept peace.' The despatch (translated) is in the N. Y. Docs. vol. iii. p. 151.
[3] *Ib.* p. 130.

force, the Governor sent a band of Jesuit missionaries, escorted by the Mohawks who had come to Quebec.

Nicolls saw that he had no ground for opposing this peaceful invasion. When the Jesuits, in their eagerness to check the trade in spirits among their new converts, begged for an interview with the English authorities, Nicolls acceded, and sailing up the Hudson to Schenectady gave them an audience there.[1]

Simultaneously with the treaty of Breda peace was made between France and England. The terms of the peace guaranteed to the French Crown secure possession of the disputed territory of Acadia. But nothing was said of the country between Canada and the upper waters of the Hudson, and though Nicolls might acquiesce in the advance of the French missionaries, yet he and every other thoughtful Englishman must have seen that in that region the American battle of the two great nations would be fought out.

The hostility of France and Holland was not the only danger which Nicolls saw threatening his province. The reckless profusion of the Proprietor and the unscrupulous greed of Berkeley and Carteret had dismembered the territory almost before it was acquired. Before his authority over the conquered province was a year old, Nicolls heard of its partial alienation. The territory on the Delaware might have been spared. It lay at a distance from the seat of government, and the rival claims of Maryland lessened its value. But to lose the land on the West of Manhattan Bay practically reduced the colony to Long Island and the valley of the Hudson. With the intermediate land gone, the Proprietor could never exercise any official control over the territory on the Delaware. Let the grantees, Nicolls at once proposed, consent to

The grant to Berkeley and Carteret.

---

[1] I can find no particulars of this affair beyond those given in Brodhead, vol. ii. p. 130. He refers to the Jesuit relation in a report for 1668.

CARTERET'S GRANT. 159

an exchange.[1] On the Delaware they might have a hundred thousand acres, ' a noble tract.' With courtier-like tact, Nicolls assumes that neither Berkeley nor Carteret would have dreamt of asking for such a grant if they had known what it really cost the Duke : it must have been the work of that agent of evil, Scott. Scott's whole career from the day when he figured as a rebel on Long Island showed that he might plausibly be saddled with any misdeeds. But that shrewd observer Pepys had ample opportunities for forming a judgment of Carteret. It is clear that he in no way rose superior to the average standard of public men in that scheming and self-seeking age, and he was not likely to care how much he damaged the Duke's province. The man, too, of whom Pepys said that ' of all about the court, he gave himself most to business without any desire of pleasure or divertisement,' was sure not to be slothful in turning his privileges to practical account. The first answer which Nicolls got to his protest was the arrival, in July 1665, at New York of an agent with full authority and material for establishing a settlement.[2] The Proprietor's choice had fallen on the grantee's own kinsman, that Philip Carteret whose marriage forms such a conspicuous and characteristic incident in the pages of Pepys.

That sound sense and business-like capacity which were recognised even by Carteret's enemies were fully shown in his dealings with his newly acquired territory. He at once set on foot a practical working constitution. This was embodied in a document entitled ' the Concessions and Agreements of the Lords Proprietors of New Jersey to and with all and every of the adventurers and all such as settle and plant there.' The constitution was of the usual

The New Jersey concessions.[3]

---

[1] Nicolls's letter, incomplete and undated, is in the N. Y. Docs. vol. iii. p. 105.
[2] Brodhead, vol. ii. p. 85.   [3] Leaming and Spicer, pp. 12–31.

pattern—a governor and council, and an elected body of representatives. Laws passed by the two chambers were to be in force provisionally for one year, pending the approval of the Proprietors. No tax was to be levied without the consent of the representatives. The right of laying out and granting land was vested in the council. All settlers must swear allegiance to the King, and fidelity to the Proprietors. The country was to be laid out in parishes, each with a glebe of two hundred acres, and with beside a rate for the maintenance of the minister. The recognised religion was apparently that of the Church of England, but freedom of conscience was to be granted to all individuals. Every emigrant who equipped himself with a proper fire-arm and food for six months was to have a hundred and fifty acres of land, and as much more for every man-servant that he brought out, with half that quantity for every female over fourteen years. Hired servants also were to receive seventy-five acres at the end of their term.

The whole body of emigrants who accompanied Philip Carteret numbered only thirty, most of them German salt-refiners. The Proprietors, however, did not rely exclusively or mainly on direct emigration from England. Their invitation was addressed not merely to those who should accompany, but to those who should meet, their agent. The Proprietors counted on incorporating miscellaneous populations of Dutch, Swedes, and Finns, who were already to be found scattered over their territory. Nor was that all. The concessions were distributed in New England. Influences were at work there which were likely enough to set on foot a tide of emigration. The authority exercised by Nicolls and his colleagues must already have made citizens of Massachusetts suspect that their old days of virtual independence were coming to an end. The inhabitants of New Haven had

Settlement of New Jersey.

even stronger motives for change. They saw themselves forced into a detested union with a colony, lax as they must have deemed it in its religious system, and polluted by its recent alliance with the restored monarchy. Hitherto such emigration as there had been from New England had found a natural and ready retreat in Long Island and the adjacent mainland. That was likely to be checked now that the territory in question had come under the authority of a Papist, the heir to the Crown. From early days the enterprising traders of New Haven had been only withheld by Dutch vigilance from forcing their way into the upper waters of the Delaware. Now that it was secured and thrown open to them with special inducements, they naturally turned thither. It was within the territory of Carteret and Berkeley that the settlers of Brainford found the new home, whither they bore their church records, the most effective symbol of their past corporate life.[1]

Before the tidings of the Proprietor's grant to Carteret and Berkeley had reached Nicolls, he had taken some measures towards asserting his authority over the tract in question. He had sanctioned the proceedings of isolated settlers who had established themselves there on the land purchased from the Indians.[2] But he saw when Carteret landed that the Duke's surrender had been too complete to be redeemed or contested. Nor was it a time to introduce anything like disunion among the English settlements. Philip Carteret was received with courtesy. From New York he went on to his territory by the Delaware, where according to his orders he called together the settlers

---

[1] *English in America: Puritan Colonies*, vol. ii. p. 162.

[2] In the fragmentary letter just referred to Nicolls says: 'Upon this tract of land several new purchases are made from the Indians since my coming, and three towns beginning.'

and laid the foundation of a settlement, named, in honour of Lady Carteret, Elizabethtown. Henceforth the colony of New Jersey has a history of its own, apart from that of New York.

The establishment of Carteret's colony made the conquered territory on the south bank of the Delaware even more than before an outlying dependency, nowise integrally connected with New York. It was seemingly left under the control of Carr, acting upon general instructions from Nicolls. A complaint that the delay in forming any fixed plan about the territory made it difficult for him to deal with it,[1] certain notes as to the transfer of land from Dutch officials, who had departed, to their English successors—these are all the information that our records contain as to the state of this territory during Nicolls's period of office.

Condition of the Duke's territory on the Delaware.

In 1668 Nicolls resigned his office and never again bore any part in American politics. His retirement marks an evil feature in the administrative system which was just beginning. Henceforth there is scarcely an instance of an official devoting his life to the service of a single colony, nor indeed with one or two exceptions to the colonial service generally. For the future, the governor was not to be a man whose permanent home and whose hopes of a career were in the colony. He was an official, having a temporary and limited interest in the province which he governed.

Retirement of Nicolls.

The comparatively small sphere in which Nicolls worked and the short period over which his labours extend forbid one to speak of him as a great man. But we may at least say that he succeeded where men who have a fair claim to be called great would have failed. Mere administrative

His official career.

[1] N. Y. Docs. vol. iii. p. 113.

power may not be a gift of the highest order. But such as it is Nicolls assuredly possessed it to the very full. He was not one of those decorously blameless officials who escape all active errors by shirking difficulties and transferring responsibilities. Nor was he one of those whose character is built up on the efficiency of well-selected colleagues. Both in New England and New Netherlands his work suffered in proportion as it was delegated.

The personal character of the man is less easy to grasp. Many of his colonial contemporaries who played a far less conspicuous and less worthy part have left a more definite impression in history. The eulogies of him are unanimous and obviously sincere, but they are somewhat conventional. Nor does the man himself stand out very clearly and vividly in his despatches. As business-like statements they are admirable; if we look at them as revelations of character, perhaps their most conspicuous feature is their desponding and even sombre tone. Such rapid success as Nicolls achieved in his principal work would have filled many men with light-hearted confidence. Of that his despatches do not show a trace. He saw clearly that if the conquest of New Netherlands had added to the greatness and to the opportunities of England it had added, too, to her responsibilities. Not less clearly did he see all the hindrances which lay in the path. He saw that England and France were brought face to face in America, each with aims and ambitions which could not stand together. He saw that colonial union was needed, and he saw, too, how far off it lay. His experience in New England had shown how little zeal and loyalty might be expected from the subjects; the dismemberment of New Netherlands taught him how little foresight and deliberate policy might be looked for in the rulers.

His personal character.

CHAPTER III

THE DUTCH RECONQUEST

LIKE Nicolls, his successor, Francis Lovelace, had served with distinction for the cause of which his better-known brother was the soldier and the poet.[1] In energy and capacity he was assuredly no match for his predecessor. Yet it is no slight praise that he did not alienate or disappoint the men who had become accustomed to Nicolls, and that he did not create any sense of a loss of administrative power. In one respect fortune dealt kindly with him. The great calamity of his governorship, the recapture of his province by the Dutch, may not have been due to any culpable misconduct on his part. But, as we shall see, it is impossible wholly to acquit him of blame either for his own conduct or still more for his choice of a subordinate in a place of special trust. Circumstances for which he could claim no credit prevented the calamity from becoming serious. But for that Lovelace would undoubtedly have gone down to posterity as one of those who have played on a small stage the part of Galba, and who would have been deemed fit for command if they had never commanded.

The general attitude of the colony goes far to excuse Lovelace for any lack of watchfulness. As under Nicolls, such symptoms of disaffection as were to be seen made themselves felt not among the conquered Hollanders, but among the English on Long Island. In the autumn of 1669 they

Lovelace becomes Governor.

Disaffection on Long Island.

[1] The geneology of the Lovelace family is set forth by Mr. Grant Wilson in a monograph published in the papers of the American Historical Association for 1892.

addressed a petition to the Court of Assize. They demanded, as a right enjoyed by all other subjects of the King in the colonies, to appoint deputies representing the freemen of each township who should advise and approve of the laws enacted by the Governor and Council.[1] They did not rest this claim on any general constitutional principle, but on a specific promise made by Nicolls. To prove a negative is hard, and it is not impossible that Nicolls's eagerness to conciliate may have made him hold out some vague hopes of representation in the future. But it is very certain that there was no promise which could serve as a basis for a demand. The answer was that the settlers must for the present be content with the Court of Assize and the existing laws.

A general demand for constitutional rights is seldom effective. It was followed in this case by that which is far more likely to be productive of good, a dispute on a practical detail. Resistance to arbitrary taxation was, as usual, the first standing ground from which the subject could press his claims. A rate was levied on the Long Island towns for the repairing of the citadel at New York, now called, in honour of the Proprietor, Fort James. In the days of Dutch supremacy the citizens had protested against being taxed for a like purpose. Their protest, however, was based on the contention that the fort existed only for the good of the Company. That plea no longer existed. The refusal now was on the ground that the precedent would be dangerous. On the same principle they might be required to maintain the garrison. There was a lack of absolute unanimity in the attitude of the settlers. Three towns—Heemstede, or as it was now called Hempstead, Flushing and Jamaica—contented themselves with a protest. The demand, they said, was

[1] Brodhead, vol. ii. p. 160.

unconstitutional, but they would accede and appeal to the King. Three other towns—Southold, Southampton and Easthampton—consented to pay, but with the vague stipulation that they must enjoy the same privileges as the townships of New England. The men of Huntington, Hampden-like, met the demand with flat refusal. Though this want of unanimity may have made the protest less effectual, yet it was a healthy sign. It showed that there was an independence and spontaneity about the resistance, that it had in it nothing mechanical.

The Council regarded the refusal as a declaration of seditious intentions, and ordered that the resolutions in which it was embodied should be burnt. Inquiry was to be made and the principal offenders to be punished. There is no trace, however, of any penal proceedings.[1]

As so often happens, the spirit of resistance thus kindled quickly found a fresh field. Nicolls had adopted, and in a great measure enforced, the principle that the conquest annihilated all pre-existing rights in the soil, and that all settlers must get a title by a fresh patent from the Duke. In the case of the Hollanders Nicolls had, as we have seen, relaxed this provision. But it was rigidly enforced by him against the Long Island settlers. One of those townships, however, Southampton, had either evaded the demand or, more probably, owing to an influx of settlers, required an extensive enlargement of territory. The settlers there pleaded a title based on the obsolete grant from Lord Stirling in 1640; when that claim was disallowed, and the town was again commanded to take out a fresh patent, some fifty of the citizens, those not improbably whose arrival and consequent need for land had raised the question, sent a written protest. Unwisely they did not confine themselves to the matter

Disputes about titles to land.[2]

[1] Brodhead, vol. ii. pp. 171-3.   [2] *Ib.* p. 173.

in hand, but referred to certain vague and unfulfilled promises made to them by Nicolls and his colleagues at the time of the conquest. Lovelace, in a timid and compromising spirit, gave the remonstrants some excellent moral advice, backed by a text on obedience, and appointed a commission of inquiry. The appointment of the commission meant, as it is apt to mean, an indefinite delay.

The men of Southold were not content with that. Two years later they, in conjunction with the townships of Southampton and Easthampton, lodged a complaint with the King. They were, they said, heavily taxed and unrepresented; their enjoyment of the soil was restricted as the government claimed the right to cut timber. To free themselves from the claims of the Proprietor, they were willing to be annexed to Connecticut or to be an independent corporation under the King. It is strange to find townships which had their origin in New England turning to the sovereign for redress, and still stranger to find them voluntarily offering to become a Crown colony. To revoke or curtail a grant of land made only eight years before would have been manifestly both unjust and a hopeless confession of weakness, and, as might have been expected, the three townships had to be content with having asserted their alleged rights, and thereby done something to create a precedent in their own favour.[1]

The policy of James as Proprietor of New York was in some measure an anticipation of his policy in England. As a whole it was far better. As a colonial administrator all his best points stood out, all his faults were toned down. He chose business-like, capable and, as times went, honest officials. If he claimed arbitrary power he did not

<small>General policy of the Proprietor.</small>

---

[1] The Order in Council dealing with this petition is in the N. Y. Docs. vol. iii. p. 197. The substance of the petition is set forth in this document.

enforce it cruelly, nor, in his early days as a Proprietor, wantonly. At the same time in the colonies, as in England, he never dreamt of granting to the governed any systematic check over the governor; he could not in the least understand the spirit which demanded such a check. Yet in his colony, as afterwards in the mother country, he blundered by some strange and inexplicable inconsistency into a policy of toleration. And in the colony it was not necessary as in England to carry out a policy of toleration by a glaring disregard of civil rights. Under Lovelace Calvinist, Lutheran and Independent lived together in harmony. The Presbyterian Church of New York remained in dependence on the Classis, the governing body at Amsterdam. At the same time Lovelace used his personal influence with the Council to secure the minister of that Church an annual grant from the exchequer of the colony of a thousand guilders, a little over a hundred pounds in English money.[1] Wherever Lovelace did interfere in religious matters, it was to check some display of ecclesiastical tyranny. When an Independent minister from New England refused to baptize a man's children, and yet afterwards distrained on that same man for payment of his salary, Lovelace reminded him that he held his own position only by sufferance.[2] When the Calvinist sexton at Albany claimed to bury and to be paid for burying all who died, whether members of his own sect or not, an order was passed in Council authorizing the Lutheran minister to bury his own dead.

Meanwhile the grant to Carteret and Berkeley was breeding results which justified Nicolls's protests. At one time it seemed as if the exchange which Nicolls recommended would be carried through. Carteret and

---

[1] Brodhead, vol. ii. p. 175. Mr. Brodhead quotes the text of Lovelace's order.
[2] Letter from Lovelace, published in O'Callaghan, vol. iii. p. 209.

Berkeley both professed themselves willing to exchange their grant for a tract on the Delaware. That this was not effected may have been in part due to the claims of Maryland to the Delaware territory. But there was an even more serious difficulty. The new settlement soon fell into anarchy, a result partly due in all likelihood to the incompetence of Philip Carteret. The settlers there had precisely the same grievance as those on Long Island. The Proprietors required that those who had been already established there, Swedes and others, some who had purchased their land from the Indians, others who had grants from Nicolls, should take out fresh patents. Just as discontent was making itself felt, one appeared on the scene who saw his chance of turning it to account. In that grotesque constitution which Locke had fashioned for Carolina, a place as landgrave had been given to James Carteret, a younger son of Sir George. Instead of going straight to his own colony he touched at Elizabethtown. The malcontents held a convention, deposed Philip Carteret, who fled back to England, and replaced him by his cousin.[1]

Affairs of New Jersey.

A like spirit of disaffection had already extended to the southern side of the peninsula. Carr's incompetence, his greed, and in all likelihood the looseness of his private life, had disgusted the settlers on the Delaware. In 1669 an insurrection broke out headed by an impostor, who passed himself off as a son of Count Konigsmark, and who went commonly by the name of the Long Finn or the Long Swede. The advice which Lovelace gave Carr at this juncture is as full a proof as could be wished of the loss which the colony had sustained in the retirement of Nicolls. 'Follow,' he says, virtually, 'the policy of the Swedish Government when it administered the

Insurrection on the Delaware.[2]

---

[1] O'Callaghan, vol. iii. p. 525; Brodhead, vol. ii. p. 189.

dependency. Keep the people down by such taxes as shall keep them hard at work, and give them no time for political agitation.' Such instructions given to an arbitrary and unpopular subordinate show that it was good nature and rule-of-thumb shrewdness rather than any real spirit of statesmanship which kept Lovelace within the paths of moderation and common sense. The disturbance was quelled without difficulty. The pseudo-Konigsmark was whipped, branded, and sold as a slave to Barbadoes; his chief accomplice, Henry Coleman, took refuge among the Indians, and at a later day figured as a landholder in Penn's colony.[1]

Disaffection within was not the only trouble which beset the colony or, as one might rather call it, the outpost on the Delaware. In 1669 an attempt was made on behalf of Lord Baltimore to assert authority over the settlers there, and three years later they were attacked and pillaged by a party of raiders from Maryland.[2] They plundered the unhappy settlers on the Hoarkill, and destroyed their crops, reducing them, if we may believe an almost contemporary witness, to such straits that, as in Samaria in the days of Joram, women ate their own children.

Attack from Maryland.

A document is extant which shows that there was no desire among the inhabitants of Newcastle to detach themselves from New York, while at the same time it illustrates the difficulties which ensued from the position of the settlement on the Delaware as a detached dependency of New York. In 1671 the settlers at Newcastle petitioned Lovelace to allow them to erect a blockhouse at Newcastle for the defence of the town. They also petitioned that no ships should be allowed to go up the river above Newcastle, so that the town

[1] N. Y. Docs. vol. xii. pp. 463-71 ; Council Minutes, vol. ii.
[2] This raid is referred to in the travels of Dankers and Sluyter, the Labadists.

might practically enjoy a monopoly of the trade in corn and fur. They also petition for restrictions on the distilling and selling of strong drink; they wish the authority of the constables to be strengthened by furnishing them with staves bearing the King's arms, and in the same spirit they ask to be allowed to put up the King's arms in the courts of law. They propose the appointment of a public inspector of grain so that the colony may not be discredited by the exportation of foul corn. It would seem that the feud between Maryland and the settlers on the Delaware was now at rest, since the former colony has offered to make one half of a road connecting the two districts if their neighbours will make the other half. Lovelace is asked to enforce this arrangement.

All these requests were favourably received. The interest of the matter lies in the picture which it gives us of the condition of things on the Delaware. We have at Newcastle a coherent community, anxious to enforce order and to secure material prosperity among a scattered rural population, and unable to do so for lack of administrative authority, and obliged to turn for help to a distant superior.[1]

Another illustrative incident occurred soon after. An Indian murdered a white settler on the Delaware. A council was held at New York to consider what steps should be taken, and the two Carterets, Philip and James, both attended.[2] In short, at a special emergency a sort of federal system for the Delaware and Hudson settlements had to be extemporized.

All these events must have impressed on colonial administrators the need for some common control. As Lovelace said in his remonstrance addressed to Calvert,

---

[1] The petition and the answer are in the Pennsylvania Archives, 2nd series, vol. v.
[2] This also is told in the Pennsylvania Archives, same volume.

'these portending troublous times, wherein all true-hearted Englishmen are buckling on their armour, were no seasons for such disputes.'[1]

Lovelace's words were soon to be verified. In the summer of 1672 the colonists learnt that England and Holland were again at war. If anything were needed to prove how little spirit of nationality there was among the Dutch colonists, the policy now adopted by Lovelace would show it. He plainly had no dread of internal dissensions. In his arrangements for strengthening the defences of the colony, Dutch officers were without fear placed in positions of trust. All that Lovelace dreaded was invasion from the sea. That he saw must be guarded against by acting in concert with New England, and to that end he applied himself to establishing a post between New York and Boston. His proceedings and intentions in this matter are described in a despatch sent to Winthrop of Connecticut, somewhat wordy and ornate after the manner of Lovelace's letters.[2] The New Englanders will, he trusts, enter into the scheme with the same 'ardent inclinations' as he does. He has secured a postman, 'active, stout, and indefatigable.' But if his language strikes one as somewhat out of place on such a plain question of business, he was beyond doubt right in thinking that his scheme was 'the most compendious means to beget a mutual understanding.' Unfortunately his anxiety to carry out the scheme led him to leave his post at this crisis, placing the garrison of New York under a subordinate, one Manning, in whom it is plain he had but little confidence. In July 1673 Lovelace was at Hutchinson Bay, near the Connecticut frontier, making arrangements for his postal scheme. A messenger came from Manning

[1] Brodhead, vol. ii. p. 190.
[2] Ib. pp. 196-8. Mr. Brodhead quotes the letter textually.

to tell him that a Dutch squadron was off the coast, and that his presence was needed. So little faith had Lovelace in the deputy whom he had appointed that he treated the report as a false alarm, and instead of returning, actually went on to Connecticut. Though Manning's alarm was fully justified, and though Lovelace showed gross carelessness, yet one may well doubt whether his presence could have availed anything.

In the winter of 1672 a Dutch fleet of fifteen vessels with troops on board was sent to attack the English shipping in the West Indies. It was joined by a force of four more sail under a separate command. After doing much damage to English merchantmen off Jamestown they fell in with a New York vessel. They captured her, and examined the captain as to the defences of the colony. He must have rated their local knowledge exceedingly low when he assured them that Lovelace could at any moment raise five thousand men, and that the fort was guarded by a hundred and fifty guns. Unluckily there was on board one Samuel Hopkins, of Elizabethtown. He, being anxious to secure the friendship of the Dutch, mercilessly knocked over this noble fabric of invention. The garrison of the fort, he said, numbered seventy, and it would take Lovelace three or four days to raise as many hundred men. The Dutch commanders at once decided on their course. Such opposition was nothing to a fleet of over twenty sail, with sixteen hundred men on board. Moreover they might reckon on the inhabitants, if not for support, at least for benevolent neutrality. In less than a fortnight the Dutch fleet was riding at anchor off Staten Island, and was in

A Dutch fleet threatens the colony.[1]

---

[1] Basnage. *Hist. of the Netherlands*, vol. ii. p. 456. Statement of Nathan Gould and affidavit of William Hayes, N. Y. Docs. vol. iii. pp. 200, 213. Ludwell (Secretary of Virginia) to Arlington, N. Y. Docs. vol. iii. p. 364. Report of Amsterdam Board of Admiralty to States-General, N. Y. Docs. vol. iii. p. 527.

active communication with the adjacent Dutch settlements.

Manning seems to have done his best under the circumstances. He hurried off a messenger to Lovelace, but a governor who was in New England could be of little use when a few hours' sail would bring the enemy within gunshot of the fort. The one chance had been lost when the first alarm had failed to collect a strong land force from New England and from the English towns on Long Island.

Bloodless captures seemed destined to recur in the history of New Netherlands, to use the name which had once again become appropriate. On August 9 the Dutch fleet anchored off New York, as Nicolls's fleet had anchored nine years before. The whole drama reproduced itself with one important exception. Manning, unlike Stuyvesant, did not even make show of a determination to die at his post. Practically, however, he did as much as the Dutch commander in the way of defence: when the enemy opened fire, the fort replied and riddled the enemy's flagship. But the captains of the invading force, following the precedent of Nicolls, had detached the civil population by a promise of immunity.

Capture of New York.[1]

As before, too, a land force was threatening the town from the north. Resistance would have been a wanton and culpable waste of life. Manning showed a flag of truce and demanded a parley. His second in command, John Carr, a son of Sir Robert, on his own responsibility as it would seem, lowered the English colours. Practically he did only what Manning would have been forced to do. The garrison marched out with military honours, and the town peacefully submitted.

[1] As authorities for the capture of New York, we have various unofficial reports in the New York Documents.

Lovelace was now on his way home, and had reached New Haven when he heard that his colony was lost. His first thought was to raise a force on Long Island, and to strike a blow for the recovery of the town. A Dutch clergyman was sent to him, apparently in a semi-official capacity, and induced him to visit the town and have an interview with the commanders of the invading fleet. The result was creditable neither to the dignity and wisdom of Lovelace nor to the generosity of the conquerors. He was arrested for debt. This was made more serious by the policy of the Dutch commanders, who had excepted English officials from the general protection granted to private property. The arrest does not seem to have been pressed, but the unfortunate Governor left the colony a beggar.[1]

The conditions of the conquest left the Dutch officials a free hand. They had been merely sent out with general instructions to annoy the English settlements; they had not, like Nicolls, any specific orders for the reduction of New York, and as a necessary consequence in dealing with it they could only consult their own discretion. They were at least justified in assuming that the two conquests annihilated all the right of the West India Company. Henceforth as long as the colony was Dutch territory it would be in direct dependence on the United Provinces.

Action of the Dutch commanders.[2]

Clearly then any constitutional arrangements made by the Dutch commanders could only be of a provisional nature. They showed, however, no fear of responsibility. The two commanders, Evertsen and

---

[1] Brodhead, vol. ii. p. 213. Mr. Brodhead quotes a letter written by Lovelace, but does not say to whom it was addressed, nor where it comes from.

[2] The Minutes of the Council, translated into English, are in the N. Y. Docs. vol. ii. pp. 569-730.

Birckes, together with three captains named by themselves, sat as a temporary council. But the fleet could not stay locked up in Manhattan harbour, and it was needful to organize a government which should act after the ships had sailed, and till the home authorities took measures for the management of their recovered dependency. The council conferred the office of governor on one of the three co-opted councillors, Anthony Colve. To grant representative government as part of a mere temporary arrangement would have been absurd. But the method of choosing an executive showed a want of confidence in the inhabitants which can hardly have been necessary, and if unnecessary was certainly impolitic. Six of the principal inhabitants were instructed to prepare a list of eligible citizens, wealthy and of the Reformed Christian religion. Out of these the council chose three burgomasters and four schepens.[1]

The conquest of the capital was followed by the reduction of the outlying portions of the settlement. Albany at once yielded. As New York was renamed Fort Orange, so Albany in honour of the young stadtholder became Willemstadt.[2] The inhabitants of New Jersey had not so fared under the Proprietors as to give them any interest in resisting the assertion of Dutch rule, and the new supremacy was at once accepted. Courts of justice were established, officials were appointed or formally approved, and the oath of allegiance to the republic administered to the citizens. The outlying settlements on the Delaware were dealt with in a like manner, and placed under the control of Peter Alrich as schout or commandant.[3]

Hopkins's treachery was rewarded by his being appointed clerk of the court at Elizabethtown.[4]

---

[1] Minutes, p. 574.   [2] *Ib.* p. 593.   [3] *Ib.* pp. 604–5, 607.
[4] Mr. Brodhead states this in a note to Hayes's affidavit referred to above.

One article in the instructions given to Alrich might have furnished a basis for religious persecution. The pure, true Christian religion according to the Synod of Dort is to be taught and maintained in every proper manner, without suffering anything to be attempted contrary thereunto by any sectaries.

In September the fleet sailed away. The inhabitants pleaded urgently their defenceless condition and the likelihood of an attack. Not only had the English Crown an interest in the recovery of the colony, but that interest was shared by the Proprietors, by those who had claims on New Jersey, and by the New England settlers. Accordingly two ships were left to guard against invasion.[1]

The colony under Colve.

In two matters the system of government adopted by Colve must have contrasted unfavourably with that of the late Proprietor. The municipality of New York was no longer a corporation, kept continuously alive by self-election. Colve reverted to the earlier Dutch method, and required the outgoing magistrates to frame a list, of which one half were nominated by the Governor.[2] Moreover, Colve at once swept away that freedom of worship which Nicolls had established and Lovelace continued. The Reformed Christian religion as established by the Synod of Dort was to be maintained in every township, and no other sect was to be permitted to attempt anything to the contrary.[3] By a special indulgence the Lutherans at Albany were allowed to keep their church and their worship.[4] But at the capital, the destruction of the Lutheran church, though defended by the plea that the ground was needed for fortification, was a melancholy evidence of the changed system.[5]

Amongst the purely Dutch settlements on Long

[1] *Minutes*, pp. 598–600.   [2] *Ib.* p. 680.   [3] *Ib.* pp. 618, 620.
[4] *Ib.* p. 622.   [5] *Court Minutes*, vol. vii. p. 13.

Island and the opposite coast, the change of sovereignty was accepted not with any special enthusiasm, but with acquiescence. Among the towns of New England origin it was different. There, it was soon manifest, the conquest would have to be carried through step by step if it was to be effectual. In the autumn of 1673 Colve sent a commission to those parts to enforce the oath of obedience, and to remind the inhabitants that resistance would bring with it confiscation of property.[1] Some of the settlements acceded. Easthampton and Southold temporized, while Southampton, trained in stubbornness by its dealings with Lovelace, stood fast and refused its allegiance to a foreign Power.[2]

{Disaffection among the English-speaking settlers.}

Colve's first impulse was to send an armed force and punish the recalcitrant towns as rebels. His advisers, however, bore in mind what he, a new comer to the colony, not unnaturally overlooked. The men of Southold and Southampton did not stand alone. There was even reason to think that their action was not wholly spontaneous, but that they were incited to resistance by emissaries from Connecticut. That colony, ever aggressive, energetic and self-reliant, was certain to seize such an opportunity of pursuing its territorial claims. Harsh dealings with the Long Island townships would in all likelihood be the signal for war with New England. This view prevailed, and a second commission was sent to bring about if it might be a peaceful settlement.[3]

While these second commissioners were sailing for Long Island the government of Connecticut was giving the English township something more than secret encouragement. Representatives from the three towns

[1] *Minutes*, pp. 620, 626.
[2] The respective answers of the three colonies are in the *Minutes*, pp. 639–40.
[3] *Minutes*, pp. 642, 648.

had openly visited Hartford and been received with favour.¹ The government of Connecticut wrote to Massachusetts to enlist that colony in a scheme for recovering the Long Island towns.² The traditions of Massachusetts were all against a policy which could strengthen Connecticut or extend her territory southward. Moreover the Court of Massachusetts had just shown how indifferent they were to any question of Dutch or English supremacy. In September 1673 Clayborne, the commander of an English frigate, touched at Boston and asked for men and supplies with which to make an attack on New Netherlands. The Court might reasonably have refused on the ground that the enterprise was too serious for the commander of a single ship acting on his own responsibility. They took a less intelligible and less creditable position. They would lend a hand if Clayborne would guarantee them the possession of the captured territory. But they did not care to win it back for the Proprietor. Rather than see it again under Lovelace they would prefer that it remained in Dutch hands.³ When we condemn the policy of Charles II. and his successor towards Massachusetts we must not forget that incident. It not only showed in the colony a lack of any patriotic sentiment on behalf of the mother country; it showed, what was far more dangerous, an inability to understand the need for connected action against a foreign Power.

The backwardness of Massachusetts did not hinder Connecticut from taking prompt measures. A despatch was sent to Colve, telling him that if he pressed the oath of allegiance on the Long Island towns, Connecticut would interfere. Colve was not to be turned aside

[margin note: Dealings with Connecticut.]

---

¹ Connect. Records, 1665-77, p. 212.   ² *Ib.*
³ Resolution of the General Court of Massachusetts quoted textually by Mr. Brodhead, vol. ii. p. 229.

by vague threats. The bearer of the letter was at first detained, and then sent back to Hartford with an answer which was virtually a defiance. A paper, Colve said, had been handed to him by a man who called himself John Bankes. It was signed by one John Allen, claiming to be Secretary for the colony of Connecticut. But Colve cannot believe that such an impertinent and absurd writing emanated from persons bearing the name of Governor and General Court, and he has therefore deemed it unworthy of an answer. Nor did Colve confine himself to this: in his interview with the English emissary he plainly met threats by counter-threats, warning him that reinforcements were expected from Holland, and that the citizens of Hartford might find that it was not a question of winning back Long Island, but of holding their own territory.[1]

At the same time that they sent this message, Connecticut despatched two commissioners to the threatened townships to watch the interests of the colony, and to see that the Dutch officials took no prejudicial steps. The two parties, the commissioners from Connecticut and those sent by Colve, met at sea near the coast of Long Island. After an exchange of civilities they went together to Southold. The inhabitants were already in arms. The Dutch officials soon saw that the current of feeling ran dead against them, and they went straight back to New York without even visiting any of the other townships.[2]

A month later, in November 1673, Connecticut sent a volunteer force under Winthrop's son, Fitz-John, to help the settlers of Southold. Bankes on his return from his embassy described Colve as 'a man of resolute and passionate spirit.' His career as a whole may

[1] The letter is in the *Minutes* together with Colve's reply. Bankes's report of his interview is in the Connecticut Records, 1665–77, p. 565.

[2] A very full report, in the form of a journal, by the commissioners is in the *Minutes*, pp. 654–8.

justify the description, but his dealings with Southold hardly deserve the praise of resolution. Three times did he take measures just decided enough to irritate, and so ineffective as to give every encouragement to resistance. At the end of February he despatched a fleet of four vessels [1] to collect stores from Long Island for the use of his troops, and to summon Southold to submit to Dutch authority. The fleet anchored off Southold, and the commander, Nathaniel Sylvester, called on the town to surrender. If not, it must prepare for an immediate attack. All he got for answer was a command not to interfere with English subjects. Shots were exchanged without effect, then Sylvester came to the conclusion that his force was not equal to the task in hand, and he returned to New York.

{The Dutch fail to reduce Southold.}

During the winter trifling hostilities were carried on at sea. But it was clear that neither New England nor New Netherlands had the will or power for any serious operations. The battle for the possession of Long Island and the Hudson valley was to be fought out not on the coast of America, but in the council rooms of Europe. The Dutch Government had stronger motives now for making an effort to retain the colony than in the days when it had been so cheaply won by Nicolls. The title of the Company was extinct, and whatever was acquired now was acquired for and by the whole nation. The gain which the colony might thus be, had been strongly set forth in a letter sent by the municipal authorities of New York to the States-General immediately after the capture. The place had, they pointed

{Motives for the retention of New Netherlands by the Dutch.}

---

[1] A man-of-war, a ketch, and two sloops. This is stated in a letter from Fitz-John Winthrop to Allen. This letter is the chief authority for the expedition. Winthrop speaks of Sylvester's 'great civility' in a manner which suggests that, while nominally serving the Dutch, his sympathies were English.

out, both military and commercial value. In Holland thousands of homes had been laid desolate by the late French invasion; the outcasts might find a refuge in Dutch territory beyond the Atlantic. Beside the profit of the fur and tobacco trade, the colony would supply grain to the Dutch settlements in the West India Islands. Placed in the midst of English territory it would serve as a constant check on England and on any sudden extension of English naval power.

Before that letter could reach Holland, before the Dutch even knew that their colony had been won back, the fate of New York had been settled by diplomacy. In August 1673, Spain intervening on behalf of the States-General laid down as a condition of agreement that all territorial conquests made during the war should be restored. The treaty was not finally accepted and signed till the following February. In the meantime the States-General made certain provisional arrangements for the government of the colony. But in doing so they can have been merely reckoning on the bare chance of negotiations falling through. In truth Dutch statesmen must have seen by this time how untenable was the isolated province on the Hudson. Surrounded by English settlements it could only be held at a cost which it could in no way repay. If, too, they wished to see France held in check, that could be done far more efficiently when the valley of the Hudson formed part of a continuous English territory. That may have done something to reconcile Holland to the sacrifice. To thwart France was the one supreme motive which dominated William's policy, and she could best be thwarted by the union of New Netherlands with the English colonies. To perceive and act on that view was in no way beyond the clear foresight and steady purpose of the young Stadtholder.

Final cession by Holland.

CHAPTER IV.

NEW YORK UNDER ANDROS AND DONGAN

As between England and Holland the treaty of Westminster simply restored existing relations. But it did not leave things as they had been between England and the recovered dependency. Just as the English conquest in 1664 wiped out the claim of the Dutch West India Company, so did the loss and recovery of New York wipe out the Proprietor's title. Just as New York when reconquered by the Dutch passed at once under the direct dominion of the States-General, so after the treaty of Westminster it at once returned to the English Crown.

Altered position of New York.

There was nothing in that theory at variance with equity. The officials appointed by the Proprietor had lost the colony. When it was recovered, the recovery was simply part of an arrangement to indemnify the nation for what it had spent on the war. In this case the theory was acceptable not only to grantor, but to

---

[1] For this period we have two fresh authorities of value. In 1679 two Dutchmen, members of the French Protestant sect the Labadists, so called after their founder Jean Labadie, visited New York and New Jersey, and left a very clear and valuable record of what they saw. A translation of their journal, with a preface and notes made by Mr. H. C. Murphy, was printed in 1867 by the New York Historical Society. It is of special value for New Jersey affairs, and for the dealings of the rulers of New York with that colony.

Another authority is the Rev. Charles Wooley, who went to New York in 1678 as chaplain to Andros. His journal with notes by Mr. O'Callaghan was published in 1860 in Gowan's *Bibliotheca Americana*.

grantee. There was no fear that the reconquest would be used as a pretext for any substantial interference with the Duke's proprietary rights. All that was taken could be and was sure to be at once re-granted. And there were reasons which made it distinctly to the interest of the Duke to accept this view. If it wiped out his existing rights, it also wiped out his existing obligations. He was sure of the recovery of the former, the restoration of the latter was at his own pleasure. The annihilation of the Duke's title would effectually undo that alienation of territory to Berkeley and Carteret which had so vexed Nicolls. It might even enable the Duke to reopen the boundary question with Connecticut. Not, indeed, that the two matters were on the same footing. The proprietors of New Jersey enjoyed their rights under a concession from the Duke. The claims of Connecticut as against the Duke were decided by the interpretation of a legal instrument, the charter of the colony, and it could not be pretended that either the Dutch conquest or the treaty of Westminster affected that instrument. It might be urged, however, that there was a taint of fraud in the process by which Connecticut had obtained her existing boundary. The question might be regarded not as one of legal right, but as an open question to be settled by diplomacy, and if so the change no doubt put the Proprietor in a stronger position. The extinction of Berkeley's and Carteret's rights could not be regarded as in any way inequitable. Just as much as the Proprietor himself they were responsible for the loss of the territory. The real hardship would fall on private persons who had titles to land dependent on the territorial rights either of the Duke of York or of the New Jersey proprietors.

In June 1674 a new grant was issued to the Duke. The extent of territory and the political privileges conceded were identical with those given by the earlier instrument. But the one instrument was in no sense a prolongation or a confirmation of the other. The second grant ignored any territorial title of English Proprietors as completely as the first overlooked the rights of Dutch inhabitants.[1]

<small>Fresh grant to the proprietor.</small>

It might have been expected that the warnings given by Nicolls would at least have saved the Proprietor from repeating his error, and again dismembering his province. But the same deliberate forethought which had led Carteret nine years before to secure a contingent interest in the province yet to be won did not now desert him. Between the treaty of Westminster and the second grant to the Duke of York, Berkeley and Carteret had each of them taken steps for saving their rights. Each had practically asserted the view that the Dutch conquest had left their grants unimpaired. In March 1674 Berkeley transferred his interest to two Quakers, Bylling and Fenwick. He must have known at the very time that he made the grant that the treaty of Westminster imperilled, if it did not annihilate, his title. We can hardly doubt that he was simply getting out of an unsafe investment, and leaving to the purchasers and his partners the risks of litigation or the cost and trouble of securing a fresh title. We may reasonably believe, too, that the troubles in the colony had their share in disgusting Berkeley with his speculation.

<small>Position of Carteret and Berkeley.</small>

Carteret adopted the bolder policy of holding on to his property and securing it in the face of the Duke's interest. In June he obtained a letter from the King which established his claims to the territory of New Jersey. The form of it was peculiar and ingenious. It did not confer a grant of land on Carteret. It was an injunction to the inhabitants of the province,

<small>Carteret obtains a fresh grant.</small>

[1] *Col. Papers*, 1667-74, p. 1308.

ordering them to obey Carteret. His authority was assumed as a pre-existing condition. Nothing was said of its origin. The letter only stated that 'the said Sir George Carteret' 'hath the sole power under us to settle and dispose of the said country, upon such terms and conditions as he shall think fit.'[1] This was practically a grant, not indeed made in legal form nor fenced in with the necessary precautions, but one which an astute and resolute man could convert into an efficient basis for something more valuable. Within a fortnight of the day when this letter was written the grant was issued to the Duke of York. Thus, within three months, three distinct and incompatible titles had been called into existence. The Duke's patent vested the soil of the whole province absolutely in him; the King's letter to Carteret gave him at least an equitable title which vested a portion of the soil absolutely in him; the conveyance made by Berkeley gave the purchasers an undefined interest in Carteret's estate.

The question between the Duke and Carteret was soon settled. The Duke, heedless of Nicolls's warnings, and regardless of the legitimate means of escape offered to him, fell again into precisely the same trap. In July he issued a grant, setting forth his own title under the fresh patent, and then by virtue of that title granting to Carteret and his heirs the eastern moiety of New Jersey.[2]

The multiplication of territorial titles was not the only complication to which this gave rise. There was a further matter of dispute. How far were the Duke's rights of political sovereignty over his territory transferred to his grantees, and how far again transferred by Berkeley to the Quaker purchasers? The difficulty

---

[1] *Col. Papers*, 1669-74, p. 1305.
[2] The warrant for the preparation of this grant is in the N. Y. Docs. vol. iii. p. 223.

was precisely like that which constantly arose in the Middle Ages when territorial grants carried with them certain limited rights of sovereignty. The further course of that dispute belongs to the history of New Jersey, and will be better dealt with hereafter.

The Governor to whom the Proprietor now entrusted the colony had none of the administrative ability of Nicolls. He had not even the lower merits, the activity and enterprise of Lovelace. He was a mere soldier of a respectable type, whose idea of government was to perform certain prescribed acts and to enforce discipline, observing as far as might be courtesy and humanity. That phase of his career by which he is best known to the world is his governorship of New England at the time of the Restoration. There we see him at his worst, enforcing a crude despotism, which abounded with unnecessarily irritating incidents. At Boston the merits of Andros as well as his faults made against him. He was too loyal and conscientious a servant to shirk the duties assigned to him; he had not the sympathy or the adroitness by which another man might have made the system of government tolerable. But if he had never returned to America after his first governorship of New York, he would have taken rank as a highly respectable, commonplace, and somewhat hardly used official.

<small>Andros appointed Governor.</small>

In October 1674 the ship which brought out Andros anchored off Staten Island.[1] According to the treaty of Westminster, Colve had no duty nor option but to hand over the territory. He was, however, determined so to use his position as to secure, if might be, the rights of his fellow-countrymen against any possible encroachment. On no conceivable ground had Colve any claim to stipulate. Under

<small>He arrives at New York.</small>

---

[1] See Andros's letter to Colve, dated October 22, 1674, in O'Callaghan, vol. iii. p. 45.

the treaty of Westminster he was but a private Dutch citizen. But a quick and resolute man was dealing with a slow and irresolute one. Nothing is more marked throughout the career of Andros than his lack of resource in any unlooked-for emergency.

Colve drew up and submitted to Andros what may be called a treaty of surrender under eleven heads.[1] He asked that there should be no hindrance to the settlement of any unfulfilled contracts between officials and private citizens; that Andros should accept as valid all the judicial acts of the late Dutch government; that private property should be respected; that certain Dutch usages as to poor rates and inheritance should be maintained; that the Dutch should retain their rights to freedom of worship; that the system of excise and of public-house licenses in force should be continued; and that the existing arrangements for paying off a debt on the fortification should not be altered.

Negotiations with Colve.

The letters, if any, which accompanied these demands of Colve do not seem to be extant, and we can only judge of them by the tone of Andros's answers. From those one would certainly not infer that Colve asked Andros to grant these conditions as an act of grace. Yet he was in no position to negotiate. He might name conditions, but if Andros refused them, how could they be enforced? But every incident in the career of Andros showed that he was unequal to such a crisis. His despatches, too, show that incapacity for clear and decided expression which often accompanies indecision in action. Hesitating and rambling answers to Colve's demands were the prelude to complete concession. The conduct and temper of Andros were always better than his judgment, and even at his worst in New England he always showed personal courtesy to his opponents. It is not a little to his credit that during

[1] O'Callaghan, vol. iii. p. 49.

these negotiations, when some English soldiers were arrested by Colve for being drunk in the streets, Andros made no protest, but civilly asked that they might be pardoned.[1]

On November 10 the final surrender was made, and the long-debated land became finally a British province.[2] The peaceful reassertion of the Proprietor's authority at Albany followed as a matter of necessity. On November 9 Andros in anticipation of the formal surrender declared the constitution of the province. The Duke's laws were to be in force, and all grants and estates which had existed before the Dutch conquest were to revive. At the same time legal proceedings during the Dutch occupation were not to be invalidated.[3] One important change, however, was introduced. Henceforth the Records of the Town Council were to be kept in English, and as far as might be its judicial proceedings were to be carried on in that tongue.[4]

Though an indemnity was granted to all Dutch subjects for what had been done during the late occupation, one English offender did not escape.

Court-martial on Manning. A court-martial was held on Manning. He pleaded guilty to neglect of duty, urging as an extenuation a 'broken head and disquieted spirit.' He was deprived of his commission, and declared incapable of military service or of civil employment within the colony.[5]

But for his plea there would be little in the case, as it comes before us now, to condemn Manning. He may have been guilty of errors in detail, but it is not easy to see, with such resources as he had, what could have resulted from resistance but wholly profitless bloodshed.

[1] Letter of Andros, October 28, 1674, given by Mr. Brodhead in an Appendix, vol. ii. p. 655.
[2] O'Callaghan, vol. iii. p. 51. [3] N. Y. Docs. vol. iii. p. 227.
[4] Brodhead, vol. ii. p. 274.
[5] For the details of Manning's trial see O'Callaghan, vol. iii. pp. 52-65.

And it is certainly surprising that no punishment should have overtaken Carr. If Manning was to blame for surrendering at his own discretion, Carr was assuredly far more to blame for hauling down the flag in defiance of orders.

Nicolls in his short colonial career had shown powers of administrative statesmanship. So, too, had Lovelace, on a smaller scale and with less satisfactory results. Andros showed himself nothing more than a docile and respectable servant of the Proprietor. Yet, to do him justice, he seems in one important matter to have had views of his own at variance with those of his employer. The demand for a system of representative government which had been made to Lovelace was renewed almost immediately on the arrival of his successor. The demand was communicated by Andros to the Duke.[1] The Duke's reply formed one of those many links by which his policy as a colonial ruler is instructively connected with his later policy as a king. He shows an honest wish to understand the matter fully. Andros has not told him 'what qualifications are usual and proper to such Assemblies'—that is, we must suppose, how the system worked in other proprietary colonies, and what safeguards were there imposed. However, if Andros thinks the matter worth further discussion the Duke will give him a fair hearing. But without fuller details he cannot approve of the demand. His refusal is supported by most characteristic reasoning. An Assembly would probably encroach on the rights of the existing government. Besides what do the settlers want that they have not got? Even if the council fail to govern according to the laws established, there is an

_{Demand for representative institutions.}

[1] The letter or letters of Andros on this point do not seem to be extant. Their general tenor may be inferred from the Duke's answer. N. Y. Docs. vol. iii. p. 235.

appeal to the Proprietor. And what difference would there be between the General Court of Assize as established and a representative Assembly? There 'the same persons are usually present, who in all probability would be their representatives if another constitution were allowed.' That men should feel safer if their affairs were in some measure in their own hands seems never to have occurred to James. It is not fair to call him an unscrupulous ruler as his brother was. He would have admitted as readily as any member of the Long Parliament or of the Convention of 1688 that a king was bound by moral obligations to his subjects. It seems strange that the brother of Charles could not see that a king may be an unprincipled self-seeker. It is perhaps less strange that he should not have seen that he might be a fanatic, with a narrow brain and a distorted conscience. It is at all events certain that neither as proprietor nor king did James show the slightest power of understanding that men could reasonably demand any security for their political rights beyond the personal good-will and upright intentions of the ruler. The practical result of James's government is the best comment upon the fancies of the Patriot King.

One thing we must not forget in estimating the amount of freedom enjoyed by the Duke of York's colony, and the motives which led the citizens to acquiesce in so arbitrary a system. As freemen of their various townships they enjoyed that liberty and those rights of self-government which were withheld from them as citizens of New York.

The views here expressed by James are reaffirmed in a letter written to Andros in the following January. The Proprietor evidently suspects his deputy of viewing the popular demand for representation with too much tenderness. 'Unless you had offered what qualifications are usual and proper to such Assemblies,

I cannot but suspect they would be of dangerous consequence; nothing being more known than the aptness of such bodies to assume to themselves many privileges which prove destructive to, or very often disturb the peace of, the government wherein they are allowed. Neither do I see any use of them which is not as well provided for whilst you and your Council govern according to the laws established (thereby preserving every man's property inviolate), and whilst all things that need redress may be sure of finding it either at the Quarter Sessions or by other legal and ordinary ways; or, lastly, by appeals to myself. But howsoever, if you continue of the same opinion, I shall be ready to consider of any proposals you shall send for that purpose.' In the same letter the Proprietor approves the action of Andros in allowing American goods to enter the colony duty-free for three years. He also asks for a more exact account of the finances of the colony. Andros, he says, has held out hopes that it may be at least self-supporting, not a burden as hitherto.[1] A few days later we find the Duke's secretary, Werden, remonstrating with Andros for deviating from the practice of his predecessors, and allowing goods to be carried past New York and sold at Albany.[2] In other words Andros is to uphold a system which should make Albany dependent on New York, and thus give the latter a monopoly of the rich trade of the Hudson. So rigidly was this monopoly fenced in that it was only after three years' residence apparently that a New York merchant was allowed a share in the trade with Albany.[3]

One important assertion of the proprietary authority Andros did effect. The townships of Southold and Southampton yielded to the demand made ten years before and took out patents for their land. But by

---

[1] *Col. Papers*, 1675-6, p. 513. [2] *Ib.* p. 803.
[3] *Travels of the Labadists*, p. 284.

far the most important part of his official career, that which had the most abiding influence on colonial history, was his dealing with New England. As we have seen, the boundary between the Duke's territory and Connecticut had been drawn by mutual consent in 1664. Owing to an error or a fraud in surveying, that line had been drawn in a fashion more favourable to Connecticut than was intended. Andros now contended that the Duke's new patent wiped out the settlement made by Nicolls. The new grant had for its eastern boundary the Connecticut river. If strictly interpreted that would have dismembered Connecticut. The Connecticut charter was in its geographical provisions a vague document. But we may be at least sure that it meant to give the colony secure possession of the townships on the western bank of the Connecticut, to say nothing of Guildford and New Haven. No court of equity would have given effect to a document by which the grantor tacitly revoked that grant. On the other hand there is no doubt that when the frontier line was drawn Nicolls and his colleagues were imposed on; nor would Andros have been doing his duty by his principal if he had not striven to put that right. Andros, however, without attempting to negotiate or to invite a compromise, made in person a crude assertion of the Duke's alleged rights, in a form so unqualified and impracticable that it was impossible for the colony to acknowledge them without danger, and without a total loss of self-respect. I have told elsewhere the details of the dispute.[1] It had no immediate practical result. But it did this: it taught Connecticut what manner of man Andros was, and when his time of authority over them came thirteen years later the lesson was not forgotten. They must have seen that he was a man withheld from being for-

[1] *Puritan Colonies*, vol. ii, pp. 237-41.

midable alike by his merits and his failings. He was no tyrant, but a fairly good-humoured English gentleman, carrying out a harsh measure ungraciously, but not roughly or brutally. In caution, in diplomatic tact, in all that could really make him dangerous, Andros was wholly wanting, and the dispute with Connecticut displayed that want to the full.

At the same time Andros was learning something of the character of New England, not only in his dealings with Connecticut, but also from the conduct of Massachusetts in relation to the Indian war. There he saw the Puritan polity on one of its weak sides, weak, too, in a way which to a practical soldier and an English official was peculiarly offensive. He saw their hesitation, their inability to co-operate readily, their suspicious jealousy of English interference. He had not before his eyes, nor, if he had, could a professional soldier estimate at its due worth, that stubborn spirit of local resistance, whose isolated efforts were the brightest feature of the war. That hostility between Andros and the people of New England which at a later day had such important effects was in no small measure due to the events of his first term of office.

In the opposite direction Andros was entangled in disputes with the patentees of New Jersey. Those disputes will come before us as part of the history of that colony. For the present it is enough to say that Andros asserted certain undefined rights of sovereignty over the territories which the Duke had alienated, and that he attempted to put in force his claims by deposing Carteret and issuing writs for the election of an Assembly, and by so doing raised the whole question as to the completeness of the Duke's surrender of his rights over New Jersey.

<small>Andros recalled.</small>

One of the most important features of Andros's administration was that the ecclesiastical constitution of the colony began to take on that form which gave it so singular and anomalous a character. In none of the colonies was the system of a State Church dependent on that of the mother country less adapted to the origin and composition of the community. In none except South Carolina was it carried out so rigidly.

<small>Ecclesiastical matters.</small>

The ecclesiastical constitution introduced by Nicolls after the conquest was obviously one which contemplated a system of concurrent endowment. At the same time it had none of that definiteness and that precision which were absolutely necessary to secure permanence for a system so complex and so unfamiliar.

The Duke's code of laws assumed the existence of parishes. It provided for the building of a church in every parish, and the maintenance of a minister by a public rate. The minister was to be chosen by the freeholders, and inducted by the Governors. It was further provided that he must have received ordination from some Protestant bishop or minister within the British dominions, or within the dominions of some foreign prince of the Reformed religion.

In 1675 Andros, regardless of the stipulation, introduced one Nicolaus van Rensselaer to share the ministry of the Reformed Church at Albany with Dominie Schaats, the minister who already held office there.

Van Rensselaer was by birth a Dutchman and an ordained minister of the Lutheran Church of Amsterdam. But circumstances had associated him with England. It is said that when Charles II. was a fugitive Van Rensselaer, preaching before him at Brussels, had assured him of his impending restoration. The preacher came over to England, was ordained deacon and priest in the diocese of Salisbury, and was then placed in charge of the Dutch church at Westminster. His appointment at Albany was protested against by Van Niewenhuysen, the Lutheran minister at New York. He could not deny that Van Rensselaer was an ordained minister in the Dutch Church. But he apparently took the view that Van Rensselaer's ordination in the Church of England vitiated his Lutheran orders, and that he was ineligible for a ministry in New Netherlands since he was no longer amenable to the Classis at Amsterdam. The matter was brought before the Council. They with singular compliance accepted this view, and Van Rensselaer was allowed to retain his office on condition that he conducted his ministry 'conformably to the public church service of the Reformed Church of Holland.' The chief historical value of the incident is the moderation shown by Andros.

The next incident in the career of Van Rensselaer is also of interest as throwing light on the character of two conspicuous figures in New York history. For certain words used by Van Rensselaer in a sermon at Albany he was charged before the Albany magistrates of 'false preaching.' His accusers were Jacob Leisler, a German brewer, then a deacon in the church of New York, and Leisler's son-in-law, Jacob Millborne, an Englishman. The Albany magistrates found Van Rensselaer guilty and imprisoned him. He appealed to a court composed of the Governor, Council, Mayor, Aldermen and Ministers of New York. They referred the matter back to Albany. The magistrates, therefore, after further deliberation withdrew their condemnation, and ordered mutual forbearance. All differences were to be consumed in the fire of love. Thereupon the Court at New York which had previously dealt with the question showed their view of the merits of the case by ordering Leisler and Millborne to pay all costs, 'as giving the first occasion of difference.'[1]

[1] All the authorities on these questions are brought together by Mr. Brodhead, vol. ii. pp. 288, 360. Mr. Brodhead takes the view that the

By his good measures and his bad alike, Andros had incurred unpopularity with the colonists. He was *Grievances of the colonists against Andros.*[1] charged with favouring Dutch traders at the expense of English, and the Duke was told that he might by farming the revenue of the colony make more of it than was made by his present representative. The Governor also set his face against that unfair and wasteful system, whereby favoured capitalists were allowed to occupy large tracts of land and leave them unreclaimed.

In other matters Andros had more justly earned his unpopularity. He was charged with setting aside the verdicts of juries. Especially had he offended the trading classes by ill-judged interference, if nothing worse. He himself, it was alleged, kept a store and thus became a rival to the New York traders. He anticipated in a crude fashion the mercantile policy of the next generation which fettered colonial industry in the interests of the English manufacturer. Tanning was an important business in the colony. The shoemakers, thinking themselves overcharged, were foolish enough to invoke the help of Andros against the alleged monopoly of the tanners. He thereupon entirely prohibited tanning. Henceforth all hides had to be sent to England and tanned leather re-imported. It can hardly have been the same motive, but rather a belief that government could better trade, which led Andros to the most unpopular of all his measures—interference with the staple product of the country, grain. He prohibited distilling within the colony. This had two

right of the Amsterdam Classis to control clerical appointments in the colony was secured by the eighth article in the capitulation to Nicolls. I can see no evidence of this. The article simply says : ' The Dutch here shall enjoy the liberty of their consciences in Divine worship and Church discipline.' Col. Docs. vol. ii. p. 251.

[1] All these are set forth by the Labadists in their account of their travels.

effects. It led the settlers to import Barbadoes rum. This was at first brought by way of Boston. That, however, Andros prohibited, thinking probably that the resources of the Duke's colony ought not to go to enrich disloyal New Englanders. The increase in the price of spirits was not the worst effect of Andros's legislation. The demand for grain was lessened, and the farmer could only find a market for it abroad. Andros then proceeded to fence in the export trade with vexatious restrictions. He prohibited all exportation except from New York itself, and he insisted that the grain before exportation should be assayed lest the colony should be discredited by an inferior article. The state of things in the colony may have made this needful. But it was sure to be unpopular, and Andros had no gift for lightening such administrative difficulties.

The questions in dispute between Andros and the patentees of New Jersey made his presence in England necessary. In the autumn of 1680 he left the colony. He entrusted affairs to his military subordinate Brockholls, under the title of Commander-in-chief and with the powers of Deputy Governor. A strange administrative oversight of which Andros was guilty had an important effect on the constitutional history of the colony. The customs duties fixed by the Governor in 1677 expired after a term of three years, and Andros neglected to make an order continuing them.[1] The collector of customs assumed that the renewal took effect as a matter of course. The New York merchants held that the obligation to pay was suspended. A test case soon arose. In May 1681 the consignees of an incoming vessel refused to pay the duty demanded, whereupon the custom-house officials seized the goods. The matter was brought before the Council, who gave

Dispute about customs.

[1] Brodhead, vol. ii. p. 351.

it as their opinion that no duty could be exacted by any official without the express approval of the Proprietor. Thereupon a civil action was brought against the collector of customs, and a verdict given which compelled him to yield the goods.

The merchants were not content to stand merely on the defensive. Dyer was indicted for high treason on the plea that he had illegally exercised authority over the King's subjects. His position increased the moral effect, if not the constitutional importance, of the attack. Dyer was not only collector of customs, but also mayor of New York. Proceedings were taken in due form, a jury was empanelled, and witnesses examined. But after putting in a plea of not guilty, Dyer demurred to the jurisdiction of the Court. It had no power, he said, to try an official acting under a commission from the Crown. The Court accepted that view. Dyer was sent to England and his case referred to the Privy Council. At the same time the merchant who had prosecuted him was bound in a surety of five thousand pounds to follow up the matter in England.[1] On Dyer's reaching England the case was brought before the Privy Council, and after, as it would seem, a perfunctory inquiry was suffered to drop.[2]

The personal aspect of the case was the least important part of it. The impulse that has prompted resistance to an isolated exercise of arbitrary power seldom stops there. If the community has had no political training, if resistance cannot fasten on certain specified constitutional remedies and demand them, then follows a mere destructive revolution. Wat Tyler begins by resisting the tax-gatherer, and ends as the leader of purposeless and predatory rebellion. If, on the other hand, the community has already travelled some way in the path of self-government, if its traditions and

<small>Demand for representation.</small>

[1] N. Y. Docs. vol. iii. pp. 287-9.   [2] Ib. pp. 318-21.

its associations enable it easily and naturally to adopt fresh institutions, then isolated resistance will be the signal for constitutional reform. The protest against the Stamp Act lays the foundation of the American confederacy.

The drama now enacted on the small field of New York followed the latter course. Brockholls, Andros's deputy, a man neither firm enough to control the people, nor intelligent enough to sympathize with them, sent home deplorable accounts of the prevailing anarchy, of his inability to get any duties paid, and of the seditious temper which pervaded the colony.[1] The sole justification, as it would seem, for his outcry was that the settlers were demanding, in no intemperate or dangerous fashion, an extension of their rights of self-government. On every side of them they saw communities enjoying a system modelled on that of the mother country. The oligarchy of Massachusetts, factious and disloyal, enjoyed a system harsh indeed as against those whom it excluded, but which made it in all but name independent of the Crown. The line which separated New York from Connecticut was even still a matter of dispute. Yet on one side of that line men enjoyed the full privileges of English citizens, but lately confirmed in express terms by royal charter. How could the freemen of Southold and Southampton be expected to acquiesce in a system which placed them under the arbitrary control of the Proprietor? The peaceful loyalty with which they had accepted English supremacy deserved some recognition. By slow, faltering, and imperfect steps the colony had been working its way under Dutch and English rule towards self-government. The oversight of Andros in the matter of the customs gave the final impulse that was needed.

[1] Brockholls's letter is quoted by Brodhead, vol. ii. p. 355.

The connexion between the attack on Dyer and the demand which it suggested was direct. The same grand jury which indicted him called the attention of the Court of Assize to the absence of a representative Assembly.[1] The conduct of the Court shows that there was a certain rough truth in James's view, that the magistrates were really effective guardians of popular rights. It assuredly proves that the mere distribution of political power is in itself a gain to popular liberties. The Court presented to the Duke a petition setting forth in strong language the grievance which the colony suffered from the want of a representative Assembly. They were taxed by arbitrary and absolute power, while all about them they saw communities flourishing under systems of government modelled on that of the mother country.[2]

Happily for the colony the Proprietor was not left to the vague and inactive policy of Brockholls, nor to that of a respectable disciplinarian such as Andros. Among the Duke's chief advisers was one whose counsel at such a time was sure to make for peace and moderation. In later times the influence of William Penn over James may have been an evil one. The political theory and sentiments of the two men had too much in common. Penn, like James, was too ready to measure a political system by its immediate application, without taking into account the abuses of it which were possible. But so far his own views on colonial government plainly were that concessions such as those asked for by the Court of Assize were safe and expedient. That he was soon to show by his treatment of his own colony, Pennsylvania. We can hardly err in believing that it was in no small measure due to him that the Duke received the petition of the

Probable influence of Penn.

---

[1] Brodhead, vol. ii. p. 354.
[2] The petition is given by Mr. Brodhead in an Appendix, vol. ii. p. 658.

Court of Assize with approval, and with a promise that their demand should be speedily regarded. The intention was notified to the colonists through Brockholls. They were told at the same time that funds must be provided by the colony for the maintenance of the government and for military purposes.

The change of system brought with it, almost of necessity, a change of governor. It could hardly be said that the relations between Andros and the settlers were hostile, but he had neither the breadth of mind to carry out a policy of reform, nor the temper to work cordially with a popular body. A post was found for him in the Island of Jersey, and the governorship of the newly enfranchised colony was bestowed on an Irish soldier, Thomas Dongan.

When appointed Governor of New York, Dongan was forty-eight years old. He in all likelihood owed his preferment at the outset to the fact that he was the nephew of Richard Talbot, Earl of Tyrconnel. In those traits of character by which Tyrconnel is best known in history, Dongan had no share. He had nothing in common with the boisterous libertine who figures in the pages of Grammont, or with the unrestrained and truculent partisan whose Irish administration disgraced the Jacobite cause. Yet in one or two important features Dongan was a decorous copy of his kinsman. He did not fly into the frenzies of a spoilt child and vent his fury on his own wig. But his diplomatic correspondence plainly shows traces of a sharp and arbitrary temper. Compared not merely with Tyrconnel, but with the average public men of that day, Dongan was honest and disinterested. Assuredly he was not wholly and absolutely indifferent to personal gain. Such indifference was almost unknown among the public men of that generation. Dongan would serve his master faithfully, but if a chance of profit offered itself as an incident of good service it would not be neglected. As usual mammon worship proved as incompatible with civil as with spiritual obligations, and Dongan found himself exposed to charges and involved in difficulties which a purely disinterested man would have escaped. But in spite of such drawbacks the New York settlers had good reason to be thankful for James's choice. The difficulty would have been to find among James's followers not one free from Dongan's faults, but one in whom they were so slightly developed. Taking them at their very worst they were far outweighed by his merits, his common sense and his clear perception of what was practicable, his energy, ubiquitous yet not meddlesome, and persistent without being obstinate. His nationality, too, and even in some measure his religion, were in his favour. The history of India and of the British colonies has shown by many instances that in the task of ruling alien nations all the best faculties of the Irishman come into play. The presence of a violent Papist in high office would no doubt have been a source of discord and danger. But it is clear that Dongan's Romanism was of a sober and somewhat conventional kind. Beside, it was no small matter to have a man who was bound by no ties of connexion or sentiment to the settlements of New England origin. One fear no doubt there was : a papist, the nominee of James, was in danger of being amenable to French influence. In the coming struggle for the supremacy of America, the Jesuit missionaries were the advanced guard of France, New York the key of the frontier to be held by England. Luckily Dongan's experience had qualified him to understand the designs of France and had taught him to distrust them. He had been colonel of an Irish regiment which was transferred by Charles II. to the service of the French Crown. Strange to say, he does not seem during his service to have acquired enough knowledge of the French language to embolden him to correspond in it. But we may be sure that he had studied the policy and the resources of France. Moreover, though not actually dismissed from the French service, his career there was brought to an end in a manner which he plainly felt a grievance. When in 1678, after the treaty of Nimeguen, all British subjects in the French service were ordered by the English Government to return to England, the French King endeavoured by liberal offers to retain Dongan. He refused and, as he stated, in consequence never received his arrears of pay, sixty-five thousand livres—in English money upwards of five thousand pounds.[1] He set sail for his province in a frame of mind no wise trustful of French promises nor tolerant of French pretensions.

Such was the Governor to whom was assigned the task of introducing representative government into New York. His instructions were a complete fulfilment of the pledges which the Proprietor had given to the colonists. Dongan on his arrival was to issue writs for the election of a representative Assembly, to be chosen by the freeholders. The number of representatives was limited to eighteen. Apparently the apportionment of these members was left to the discretion of Dongan and his Council. All Acts passed by the Assembly and confirmed by the Governor and the Council became law provisionally, pending the approval of the Proprietor. The power of levying rates was exclusively vested in the Assembly.

Dongan's instructions.[2]

The same instructions clearly defined the functions of the Governor. He might establish law courts and custom-houses, and grant lands. He was to have

---

[1] See a letter by Dongan quoted by Mr. Grant Wilson in his *Memorial History of New York*, vol. i. p. 399.

[2] N. Y. Docs. vol. iii. p. 369.

military authority for defensive purposes such as fortification and the control of the militia, but he had no power to make war except by command of the Proprietor.

There was plainly no absolute security that the system of representation, thus granted, was to be permanent. It was conceded as a favour, not a right. Practically, however, when representative machinery has once been established, it contains within itself, if there be in the community the needful instincts and conditions for freedom, a power of self-preservation. It was a great matter, too, that the Proprietor should recognise and approve a representative Assembly not as a special arrangement to meet an emergency, but as part of the every-day working system of the community.

In August 1683 Dongan reached New York.[1] In less than three weeks from his arrival the freeholders were apprised of their new privileges and were instructed to prepare for an election.[2] The announcement was received with a somewhat florid declaration of gratitude by the Court of Assize. Their sense of the Duke's benevolence was 'larger and more grateful' than they could express. They would 'always be ready to offer up their lives and fortunes' against all enemies, whether for the King or the Proprietor.[3]

The first Assembly summoned.

This spirit, however, was not universal. One township (Easthampton) regarded the change not as a concession on the part of James, but as an encroachment by him upon their constitutional rights. They elected representatives, but they protested against the issue of any writ in the Proprietor's name. It might seem an illogical proceeding to elect representatives and then to

---

[1] Brodhead, vol. ii. p. 375.　　[2] *Ib.*
[3] *Ib.* p. 380. Mr. Brodhead, as usual, gives the actual text.

deny the efficiency of the instrument under which they were elected.[1] But to guard against this argument the representatives were expressly to declare that the town had elected not in obedience to the Proprietor's command, but because the freemen would not lose an opportunity of defending their own rights.

It is difficult to see what ground the freemen of Easthampton had for their contention. The Proprietor's patent distinctly gave him power ' to govern and rule,' terms amply wide enough to cover the issue of the writ. Yet the temper which made the men of Easthampton scrutinize a concession instead of accepting it eagerly and unquestioningly had its good side. It was an exaggerated and ill-judging display of the same spirit which five years later made the wiser Nonconformists reject the Declaration of Indulgence.

In October 1683 the deputies, eighteen in number, met. It is to be noticed that the Dutch part of the colony was represented out of proportion to its population. *Composition of the Assembly.*[2] The capital alone returned four, Esopus two, Albany, with which was joined the adjacent hamlet of Rensselaerwyck, the same number, Schenectady and Staten Island one each. Thus every one of the Dutch townships on the Hudson was represented. Long Island, on the other hand, was represented not by towns but by its three ridings, two members to each. Each of the three outlying dependencies, as we may call them, Pemaquid, Nantucket, and Martha's Vineyard sent a representative. If any question should arise affecting the rival interests of the two nationalities, it is plain that the Dutch side of the house, as one may call it, would both outnumber the English and be bound together by a stronger principle of cohesion.

[1] Brodhead, vol. ii. pp. 381-2. Here again our author quotes the actual text.
[2] *Ib.* p. 382.

The first proceeding of the Assembly was to pass a measure analogous to a Bill of Rights. This was entitled 'The Charter of Liberties and Privileges, granted by his Royal Highness to the inhabitants of New York and its dependencies.' This settled the future constitution of the colony. The executive power, however, was still to be vested in the Governor and his Council. There was to be an Assembly which must meet not less than once in three years, to which every freeholder and every freeman of a town corporation should vote for a member. The colony was arranged in electoral districts, corresponding closely to those which had returned members to the extant House. The only noteworthy changes were that Martha's Vineyard and Nantucket were combined into a single constituency, and that the representation of the Dutch part of the colony was increased by two. The scheme for the distribution of representatives was confirmed by another Act, passed in the same Assembly, dividing the colony into twelve counties. General principles were laid down as to procedure and as to the privileges of members, substantially identical with those which apply to Parliament.

The Assembly did not limit itself to framing a representative system. It also declared certain general constitutional principles. No tax of any kind was to be levied except by the Governor, Council and deputies sitting as the general Assembly. No man was to be punished arbitrarily or otherwise than by due course of law. Trial by jury was provided for, and it was also enacted that the English law of real property should be in force.

Not the least important clause was the last. It provided that no one who professed his faith in Jesus Christ and abstained from disturbing the peace of his

[1] This is given by Mr. Brodhead in an Appendix to vol. i. p. 659.

neighbours should be molested for his religion. This, however, was not to exempt Dissenters from the payment of ecclesiastical dues, nor to interfere with the existing arrangement whereby in every township a minister, chosen by two-thirds of the freemen, was maintained by a general rate.

The clause which claimed for the Assembly the right of taxation was not left a mere abstract resolution. On October 30 an Act was passed granting to the Proprietor certain specified duties. The very next day the representatives formally communicated to their constituents the victory, as they considered it, which had been won for them. The people were summoned by sound of trumpet to the town hall, and there in the presence of those officials who formed the government of the colony and of the municipal government of the city, the charter of liberties, together with the appended Act assigning a revenue to the Proprietor, was formally published. Immediately afterwards the obligation to pay such duties was notified by proclamation.[1]

<small>Revenue Act.</small>

It is hardly needful to point out these enactments were worthless without the sanction of the Proprietor. Nor did the Assembly pretend that it was otherwise. The liberties specified by the charter were not what the colonists actually claimed as their right, they were only what they hoped the Proprietor would confer on them as an act of grace.

Perhaps the most striking feature of all in the charter is its intensely English character. There is nothing in it abstract or general, not a line of it that is not distinctly modelled on English precedent. The whole phraseology is English, it implies a perfect familiarity with English constitu-

<small>Growth of English feeling and influence.</small>

---

[1] Brodhead, vol. ii. p. 384. I rely upon the same authority for the remaining enactments.

tional usage in those who drafted it, a constant reference to English law in those who were to use it. Yet, as we have seen, the Assembly which drafted it was one in which the Dutch portion of the community preponderated. Nor was that all. It is almost certain from the manner in which the Act was proclaimed that the Assembly knew that it would be received with enthusiasm among the Dutch inhabitants of the capital. Nothing could show better how effectively Nicolls and his successors had done their work, with what almost incomprehensible speed the colony was becoming Anglicized. It may seem paradoxical to say that the very plurality of nationalities made this all the easier. Yet in truth it was so. A solid Dutch nationality might have held its own against English influence. There was no such power of resistance in the miscellaneous population of which the colony was made up. That feature was clearly recognised, probably increased, by one of the Acts passed by the Assembly. It ordered that any free man, who was ready to profess Christianity and to take the oath of allegiance to the King and fidelity to the Proprietor, might without any further ceremony become a naturalized citizen. Naturalization did not merely carry with it political privileges. The unnaturalized foreigner residing in New York laboured under material disadvantages. He might only deal with merchants and might not carry on retail trade.[1]

One practical result of this naturalization Act was certain to be an immigration of fugitive Huguenots whom the bigotry of Lewis was driving from French soil. At the same time the colony was divided into counties, and courts of justice were instituted. There were to be four separate tribunals in New York: monthly Town Courts to decide small cases; quarterly or half-yearly County Courts; a General Court of Oyer

[1] *The Labadists*, p. 260.

P

and Terminer, and a Court of Chancery. From all these an appeal was to lie to the Crown.¹

Hitherto such freedom as had been enjoyed by the inhabitants of New York had rested chiefly on the municipal privileges of individual townships. Now that the whole community had at length, as it seemed, acquired rights of self-government the peculiar privileges of the city were not overlooked. Special attention to them was indeed enjoined on Dongan by his instructions. Henceforth the city was to be incorporated by charter and to enjoy an elaborate municipal constitution. It was to be divided into six wards, each electing one alderman. The corporation, however, was not to be wholly self-governing, since all officials but the treasurer were to be nominated by the Governor and Council.²

The city of New York to be incorporated.

Dongan, like Nicolls, clearly saw the administrative evils which resulted from the separation of New Jersey. His remonstrances, however, were of no more avail than those of his predecessor. Even if Carteret had been disposed to give way, there were now so many vested interests created in the territory that it was wholly impossible for the Proprietor to recover his rights. The situation, with its tangle of political and territorial claims, reminds one what must have been the practical working of feudalism under a liberal and easygoing sovereign.

Difficulties about New Jersey.

All that Dongan could effect in the direction of New Jersey was to thwart an unscrupulous attempt to annex Staten Island. The history of that dispute belongs rather to New Jersey than to New York.

Retention of Staten Island.

Dongan was equally resolute in dealing with ter-

¹ Brodhead, vol. ii. p. 386. Cf. Dongan's report in March 1687, *Col. Papers*, 1685–8, 1160.
² Brodhead, vol. ii. p. 390.

ritorial aggression in the opposite quarter and equally successful. The fraudulent encroachment, as one may not unfairly call it, made by Connecticut had hitherto gone unresisted. But Dongan insisted that the error made in striking the line must be set right, and that they must go back to the original settlement by which New York was to have a tract of twenty clear miles north of the Hudson. Connecticut had learnt what might be gained by standing well with the Crown. It would have been a violation of all her traditions to irritate the heir presumptive. We cannot doubt that if any of Dongan's predecessors had taken as firm a line they would have been equally successful. On the other hand Dongan saw that it was worth some slight sacrifice of the Duke's rights to secure the good will of Connecticut. Moreover, a strict adhesion to the twenty miles condition would have incorporated with New York townships which had grown up as part of Connecticut, and Dongan was too much of a statesman to wish for such a measure. In November 1683 a new line was struck. The instructions of the Connecticut Assembly to the commissioners who acted for them in the matter show that they made the surrender grudgingly. But they had the grace to acknowledge to their fellow-citizens their approval of Dongan's own conduct. It was not till fifteen months later that the agreement was ratified by the Governors of the respective colonies, nor were the boundaries formally acknowledged by the English Government till the twelfth year of William's reign.[1]

The instructions given to Dongan on the subject of commerce were on the same lines as the policy prescribed for Andros. No goods were to be allowed to

[1] All the details of this negotiation are to be found in the Connecticut Records, 1678–89. Dongan's original letter of demand and the final agreement are printed in an Appendix, pp. 329–32.

pass up the river without paying duty at New York. If the settlers in New Jersey attempt to open up any other route for Indian trade, Dongan must do his best to prevent it, ' as I wish to preserve the Indian trade for the benefit of New York above all others.'

<small>Dongan's instructions about trade.</small>

The Act whereby the Assembly declared, and as far as it could perpetuated, its own existence and rights met with a favourable reception from the Proprietor. His approval was given, and there seemed every reason to believe that New York would enjoy a system of representative government as complete and as effectually secured to it as that of Connecticut. But, near as the cup was to the lip, the slip came. Within a month of the accession of James, Dongan received fresh instructions. There was nothing in them to excite any apprehension of change, everything to make the colonists believe that the policy of granting representative institutions was to be followed. There was to be no change of officials, and Dongan was to inform the settlers that their proposals were under consideration of the Privy Council, and that they might 'expect a gracious and suitable return, by the settlement of fitting privileges and confirmation of their rights.'

<small>Effect of the Proprietor's accession.</small>

The Assembly adjourned in October 1684, intending to meet in the following September. It was held, however, that the demise of the Crown ended their existence. Dongan issued fresh writs, and in October the Assembly met again. This time eight days apparently sufficed for all its legislative work.[1]

There was nothing in the policy of Dongan to excite a suspicion that the altered position of the Proprietor would bring with it any change in his dealing with the settlers. The municipal privileges of New York were confirmed in December 1686

<small>Incorporation of New York and Albany.</small>

[1] Brodhead, vol. ii. p. 427.

1686 CHARTERS FOR NEW YORK AND ALBANY. 213

by charter.[1] That was obtained or it might perhaps be fairer to say accompanied by payment of three hundred pounds to Dongan as an official due.[2] There is nothing to show that Dongan was ever induced by any prospect of gain to betray his master's interests or those of the provinces. But he did not rise above the morality of the day, which regarded such perquisites as part of the natural gain of an official career.

In the following summer, Albany was likewise created a municipality with a mayor and seven aldermen. The mayor, sheriff, and other officials were to be nominated by the Governor, the aldermen to be elected by the freemen. Here again Dongan was to receive three hundred pounds, a transaction which was described in the despatch of a Canadian official as a surrender by the Governor of the chief privilege of the Crown, that of nominating magistrates. The Indian trade was entrusted to the city government, a dangerous measure considering all that was involved in the Iroquois alliance.[3]

In receiving his six hundred pounds from New York and Albany, Dongan no doubt felt that the settlers got good value for their money, and that his patron was in no way prejudiced. But for another part of his policy we can hardly urge that excuse. In March 1684 an order was issued, not by the Proprietor, but by the Governor or Council, that the townships in the colony should take out new patents for their land.[4] Bad as interference with established titles is anywhere, it is specially so in a new country where security of title is an absolutely needful condition of improvement.

Fresh land patents required.

---

[1] Brodhead, vol. ii. p. 438.
[2] Dongan himself admits this (N. Y. Docs. vol. iii. p. 412). He also says (p. 411) that he was promised the same sum in connexion with the Charter of Albany. He does not say that it was paid.
[3] Brodhead, vol. ii. p. 439.
[4] *Ib.* p. 437. Here again we have Dongan's own admission, N. Y. Docs. vol. iii. p. 412.

It is impossible to acquit Dongan of introducing this measure to put fees in his own pocket, and in those of the officials about him. An even worse feature of the transaction was the fact that, in two cases, the grant of the patent was preceded by a large gift of land from the township to the Governor.

But with all this there was nothing to show the settlers that a wholesale attack on their privileges was at hand. The Massachusetts patent had indeed been revoked. But from its very outset, that document had Change of policy. been tainted by a suspicion of misrepresentation attaching to its origin, and for nearly twenty years there had been a smouldering feud between the colony and the Crown. The constitutional rights of New York were the fresh creation of the King's own hands. Yet in the summer of 1686 a new commission was issued to Dongan, which, coupled with the instructions accompanying it, utterly shattered the constitution of the colony. By the commission, the functions which the Assembly had claimed, and had been permitted to exercise, were transferred to the Sovereign, and a council of seven nominated by the King. They were to make laws subject to the King's approval, to impose taxes, and to create courts of justice.

The instructions to Dongan added various details as to the practical administration of the system thus *The representative system annulled by Dongan's new instructions.*[1] created. The fate of the charter was virtually sealed by the commission, but the instructions explicitly declared it null and void. Henceforth, the style of all laws was to be 'by the Governor and Council.' Toleration was explicitly continued to all men of whatever religion who abstained from disturbing the public peace, or

---

[1] For the new commission see N. Y. Docs. vol. iii. pp. 377-82, and for the instructions, *ib.* p. 369. The commission is dated June 10, the instructions twelve days earlier.

molesting those of other denominations. But instead of the system whereby every township appointed a minister of its own denomination, the Church of England was to be established throughout the colony, and no minister of religion nor any schoolmaster admitted without a certificate from the Archbishop of Canterbury, stating that he was conformable to the doctrine and discipline of the Church of England. Liberty of the press was strictly fenced in by a system of licensing. No man might keep a printing press, nor might any book, pamphlet, or paper be printed without the approval of the Governor.

That a ruler who had but three years before set on foot a liberal system of popular government should thus, without reason or provocation, withdraw all the privileges then granted seems in the face of it inexplicable. One is tempted to fancy some intrigue under the surface, or, if not, to set down the change as the wayward caprice of a madman. That James certainly was not, nor is there any trace of secret influence at work. In real truth no such explanation is needed. In the eyes of James, constitutional government was but a method, not a principle. That men should value it for anything but its immediate and tangible results was to him unintelligible. His obtuse incapacity for entering into the feelings of his subjects prevented him from seeing that his previous liberality made his present policy seem all the harsher. To revoke privileges just granted was morally, if not technically, a breach of faith. Deliberate treachery was not one of James's failings. But a man who has neither the power nor the wish to understand those with whom he deals is almost certain to expose himself to such a charge.

No doubt another motive operated with James. He had in all likelihood already conceived the scheme of bringing the whole of the American colonies under one centralized system of administration. Already the first great obstacle to that, the charter under which Massachusetts enjoyed the privileges of self-government, had been swept away. The policy of Clarendon had been to strengthen the loyal colony of Connecticut as a check on Massachusetts. The dealing of James with the colonies went on an entirely different principle. Local rights were to be swept away to make room for a comprehensive system of despotism. Under a consolidating system of administration such as James now aimed at, the liberties just granted to New York could find no place.

James's policy of consolidation.

Such an attack on the constitutional rights of a New England colony would have called forth a whole literature of pamphlets. The citizens of New York seem to have acquiesced in it with that tranquillity with which they bore their various changes. Something of this no doubt was due to the tact and capacity of Dongan.

We may well believe that in the eyes of the Governor himself the change was but a detail of administration, trivial in comparison with the main objects which he had in view. He was the first of English public men who clearly saw, what had long been manifest to the French rulers of Canada, that a struggle was at hand in which the whole future of the English colonies was at stake. He points out the importance of La Salle's ('Lassel's') discovery. 'It will prove very inconvenient to us, as the river runs all along from our lakes by the back of Virginia and Carolina. The alliance of the Five Nations is our one security.' He saw, too, that a merely defensive policy would not

Dongan's anti-Canadian policy.[1]

---

[1] See Dongan's despatch, N. Y. Docs. vol. iii. pp. 389-415. It is not dated, but evidently belongs to the latter part of Dongan's term of office. The editor of the Documents assigns it to February 22, 1687, but without giving any reason.

suffice. As an inevitable result of such a policy the French would deal with the Five Nations as they had already dealt with the Algonquins: Jesuits, hunters and traders would permeate the country with French influence; mission stations would be supplemented by forts; with the French and Mohawks on the border united in enmity, the English colonies must abandon all hope of peaceful and secure development. To meet this danger, Dongan clearly saw, England must borrow the tactics of her rival. Missionaries must be sent among the Indians; the communication between the upper waters of the Hudson and the Canadian lakes must be secured by a line of forts; above all the English must assume towards the Five Nations a constant attitude of friendship and protection; the savages must be treated as the dependents of the English Crown; it must be understood on all hands that they would be supported against invasion. In Dongan's own words, the Five Nations were to be the bulwark of the English colonies, and they were to have no intercourse with any Christians save at Albany, and that by license of the English.

Placed as the various parties were, the policy contemplated by Dongan was quite incompatible with the maintenance of any real friendship with France. There might be a conventional exchange of diplomatic courtesies, but the attitude of the two nations could only be one of watchful jealousy, with possibilities of war always near at hand.

One of the first difficulties which stood in the way of Dongan's policy was the assumption by the French <small>Relations between the French and the Iroquois.</small> of some sort of authority over the Five Nations based on treaty. In the case of a civilized and a savage nation, an attempt to define relations in precise language is only misleading. But it certainly could not be held that the French had by the negotiations in 1666 and 1667 established any claim over either the Iroquois territory or its inhabitants, which the English were bound to respect. This was practically admitted by the French Government in the instructions given to Frontenac upon his appointment as Governor of Canada in 1673. He was to hold himself in readiness to repel, and if need be to attack, the Iroquois—language which could hardly have been used of a nation bound by treaty obligations. Frontenac's abilities might have given him a place among those generals who, like Demosthenes and Dundee, Clive and Gordon, have employed and controlled with unsparing energy and clear insight the military resources of barbarism. But such work needs above all things a free hand, and Frontenac, happily for England, was fettered at every turn. His colonists were animated by no unity of purpose, no steady loyalty to a common cause. He laboured under a cumbrous system of dual government. He as Governor was responsible for the general administration of the colony. But he had at his right hand the Intendant, an officer appointed to protect the financial interests of the Crown, and to act as a check and a spy on the Governor. As a writer, who, above all others, has fathomed the inner meaning of the history of French Canada, says, the relations of the Governor and the Intendant ' to each other were so critical, and perfect harmony so rare, that they might almost be described as natural enemies.'[1] Even the clergy, who virtually formed Frontenac's staff of Indian diplomatists, were not allies on whom he could reckon with certainty. The indefatigable zeal and energy of the French missionaries were marred by the jealousy of rival orders of Jesuits, Sulpicians and Recollects, each working under a different command, and in some measure on different systems.

[1] Parkman, *The Old Régime in Canada*, p. 266.

Frontenac at once saw that in the inevitable struggle with England the Iroquois country was the key of the situation, and that the position of France would be hopeless unless the Five Nations could be cowed or propitiated. Luckily for the Governor, his political schemes and the commercial interests of his subjects pointed to the same path. The Iroquois were at this very moment threatening those Algonquin tribes on the north-west on whom the French depended for their supply of furs. The fur trade itself was a Government monopoly, but the profits of the middleman and the various indirect advantages were enough to give the whole body of citizens an interest in it.

Policy of Frontenac.

Frontenac lost no time in establishing his influence over the Five Nations, and in impressing them with a sense of the power of France to punish and to protect. In the summer of 1673 he made a progress up the St. Lawrence and visited the shores of Lake Erie.[1] The scanty resources of the colony were used to bring home to the savage the material splendour and strength of civilization. The boats which bore the Governor and his little force were gorgeously painted and armed with cannon. The Iroquois at first proposed that the Governor should visit them in their own woodland fortresses. Some of Frontenac's counsellors would have had him accede. He himself, guided both by sense of personal dignity and insight into the savage character, sent back word that the Mohawks were the children of the French ruler, and that it behoved the father, not the son, to dictate the place of meeting. He prevailed, and the envoys of the savage confederacy came to him on the shores of Lake Erie. Friendly speeches were made, and gifts exchanged. Frontenac assumed the title of Father of the savages. The claim was not

[1] The journal of Frontenac's expedition, translated, is in the N. Y. Docs. vol. ix. pp. 95-114.

merely accepted but approved. Other French governors, so said the Indians, had claimed to be their brother, none had granted them a title so honourable as that of children. This may in itself be taken as proof that the Indians at least did not look on the relation thus asserted as one of sovereign and subject.

Frontenac was far too shrewd and resolute to rely on the unsupported influence of friendly words. Before his interview with the Iroquois the foundation of a French fort had been laid on the shores of Lake Erie. The choice of a site had been made by La Salle, not yet the explorer of the Mississippi or the discoverer of Louisiana, but already a daring and brilliant pioneer in the Western Wilderness. In him Frontenac saw a kindred spirit, one who could carry out with patient toil schemes conceived with the imaginative enterprise of a knight-errant. Advised by him, Frontenac gave orders for the building of a fort near the present site of Kingston. There the Algonquin hunter might bring his furs and meet his French customers, safe from the attack of the Iroquois. It would serve too as a visible symbol of the French advance, and as a protection to the missionaries who were carrying their spiritual invasion into the country of the confederated tribes.

By July 1673 the fort was built and garrisoned. The command of it was entrusted by Frontenac to La Salle. Two years later La Salle's position was confirmed and improved by a grant from the King. This established him in a position of something like sovereignty. He was ennobled; the fort itself and a tract of land round it were granted to him; he was to maintain and garrison the fort, and to establish a mission station there at his own cost. The wooden palisades were replaced by stone walls, and three Franciscan fathers were settled there. It is not out of place to dwell on the establishment of Fort Caratacouy, or as it was now called Fort Frontenac, in connexion with New York. Fort, factory and mission station in one, it represented the various influences which were at work doing battle for France in the coming struggle.

In other quarters French missionaries were winning a hold on the Five Nations. In 1667 permanent mis-sions were established by the Jesuit order among the Mohawks and the Oneidas. Within the next five years as many more mission stations were set up through the Iroquois country. There were marked differences in the readiness with which the various members of the confederacy accepted the Gospel. Among the Oneidas a leading chief, Gara-kanthie, became a zealous convert, and in that tribe the labours of the missionaries bore some fruit. So also they did among the Cayugas and the Oneidas. The Senecas and, what was still more important, the Mohawks were for the most part obdurate. But in no case did the French missionaries obtain such a hold upon any of the Five Nations as to be able materially to influence their policy.

French missions among the Iroquois.

There may have been isolated cases of real con-version. But if such conversions were real, their very reality made them less valuable as instruments of French political aggression. The Hurons were 'con-verted in platoons and baptized in battalions.' At one swoop a whole village became nominal converts to the faith of Christ, very real converts to the French alliance. The spectacle of the isolated Christian among the Mohawks would rather tempt his brethren to suspect and dislike those who had perverted him from the faith of his fathers.

At length the French had in the case of the Iroquois to be content with the policy adopted by the New England missionaries, and to withdraw a certain number of converts from the influence of the surrounding barbarism. At first some gave effective proof of the reality of their conversion by joining a Christian village in the country of their enemies the Hurons. In 1669 a separate village of Iroquois Christians was formed on the south bank of the St. Lawrence, opposite Montreal. This was afterwards moved further up the river. Another like community sprang up on the shores of the basin north-west of Montreal, known as the Lake of the Two Mountains, while a third on the shores of Lake Ontario was formed of Cayuga converts.

Such a system instead of strengthening French political influence among the Iroquois rather alienated and exasperated the chiefs, who saw a portion of their subjects thus withdrawn.[1] Far more could have been done by the presence of such a one as Frontenac, genial in his sympathy, yet daring and masterful in his self-assertion. But in an evil hour for France, a happy one for her rival, Frontenac was withdrawn for a while from Canada. His successor, De la Barre, brought out with him a good reputation as a soldier. His policy towards the Iroquois was from the outset an aggressive one, yet he wholly failed to strike any terror or to inspire his own supporters with any enthusiasm. On his arrival he found the Iroquois at war with the Illinois and the Miamis, Algonquin tribes and recognised allies of France. The Senecas and the Cayugas, too, had plundered the canoes of fur traders on the St. Lawrence and had attacked a French outpost.[2] De la Barre's policy was to divide the savage confederacy, and deal differently with its various members.[3] The chief offenders, the Senecas and the Cayugas, were to be at once attacked. Jesuit mission-

Frontenac replaced by De la Barre.

---

[1] Thus, in a conference with Dongan at Albany in 1687, a Mohawk chief says, ' We are much inclined to get our Christian Indians back again from Canada.' N. Y. Docs. vol. iii. p. 444.

[2] Memorandum by De la Barre, N. Y. Docs. vol. ix. p. 239.   [3] Ib.

aries were sent to enter into friendly relations with the other tribes. The English Court was asked to bind its representatives to a policy of neutrality, and a letter was sent to Dongan telling him what was intended, and asking him to prevent the sale of arms and ammunition to the Iroquois.[1]

Dongan's answer was alike guarded and firm. The Iroquois country, he affirmed, was English territory, its inhabitants English subjects. He would be responsible for their good behaviour towards the French.[2] At the end of July 1684 Dongan, in accordance with this declaration, met the chiefs of the confederacy at Albany. With him was Lord Effingham, who as Governor of Virginia had separate grievances of his own against the Five Nations. These were satisfactorily settled. It was then arranged, at the request of the Iroquois themselves, that the arms of the Duke of York should be set up over their forts. Furthermore the Senecas claimed that Dongan promised them aid—four hundred horse and as many infantry—in case of a French invasion.[3]

Attitude of Dongan.

Dongan at once communicated the result of the conference to De la Barre.[4] The Senecas were to be considered under the protection of England. All territorial disputes were to be settled by the two Home Governments. De la Barre answered that he had no intention of allowing territorial conquest. He is only concerned with the Indians, and he reaffirms his purpose of attacking the Senecas and Cayugas.[5]

Following up this declaration the French Governor marched from Quebec with a force of twelve hundred

---

[1] N. Y. Docs. vol. iii. p. 447.
[2] *Ib.* p. 448.
[3] This was stated by the Senecas to De la Barre in a conference hereafter mentioned, N. Y. Docs. vol. ix. p. 243.
[4] N. Y. Docs. vol. iii. p. 458.   [5] *Ib.* p. 459.

men. The expedition did not get beyond Fort Frontenac. There fever broke out among the troops. Alarmed by this, and disheartened by the reports brought in by his Jesuit emissaries, De la Barre gave up his scheme. Instead of a military force, a peaceful envoy was sent to bid the Seneca chiefs and their confederates to a conference.

<small>De la Barre's expedition.</small>

Meanwhile Dongan had also despatched an envoy, Arnout Viele, to secure the Indians in their allegiance to the English. In the Onondaga village, where the sachems of the Oneidas and Cayugas had come to hold counsel, Viele met the French agents. They had already won over one of the leading chiefs among the Oneidas, whose reputed eloquence had earned him a name translated by the French into Grande Gueule, and thence corrupted into Grangula. In a speech delivered before the envoys he set forth the attitude of the Iroquois to their civilized neighbours. His words are noteworthy, they give the key to the Iroquois policy, and they show the difficulties with which both French and English had to contend. According to recognised customs he personified the French and English by the names of Onontio and Corlaer. Onontio was the father of the Five Nations, Corlaer their brother. When the father and one of the sons came to blows it was for the rest of the family to interfere. The Onondagas must stop the battle between Onontio and the Senecas. If Corlaer was true to his brotherhood he would support the Onondagas. But though Onontio might be the father of the Iroquois and Corlaer his brother, neither was his master. He was a free man, the land in which he lived was his own.

If the Iroquois did not accept that position of vassalage in which Dongan would fain have placed them, yet he had in practice no cause to be dissatisfied with their attitude towards the French. While these negotiations were going on, De la Barre's force was encamped at Fort Frontenac, wasting away under a malarious fever. At the outset Meules, the French Intendant, had written a despatch to the colonial minister at home, warning him that De la Barre's designs would come to nothing. He would journey as far as Fort Frontenac and then make peace with the Senecas. His warlike preparations were but a blind to deceive the Canadians and the authorities in France.

<small>Policy of the Iroquois.</small>

Whatever may have been De la Barre's original intentions, Meules' prophecy was more than fulfilled in fact. Frontenac had refused to treat with the Indians in their own territory, deeming that he would thereby lower the dignity of France. De la Barre had no such scruples. He crossed Lake Erie and met the delegates of the Five Nations at Fort Famine on the far bank. Bruyas, a missionary acting as interpreter, charged the Iroquois with divers wrongs done against France. They had molested Frenchmen who were trading among the Algonquins, and had introduced English merchants as their rivals.

The answer of Grande Gueule was an open defiance. Taunting De la Barre with the condition of his troops, the savage told him he was dreaming in a camp of sick men, whom the Great Spirit suffered to live instead of slaying them by the sword. It was true that the Iroquois had brought English traders into the Algonquin country. So their own country had been explored by the French. Emphatically did Grande Gueule declare again that he was one of a free nation, dependent neither on Corlaer nor on Onontio. So long as they themselves were unmolested, so long and no longer would they keep the peace with both nations.

The interview ended better than might have been expected from the beginning, thanks to the pacific temper of De la Barre. He withdrew his force, having

Q

received from the Iroquois a pledge that in their attack on the Illinois they would not molest the French.[1]

One can hardly wonder that when the official report of these proceedings reached France, Seignelay, the colonial minister, should have endorsed it with the words 'to be kept secret,' and that De la Barre should have been replaced. His successor, the Marquis de Denonville, was sent out to carry through a definitely anti-English policy.[2] The English must be excluded from the Algonquin territory. At the same time French influence was to be used with James that the English arms should be removed from the Iroquois forts.[3]

De la Barre replaced by Denonville.

The first despatch sent home by Denonville showed that he entered thoroughly into the policy prescribed for him. The Five Nations must be controlled by force of arms and by a chain of forts along the lakes, and English traders who were already visiting the Huron country must be expelled. Denonville pointed out, too, that there was an easy communication between the valley of the Hudson and the lakes. Let the English only secure the friendship of the Iroquois, and they could set up trading houses on the shore of Lake Ontario. He added the suggestion that the King should buy the province of New York from England; then France would hold the whole Iroquois country and its fur trade. James is known to be necessitous. That he may be held back from such a sale by any patriotic scruples never seems to occur to the French diplomatist.

Policy of Denonville.[4]

Meanwhile Dongan was taking effective measures to neutralize French influence among the Iroquois. In the autumn of 1686 the confederate tribes, going

---

[1] For all these transactions see the N. Y. Docs.; cf. Colden, *History of Five Nations* (ed. 1750); also Parkman's *Count Frontenac and New France*.

[2] For his instructions see N. Y. Docs. vol. ix. p. 271.

[3] Seignelay to Barillon (the French Ambassador in England), *ib.* p. 269.

[4] *Ib.* p. 280.

further than they had yet done in the direction of friendship with the English, sent delegates to a conference at New York. Dongan promised them English missionaries of the Romish faith. He exhorted them not to visit Fort Frontenac, and to arrest and send to New York any Frenchmen who might be found in their country. Most important of all, he promised that if the Iroquois were attacked by the French, help from New York should at once be forthcoming.[1]

<small>Dongan's dealings with the Iroquois.</small>

As might have been foreseen, Dongan and Denonville soon found themselves engaged in an unfriendly correspondence. The outward show of courtesy was maintained. Dongan promised to do his best for the safety of the French missionaries among the Iroquois. When Denonville protested against the English traders who debauched the natives with rum, Dongan contented himself with retorting that English rum was at least not more harmful than French brandy.[2]

But there was no real attempt to conceal or ignore the antagonism of the two on vital points. Dongan's attitude was perfectly definite and simple. The Iroquois were English subjects and their territory English territory. Any attack on the one or the other would be treated as a *casus belli*. Any dispute arising to this claim must be settled by the two home Governments. Dongan's duty as interpreted by himself was simply to accept and guard a certain frontier.

It was no light task to impress this policy on a King with strong French prepossessions, swayed by the influence of astute and unscrupulous French diplomatists. For a while it seemed as if Lewis and Barillon

---

[1] This conference is shortly described by Dongan in his report above referred to (N. Y. Docs. vol. iii. p. 395), and with more detail in a letter written by Lamberville to his colleague Bruyas (*ib.* vol. ix. p. 489).

[2] For this correspondence see N. Y. Docs. vol. iii. pp. 455–78.

had won the game. The treaty agreed on at Whitehall in November 1686 seemed to rob Dongan of all for which he had striven. It was agreed that, even if war broke out between England and France in Europe, peace should be preserved in America. Neither nation was to fish or to trade within the territory of the other, and neither was to assist any Indian tribe with whom the other might be at war. In accepting those terms the English Government wholly abandoned the policy of Dongan, since the very keystone of that policy was a defensive alliance with the Iroquois. It was well for England that her representative in this crisis was something more than a mere commonplace official. Fortunate in that, she was even more so in her opponent. Dongan had clear views and no dread of responsibility. But his resolute resistance to the pretensions of France might have availed nothing against a wiser opponent.

Treaty of Whitehall.

I have alluded elsewhere to the folly, at once a crime and a blunder, by which Denonville threw away the advantages secured by French diplomacy. Fifty Iroquois chiefs were invited to a conference, and were then kidnapped and sent to France as galley-slaves. Denonville's folly was made complete by his choice of an agent. It was Jacques de Lamberville, a French Jesuit missionary, who, himself as much the dupe as any of the victims, was employed to lure the Iroquois to the meeting. The Indians acquitted him of guilt, and with rare forbearance the elders of the tribe escorted him in safety to Fort Frontenac lest he should fall a victim to the violence of any younger warriors. But hitherto trust in the missionaries had been the strongest agency by which the French could work upon the Iroquois, and that spell was now broken.

Dealings of Denonville with the Iroquois.[1]

---

[1] See authorities in N. Y. Docs. vol. ix.; cf. Parkman, *Count Frontenac*, p. 140; Brodhead, vol. ii. p. 476.

In July 1687 Denonville, with a force of French soldiers and an auxiliary force of Indians, marched into the Iroquois country. One skirmish in which the French would probably have been repulsed but for their Indian allies, the capture of a few bedridden Senecas who could not be removed and who were handed over to the Hurons, and the destruction of much corn, a loss however which in July cannot have been irreparable—this was all that Denonville could show as the fruits of his invasion.

<small>Denonville attacks the Iroquois.[1]</small>

It had, moreover, the effect of bringing him into collision with the English. Two English parties trading on the borders of the Algonquin country were arrested and sent as prisoners to Montreal.[2] Dongan at once had a conference with the Iroquois chiefs at Albany. He bade them remember that they were the subjects of the English King, and that they must have no dealings with the French without the approval of Corlaer. There could be no need for French missionaries, he himself would send them English priests; let them make peace with the Algonquins, and let them recall those converts who had gone to live in Canada. Of all Dongan's declarations perhaps the most important was his offer to build a fort on Lake Ontario, on a spot to be chosen by the Iroquois.[3]

<small>Anti-French policy of Dongan.</small>

Abortive as had been the warlike operations of De la Barre and Denonville, yet they had done enough to make the Iroquois feel the value of the English alliance. Dongan's appeal was received with hearty approval. The French were aiming, so the Iroquois said, at the total destruction of the Five Nations, and at gaining

---

[1] Denonville's own report of the expedition is in the N. Y. Docs. vol. ix. pp. 336-44. He does not mention the number of his force.

[2] This is stated by Champigny (the Intendant) in a letter to Seignelay, N. Y. Docs. vol. ix. p. 332. Denonville also refers to it.

[3] There is a full report of this conference drawn up by Livingstone, the secretary to the colony, N. Y. Docs. vol. iii. pp. 438-41.

entire control of the beaver trade. Surely the great sachem beyond the sea would not suffer the Iroquois to be extirpated, and their lands to become French territory. They themselves could no longer receive French missionaries, and would do their best to withdraw the converts, and their dealings with the French should be subject to the approval of Dongan.

The result of the conference did not end in mere friendly words. Dongan furnished the Senecas with a supply of arms and ammunition. In so doing Dongan was undoubtedly breaking the treaty of Whitehall. He might have urged with a good show of reason that it was impossible by any other means to guard his own frontier. To suffer the French to overpower the Iroquois was to lay the north-western border of New York open to invasion.

The soundness of Dongan's policy was soon illustrated. A rumour spread abroad that Denonville was preparing a force of fifteen hundred men to march in snow-shoes as soon as winter came. They were to overrun the Mohawk country, and then to attack and extirpate the settlers at Albany.[1] Thereupon Albany and Schenectady were palisaded, Dongan himself took up his residence at the former place, leaving a deputy to act for him at New York, and the Iroquois were bidden to place their non-combatants in safety within the English border.[2] While Dongan was thus acting on his own responsibility, he was doing his best to force the English Government to accept his policy. In the autumn of 1687 he sent home an officer, Captain Palmer, to explain to the English Government the state and the needs of the colony. He was to submit a scheme

---

[1] Stated in a letter from Schuyler to Dongan, September 2, 1687. N. Y. Docs. vol. iii. p. 478.

[2] *Council Minutes* in O'Callaghan, vol. i. pp. 162, 166. Dongan to Sunderland, N. Y. Docs. vol. iii. p. 477.

for a complete chain of border forts, and also to press on the English Government the advantage of sending missionaries, and the need for some scheme of consolidation which should bring Connecticut, New York and New Jersey under one common scheme of defence.[1]

Dongan's persuasions were not wasted. Barillon, the French Ambassador in London, and De Bonrepos, who was associated with him as special commissioner for negotiating on the American question, did their best to keep the advantage which had been gained and to persuade James to force Dongan to a neutral policy. Through all the dealings of James with France ran a faint spirit of independence, wayward indeed and uncertain, yet at least rising higher than the deliberate and selfish servility of his brother. Instructions were now sent to Dongan adopting his policy with a thoroughness which must have surprised its proposer. The Iroquois were to be distinctly acknowledged as English subjects, and as such protected. Dongan was furthermore authorized to build forts on the frontier at such places as he should select, and to require help from the other English colonies. The Governors and Proprietors of such colonies had been or would be notified of this. In fact there was for the first time something in declaration by the English Government of a definite anti-French colonial policy. At the same time the French commissioners were informed of this policy. They contented themselves with a somewhat hesitating protest declaring that the claim now made by the English Crown was at variance with previous admissions, and urging that the Iroquois had repeatedly acknowledged French sovereignty. With this protest they signed an agreement of neutrality, which provided that no commander either in Canada

James supports Dongan.

---

[1] Palmer's instructions are in the N. Y. Docs. vol. iii. p. 475.

or in the English colonies should invade the territory of the rival nation.¹

One cannot doubt that the course which James thus took was for the good of the English colonies. In all likelihood it saved them from irreparable evil. How far such a course could be reconciled with the pledges given a year earlier is a question perhaps best left in the region of speculative casuistry.

Fortified with this declaration of policy Dongan met the Iroquois chiefs at Albany, and bade them henceforth look on themselves as the children of the English King.² His great point seemed gained. Henceforth he might use the confederate tribes as a defensive weapon against France without any fear that his hands would be fettered by the timid or fickle policy of the English Court. Emboldened by that knowledge he demanded that the French should demolish their forts at Niagara and at Frontenac.³

Dongan was not fated, however, to have the satisfaction of himself wielding the weapon which he had forged. French diplomacy failed of its main end, but it at least had the satisfaction of seeing the man to whom it owed its defeat swept out of its path. Dongan's removal from office was indeed in a curious fashion a consequence of the policy which he had himself advocated. It would probably be unjust to James to suppose that he would have sacrificed a faithful servant to the vindictiveness of France. But among the measures which Dongan had urged was a consolidation of the colonies for purposes of defence. New York was to be strengthened by the addition of Connecticut on the north and of New Jersey on the south.⁴ In this

---

¹ The negotiations with the French commissioners are to be found in the N. Y. Docs. vol. iii. pp. 505-10. Dongan's instructions are in the same volume, p. 503.

² N. Y. Docs. vol. iii. p. 533.   ³ *Ib.* vol. ix. p. 389.

⁴ *Col. Papers,* 1685-8, 1160, 1262.

proposal Dongan did but give definite shape to views which were floating through the mind of every man who took an interest in colonial politics. The colonial policy of Clarendon by strengthening the administrative control of the mother country had done something to break down the barriers of local peculiarity which severed colony from colony. The aggression of France had done still more to create a sense of common interests and of the need for joint action. In these days the occasion would have called out a society to promote colonial union with an organization and literature of its own. As it was, one can hardly take in hand a batch of Colonial State Papers between 1690 and 1720 without lighting on some trace of such a project.

Beyond doubt, the great obstacle to such schemes lay in the mental and moral isolation of New England, above all of Massachusetts. Fortified by a not unfounded confidence in her power of independent action, by an exaggerated and arrogant, but not wholly erring, sense of aims and principles higher than those around her, the Puritan Sparta was as yet both unwilling and unfit to join in corporate life with colonies which were, by comparison with herself, but temporal unions, living for material objects. But to one like James such unfitness and such unwillingness went for nothing. The ruled were mere puppets to be ranked and marshalled by the superior wisdom and benevolence of the ruler. James doubtless believed in all honesty that he had taken a step towards accomplishing the policy prescribed by Dongan, when he placed the whole territory which had made up the New England confederacy, together with New Hampshire and Rhode Island, under the governorship of Andros. It was a mere question of mechanical convenience to extend that further, and to incorporate New York with that province. The question then rose, was New England to be attached to the government of Dongan, or New York to that of Andros? We can now see how that, whereas the attempted union under Andros was nothing but a source of irritation and disappointment, union under Dongan might at least have fulfilled the main object to be aimed at, and might have erected an efficient barrier against France. But what was with Dongan the supreme motive for colonial union, was with Dongan's master but one of several motives which made such union expedient. To bring the whole body of colonies under a uniform fiscal system was a perfectly legitimate aim. To crush out that spirit of isolation and independence which by its good and its evil made Massachusetts odious to men like Randolph was an object, not perhaps so fully acknowledged by James even to himself, but which went far to determine his policy. We judge, too, of Dongan and Andros by fuller light than was enjoyed by James and his advisers. We know the result, and the antipathy of New England to Andros seems wiser, the confidence of James more foolish, than each really was. We measure Andros by the Boston rebellion, Dongan by the events of the next half century. Those who had to make the choice could not see the policy and character of each man as a whole.

There was, moreover, one insuperable objection to Dongan as a governor for New England in his religion. Odious as Andros might be, he would be far less so than a governor who was taking measures to supply the Five Nations with Jesuit missionaries. To choose a ruler for the newly combined group of colonies who should be at once efficient and acceptable was a task which might have baffled a wiser king than James.

In March 1688 Dongan was recalled, and replaced by Andros. There is no reason to think that French influence counted for anything in this change. But the temptation to make capital out of it, by representing it as a measure friendly to France, was irresistible. We find Seignelay writing to Denonville a cheering assurance that the King of England would no longer support 'the chimerical pretensions' of Dongan.[1] In such a case the appearance of concession was almost as bad as the reality. It was not enough to resist the aggression of France and her savage allies. If that policy was to be effective the intention of resistance must be plainly and emphatically declared.

[1] N. Y. Docs. vol. ix. p. 372.

CHAPTER V.

THE REVOLUTION IN NEW YORK.[1]

Constitution of the new province.[2]

THE dismissal of Dongan was at once followed by the appointment of Andros. That appointment did not take the form of a separate commission. Andros was not like Bellomont, at a later day, simultaneously Governor of New York and of Massachusetts, by different titles. The whole territory from the west bank of the Delaware to Pemaquid was

[1] The chief authorities for Leisler's rebellion:—1. Letter from Stephen Van Cortland to Andros, July 9, 1689, N. Y. Docs. vol. iii. p. 590. 2. 'A modest and impartial narrative of several grievances and great oppressions that the peaceable inhabitants of New York lie under by the extravagant and arbitrary proceedings of Jacob Luysler and his associates.' Printed at New York and reprinted in London, 1690. N. Y. Docs. iii. 665. 3. A memorial signed by Bayard, entitled : ' A brief deduction and narrative of the several disorders, abuses and enormities and insolencies lately committed by Jacob Leyseler and several of his associates at New York since the 28th of April, 1689.' N. Y. Docs. iii. 636. 4. A short memorial in French, dated from the Hague, addressed to William and Mary, and signed by certain adherents of Leisler, entitled : ' Memoir and relation of what occurred in the City and Province of New York, in America, in the years 1690 and 1691, which the relatives and agents of the good people of that city residing in Holland have been requested to communicate in a most humble address by all possible means to their Majesties of Great Britain, protectors and defenders of the Faith.' This last is a secondhand *ex parte* statement. O'Callaghan also publishes in his Documentary History, vol. ii., a number of documents, including the minutes of the Council during Leisler's usurpation. There are also documents of value in the Col. Hist. Papers. There is a very brief official report of Leisler's Trial in Col. State Papers, 1691, p. 1379. There are also four contemporary pamphlets in the Dutch Museum under the head Leisler. None of them throw any new light on the subject.

[2] For Andros's commission and instructions, see N. Y. Docs. vol. iii. pp. 537–49.

formed into a single province, called New England. One may almost say that every element in the government of the various members of the new province was uprooted. The appointment of law officers was vested in the Governor himself. The work of legislation and taxation was entrusted to a council of forty-two, chosen from the whole province. Events showed what might easily have been anticipated, that such a system would be received very differently in New York and in New England. To the former the change was a mere legislative encroachment, such as a colony must expect and make the best of; to the latter it was an act of sacrilege. It is easy to contrast the sobriety and moderation of New York, at this juncture, with the petulant self-will, the disposition to enlarge on and even manufacture grievances, the diplomatic sharp practice of the New Englanders. But we must not forget that the provocation and the stake were in each case wholly different. Nor must we forget that Massachusetts, with all the needful political instincts developed and highly trained, at once showed herself able to supply an efficient substitute for the government which she overthrew, while New York, for lack of such training, became the prey of a disreputable adventurer, who neither understood the wants nor represented the wishes of the colony.

The system which vested the supreme authority in a council chosen by the Crown from the whole body of incorporated colonies could not work smoothly. It failed to secure the rights of the colonies not only as against the Crown, but also as against one another. If union were to be carried out effectively it must be by a system which should give each colony a due share of representation in the common government. To do that equitably and effectively was the real difficulty. James and his advisers cut the knot by sweeping away all representation. To

Evils of the system.

such a system no colony could be loyal since it offered to none any safeguard for its own special interests.

Yet the attitude of New York to the government of Andros was one of discontent only, not of vigorous hostility. Of Andros himself New York saw but little. Administrative difficulties at Boston and military duties on the frontier kept him fully employed. The government of New York was left to his deputy, Nicholson, and three councillors Far above Andros in intelligence and power of expression, Nicholson was not greatly superior in decision and practical capacity, and much inferior in moral character. His three assistants, Philipse, Van Cortland and Bayard, were all Dutchmen of wealth and good station.[1] Their nationality is a point of importance, as it clearly shows that the insurrection which followed was not, as some have held, an uprising of the old Dutch settlers against English domination. Philipse seems to have been a nonentity. Van Cortland was at the time of his appointment Mayor of New York. Protestant though he was, his demonstrations of loyalty at the rejoicings for the birth of the Prince of Wales were so exuberant as to discredit him at a later day with the followers of William. Bayard's after career showed energy and ability. But up to this time he had little scope for displaying those or any other qualities.[2] He held the colonelcy of the city train-bands, and the vindictive hostility of one under his command soon entangled him in what proved a death struggle for the assailant, and little less for Bayard.

The colony under Andros.

Before the abdication of James could become known in America, it had materially influenced the prospects

[1] Brodhead, vol. ii. p. 558.

[2] In 1675, just after the re-establishment of English rule, Bayard and others were prosecuted for signing a seditious petition. The purpose of the petition was to urge the rights of the Dutch inhabitants. The prisoners were dismissed on giving security for good behaviour.

of New York by the change which it wrought in European politics. There was no longer anything to restrain <small>French scheme of invasion.</small> Lewis from carrying out to the full those schemes which the rulers of Canada had been for years maturing. Such projects would now serve a double purpose. The aggressive policy of Frontenac would no longer entangle his country with a friendly power. The action, which would secure for France the dominion of the New World, would at the same time avenge James of his enemy. Accordingly in the spring of 1689 a scheme of attack was planned. A land force was to carry out, but somewhat more effectively, the policy of Courcelles and Tracy, and to invade New York by the line of Lake Champlain and the Hudson. At the same time a French fleet was to attack from the sea.[1]

The intended invasion was hindered by events in which no Englishman had any share. In August 1689 <small>The French invaded by the Mohawks.</small> Denonville's treachery met its appointed reward. Although there was on the frontier an exasperated enemy with every means of making a sudden attack, yet the French seem to have taken no special precautions. On a stormy night, which concealed their preparations, fifteen hundred Mohawk warriors in canoes crossed the St. Lawrence. Their point of attack was the prosperous village of La Chine, nine miles above Montreal. No blow so terrible had ever befallen civilized men at the hands of the American savage. La Chine was burnt and its inhabitants to the number of two hundred were massacred. The invaders swept on, destroying everything in their path. Montreal itself was devastated. The total loss of life was estimated at a thousand; of the invaders only thirteen fell. The fort at Caratacouy was abandoned; at one blow all the work of Tracy and Frontenac was undone.

[1] De Callières (Governor of Canada) to De Seignelay. N. Y. Docs. vol. ix. pp. 404-28.

Before the effect of this diversion was known vague rumours of the intended attack by the French reached the English colonies. Nothing could be more calculated to shatter all confidence among a community disunited in itself, justly distrusting the efficiency of its rulers, naturally, though perhaps not justly, distrusting their loyalty. To the citizens of New York, thus unsettled, came tidings even more calculated to rouse vague expectations and vague fears. In February a merchantman from Virginia reached New York with the news that William had landed in England. Nicholson scoffingly foretold that the attempt would but repeat Monmouth's. The very prentice boys of London would drive out the would-be usurper. Like Andros in New England, Nicholson determined that the matter was to be kept a secret from the people.[2] How far he succeeded does not appear. One can hardly suppose that neither by way of England nor of Holland did any rumour of William's enterprise reach the citizens of New York; nor, wanting though they were in political and national enthusiasm, can we doubt that the success of their countrymen would have been welcome tidings. Be that as it may, while the citizens of Massachusetts were declaring themselves once again a self-governing province, no measure of resistance was carried out, nor as far as we can learn meditated, at New York.

In April the citizens of New York learnt that Andros was a prisoner at Boston.[3] The position of Nicholson was even more pitiable than that of his chief. Andros at least was divested of responsibility. Nichol-

---

[1] An official summary of these events taken from the despatches of colonial officials is in the N. Y. Docs. vol. x. pp. 424, &c.

[2] Deposition of Andries Greveraet, Dec. 13, 1689, in N.Y. Docs. vol. iii. p. 660.

[3] Nicholson to Board of Trade, May 15, 1689. N. Y. Docs. vol. iii. p. 574.

son and his council were left, at a crisis when invasion from without and insurrection within were alike possible, ignorant under what king they were really serving. France they heard had declared war against England. But war against England now might mean alliance with one who would soon again be the king of England. How at such a crisis were Crown servants in a distant dependency to shape their course?

Nicholson's first step showed no lack of judgment. On the arrival of the news from Boston, the Aldermen and Council were called together. Next day, when it was reported that France had declared war, the militia officers were invited to join. All were to act as a General Convention.[1] To make the people as far as might be partners in his responsibility was doubtless Nicholson's best course. Unluckily it was a course slowly taken and soon abandoned.

Attitude of Nicholson.

With all Dongan's strenuous exertions for the defence of the frontier, he seems to have culpably neglected the safety of the capital itself. The fortifications were, if Nicholson may be believed, ruinous beyond all possibility of repair, and there was no money in the treasury to meet the cost of rebuilding.[2] The Council accordingly decided that the import duties should be applied to purposes of defence. This proposal at once called out resistance. This was made dangerous by the position rather than the character of the chief opponent. Jacob Leisler was a German emigrant, prosperous in his trade as a brewer, and holding office as a captain in one of the city trainbands. He chanced to own a valuable cargo of wine, liable for duty to the amount of a hundred pounds There is nothing to show that personal cupidity was

Dispute with Leisler.

[1] Cortland's letter to Andros, N. Y. Docs. vol. iii. p. 590.
[2] Nicholson to Board of Trade, May 15, 1689, *ib.* vol. iii. pp. 575-637; cf. Cortland to Andros, *ib.* p. 592.

R

among Leisler's failings. He was a fanatical Protestant, and on that ground bitterly opposed to the existing government, overbearing, noisily and ostentatiously ambitious. In such a man the chance of playing the part of a colonial Hampden overpowered every thought for the public welfare. Leisler refused to pay customs, basing his refusal on the technical ground that the collector was a Papist, and that therefore his commission was invalid.[1]

Leisler's action seems to have been imitated by others.[2] Even if it had stood alone, such conduct on the part of a prominent citizen must have perilously weakened the government. Meanwhile danger was showing itself in another quarter. Though there might be no active sympathy with the Dutch usurper, there were many who were ready at once to make common cause with New England malcontents. Leisler's attack on the government might have died down for lack of support. The English settlements on Long Island were the real spring of disaffection. On Long Island and on the mainland bordering Connecticut the people, acting in their townships or counties, displaced the civil and military officials.[3] Delegates were sent to Nicholson to demand that the fort should be placed in the hands of persons chosen by the commons.[4] Most alarming symptom of all, the militia, whose pay was in arrears, assembled under arms at Jamaica, and vague rumours began to spread about New York that the city would be attacked and plundered. Impoverished as the treasury was, that danger was averted by payment of arrears due.[5]

Disaffection on Long Island.

[1] *Modest Narrative*, p. 667. I do not find any contradiction of this by the Leislerian party. [2] Nicholson to Board of Trade, *v.s.*
[3] Nicholson as above, N. Y. Docs. vol. iii. p. 575.
[4] N. Y. Docs. vol. iii. p. 577.
[5] Cortland to Andros, *ib.* p. 592. *Modest Narrative*, pp. 665-6. I infer from Cortland's account that a night intervened. But he is not quite clear on the point.

The demand for control over the fort was met by a partial concession; the counties might send representatives to New York to act with the council.¹ To share the responsibilities of government at such a time was not a tempting offer, and no delegates came.

Nicholson's hot temper and lack of judgment brought matters to a head. A dispute broke out between him and Henry Cuyler, a lieutenant of militia, as to the right of the latter to post a sentry. In the course of the dispute Nicholson, it is said, was misguided enough to use the words 'I would rather see the city on fire than be commanded by you.' Instantly a rumour went abroad that the Deputy had endeavoured to enforce his authority by a threat to burn New York.² Vague discontent and alarm found a representative and spokesman in Leisler. Either, however, the enthusiasm of the people somewhat outran his own intentions, or he had enough tact and self-restraint to see the advantage of keeping for a while in the background. On the day following the dispute Nicholson called together the militia, and denied the charges against him. Cuyler repeated them, whereupon the Deputy deprived him of his commission.³ Cuyler's cause was at once taken up by his fellow-soldiers and the citizens at large. Rising under arms they demanded and obtained the keys of the fort. Up to this point Leisler seems to have taken no part in the mutiny. He now came forward and drew up a declaration on behalf of the mutineers. It set forth the Popish character of the previous government. On that ground Leisler and his followers would hold the fort till it could be delivered over to the Protestant authority in England.⁴

(margin note: The malcontents seize the fort.)

[1] N. Y. Docs. vol. iii. p. 575.
[2] *Doc. Hist.* vol. ii. p. 7. Declaration of inhabitants, &c. Col. Papers, 1689–92, p. 160.
[3] *Modest Narrative*, p. 669. [4] *Doc. Hist.* vol. ii. p. 7.

Even yet the game was not so far lost that resolute action on Nicholson's part might not have retrieved it. On the day following the seizure of the fort a demand was made by a number of the inhabitants that Bayard should take the command. This he refused to do on the plea that the fort had been occupied by the malcontents without authority, and that by taking the command he should be condoning their action.[1] In form, no doubt, he would have been violating Nicholson's authority by consenting. Practically, Bayard would thereby have given the Deputy all the standing ground which he needed till help came from England. While Nicholson and his supporters remained passive, Leisler was kindling popular feelings by appeals to Protestant sympathy, and by spreading rumours that a French fleet was in view. Acting on this alarm the train-bands assembled before the fort. Then by Leisler's order they marched in and took possession. Many of the officers, it is said, hung back and were only forced in by threats of punishment. A declaration was then drawn up and signed by all six captains and by four hundred of their men. This pledged them to hold the fort till they could hand it over to some person authorized by the Prince of Orange. It is to be observed that this declaration did not accept the English Revolution as a fact and pledge the colonists to abide by the result of it. It put the government of the colony in the position of Whig partisans, pledged to the Prince of Orange. They were to obey him not as the *de facto* Sovereign of England, but as a Dutchman and a Protestant. So far it is true that the movement was a national one, representing Dutch feelings and interests as against English. But it certainly could not be looked on as a spontaneous outburst of national feeling. Excepting Nicholson, the authorities

Progress of the Revolution.

[1] Col. Papers, 1689, p. 173.

against whom Leisler rebelled were Dutch, while Leisler himself was a German acting in obedience to that natural law, as it would seem, whereby one who has adopted a nationality always outdoes those born to it.

If Nicholson, immediately upon learning the success of William and Mary, had declared in their favour and announced that the government was to be carried on in their name, he would have cut the ground from under Leisler's feet. Instead, on June 24, he took ship for England.[1] That incapacity for political action which the rule of the Company had created and which the later rule of England had done little to remedy, now left the colony at the mercy of an aggressive and self-confident usurper. Leisler summoned a convention. Thanks, too, to Nicholson's action, Leisler was able to represent his own attitude as no more than a proper and legitimate adhesion to William and Mary. Nicholson by his flight left in force the commissions made out in the name of James. These Leisler declared void. To annul a Jacobite government and to substitute for it one loyal to the Protestant interest was but a mere following in the footsteps of the revolutionary convention at home. Had Leisler gone no further he could have had nothing to fear save in the unlikely chance of a Jacobite counter-revolution. Even the declaration with which Leisler overbore his colleagues, 'Do you talk of law? The sword must now rule,'[2] might be pardoned in one whose cause was morally, but not yet legally, a good one.

There can be no doubt that the insurgents in New York had been encouraged by the example, if not by the direct counsel, of their neighbours in New England. Connecticut sent two representatives to advise the

[1] N. Y. Docs. vol. iii. pp. 585-95. It is only fair to Nicholson to say that his council seem to have advised him to take this course.

[2] *Modest Narrative*, p. 671.

citizens of New York. The three Councillors whom Nicholson had left behind him met the delegates from Connecticut and, taking the part which the Deputy-Governor should have taken, proposed the proclamation of William and Mary. The Connecticut delegates instead of now recognising the Councillors as the repositories of legal authority chose to confer with Leisler.[1] He then by their advice proclaimed the new Sovereign.[2] Thus, one may say, his New England advisers urged him to the first step which put him in the wrong. The Councillors having expressed themselves willing to accept the authority of William and Mary, became the representatives of the Crown, and in refusing to acknowledge them Leisler was taking the first step in the direction of treason. It was a short stage onward to active disobedience. A proclamation by the new Sovereigns issued on February 19 confirmed the appointments of all existing officials in the colonies.[3] This was published by Van Cortland. Acting on the authority thus conferred he and his colleagues removed the collector whose religion had been an offence to Leisler, and substituted provisionally four commissioners of customs. Leisler thereupon, accompanied by a troop of soldiers, seized the custom house, deposed the commissioners and substituted a creature of his own.[4]

Assumption of authority by Leisler.

On June 26 a convention met at New York. The composition and action of the convention soon showed what was the real state of affairs in the colony. There was nothing like widespread enthusiasm on behalf of Leisler. But he had at his

The New York Convention.[5]

---

[1] The advice of the Connecticut delegates was given by a memorandum dated June 26, 1689. N. Y. Docs. vol. iii. p. 589.

[2] This is stated in a letter from John Tuder to Nicholson. Tuder was a lawyer who had held office under Dongan.

[3] Col. Papers, 1689, p. 22. [4] Cortland to Andros as above, cf. p. 608.

[5] *Ib.* Cf. Tuder's letter as above.

back a solid body of partisans. These may have been in part moved by a national Dutch feeling which had not been strong enough to prevent the English conquest, but which resented it. More manifest elements in the attitude of the Leislerian party were the desire of the New England immigrants for such self-government as they had enjoyed at home, and a hatred of James which would be satisfied with nothing less than the displacement of his whole official staff. It is almost certain that those who supported Leisler were a minority. But they were an earnest and resolute minority with definite views. Their opponents had no convictions to bind them together or to waken enthusiasm.

As to the actual numerical strength of parties it must be remembered that we derive our knowledge mainly from Leisler's successful opponents. But there is nothing to discredit the statement that not more than a third of the inhabitants took part in electing a convention. When one thinks of all the suffering that might have been saved by timely resistance to Leisler one feels the justice of the Greek view, that in civil strife abstinence is itself a crime. New York wholly lacked that feeling which in New England existed with morbid intensity, that the State was an inheritance wherein every citizen had a share, for which he must render an account.

In one instance the disaffection of a colony from New England took the form of demanding to be restored to its parent stock. The settlers in Suffolk county sent no delegates to the convention, but petitioned the government of Connecticut to reannex them. Connecticut had learnt the value of royal favour too well to risk it by compliance.[1]

Eighteen delegates from seven towns formed the

[1] Brodhead, vol. ii. p. 573.

convention. Not only did the convention represent a minority, but the acting part of it was little more than a minority of itself. Two delegates, seeing that the convention intended to vest supreme authority in Leisler, formally withdrew.[1] Six more seem to have stood aloof. Finally, ten delegates representing nine towns formed themselves into a committee of public safety.[2]

The one act of the convention was to vest all authority in Leisler. He was appointed Captain of the Fort, with full power to suppress any foreign enemy and to check any internal disorder. Never did a party in the act of claiming its freedom make a more full and frank confession of political incapacity.

Position of Leisler.

Leisler's own position was thoroughly and hopelessly illogical. Claiming to be the representative of the new Whig Government of England, he showed not the least anxiety to learn the wishes of that Government or to comply with its principles. His policy in New York was not even a crude and clumsy imitation of William's policy in England. For its counterpart we must look not among the recognised political parties, but among that fringe of Protestant malcontents who denounced William as a Gallio and worshipped Oates as a martyr. One of the first incidents of Leisler's rule was an anti-Papal panic, as extravagant, though happily not as bloodthirsty, as any which had terrified Londoners in 1678. Four students from Cambridge in Massachusetts appeared in the colony. Leisler suspected, for some unknown reason, that they were on friendly terms with certain of the deposed Jacobite officials in New England, and from this he deduced the opinion that their presence

Anti-Papal panic.

---

[1] *Modest Narrative*, p. 670.
[2] Only ten signed Leisler's commission. Col. Papers, 1689, p. 217.

was a danger to Protestantism and to himself. Dongan, too, had not yet left the colony,[1] and this fact, coupled with the recent attempt of Andros to escape, seems to have increased Leisler's alarm. He appears, indeed, to have worked himself into a frame of mind easy to an uneducated fanatic of meagre abilities. He believed that his own safety and that of the State were bound up together, that every public enemy took that view, and that he was therefore menaced on every side. Thus, while claiming to be the representative of the people's wishes, he never threw himself with loyal confidence on popular support.

The four unfortunate scholars were arrested; four hundred of Leisler's supporters turned out in arms, and certain leading citizens thought to be unfavourable to the usurper were summarily imprisoned. The supposed danger was furthermore made a pretext for enlarging Leisler's powers. The committee of ten granted him a commission as Commander-in-Chief of the province. He was thereby empowered to administer oaths, to issue warrants, and 'to order such matters as shall be necessary and requisite to be done for the preservation of the peace of the inhabitants, taking always reasonable advice with militia and civil authorities as occasion shall require.' The commission, however, premised that this was done in the uncertainty 'whether orders shall come from their Majesties.' This view of Leisler's position made his authority merely provisional pending the formal claim of sovereignty by William and Mary. But Leisler's more enthusiastic adherents were not content with that. According to them Leisler's authority rested on popular choice, just as William's own authority did in England. That such a contention carried with it a denial that the sovereignty of England

---

[1] Leisler to Burnet, Col. Papers, 1689, p. 690.

included the sovereignty of her colonies probably never once occurred to those who put it forward.

Leisler's government was in real truth that of a faction ruling by the sword, and resting on the sympathy of an eager minority and the inertness of the rest. Yet he saw the expediency of observing, so far as he could, certain forms of popular government. Constitutional forms one cannot call them, since such political rights as New York had yet enjoyed only existed by the pleasure of the monarchy which had been overthrown, and could only be revived by its successor. In September the counties were ordered to choose civil and military officers, and did so. At the same time the freemen of the city were called on in accordance with the charter given them by Dongan to elect a mayor and aldermen. But while Leisler availed himself of the charter to hold an election in defiance of its provisions, he restricted the election to Protestants.[1]

Elections held under Leisler.

The effect of these elections was to place the municipal government of New York and the local government of several of the counties in the hands of Leisler's partisans. If these elections had been so carried out as to secure a real expression of the popular will they would not have made Leisler's position legally valid, but they certainly would have made it morally strong. But it is clear from statements which Leisler's advocates never denied that the New York election was a mere farce. Of the whole body of freeholders not one hundred voted.[2]

In New York Leisler ruled by the power of the sword. In the county districts so far as he could be said to rule it was by the apathy of those who might have opposed him. There was, however, one

---

[1] Bayard's *Narrative*, p. 645; *Modest Narrative*, p. 675.
[2] Bayard states this.

portion of the colony which looked on Leisler with neither indifference nor fear. Albany had been incorporated under a charter from Dongan. Commanding the upper navigation of the Hudson, it became the centre of the fur trade, while at the same time it was the key of the Mohawk country and the approaches to Canada. Unlike New York, its sense of corporate unity was not impaired by a constant influx of alien nationalities.

Position of Albany.

If Leisler had any claim to represent Dutch feeling as against English, Albany should have been a very stronghold of his partisans. Nor was there any lack of Whig zeal there.[1] The news of William's landing was gladly received and the new Sovereigns were proclaimed with public rejoicings. Albany, too, was far more than New York exclusively Protestant. But the citizens of Albany were nowise minded to come under the control of a German adventurer. They had, indeed, special ground for their mistrust of Leisler. Menaced as they were by the prospect of invasion at the hands of the French and their savage allies, internal unity was of vital importance.

On August 1 the Mayor, Aldermen, Justices of the Peace, and military officers at Albany met. They gave themselves the not wholly appropriate name of a convention. The really significant point, however, is that the Mayor and Aldermen were chosen by the townsmen, that the convention included a definitely popular and representative element, and that there is no trace of any attempt to resist the authority of the convention. The first act of that body was to vest the government of the colony in

The Albany convention.[2]

---

[1] This point is emphasized in a memorial presented by certain inhabitants of New York to the Crown, N. Y. Docs. vol. iii. p. 764.

[2] For the composition and proceedings of the convention, see *Doc. Hist.* vol. ii. p. 46.

the existing officials until orders should arrive from the King and Queen of England. As an evidence of loyalty all the civil and military officers took an oath of allegiance to William and Mary. No course could have been taken more embarrassing to Leisler. His authority either rested on the approval of the citizens generally, or was exercised provisionally pending some definite action by the English Government. On the former view he could not claim to override the express wishes of the inhabitants of Albany. On the latter the course taken by them was practically identical with his own. His nearest approach to a justification was the plea of necessity, and what necessity could there be for him to force his authority on loyal English subjects against their will? One need not, however, suppose that Leisler was consciously setting up his own authority against that of the Crown. A passionate temper and a confused mind had led him to identify the success of the Protestant cause with his own ascendancy, and to believe that whatever thwarted the one must be an enemy to the other.

The men of Albany were assuredly justified in thinking that it was no time to fritter away their energy and resources in the stage antics of Leisler's grotesque imitation of sovereignty. A force of Canadians and Mohawks might at any moment appear before the gates. The church was temporarily converted into a magazine. There every member of the convention was to deposit a gun and a supply of ammunition ready for an emergency.[1] There seemed some fear that the dread of invasion would lead the inhabitants to desert the town. To guard against this an order was issued that no ablebodied inhabitant should leave without special permission.[2]

Preparations against a French invasion.

[1] *Doc. Hist.* vol. ii. p. 46.   [2] *Ib.* p. 48.

The news of the Iroquois invasion of Canada removed these apprehensions. But to some extent it merely substituted one alarm for another. The lust of plunder and bloodshed once kindled among the savages might flow into unlooked-for channels, and the very fact that the Iroquois were set free from fear of the French might make them a source of danger.

All attempts to obtain help from Leisler failed. He showed plainly that unless Albany was defended in accordance with his wishes and in deference to his authority he would rather not see it defended at all. After some ineffectual attempts to persuade the citizens of Albany by letter to accept his authority he decided to use force. A letter [1] addressed by Leisler at this time to the Assembly of Maryland is a most significant document, full of self-revelation. At a time when the very existence of the British colonies depended on effective common action, Leisler's uppermost thought is to prevent the 'Papists and popishly evil-affected adversaries to effect and bring to pass their wicked designs against their Majesties' loyal Protestant subjects.' That anyone can oppose him except under some evil influence is to Leisler utterly unintelligible. He has 'done all the diligence possible to join Albany to us, and has caused their Majesties to be proclaimed there, but they are lulled asleep by some of the former creatures to the late government.'

Albany makes itself independent of Leisler.

When these attempts at persuasion failed Leisler sent three sloops with an armed force of fifty men under one of his chief partisans, Millborne, to take possession of the town.[2]

As soon as the news of Leisler's purpose reached Albany the citizens took measures of defence. By a

---

[1] *Doc. Hist.* vol. ii. p. 19.

[2] *Bayard's Narrative,* p. 646; *Modest Narrative,* p. 675; *Doc. Hist.* vol. ii. p. 63.

popular vote the Mayor, Peter Schuyler, was formally installed as Commander of the Fort. On November 9 Millborne landed. He was admitted to the city and allowed to address the citizens. He told them that their charter was null and void as it had been granted by a Jacobite and a Papist. The Recorder, Wessels, speaking on behalf of the city, at once put the case clearly and effectively. They would accept the authority of King William if it could be produced, but not that of a company of private men at New York.[1]

For three days Millborne, as it would seem, contented himself with attempting, not wholly without success, to raise a party among the citizens. But though he was able to prove that the citizens of Albany were not absolutely unanimous in their acceptance of the convention, he could not secure any effective support. After an undignified and futile attempt to enter the fort and read his commission, he withdrew.

Millborne's departure seems to have been accelerated, if not caused, by a somewhat singular intervention. A party of Mohawks were encamped outside the town. They, apparently regarding the men of Albany as their friends, and Millborne as a spy and an invader, sent a squaw into Albany with a message. Unless Millborne at once withdraws they will fire on him. Thereupon the Mayor sent out the minister, Dr. Dellius, with the Recorder, to pacify the Indians, and to assure them that 'the business was that a person without power or authority would be master over the gentlemen here.' The Indians then sent a message to say that if Millborne showed himself they would shoot him.[2] Nothing could illustrate more forcibly how the Mohawk alliance, the very corner-stone of English colonial policy, was imperilled by the dissensions among the colonists.

[1] *Doc. Hist.* vol. ii. pp. 63-67.   [2] *Ib.* p. 73.

Within a fortnight of Millborne's departure a troop of eighty-seven men arrived, sent by Connecticut to help in guarding Albany against French or Indian attack. This at least shows that the government of Connecticut, whose natural prejudices would have been in favour of Leisler, did not condemn the attitude of Albany.¹

Meanwhile, Leisler was at every stage more and more thrusting his own authority into the foreground, and ignoring that of the English Crown. Before Millborne returned from Albany Leisler had called upon his adherents to form an association, pledging themselves to obey the Committee of Safety, and himself as its representative. There was, indeed, a reservation of fidelity to William and Mary, but there was no attempt to show that Leisler was acting under any commission from the Sovereigns.²

Further encroachments of Leisler.

One cannot acquit the home Government of having by its heedlessness played into Leisler's hands. When the news of the Revolution at Boston and the capture of Andros reached England, the Privy Council at once took measures to supply the vacancy. Nicholson was instructed to proclaim William and Mary. There was also sent him what was virtually a commission as governor, pending other arrangements. This was embodied in a letter from the King, authorizing Nicholson to call to his assistance such of the principal freeholders and inhabitants as he should think fit, and with their help to act as Lieutenant-Governor and Commander-in-Chief of the Province. This letter was addressed to Nicholson, and in his absence 'to such as for the time being take care for preserving the peace and laws' in the colony.³ Before this could be sent Nicholson himself arrived in England. One would

Proceedings of the home Government.

¹ O'Callaghan, ii. 74.
² Bayard's letter, p. 648.
³ Col. Papers, 1689, p. 307 ; N. Y. Docs. vol. iii. p. 306.

have supposed that this would have brought with it of necessity a revocation of the commission, or a complete change in its terms. Nevertheless the letter was despatched, apparently on the assumption that the Councillors whom Nicholson had left behind him were his representatives and would receive and act upon the commission. The bearer of the letter was that John Riggs, a follower of Andros, to whom we owe a large share of our knowledge of the Revolution at Boston.[1] He did not reach New York till December. He then, as might have been expected, proposed to deliver his letter to the three Councillors. Leisler at once interposed. They, he said, were Papists, and as such could exercise no authority. The plea was good neither in fact nor in law. Leisler then claimed that the letter should be delivered to him. The letter, he said, was addressed in Nicholson's absence to the *de facto* governor of the colony, and he was the only person who could be so regarded.

If Leisler had really ruled by free popular choice there would have been some moral weight in his plea. His next step showed how little ground there was for that contention. He had used the alleged approval of the citizens as a ground for seizing on the royal commission. He now used that commission to fortify his position with the citizens. To have published the King's letter would have been a fatal acknowledgment that he had been superseded, and that power was vested in the very men to whom he refused to allow any share in government. We may be sure that if the real state of things had been known, many who were now apathetic would at once have dissociated themselves from a usurper whose authority

Leisler usurps the governorship.

[1] It is clear that Riggs had not sailed on August 26, 1689, since his pass is dated that day. Col. Papers, 1689–92, p. 323. Nicholson was then in England

could be but temporary. The true secret of the letter was confided only to those who were too deeply committed to retreat; to the public it was announced that Leisler had received a commission as Lieutenant-Governor.[1]

Leisler's career shows no trace of real administrative power. But one quality at least he had, fruitful of temporary success, promptness: the promptness, of a fanatic honestly convinced of the justice of his cause and its final success, never caring to qualify his actions or to secure himself possibilities of retreat. At once and without hesitation he took upon himself all the rights and all the outward forms of his alleged office in a manner which could not fail to impress the popular imagination with a sense of authority. He nominated a council from which all who had opposed him were excluded. He established courts of justice. All civil and military officials who had held commissions from Andros were compelled to surrender them, and fresh appointments were made. A seal was struck. On one point, however, Leisler could not avoid coming into conflict with popular feeling. He issued a proclamation declaring that all public rates previously in force should still be paid. The refusal to pay duty had been Leisler's first overt act of resistance to authority. He had, it is true, based his refusal on the ground that the collector was a Papist. But, though the seeming inconsistency might be explained away, it could not fail to impress the popular imagination unfavourably. The difficulty was just one of those which the agitator turned official has inevitably created for himself. The proclamation was torn down. Leisler at once replied by another proclamation making it henceforth illegal to remove

---

[1] *Bayard's Narrative*, N. Y. Docs. vol. iii. p. 648. Certificate of Plypse (Philipse) and Van Cortland, *ib.* p. 649. *Modest Narrative*, Memorial, *ib.* p. 764. *Letter from a gentleman*, *Doc. Hist.* vol. ii. p. 264.

an official notice. This was enforced by imprisonment, and those who refused to pay the dues required suffered distraint by order of a court specially called into existence by Leisler. While Leisler was thus using his pretended authority from the Crown to overawe the citizens of New York, he was endeavouring to strengthen his position in England by representing himself as ruling by the choice and approval of the people. He sent home a despatch to the King[1] with a short and formal report of his proceedings.[2] For fuller information he refers the King to a letter, sent at the same time to Burnet. The letter contains nothing beyond vague denunciations of Leisler's opponents and the repetition of the old charges against Andros and Nicholson. Everyone who opposes Leisler is a Jacobite, and if not a Roman Catholic, at least a traitor to the Protestant religion. One part, however, stands out plainly, that Leisler was losing rather than gaining ground with his fellow-citizens. 'Though our numbers were lessened we still keep the major part.' 'We then settled the magistracy, appointed courts of judicature and proceeded to establish the militia, in all which we met in the circumstances with indifferent success.'

In a second letter to Burnet, written some two months later, Leisler complains in the same strain that he 'finds the people very slack in bringing up money;' they will not convene us an Assembly to levy the same, though our writs were long ago issued to the various counties for the purpose.[3]

It is to be noticed that Leisler speaks of the Quakers in New Jersey and Pennsylvania, and especially of Penn, as bitterly as he does of Andros and the supposed Papists. That may be looked on as in a certain sense

---

[1] Col. Papers, 1689-92, p. 689.
[2] *Ib.* p. 690. N. Y. Docs. vol. iii. p. 664.
[3] Col. Papers, 1689-92, p. 805.

prophetic. Throughout the coming century the Quaker colonies were often insubordinate in their attitude to the Proprietors and to the British Government. They can hardly be said ever to have come into line with the other colonies, or to have joined heartily and unreservedly in any movement of resistance.

The change in Leisler's position forced action upon his opponents. Hitherto they might feel that they were only suffering under a transient tyranny made possible because those in authority in England had no knowledge of the state of affairs in the colony. Now the blunder of the English Government, backed by the audacity and good luck of Leisler, had so altered affairs that a mere policy of delay would no longer suffice. The English Government must learn that the popular approval which Leisler claimed was really an unwilling obedience extorted by misrepresentation and terror. Accordingly some of Leisler's chief opponents, including Bayard and Van Cortland, drew up letters to be sent to the authorities in England. Dishonesty does not seem to have been naturally one of Leisler's failings. But by yielding to the temptation of opportunity he had forced himself into a position which could only be maintained by continued deceit. To his fellow-colonists he assumed the position of a public servant, responsible only to the Crown. To the English Government he assumed the position of a popular leader forced into power at a crisis by the general will. Such a game of double pretences could only end in ignominious discovery. An experienced and sagacious intriguer might have been glad to retreat. But the wit to discern a hopeless position and the moral courage to abandon it were qualities not to be found in company with Leisler's vulgar audacity and brutal self-confidence. He might at least delay the evil hour by hindering communications between his enemies in the colony and the authorities at home. With this hope he intercepted and read the letters from Bayard and his allies. To attempt to discredit Leisler in England was 'a hellish conspiracy,' and the writers were at once arrested. Leisler was not of a temper to be content with rendering an opponent innocuous. Bayard was refused bail; he was publicly exhibited to his fellow-citizens in chains, and his house was pillaged by a mob of Leisler's followers.[1]

Meanwhile the men of Albany were holding their ground stubbornly against the usurper.

Evils were at hand worse than internal disunion. During the autumn of 1689 Frontenac made strenuous attempts to win over the Five Nations. The task of counteracting him was left to the self-appointed rulers of Albany. At the beginning of 1690 a great council of the Five Nations met at Onondaga to consider what policy should be adopted towards the rival powers. Before they met messengers were sent to Albany to confer with the English. They returned bringing the message that a governor sent from England was every day expected, and that his arrival would be the signal for an attack on Canada. They were accompanied by an interpreter, so that the English might know what passed in the councils of their allies.[2]

Dealings with the Five Nations.

Never had that alliance, the keystone of English supremacy, and almost a needful condition to the existence of the English colonies, been in greater danger. Peter Millet, a Jesuit missionary who for twenty years had lived and laboured among the savages, was now with the Iroquois striving not unsuccessfully to undo the mischief wrought by the

---

[1] Leisler himself in a private letter (*Doc. Hist.* vol. ii. p. 36) reports the arrest of Bayard and his associates. For the other incidents see *Doc. Hist.* vol. ii. pp. 37-246, and the *Modest Narrative.*

[2] Colden's *History of the Five Nations* (ed. 1750), pp. 108-10.

timidity of De la Barre and the treachery of Denonville. His labours were in part successful. The members of the savage confederacy had more than once shown that they could act independently, and the Oneidas and Cayugas now refused to follow the other three tribes. But the rest of the confederacy accepted eagerly the policy suggested from Albany. They would not send an embassy to meet Frontenac. They called loudly for an aggressive policy against France. Let the English no longer content themselves with lopping off the branches; let them strike at the root by the capture of Quebec, and the tree of French colonisation would at once wither.[1]

Unhappily the English colonies, disunited and distrustful of their rulers, were in no condition for such measures. This Frontenac doubtless knew. He saw that the wavering allegiance of the Five Nations might be yet further shaken by bold measures, and that it was his true policy not to wait for the blow but to anticipate it. The season made it impossible to renew the scheme of the last year for a joint invasion by sea and land. He decided on a land invasion of the English colonies along three lines. The two invading parties to the north-east aimed at nothing more than harrying the frontier of New England. The third attack was the real backbone of Frontenac's scheme. It was intended to seize Albany and thus to obtain the mastery of the Hudson. The French policy of that day was identical in principle with the French policy of fifty years later, differing only in that it substituted for the arc of the Great Lakes, the Ohio, and the Mississippi, the narrower one of the St. Lawrence, Lake Champlain, and the Hudson.

French scheme of invasion.

The force designed to invade New York consisted

[1] Colden's *History of the Five Nations* (ed. 1750), pp. 108–10.

of a hundred and fourteen Canadian militia, with ninety-six Indian allies. The wisdom of that policy by which the French missionaries had detached a body of converts from the Five Nations and settled them as a separate village was now seen. Of the Indian allies only sixteen were Hurons. The rest were Mohawk converts, whose knowledge of the track and of the country to be invaded was of inestimable service.

The Indian alliance was a needful condition for French success, yet it was in some ways a hindrance. The savages were wholly indifferent to the French schemes of invasion for purposes of conquest. All that they wanted was a raid which should give them scalps and plunder. Had the French officers been left to themselves they would have marched direct on Albany. But the Indians saw an easier and more accessible prey in Schenectady. That place was guarded by only twenty-four men. It might therefore with perfect safety have been left in the rear, while an attack upon it was likely to rouse an alarm at Albany, and thus to hinder the main purpose of the expedition. Nevertheless the council of the Indian allies prevailed, and it was decided that Schenectady should be the first point of attack.[1]

When the representative whom Leisler had sent to Albany to summon the citizens to accept his authority had failed there, he had gone on to Schenectady. He had not persuaded the inhabitants to accept the authority of Leisler or to sever themselves from Albany, but he had done something to beget a sense of insecurity, and to sow mutual distrust between the citizens and the garrison. The village consisted of one long street, with a palisade running outside and a gate at each end. These the inhabitants, with incredible folly, left open. The commander of the

Destruction of Schenectady.

[1] Monseignat's report mentioned below.

garrison warned them, but to no purpose. At midnight on Saturday, February 9, the invading force reached the village. Wearied with their journey and numbed with cold they would have been powerless if they had been resolutely resisted. But twenty-four soldiers unsupported by the inhabitants could do nothing. The whole garrison perished and sixty inhabitants with them. As many more were taken prisoners, while five-and-twenty made their escape. Before dawn on Sunday morning one survivor, a wounded man on a crippled horse, reached Albany, as Brydon reached Jellalabad. The alarm was immediately given and the militia called in from the neighbouring villages. That was needless. The Indian assailants, true to their usual mode of warfare, had withdrawn after a single onslaught with their prisoners and their plunder.[1]

Leisler's action when the news reached New York was characteristic. The colony was to be saved not by suppressing jealousies and differences, and by a union of parties, but by a complete extirpation of what he would have termed the Popish faction. All persons who had held commissions from Dongan or Andros were to be arrested. As a result some of the most influential settlers fled, among them Dongan who had stayed on in the colony, but now found refuge in New Jersey.[2] Leisler's wrath

<small>Violent conduct of Leisler.</small>

---

[1] We have two accounts of the Schenectady massacre, one from the French, the other from the English side; the former is the fuller. It is contained in a report written by Monseignat, the Controller of Marine and Fortification, in Canada. A translation of it is in the New York Historical Documents, vol. ix. The translator thinks, apparently with good ground, that the report was addressed to Madame de Maintenon. There is on the other side a report by Peter Schuyler, Mayor of Albany, in the third volume of the *Andros Tracts*. Colden also describes the massacre (pp. 113–5), and there are several references to it in letters from New York.

[2] Col. State Papers, 1689-92, p. 886.

extended to all who in any way countenanced the convention at Albany. He sent a letter of almost incredible insolence to the government of Connecticut.[1]

The Governor and Mayor of Connecticut are denounced as favouring the rebellious party at Albany. Unless they immediately 'control[2] the orders they have issued for obedience to the convention, the forces belonging to them at Albany shall be declared enemies and treated accordingly.' Finally, it is demanded that Allen, the secretary for Connecticut, be dealt with as a traitor.

In February Leisler, acting on his imaginary commission as governor, issued writs for the election of an Assembly. The appeal roused no enthusiasm. East-hampton, one of those townships of New England origin where Whig feeling was strongest, declared its intention of seeking incorporation with Connecticut.[3] Leisler's dealing with the Assembly showed what indeed he had made manifest enough, that he had no real confidence in the people. Petitions came in to the Assembly from the victims whom Leisler had imprisoned. Dreading the result Leisler prorogued the Assembly after a session of a few days.[4] This was but of a piece with his treatment of Bayard and his conduct in the matter of the intercepted letters. A government claiming to exist by popular approval and yet obliged to stifle free speech is an anomaly too glaring to survive save under favourable conditions

Leisler calls an Assembly.

---

[1] The letter addressed by the Council in New York to the Governor of Connecticut, and signed by Millborne, is in the Col. State Papers, 1689-92, p. 776. Though it is signed by Millborne, we may safely credit Leisler with the authorship, at least in substance.

[2] 'Control' apparently means withdraw.

[3] Their letter to Leisler is in the *Documentary History*, vol. ii. p. 104.

[4] The fact of the petition is stated in Van Cortland's letter. Mr. Brodhead is my authority for the proroguing of the Assembly. I have not been able to verify it from any contemporary authority. There is, however, no sign of its existence between April and September.

and dexterous management. In the presence of external danger the demagogue-tyrant may make himself necessary to the community, or he may delude his subjects with forms, blinding them to the fact that the freedom underlying the forms had vanished. Leisler had not the executive power for the one part nor the diplomatic skill for the other. Whatever hold he may have had on the people was gone; his power was a bubble, ready to burst the moment that anyone with real authority from England appeared. As the year went on, the true state of affairs became more and more manifest. A memorial was addressed to the English Sovereigns, signed by thirty-six men of position, several of them ministers of religion, setting forth the tyranny which prevailed at New York, arbitrary imprisonments, banishment, and violation of private correspondence. Leisler was in this denounced as 'an insolent alien,' his supporters as a rabble.[1] Men refused to pay the dues demanded by the government, and Leisler himself was assaulted in the streets by a mob and only rescued by main force.[2] Clutching desperately at the last remnants of power, he prepared an address, pledging the citizens to be faithful to him as the representative of the Sovereign, and declared that all who refused to sign it should be treated as traitors.

Leisler's career was now varied by the one incident in it which shows some approach to statesmanlike perception and capacity. That a man assuredly not more far-sighted than the ordinary run of colonial officials should have set on foot the first working scheme for a union of the colonies is strong proof that such projects had already found general acceptance. At the summons of Leisler, Massachusetts, Plymouth, and Connecticut sent dele-

Leisler proposes a colonial convention.

---

[1] The memorial is in the N. Y. Docs. vol. iii. p. 748.
[2] Depositions in N. Y. Docs. vol. iii. pp. 740, &c.

gates to a meeting at New York. Maryland likewise was summoned. It sent no delegates, but its government entered into communication with the congress. A force of eight hundred and fifty-five men was raised, to which New York contributed half.

This first attempt at an allied expedition foreshadowed the difficulties which for more than half a century beset every like enterprise. The colonies did not contribute the contingents which they had promised. Massachusetts and Plymouth withheld theirs, pleading that all their available forces were needed at home to defend them against a French attack. Leisler at first wished to give the command to his follower, Millborne. Such an appointment, however, would have been displeasing to Connecticut; the command was given to Fitz-John Winthrop, and Millborne took the post of commissary. Winthrop was a kindly, upright man, not lacking in sense, and of unimpeachable courage and honour. But in the Winthrop family power to rule and conspicuous energy seem to have disappeared with the death of its founder. Yet one may doubt whether a more vigorous commander could have achieved anything with such material. At the beginning of August the force set forth. They were dependent on their savage allies for all the material of transport. The supply of canoes was insufficient; when the English proposed that more should be built the Indians explained that so late in the year the bark would no longer peel. The excuse may have been a good one: the English allies were evidently in that hopeless condition, dependent upon subordinates whom they distrusted, but yet could not convict of fraud. The Indians pleaded, too, that they were crippled by an outbreak of small-pox. That at least was true; the English soon had proof of it by the appearance of it in their own camp. On August 15

Failure of the campaign.

a council of war decided that the expedition was hopeless and Winthrop led his troops back to Albany.

Such small share of success as rewarded the expedition fell to the lot of New York. John Schuyler, the brother of the Mayor of Albany, was detached with a force of forty English and a hundred and twenty Indians to make an attack on a French settlement, Prairie De la Madeleine, facing Montreal. As a mere raid the attack was brilliantly successful. The settlement was devastated, six of its defenders killed and nineteen carried off prisoners, with trifling loss to the assailants. But the victory did nothing to divert the French from the defence of Quebec or to further the general purposes of the campaign.[1]

<small>Schuyler's raid.</small>

As far as the blame of failure could be laid on any one person, Leisler and Millborne were assuredly responsible for it. The former by his insolent and arbitrary attitude had alienated the men of Connecticut, and quelled the not very ardent temper of Winthrop. Millborne as commissary had done nothing to further a task which depended on good arrangements for transport and supply quite as much as on courage or military skill. Nevertheless Leisler, in the fury of disappointment, treated Winthrop as criminally responsible. At first he was put under arrest. The disapproval of the troops at this proceeding was too strong to be faced, and Leisler had to content himself with defaming Winthrop's character, charging him in despatches sent to the governments of Massachusetts and Connecticut with treachery, cowardice, and uncleanness of life.[2]

In September the adjourned Assembly again met. Its proceedings were a last despairing effort on the part of the Leislerian party to crush resistance with the strong hand. No person was to leave Albany or Ulster without Leisler's leave on pain of a

<small>The Assembly meet again.</small>

---

[1] *Col. Doc.* vol. iii. p. 753.   [2] *Doc. Hist.* vol. ii. p. 169.

hundred pounds fine; all persons who had already so left these counties must return within fourteen days. The same rule was applied to the whole colony, save that the term of grace was there extended to three weeks. Disobedience to either of these orders was made criminal, without the protection of a specified penalty.

Leisler's wrath against Winthrop was not all the result of disappointed patriotism. The failure of the Canadian expedition had deprived him of the one plea which in the eyes of his fellow-citizens could have justified his arbitrary policy. Waste and dishonesty are the vices which make a despotic government unpopular. It was reported that Leisler and his friends were growing rich, and that distraints against public offenders were so conducted as to create a profitable trade with the West Indies. The people of Queen's County and of various townships on Long Island refused to pay their taxes, and showed other symptoms of disaffection. Leisler's one policy for dealing with complaint was to gag it. Millborne, already an unpopular man and of tarnished character, was authorized to arrest disaffected persons, with power to search houses and shops. But it was impossible to stifle the complaints of Leisler's victims. Early in 1691 the Secretary of State, the Earl of Nottingham, received a memorial, drawn up in the previous November, from the inhabitants of four Long Island townships, which set forth Leisler's misdeeds, and implored the interference of the Crown.[1]

<small>Decline of Leisler's influence.</small>

It is little to the credit of William's advisers that such a petition should have been needed, and that the grievances of the New York colonists should have gone so long without redress. One cannot indeed wonder that there should have been some delay in finally settling the constitution of the

<small>Apathy of the English Government.</small>

[1] Col. Papers, 1689-92, 1170; Brodhead, vol. ii. p. 625.

colony. New York was in real truth the point on which the whole future of the American Empire of Great Britain turned. No settlement could be satisfactory which did not make some provision for a scheme of defence common to the body of colonies. James had made a crude attempt to solve the difficulty by placing the whole group of northern colonies under a government responsible only to the Crown and containing no element of representation. That was indeed a hopeless policy, yet it at least acknowledged a difficulty which William and his successors either ignored or abandoned in despair. To satisfy the aspirations of New England after self-government, and yet to retain that control which was needful for the safety of the frontier, were difficulties which might well excuse delay. But there was at least no excuse for leaving New York for two years at the mercy of Leisler. He might have been superseded by a provisional government without any attempt to settle at once the future of the colony. For, be it remembered, Leisler was something more than an arbitrary tyrant. He was a tyrant masquerading in the show of constitutional authority, bringing discredit on the Crown by professing himself its representative. We know now that his authority had no moral weight, that it was no better than a forged commission. The majority of his fellow-citizens may have been puzzled as to the origin and extent of his authority, but in a vague way they believed in its existence.

Months passed from the day that William and Mary were acknowledged Sovereigns of England before any action was taken towards New York. In November 1689 a Governor was appointed. His commission contained provisions which made it virtually a constitution for the colony. The Governor was to be assisted by a Council nominated by the

<small>Colonel Sloughter appointed Governor.</small>

Crown. He was to call an Assembly of the representatives of the freeholders. Their enactments might be vetoed in the first instance by the Governor, or later by the Crown. The apportionment of representatives was implicitly left to the Governor. The right to adjourn or dissolve the Assembly was expressly conferred upon him.[1]

The system was a mere reproduction of that in force before the attempted consolidation under Andros. There was assuredly nothing in its provisions to justify the long delay which preceded it. And while William and his advisers were to blame for the tardiness of their measures, they did not make amends by any specially wise choice of instruments. The governorship was given to Colonel Sloughter. He seems to have been a man of moderate temper and fair common sense. But he had no colonial experience, and his private character was not free from reproach.[2] There was nothing in him to call out the respect and confidence which were needed at such a time. His subordinate, on whom in case of any mishap to the Governor his authority would devolve, was Ingoldsby, a respectable official of no special capacity. At such a crisis the presence of one like Nicolls would have been invaluable. In his hands the authority of the Crown would have appeared as a moderating and restraining influence, delivering from tyranny and making the future recurrence of either tyranny or anarchy impossible. The measures which Sloughter adopted, or one should rather say to which he gave an inert and unthinking consent, may have been needful. The punishment which overtook Leisler and his associates certainly did not exceed their moral deserts. It may not have been even needlessly severe.

---

[1] The commission is in the N. Y. Docs. vol. iii. pp. 623-9.
[2] See Brodhead vol. ii. p. 594.

But it was so administered as to seem not the justice of supreme authority, but the revenge of a faction.

One thing only can be urged in extenuation. Whenever the English Government made any error, the turn of events was sure to bring out all the evil consequences in their fullest form. To have sent out a commission to Nicholson when Nicholson was actually known to be in England was a strange blunder. But it was the astounding recklessness of Leisler, perhaps in some measure the timidity and lack of promptness shown by the resident Councillors, which made the error a fatal one. So it was after Sloughter was commissioned. The demands made upon the transport service by the Irish campaign and the weakness of the English navy made it almost impossible to allot vessels for Sloughter and the troops which it was needful to send with him.

Sloughter's arrival delayed.

In October 1690 they set sail in four vessels. The same mishap befell them that befell the Virginian fleet in 1609. The frigate *Archangel* with Sloughter on board became separated from her consorts, and the three others reached New York without the Governor.[1] Ingoldsby was commander of the troops, and as such was entitled to the supreme command in the absence of his superior. That being so, the delay in Sloughter's arrival need have made no difficulty in the pacification of the province. But Leisler had made it clear that he would create every hindrance, clinging to power without a thought of consequences. Ingoldsby on landing made no attempt to exercise civil authority, but contented himself with

The troops arrive without Sloughter.

---

[1] Sloughter to Nottingham, N. Y. Docs. vol. iii. p. 756. For what followed our authorities are: (1) a letter from Chidley Brooke, a councillor who accompanied Ingoldsby to Sir Robert Southwell, and Sloughter's own despatches. These are in N. Y. Docs. vol. iii. pp. 758-62. (2) Leisler's own declaration against Ingoldsby. This was in Dutch. There is a translation in the *Documentary History*, vol. ii.

demanding possession of the fort. This Leisler refused, contending that his authority could only be superseded by that of the Governor, and that it included the control of the fort and of the troops. It is clear that Leisler had the true fanatic's gift of persuading himself of that which he wished to believe, and that the grotesque fiction by which he had acquired a pretence of constitutional authority had become in his own eyes a grave reality.

At first Leisler's tone towards Ingoldsby was moderate. He would do everything for the convenience of the troops short of surrendering the fort. The troops were to be billeted in the city. The fort could only be given up to the Governor.

<small>Defiant attitude of Leisler.</small>

If Leisler had really held the position of delegated authority to which he pretended, his contention would have been a reasonable one. Unfortunately for him Ingoldsby had a ready answer. Where was Leisler's commission? He had no formal authority in the fort, and in the absence of such authority he was bound to surrender it to the military commander. Leisler's refusal to recognise Ingoldsby's authority might not be in itself treasonable; but if in any other matter he crossed the line of treason this was certain to be regarded as an aggravation of his offence.

Leisler's refusal to surrender the fort was followed by an even grosser defiance of the royal authority. Ingoldsby demanded the release of Bayard and that of another political prisoner, Nicolls, who like Bayard was nominated to the Council. When Leisler first heard of the appointment of Bayard, Cortland, and Philipse as Councillors, he burst into a fury. They were Popish rogues. He would destroy three thousand such in defiance of the King's commission. He now refused to liberate Bayard and Nicolls.

Ingoldsby showed no wish to push matters to

extremities. For two months he took no active measures beyond quartering his troops in the town-hall. That done he waited for the arrival of Sloughter. Meanwhile Leisler was more and more drifting into the position of an armed traitor. He or some of his more extreme partisans made a wild attempt to discredit their opponents by declaring that they were Jacobites with forged commissions. The garrison of the fort was strengthened by levies introduced from New Jersey, and it was victualled against a siege. Tradition represents Ingoldsby as hasty and violent. His conduct at this stage of proceedings shows the very opposite qualities. If he was to blame, it was for inertness and dread of responsibility, for sitting with folded hands while sedition was gaining strength. By prompt action now he might have saved future bloodshed. Nothing can prove more fully the hollowness of Leisler's cause, its lack of any real hold on popular feeling, than its failure to make any head even against such patient and half-hearted opposition.

Ingoldsby, indeed, seems to have been perfectly willing to await Sloughter's arrival. It was Leisler's own deliberate act that finally led to strife. His whole attitude was so strange, his purpose so hopeless, that one can hardly impute to him a definite policy. But he would seem to have been using the respite granted to him by Ingoldsby's inaction to garrison and provision the fort, and to have decided, as soon as he was strong enough, to take active measures of attack. In the middle of March having three hundred men in the fort, Leisler sent a message to Ingoldsby and his fellow-counsellors bidding them disband their troops under pain of death.

The insolence of the demand was even surpassed by the violence of the language in which it was couched. Ingoldsby and his 'evil counsellors' are described as 'enemies to God, their present Majesties, and the peace and welfare of this people and province.'

Such a defiance to a commissioned officer at the head of the King's troops would assuredly have justified the immediate use of force. Ingoldsby contented himself with a mere warning that an attack such as Leisler threatened would be an act of treason. He did not even demand submission, but suffered Leisler and his adherents to keep the peace till Sloughter arrived, and Ingoldsby and the Council would be content.

Leisler now showed that he was ready to pass the line which separated treasonable words from treason-able acts. He may possibly have hoped to overwhelm the royal troops before the arrival of Sloughter, and thus to be able to treat with the Governor from a position of armed supremacy.

Leisler fires on the troops.

Early on March 17 Ingoldsby's answer to Leisler was handed in to the fort. In less than half an hour the garrison opened fire. The negligence of Ingoldsby had suffered his enemy to obtain an important military advantage. Not only had Leisler garrisoned the fort, but his troops also held an outwork on the landward side, probably on the high ground by the Hudson which commands the town.

This advantage, however, was sacrificed by the indecision of Leisler's lieutenant, Brasher, who had command of the outwork. He apparently shrank from the thoroughgoing policy of his commander, and leaving his post went to the fort for further orders. Before he could reach the fort he was arrested, and his troops, having the responsibility of treason thus thrown on their own shoulders, laid down their arms and abandoned their post.

In spite of this defection, the first exchange of hostilities was all in favour of the Leislerites. The musketry fire of the fort killed two men and wounded several more. Ingoldsby's artillery was less fortunate, and its only recorded result was an accidental discharge which killed six loyalists.

Discouraged probably by this, Ingoldsby seems to have contented himself with keeping his men out of fire and waiting the turn of events. The day passed with no active renewal of hostilities. But on the morrow Leisler's followers heard the unwelcome noise of cheering in the streets. Their fears interpreted the sounds: the Governor must at length have landed. It was so: after a delay of three weeks at the Bermudas the *Archangel* had reached America and was at anchor in New York Bay. The Council at once hurried to meet Sloughter with news of the state of affairs, and brought him without delay into the city. Having read his commissions and sworn in his Council, he at once sent to demand the surrender of the fort.

<small>Arrival of Sloughter.</small>

The time had now come for Leisler to show whether there was any foundation for his repeated professions of loyalty. Three times did Sloughter command him to surrender the fort. At first Leisler met the demand by equivocation. He must see direct orders from the King's own hand to himself. He could not give up the fort, but he would negotiate with Sloughter. Finally, when it was plain that Sloughter would be content with no compromise, his demand was met with flat refusal. Such conduct can only be explained in one of two ways: either Leisler was, as some of his enemies hinted, insane, or else he had wholly deluded himself as to the true state of popular feeling, and believed that even at the eleventh hour there would be some outburst on the part of the citizens which would give him the upper hand.

The nearest approach which he had made to concession had been to send out Millborne and another of his chief supporters, a lawyer, Peter de la Noy, to treat with Sloughter. They were not suffered to return, but put under arrest.

Their detention seems to have convinced Leisler that the Governor was in earnest. He now for the first time showed a wish to come to terms. He sent a message professing himself ready to yield up the fort and give an account of his conduct. But his day of grace was past. Sloughter refused to negotiate with an armed rebel, and sent a message to the fort bidding the garrison lay down their arms and withdraw. If they did so they should be pardoned, excepting only Leisler and those who had acted on his Council. The garrison at once accepted the terms offered. Sloughter's troops occupied the fort and Leisler was made prisoner without resistance. Bayard and his fellow-prisoner were set free, and, if we may believe tradition, their very fetters were used upon Leisler.

Submission of Leisler.

Sloughter's commission gave him power to constitute criminal courts. In accordance with this he appointed a court to try Leisler and his chief accomplices.[1] It consisted of three trained lawyers, Joseph Dudley of New England, Thomas Johnson and William Pinhorne, of Ingoldsby and three other soldiers, of the commander of the *Archangel*, Hicks, and of Sir Robert Robinson, an ex-Governor of Bermuda. Of this somewhat cumbrously large tribunal six were to form a quorum, provided that either Dudley or Johnson was present. The partisans of Leisler found fault with the composition of the court. Some of its members were personally hostile to Leisler, others too young to have judgment or influence. But in truth in such a trial there was little for the jury to do. The facts were all matter of notoriety. The only question at issue was the question of law: was such conduct as

Trial of Leisler.

[1] See the official account of the trial.

Leisler's treasonable? Was the alleged authority from the Crown, which he had pleaded throughout, valid? Nothing in the composition of the court showed any wish to bear hard on Leisler. None of the members had, as far as appears, any personal grievance against him. The chief fault in its composition, its unwieldy size, was certainly in favour of the prisoners. For in so large a court there was no great likelihood of unanimity, and in a criminal trial a lack of unanimity is almost sure to make for acquittal. Nevertheless Leisler, as throughout, clutching at every shift as if it contained hope, begged Sloughter to take the matter into his own hands. This he might possibly have done lawfully under the orders given him by the King in Council. Indeed, while the court was sitting on Leisler's case, Sloughter was conducting a concurrent inquiry into the charges embodied in the various reports and petitions sent home by Leisler's opponents. But to make such an inquiry with a view to reporting to the Government in England was a very different thing from trying Leisler on a criminal charge, and Sloughter's refusal to take on himself this responsibility was assuredly no grievance.

In spite of Sloughter's refusal the course of the trial did practically shift the main question on to the Governor and his Council. The principal count on which the prisoners were tried was that of traitorously levying war against the Crown. Leisler himself and nine of his chief followers were put on trial. Eight of them pleaded not guilty. Leisler and Millborne technically refused to plead. They suspended their plea till the court should have decided on the question whether the intercepted commission to Nicholson had not authorised Leisler to act as he did. This was to all practical effect a plea of not guilty. The court, however, refused to take upon itself the responsibility of deciding the question so submitted, and referred it to Sloughter and his Council. They ruled that the commission in question had given no authority to Leisler. In the face of that declaration the court could only take one course. Leisler's actions were matter of open notoriety; there could be no dispute as to fact. Leisler and Millborne now made it plain that when they refused to plead till the preliminary question of authority had been settled, they were merely adopting a subterfuge. For when the court pronounced the question settled they still remained mute. The court passed sentence. Of the ten prisoners, six beside Leisler and Millborne were found guilty and sentenced to be drawn and quartered. The court, however, appended to their verdict a recommendation that execution should be deferred till the King's pleasure was known, unless any insurrection of the people should necessitate the execution.

To let a question of life and death depend on political expediency is on the face of it a repellent policy. But to deal on such a principle with a life justly forfeited is a widely different thing from sacrificing an innocent man in obedience to supposed necessity. If ever a man of free choice played a game in which the stake was his own life, Leisler did. If we blame those who approved of Leisler's death we must blame them not for injustice to their victim, but for having misinterpreted the signs of the times, for having seen a necessity for strong measures where no such necessity existed. There were not in Leisler's case any of those conditions which may beget a conflict between public policy and reasonable human feeling. If Charles Edward had been captured his execution would have shocked the moral sense of men, because he was but carrying out a theory held by upright and humane men, and impressed on him from his childhood. The execution of the mutineers at the Nore shocks us,

The sentence on Leisler.

because they had been goaded into rebellion by the folly and wrong-doing of their superiors. Leisler was the victim neither of his own theories nor of others' wrong-doing. He threw a province into confusion, wantonly and for his own personal objects. For two years, while he had ruled as the head of a faction, his opponents had suffered under a greedy and brutal tyranny.

One plea, and one only, could be urged for mercy. It might be said that Leisler's faults of temper and character prevented him from being dangerous, that he did not embody any general feeling of disaffection which it was needful to intimidate, and that therefore imprisonment or banishment would have sufficed.

Let that be as it may, at least the blame if any does not rest on the Governor nor on any of his official colleagues. The worst that could be said of Sloughter was that he did not show sufficient firmness in resisting the cry for blood. There is no reason to doubt his statement made in a despatch to the English Government, that 'the loyal part of the colony was very earnest for execution.' He may perhaps have erred in his opinion that 'if the chief ringleaders be made an example, the whole country may be quieted, which otherwise will be hard to do.'

Sloughter lost no time in enabling the colonists to express their opinions and wishes legally and constitutionally. Early in April he issued writs for an Assembly. It was but natural that the members returned should have been enemies to Leisler and his faction. A party just beaten and discredited, whose leaders are in prison, is not likely to obtain even its due share of influence in a general election. But the Leislerites had at a later day full opportunity of making their grievances heard, and we meet with

<small>An Assembly summoned.</small>

nothing to show that the election was in any way an unfair one.

The first proceeding of the new Assembly was to pass a resolution condemning Leisler's conduct, and attributing the massacre at Schenectady to his misgovernment. Nevertheless, they declared at the same time that the question of a reprieve was one on which they could not give an opinion.

Meanwhile pressure was being brought to bear on Sloughter from various quarters to force him into a policy of severity. The Mohawks, it was said, were exasperated by Leisler's conduct in the Canadian war. They were showing an inclination to intrigue with the French: the fate of Leisler might confirm or overthrow their tottering loyalty. The anti-Leislerite party might be temperate in their public and official utterances, but in private the Governor was beset by the cry for blood, a cry, it is said, in which many women of high position in the colony loudly joined.[1]

<small>Public opinion as to the execution of Leisler.</small>

Sloughter's first intention manifestly was to divest himself of responsibility by waiting for the decision of the Crown.[2] It would obviously have been far better for his future relations with the colonists to have kept to that resolution, to have carefully avoided an attitude which even resembled that of a partisan. But he lacked the strength of will to resist the pressure which was put upon him. The enemies of Leisler knew that the policy of the Whig Government had been one of consistent clemency. They might well feel that if they once allowed the matter to come before the home Government their chance of revenge was gone. Sloughter did not wholly yield to the pressure

<small>The question referred to the Council.</small>

---

[1] Brodhead, vol. ii. p. 147.

[2] Sloughter to Nottingham, May 6, 1691. Printed in N. Y. Docs. vol. iii. p. 762.

put upon him. He would not take on himself the responsibility of the execution, but he referred the matter to the Council.[1] The Councillors, naturally less afraid of responsibility than the Assembly, were in all likelihood more amenable to the pressure put on them by Leisler's opponents. He was threatened not by the just indignation of a whole people whose constitutional rights he had violated, but by the resentment of a class in whose eyes he was an upstart and a demagogue. The opinion of the richest and best-born citizens would find voice in the Council. Their unanimous resolution was, 'that as well for the satisfaction of the Indians as the asserting of the government and authority residing in his Excellency in preventing insurrections and disorders for the future, it is absolutely necessary that the sentence pronounced on the principal offenders be forthwith put in execution.'[2] Tradition represents Sloughter as still wavering, and at last overcome by the persuasion of his wife,[3] or, according to another story, signing the death warrant in a fit of drunkenness.[4] There is little likelihood in either tale. When Sloughter had once referred the question to the Council he had virtually placed the decision out of his own hands. There has always been a tendency to clutch at any incident which may invest the dull records of colonial history with something of romance, and to that in all likelihood the legend owes its origin. Yet it contains a faint suggestion of the truth. The execution was not the work of Sloughter's own judgment; it was a policy forced on him by popular clamour.

The death warrant included only the two chief offenders. The rest were to await the pleasure of

[1] Sloughter to Blathwayt, N. Y. Docs. vol. iii. p. 759. This letter was sent, with some amendment, by the Council after Sloughter's death.
[2] Resolution of Council quoted by Brodhead, vol. ii. p. 648.
[3] Brodhead mentions this only as a rumour.
[4] Smith is the authority for this story.

the Crown. On May 16, Leisler and Millborne were hanged. Millborne was defiant to the last and denounced his enemies at the foot of the gallows. Leisler did not explicitly acknowledge his own crimes. But he admitted those committed by his followers in his name; for those he asked pardon.

<small>Execution of Leisler and Millborne.</small>

There is little need for comment on Leisler's career or his end. His was not one of those crimes where the verdict of sentiment either outruns that of reason or falls short of it. He was not a Marat sinning much against law, but far more against human feeling. He was not a Balmerino on whose fate law and human feeling inevitably speak with discordant voices. Leisler sinned against law and against human feeling. He was an unscrupulous rebel and a harsh and arbitrary ruler. But in neither matter can we say that he sinned greatly. Till almost the end his acts of rebellion were tricks and evasions, not open defiances of authority. He was to such a rebel as Monmouth what a pickpocket is to a pirate on the high seas. Nor, on the other hand, do the wrongs inflicted on Bayard and his fellows rank with the tyranny of such men as Kirke or Carrier. There was no greatness in the man either for good or evil; he was throughout the slave of events, wholly without foresight or constructive genius. If we condemn the government that put him to death, we must condemn it for reckoning such an one seriously dangerous. The worst side of the matter was not the fact but the manner of his execution. The government lost all dignity, it threw away that influence for which dignity is needful when men saw that its representative shrank from maintaining and upholding his own views, that he shifted his responsibility on to a body of heated partisans, and made himself the instrument of class terror and party revenge.

CHAPTER VI.

NEW YORK AFTER THE REVOLUTION.[1]

Effect of Leisler's rebellion.

THE general result of Leisler's rebellion was to leave the colony in a condition which went far to make good administration impossible. For if government by a representative body implies, and almost inevitably brings with it, a system of parties, it also

[1] After the Revolution the Official Documents concerning New York greatly increased in number and value. The despatches of Bellomont, Cornbury and Hunter, all to be found among the New York Documents, are of great value. We lose the guidance of Brodhead, but as a compensation we gain that of Smith, whose work now becomes much fuller and more authoritative. The author, William Smith, was the son of a William Smith who played a conspicuous part in New York politics. He (the elder) came to America with his father in 1715, being then eighteen years old. He was a successful barrister, became Attorney-General in New York, and a member of Council, and at a later date a judge. His son, the historian, was born in 1728. Like his father, he graduated at Yale, and distinguished himself at the New York bar. He became Chief Justice of that colony. His History originally appeared in 1793. As then published it only came down to 1732. But a further portion of it, coming down to 1761, remained in manuscript, and was published by the New York Historical Society in 1826. This I refer to as part 2.

The Acts of Assembly, from 1692 onwards, were published in 1725.

Colden's *History of the Five Nations* now becomes an important authority. He was a Scotchman who emigrated to New York in 1710, being then twenty-two years old. He became a large landholder, a member of Council, and at length lieutenant-general. Colden has, what is in a colonial writer the unusual quality, of enthusiastic admiration for the savages. If this sometimes makes him untrustworthy, it at least serves to balance the opposite tendency in most colonial writers of that day. The elaborate orations which he often puts into the mouth of his savages cannot possibly be historical. Colden's book appeared in 1727. This edition was reprinted in 1866. Another edition was published in 1750, and it is to this that my references apply.

requires that the issues which divide these parties should be distinctly limited, that there should be behind party differences certain general principles common to all, and that it should always be possible to overrule such differences for the common good. Above all was this needful when government was vested partly in a representative assembly, partly in a governor who could know little of the real condition of the colony, and who was therefore largely dependent on the Assembly not only for support but also for advice. The strife kindled by Leisler had rent the colony into two embittered factions. The object of each in dealing with a newly arrived governor was to possess themselves of his support and to use it as a weapon for crushing and keeping down their enemies. The colony, too, was suffering from the perils incident to its position, and to that terrible sense of insecurity which such a rule as Leisler's is certain to produce. There was a heavy public debt; men were every day withdrawing to safer and less burdened colonies—to Connecticut and Pennsylvania. The perpetual need for guarding against invasion left the settlers at Albany no leisure to attend to business, and thus the two great resources of the colony—tillage and the Indian trade—were crippled. Meanwhile the French missionaries were working their way among the Five Nations, and French emissaries were using all their unscrupulous craft to prevent any union between the confederacy and the native tribes outside its limits. To counteract that would need all the energy and adroitness of an able governor, backed with the resources of a united province.

The effect of James II.'s later policy had been to leave New York without a constitution. That want was in part supplied by the instructions issued by the Crown to its successive representatives, in part by enactments in which the Assembly definitely declared what should be the constitutional rights of the colonists. The Assembly which met under Sloughter, immediately after the overthrow of Leisler, passed two Acts which set forth, the one the nature and extent of the authority enjoyed by the Crown, the other the rights and privileges of the settlers.[1] The first was avowedly a declaration against the principles involved in Leisler's proceedings. The preamble contrasted loyal New York with its disaffected neighbours. The people had been ' poisoned from New England with the mistake that the Crown has nothing to do with the people here.' On the other hand ' there can be no power or authority exercised over their Majesties' subjects in this their province and dominion but what must be derived from their Majesties, their heirs and successors.' There clearly spoke the voice of a party exasperated by the self-constituted rule of a demagogue tyrant. With no truth could it be said that anyone speaking with any authority in the name of New England had ever declared that the colonists were independent of the Crown. The only quarter in which such a doctrine had ever been suggested even by implication was in the wild utterances of Leisler's most reckless partisans. Leisler himself had assuredly never set up such a claim, and the declaration of the Assembly did but enunciate what was regarded on all hands as a truism.

Attempts to define the constitution of the Colony.

At the same time the Assembly passed an Act which was undoubtedly intended as an equivalent to the Bill of Rights. It provided that an Assembly should be elected annually. The franchise was to be enjoyed by all freeholders worth forty shillings a year. The apportionment of representatives was also

Bill of Rights.

[1] For the Proceedings of the Assembly see Acts of Assembly, pp. 2-14.

determined. New York city and county were to have four members, each of the other counties two, Albany two, and Rensselaerwyck one. No tax was to be imposed save by the joint action of the Governor, Council and Deputies, and freedom of conscience was secured to all Christians, Papists only excepted. That clause was a sufficient answer to the charge of Popish sympathies so recklessly brought by Leisler and his allies against their opponents. The Whiggish nature of the settlement was also shown by an Act enabling persons who conscientiously objected to an oath to substitute a declaration. Existing rights, too, were secured by enacting that the land tenure neither of individuals nor of corporations, if good in equity, should be vitiated by any want of technical legality. Those rights of local self-government which were already enjoyed by various townships were put on a more secure basis. It was enacted that the freeholders in any town might hold meetings, and make orders for the improving of their respective lands and tillage, and appoint surveyors.[1]

Another clause in the General Act for protecting the rights of the colonists provided that no soldiers might be billeted on any inhabitant without his consent. This, however, was apparently fatal to the acceptance of the Act in England. Mainly in consequence of that provision, partly too from the power which it vested in the representatives, the lords of trade advised the King to withhold his consent to the Act. They recommended that instead the rights of the colonists should be set forth in a charter analogous to that granted to Virginia.[2] That, however,

The Bill vetoed.

---

[1] *Ib.* Cf. Bishop on *History of Elections in U.S.* p. 207.
[2] N. Y. Docs. vol. iv. p. 244. Inasmuch as Virginia had no charter, I find it difficult to understand what this means. Probably the words were used proleptically of some charter for Virginia which was under consideration; or it might be a clerical error for New England.

was not done, and the privileges of the colony were left to rest on the successive instructions to governors, gradually crystallizing into continuous usage.

In another matter the Assembly showed that reaction had not begotten indifference to the recognised principles of constitutional freedom. The money in the public treasury might be paid out under a warrant from the Governor. But this provision only extended over two years, and thus the Assembly retained in its own hands a check over the Governor.

Sloughter's conduct over the trial and execution of Leisler showed that he was wholly unfitted for the heavy task before him. To guard the frontier, to keep the good will of the Indian allies, to assert the authority of the Crown, and to protect the remains of Leisler's faction against their vindictive enemies—here was indeed a complex task which might tax the best ability that had ever been employed in the colonial service of England. The death of Sloughter within three months of Leisler's execution gave the King the opportunity for choosing a more efficient instrument. It is a melancholy illustration of the pitch of bitterness which party feeling had reached, that Sloughter's death was set down by rumour as the result of poison, without, as far as can be seen, a tittle of confirmatory evidence.[1] Readiness to accept such rumours shows a state of social and political morality little less diseased than would be shown by their truth.

One assuredly has no right to blame William and Mary, or those responsible for their policy, if they failed to find a governor equal to the task before him. But that plea will hardly avail for the choice of such an one as Sloughter's successor. Colonel Benjamin Fletcher seems to have been suddenly thrust

Death of Sloughter.

Appointment of Fletcher.

[1] Smith, p. 106.

into a responsible position in colonial politics without special experience, and without any of those gifts of mind or character which could make up for its absence. All that was creditable in his career was due to his advisers, and his whole policy justifies one in saying that when he did light on good advisers luck had more to do with the matter than judgment.

The instructions given to Fletcher came nearer to giving the colony a definite constitution than Sloughter's had done. The same arrangements were prescribed for carrying on government. But certain definite provisions were inserted on matters which had been before left vague. The right of taxation was not explicitly vested in the Assembly. But that was implied in the absence of any other direction for raising money, and in the provision that every Act of Assembly which granted money should contain a special reservation of the purposes for which such money might be spent.

<small>His instructions.[1]</small>

The instructions introduced a new feature in the ascendency given to the Church of England. This may be said in a certain sense to have created a religious establishment in the colony. Every minister, so ran the instructions, was to have a certificate of orthodoxy and good conduct from the Bishop of London, and to receive a stipend and glebe. This might fairly be held to mean that there was to be a body of endowed Anglican clergy. At the same time the conditions of such endowment, the mode of raising it and the liability to pay it, were left undetermined. And as a clause was added which gave liberty of conscience to all, Papists excepted, it was evidently not intended to deprive Nonconformist sects of the right to endow their own ministry.

Further provision was made for the supremacy of

[1] N. Y. Docs. vol. iii. p. 818.

the established Church, by a clause prohibiting any schoolmaster to keep school without a certificate from the Bishop of London.

The reaction against the Dutch party, and the inevitable tendency of the community after the discreditable failure of a revolution to cling to constitutional authority had ensured harmony between Sloughter and the Assembly. But these influences soon spent their force, and there was nothing to reconcile the Assembly either to the personal character of Fletcher or to the various features of his instructions which ran counter to the feelings and prejudices of the settlers. He soon found himself in conflict with the Assembly. The scheme for endowment was brought before them, and was urgently pressed by the Governor. The Assembly took the matter into consideration, and at length drafted a bill giving not a general endowment throughout the colony, but one in certain parishes. To this Fletcher and his Council apparently assented. But they introduced an amendment, which made the approval of the Governor necessary for the appointment of any incumbent. The representatives refused to accept the bill thus amended. Fletcher thereupon prorogued the Assembly, reading them a lecture on their stubbornness, their indifference to orthodox religion, and their wish to arrogate to themselves the whole of legislation.[1] Practically the Assembly carried their point in saving the endowment from being appropriated exclusively to the Episcopalian Church. For two years later, when a dispute arose as to the right of the churchwardens and vestrymen to appoint a Dissenter as their minister, the house decided that under the late Act they could do so.[2]

[1] Smith (pp. 115-8) gives a full account of this dispute, quoting Fletcher's speech to the Assembly verbatim.
[2] Smith, p. 119.

The result of Fletcher's instructions and the Act of the Assembly taken together was to bring about a state of things fraught with difficulty and complication. The one part which stood out clearly was that every parish was to have an endowed minister. Fletcher's instructions implied that it was the intention of the English Government that such endowment should be confined to the Church of England. The Act of the Assembly as subsequently interpreted by that body provided that religious bodies other than the Church of England should benefit by the endowment. To accept the former view was to recognise the right of the English Crown to impose a form of Establishment which might be wholly opposed to the wishes of the inhabitants. To accept the latter view was to vest in the Bishop of London a certain control over clergy outside his own Church. Either of these positions even if accepted without reserve would have been full of difficulty. The conflict of the two created a situation pregnant with troubles, nor, as we shall see, were they long in coming to the birth.

The best side of Fletcher's career as Governor was his dealing with the Indians on the Canadian frontier. There he had the good fortune to fall into the hands of capable and public-spirited advisers.

Fletcher's Indian policy.

One may almost say that there was now in America a school of public men strongly impressed with the need for carrying out the policy which Dongan had been the first to advocate publicly and definitely. Such was Nelson, of whose later career as Governor of Acadia I have spoken elsewhere.[1] In an able despatch, written the year before Fletcher came into office, he urged the need of meeting the French policy not by merely defensive measures, but by counter-

John Nelson.

---

[1] *English in America: Puritan Colonies*, pp. 410-35.

aggression.¹ He dwells on the advantage of creating a militia on the frontier, a scattered garrison of armed hunters answering to the *coureurs de bois* of Canada. In this he was supported by another of Fletcher's advisers, Lodwyck. More, too, must be done in the way of showing active sympathy with the Indians. Their chiefs must be brought over to England and impressed with a sense of the greatness of Britain. The settlers must, like the French, show themselves eager in embracing the quarrels of their savage allies. 'It cannot be thought that they should also expose themselves in our quarrel while we remain by our fires.' As far as mere individual courage goes we are as well off as our neighbours. Such a feat as Schuyler's raid on Prairie de la Madeleine showed that.² Nelson points out, too, the difference between French and English policy as illustrated by this incident. The French themselves admitted that such an exploit as Schuyler's would with them have been the subject of a special acknowledgment from the Court. But with the English Government it was left to be its own reward. Another point of superiority in the French policy not mentioned by Nelson is put forcibly by a colonial historian of a somewhat later date. The French had men of military skill and experience living among the Indians, and ever ready to advise them. Not only that, but every French officer quartered in Canada was liable to be told off for such duty, and thus a permanent connexion was established between the French garrison there and the Indian allies. At New York the English officers 'live like military monks, in idleness and luxury.'³

Like all who had applied themselves thoughtfully to the question, Nelson sees that the English policy can never be really satisfactory till her colonies are more

¹ Nelson's memorial is in the Documents, vol. iv. p. 207.
² *V.s.* p. 267.   ³ Colden, p. 183.

consolidated. Broken up in small governments the colonists 'in manner esteem each other as foreigners.'

The same note was sounded in a memorial from two of the Councillors, Brooke and Nicolls. In a memorial submitted to the Board of Trade they made the following specific proposals. Canada was, if possible, to be conquered. If that was too large a scheme, then a subsidy of a thousand pounds a year was to be granted to the Indian allies for arms, ammunition and clothes. A standing force of a thousand men should be kept on the Canadian frontier. A stone fort was to be built at Albany and Schenectady. Conestagawa on the Mohawk river was to be fortified. The writers were allowed to attend before the Board of Trade and explain their proposals more fully, but there is no evidence of any action taken.[1]

Brooke and Nicolls's Memorial.

So, too, almost every despatch that Fletcher sends home breathes the cry 'colonial union,' and tells of his failure to secure aid outside his own province. A general instruction had been issued by the advisers of the Crown that all colonies north of the Potomac are to help New York with men and money.[2] Fletcher, too, was invested with a commission as Commander-in-Chief which extended to Connecticut and Pennsylvania,[3] with further powers to raise a contingent of seven hundred men in New Jersey. His report of the attitude of the various colonies is a prophecy of what was to be heard for the next sixty years from every British official who strove to organize a connected scheme of colonial defence. Pennsylvania is parsimonious and slothful. Connecticut is suspicious and independent. The latter colony

Fletcher advocates consolidation.

[1] N. Y. Docs. vol. iv. pp. 183-6.
[2] Col. Papers, 1689-92, 2533, 2543.
[3] Strictly speaking not a 'commission' but 'commissions.' They were separate instruments. Col. Papers, 1689-92, 2296; 1693-6, 310. Fletcher's relation to Pennsylvania will come before us again.

is, Fletcher reports, a sort of republic; there all the better sort of people are dissatisfied and wish to be united with New York. It is not hard to tell what the 'better sort' meant in the mouth of an official of Fletcher's type. It was a view for which England had to pay dear in the days to come. Pennsylvania will only give good wishes, and would rather die than resist with carnal weapons. Nor is that all. Men are actually leaving New York, and fleeing to these unpatriotic colonies to escape the burden of war taxation.[1]

Fletcher is not alone in these complaints, nor in the remedy which he urges. Brooke, who beside being a Councillor was Judge of the Supreme Court in New York, reports that 'No way can be found to prevent the Jerseys from trading with the Indians to our prejudice except by annexing them to this province.'[2]

Colonel Lodwyck, an English official in Fletcher's confidence, goes further, and urges a comprehensive scheme for consolidating Connecticut, New York, New Jersey, and Pennsylvania into one Crown province.[3] He considered that he had strengthened his case by forwarding a somewhat curious petition from the inhabitants of Elizabethtown. They had settled, they say, under patents from Nicolls, intending to be in the province of New York. The Proprietors of New Jersey have separated them from New York, they have treated Nicolls's grants as null and void, and have either given the land to fresh grantees or compelled the occupants to take out fresh patents. Moreover, by exempting their own lands from public burdens they have impoverished all private holders.

Here, as so often in the history of the middle colonies, we are confronted with that root of all confusion and discord, the grant to Berkeley and Carteret.

---

[1] Fletcher's despatches in Col. State Papers, 1693-4.
[2] *Ib.* p. 289.   [3] *Ib.* p. 557.

Either the Crown or the Board of Trade appears to have laid to heart Lodwyck's suggestions, for in 1693 Sir John Trevor, a law officer of the Crown, was asked to give an opinion as to the status of New Jersey and its relation to the Crown. The answer was one which might well alarm that colony. He held that no grant or assignment made by the Duke of York could 'absolutely sever New Jersey from New York, but that it still remains a part thereof and dependent on the Government of New York, and liable to contribute men and provisions for the supply and protection of New York against any enemies.'

Strictly interpreted this decision would have annihilated New Jersey as a body politic. It meant that the grant of New Jersey was merely a conveyance of land, and that the Duke of York had not, as Proprietor, any power to transfer jurisdiction. The accession of James II. had put New York in the condition of a Crown colony, and the rights which the Crown had thus acquired passed with the Revolution to the new Sovereigns.

Trevor's opinion also contained a clause to the effect that, in spite of the charter of Connecticut and New Jersey, the Crown may appoint governors for those colonies, with power to raise men and supplies for necessary defence.[1]

The attack was in reality made less dangerous by being thus made more comprehensive. There was a certain amount of reason in the contention that the Duke of York had no right to transfer the political authority which had been granted to him. The fact that such authority had for nearly twenty[2] years been exercised without question made the attempt to revoke it little less than a revolution.

[1] Col. State Papers, Feb. 13, 1694.
[2] Twenty-eight if we count from the original grant to Berkeley and Carteret.

The inclusion of Connecticut in the attack went far to neutralize any real danger to colonial liberty. To attack the chartered rights of Connecticut would have been perilous in itself and at variance with all traditions, so far as there were connected and continuous traditions, of colonial policy. Trevor's business, no doubt, was to advise on the purely legal aspect of the case. But it was throughout the calamitous error of those in power in England that they put forward assertions of legal rights as against the colonies, without any regard to the effect which such claims were likely to have on colonial feeling.

There is nothing to show that Nelson had any direct influence over Fletcher. But the man whose conduct Nelson specially signals out as the type and illustration of what our policy ought to be in all likelihood had. The one creditable feature of Fletcher's policy was his strong sense of the need for defensive operations on the frontier, and the persistency with which he urged this on the home Government. If we may believe Fletcher's enemies, he was in these matters acting by the advice of Schuyler. Schuyler was far more than a brilliant backwoods fighter. He understood all the diplomatic arts needful to secure the good will of the Indians.

Fletcher advised by Schuyler.

The relations between the English and the Five Nations had of late years been such as to tax and develop the capacity of the English for dealing diplomatically with the savages. The intrigues of French missionaries on the one hand had excited the suspicions of the settlers, while the Indians not unnaturally doubted whether men so supine and disunited as the whole body of English could be in earnest and trustworthy. It is plain, too, that the Five Nations felt jealous, not without reason, of the way in which the brunt of the strife was thrown on them by

Difficulties with the Five Nations.

their allies. Thus, at a conference held with Sloughter in 1691, they complained that he said 'You must keep the enemy in perpetual alarm,' not 'we must.'[1] Schuyler's raid had no doubt done something to allay their suspicions. In 1692, during the short interregnum which followed Sloughter's death, Ingoldsby met the chiefs of the confederacy at Albany.[2] His speech to them was a repetition of Sloughter's, a strenuous warning and appeal against any peace with the French. The reply of the chief Indian speaker is possibly coloured in form by a partial historian, but in substance it has every internal appearance of probability. The Indians have no thoughts of peace. But how is it that the smaller and weaker party in the alliance is expected to do all the work of it? How is it that the Indians have to pay the English more than ever for powder, without which they can neither fight nor subsist? And even if they have ammunition what are they to do without guns? They cannot pelt the enemy with powder and shot. The Governor of Canada takes care that his savage allies are well armed. And how is it that, while all the English colonies are said to be parts of one nation and subjects of one King, there is no union among them? How is it that Maryland and the settlers by the Delaware and those of New England are taking no part in the strife? 'Has the King of England sold these subjects? or are they disobedient? Pray make plain to us this mystery! How can they all be subjects of the same Great King and not engaged in the same war?' The Indian orator was but saying what every thoughtful man who knew the condition of the colonies and was not blinded by provincial jealousy was thinking.

Meanwhile, Jesuit preachers were doing all in their power to detach the Mohawks from the English alliance.

[1] Colden, p. 25.   [2] *Ib.* p. 138.

FRENCH INVASION.

Frontenac, however, fully recognised that a spice of fear would be a strong reinforcement to the arguments of the missionaries. In the winter of 1692 he renewed his policy of three years back. This time, however, he confined his attack to a single expedition directed against the New York frontier. As before, the dead of winter was chosen as the season for the attack. In the second week in 1693 a force set forth of nearly seven hundred Indian converts, commanded by French officers. In the way of actual injury to the English the raid effected nothing. Three Mohawk villages were surprised, of which two were insignificant. The third, however, was garrisoned with a hundred warriors, and though the defenders were taken unawares the place cost the assailants thirty men before it was mastered. If Frontenac did little direct injury to the English by this attack, yet it was near having a serious influence on their alliance with the Mohawks. The French had taken with them a prisoner captured in the former attack on Schenectady, in all likelihood as a guide. He managed to escape and brought warning to his townsmen, or rather to those who had replaced them. There was no supineness now; a messenger was at once sent off to Albany for help, and fifty mounted men hurried back for the defence of Schenectady. But nothing was done to warn the Mohawks of impending danger, not even those of whom as usual there were a good number in and about Schenectady.

The disaffection thus created seemed likely to be dangerous, and it again fell to the lot of the Schuyler family to make amends for the supineness of their countrymen. This time, however, it was not John but his civilian brother, Peter, the Mayor of Albany, who

---

[1] These proceedings are described in a report from M. de Champigny, the Intendant, N. Y. Docs. vol. ix. p. 534.

headed the expedition. With a few regular soldiers and a force of colonial militia, making in all two hundred and fifty men, he marched towards Schenectady.[1] He was soon joined by a force of two hundred and fifty Indians. Their ill-armed condition justified their recent complaints, and the whole force had no more provisions with them than what they could actually carry in their pockets. Nevertheless they pressed on—some, it is said, going without food for two whole days—fell in with their retreating enemies, and harassed them in a succession of skirmishes.

Expedition under Schuyler.

They were then overtaken by a reinforcement of eighty regulars, under the command of a Captain Matthews, with a supply of provisions. What followed illustrates the difficulty which always attended the joint operations of a force of colonists and Indians acting with regular troops. The English pressed on and harried the retiring force, killing and wounding more than sixty of them and recovering over forty prisoners. Matthews thought that it would have been good policy to call upon the French to surrender. The Mohawks, as usual with Indians, were content to strike but one effective blow, and Schuyler seems to have agreed with them. The historian of the expedition adds the comment that Schuyler 'though brave was no soldier.'[2] It is possible that Schuyler and his Indian allies were better judges of the situation. Be that as it may, the incident illustrates what had been shown twenty-six years before when Andros criticized the operations of the New Englanders against Philip, what was shown far more terribly sixty years later when Braddock went sneering at colonial soldiership to meet his death. There lay the one feature of superiority in the system of French Canada,

[1] A very full account of Schuyler's expedition is given in Colden, pp. 145-8.
[2] Colden, p. 147.

a system void of any principle of civil or political developement, but which by virtue of its military merits held its own for nearly a century against the overmastering numbers and resources of the English colonies. The trained soldiers of France were not ashamed in matters of war to be the pupils of their Indian allies. The Canadian bushrangers, the *coureurs de bois*, formed a link between the regular troops and the savage allies.

The crisis enabled Fletcher to show that promptitude of action which was the best side of his character.

Fletcher's proceedings. He at once raised a force of three hundred volunteers and made his way to Albany. By the time he reached that city Schuyler was on his way back, and the invaders were out of reach. But Fletcher's liberal promises of help seem to have reassured the Mohawks, and his promptitude was acknowledged in Indian fashion by the honourable name of Cayenguirago, 'the Swift Arrow.'[1]

Yet in reading of Fletcher's dealings with the Five Nations one feels that all he was doing, all that he could *Difficulties of the situation.* do, was but a makeshift settlement, the temporary and imperfect solution of a difficulty which was only postponed, and which would have to be faced in real earnest by the next generation. The whole body of colonies acting under the supervision of the mother country might crush Canada. New York single-handed could do no more than keep her at bay. The best hope for the present really lay in the difficulties which faced the enemy. For the English colonies had this in their favour: they and the government of Canada were not playing for equal stakes. The English were genuinely acting on the defensive. The English colonists had as yet ample territory and ample undeveloped resources. All they needed was to keep New France within the limits of the St. Lawrence valley.

[1] Colden, p. 149.

But for France to be stationary meant failure. The spirit which kept her alive was the spirit of encroaching ambition. Thus the attitude of each nation to their savage allies was wholly different. For England it was enough if the Five Nations interposed a defensive belt between the frontier of her colonies and the French invader. France needed her Indians to be subservient, active, and aggressive. Thus if the diplomatic resources of France were far greater, so was the burden laid upon them. It was not enough to buy off the hostility of the Mohawks, they must be turned to account as a weapon against the English. At the same time this must be done without offending the tribes nearer home. Throughout his whole career Frontenac was face to face with this difficulty. To retain the alliance of the Hurons and the Dionondadies, and to win that of the Five Nations, was the ideal condition to aim at. But, failing that, the best thing practically was to keep up the hatred of the French allies against the confederacy. Thus Frontenac had on the one hand to labour at establishing a double alliance, on the other to keep open a possible feud between his two sets of allies. The short-sighted levity and the capricious vindictiveness of the savage made such a task well nigh impossible, and in that lay the best hope for the English colonies.

In the summer of 1693 Fletcher met the chiefs of the Five Nations at Albany, and put them in good humour by a substantial present of arms, ammunition, and clothes. The satisfaction with which they heard that Fletcher was now Governor of Pennsylvania, inferring that some common action against the enemy might be looked for, is a strong comment on the obvious need for union among the colonies.

Conference with the Mohawks at Albany.[1]

[1] Colden, p. 151.

On one point, however, Fletcher was unsuccessful.
In 1689 the Iroquois captured one of the most conspicuous of the Jesuit missionaries, Father
Millet. He was saved from death by the good
offices of a Christian squaw. Among the
Indians the prisoner whose life was spared
was usually adopted, and so it was with Millet. He
became naturalized as an Oneida and was raised to the
rank of a sachem. A Frenchman settled among the
Five Nations might become a potent influence in undermining their alliance with the English, and in the
following year the authorities at Albany tried to persuade the Indians to hand over to them their captive.
The Mohawks approved of this but could not obtain
the consent of the Oneidas. This is a significant illustration of that lack of unity within the confederacy
which helped to make their alliance an unstable one.

Negotiations between the Five Nations and the French.

Such was Millet's influence over his captors that he
induced four out of the five confederated tribes to
consider the question of the French alliance. The Mohawks, always the most warlike and the most uncompromising in their attitude towards Canada, stood alone,
and in the autumn of 1693 the rest of the confederacy
sent an embassy to Quebec. During this year and the
following was to be seen the somewhat strange spectacle
of representatives of the two greatest European nations
sedulously courting the friendship and bidding against
one another for the alliance of a body of savages.
The English overtures made through Fletcher and
Schuyler could hardly be said to be entirely successful.
It is plain that the Indians were deeply distrustful, not
of English good faith, but of the efficiency of a power
whose members were so disunited. One of the representatives of the Mohawks put this clearly enough in
a conference held at Albany in the summer of 1694.
He plainly told Fletcher that if the other colonies

would assist in pushing on the war vigorously, the Five Nations would not be backward. But if they were to be left alone, or to receive no help except from New York, then in their own interest they must make peace.

Fletcher's policy was in all likelihood influenced by this, and by a wish that the state of things should be brought home to the minds of men in all the colonies. He represented to the governments of the neighbouring provinces how urgent was the occasion, how nothing but a display of united feeling among the English could prevent an alliance between the French and the Five Nations. Accordingly, in the autumn of the same year, he succeeded in bringing together representatives from New Jersey, Massachusetts and Connecticut to meet the Indians in another conference at Albany.[1] There another Indian speaker repeated the appeal of his countrymen. He personified, according to Indian fashion, New York by the name given to the Governor. 'Cayenguirago's arms and ours are stiff and tired with holding fast the chain of alliance, while our neighbours sit still and smoke at their ease. They grow fat while we grow lean, they flourish while we decay.' 'If all had held the chain as fast as New York it would be a real terror to the French, and thunder itself would not break it. If all would join in taking up the hatchet against the French the common enemy would soon be destroyed, and there would be peace and ease ever after.' We may well believe that this was a perfectly true statement of the views and wishes of the Indians. We need not credit them with a disinterested attachment to the English. It was well within the compass of their intelligence to see that they had everything to fear from the French, little or nothing from the English. For the present their best

Another conference at Albany.

[1] Colden, p. 170.

hope would lie in an effective union of the English colonies. A day when the increasing needs of the white man would swallow up their hunting grounds was beyond their present view. It was well that the representatives of the four colonies should listen to these words and carry them to their homes. One can hardly doubt that the plain speaking of the Mohawk envoy must have done something to strengthen that desire for union which was already showing itself in so many quarters.

Meanwhile the Indians made no secret of the fact that they were receiving overtures from Frontenac, and that their envoys were being received at Quebec.[1] All the arts of French diplomacy were used to break the alliance between the English and the Five Nations. The confederates were taunted with having admitted a sixth nation to the confederacy, and suffering it to dominate their councils. The Indian envoys were daily entertained at the table of the Governor or some of the chief officers. The French sense of decorum and the French sense of the ludicrous must have been equally tried. Colden in his enthusiastic sympathy with the Mohawks gravely tells us how the chief Indian speaker Decanisora 'made a good appearance,' in a scarlet coat with gold trimmings and a laced beaver hat given him by Fletcher.[2]

Indian envoys at Quebec.

But the wiles of French diplomacy could not blind the Mohawks to their true interest. One feels that the sins of France were finding her out when one reads a speech in which an Indian orator reminded the French of the treachery of Denonville.[3]

Another characteristic incident showed the difficul-

---

[1] Colden gives a full account of the negotiations between the French and the Five Nations taken wholly from statements made by Decanisora to the English.

[2] Colden, p. 169.   [3] *Ib.* p. 172.

ties which beset the French in their Indian policy and the spirit in which they met them. It was of the utmost importance to the French to secure the Dionondadies, whose territory lay to the north of Lake Huron. The Five Nations, however, had been making overtures to them. If those succeeded and if an alliance were established, the French fort at Michillimakinac, on the strait connecting Lake Huron and Lake Michigan, would be in perpetual danger, and if that fell there would be an end of any chance of a westward extension towards the Ohio and the Mississippi. To avoid awakening the suspicions of the French all show of amity was avoided; between the Five Nations and the Dionondadies skirmishes went on, but those who were ostensibly prisoners were really ambassadors. In 1695 the Dionondadies captured seven warriors of the Five Nations. The French thereupon insisted that as the war was a joint undertaking they were entitled to a share of the proceeds. They then cajoled or intimidated the Dionondadies into yielding them up one of the prisoners. The prisoner was put to death with all the most hideous tortures of an Indian execution. A Frenchman, we are told, actually began the process with his own hands. Even if this be an exaggeration and if the French left the actual butchery to their Indian allies, it is perfectly clear that it was done not merely with the approval, but under the actual superintendence, of the French garrison. Nothing can be more illustrative of the French political morality of that day than the manner in which a contemporary historian tells and comments on the incident.[2]

The French torture a Mohawk prisoner.[1]

[1] The whole of this business is told by Colden, pp. 183-7, and also by the French historians.

[2] La Potherie, vol. iv. p. 75. His words are ' Cette conjoncture ne laissa pas de faire impression sur ces sauvages, qui virent que l'on continuait tout de bon à faire la guerre.' For the incident itself see also Colden.

When we shudder at the horrors of the French Revolution we must not forget that for generations the responsible rulers of France had been training up a nation in unscrupulous cruelty.

Cadillac's act of treachery did not even serve the purpose for which it was designed. In the next year the Dionondadies again sought the alliance of the Five Nations. They succeeded in proving that the French, not they, were responsible for what had been done. Belts were exchanged, and peace established. It is said that the main motive which influenced the Dionondadies was their wish to share in the English trade, a trade which from the superior resources of the Albany merchants was more gainful than that with Montreal.

Though the French failed in their schemes for the alliance of the Iroquois, they succeeded in obtaining an influence over two at least of the confederate nations, the Cayugas and the Senecas, which did something to weaken the position of the English. It was in all likelihood their neutrality which enabled Frontenac to carry out his favourite scheme for the restoration of the fort at Cataracouy which had borne his own name. Fletcher showed that he understood the urgency of the case by the energy with which he pressed upon his savage allies the need of preventing this. It would have been no difficult task for a competent commander with the resources of the united colonies at his back to seize upon the place before Frontenac had reoccupied it, and to use it as an effective bridle upon French aggression. The separate English colonies, each with its representative system and its strong local patriotism, were schools of statesmanship to which the world owes much. But years of needless bloodshed, of paralysing distrust and suspicion,

Frontenac restores Fort Cataracouy.[1]

[1] Colden, p. 182.

of demoralizing warfare, were the price at which that gain was bought.

The undying energy of Frontenac at once urged him to use his re-acquired possession as the base for a great invasion of the Mohawk territory. He was too subtle a tactician to believe that a mere inroad upon Indian territory not followed up by armed occupation could have any effect beyond striking terror. It is clear, too, that the expedition was far too massive in its character to have ever been designed for aiming a blow at the English frontier. It was clearly no repetition of the merciless but effective policy of 1689. We must, therefore, look on Frontenac's last expedition as a great military pageant, with something of theatrical purpose in its arrangement. The advanced guard consisted of five hundred Indian allies. Then came the colonial militia commanded by Frontenac himself, borne in a chair. In the rear came the regular troops, with an Indian contingent under French officers. Braddock fifty years later might have learnt a lesson from the policy which threw the duty of guarding against a surprise on the Indian allies, and which treated the colonial militia as the mainstay of the force. The cumbrous expedition wound its way along the southern shore of Lake Ontario into the country of the Senecas. But, unless it suited an Indian tribe to meet an invader in arms, there never was any difficulty in dispersing through the woods. The French found the Seneca villages empty; in one was an old chief, who according to tradition stayed to maintain the dignity of his nation against the invaders. As usual the Huron allies demanded their victim for the torture, and the French paid the price of their aid without scruple. The country of the Oneidas was also harried and their corn

Frontenac makes a military progress through the country of the Five Nations.[1]

[1] Colden, pp. 188-92.

destroyed. There twenty-five prisoners were taken. Père Millet, the French missionary, had gained enough influence over that tribe to raise some hopes of winning them to the French alliance. Accordingly the prisoners were brought alive to Quebec.

The scanty resources of the country could not long maintain the French army, and by the middle of August Frontenac was back in Montreal. The enemy, who had left the advancing force unmolested, swarmed out of the woods during the retreat, harassing the rear and cutting off stragglers.

The success, such as it was, was bought dear. Canada had not men enough to fill the ranks of the militia and to till the fields, and the summer brought scanty crops and famine in its train. One may fairly think that Frontenac with all his astuteness had overrated the effect of mere display on the Indian character. Such an expedition was in no way likely to intimidate the Five Nations, or to detach them from the English. As a colonial historian justly said, ' the enterprise was a kind of heroic dotage.'[1]

The real work of invasion was to be done not by large and elaborately organized force, but by small parties of raiders, such as that which had made havoc of Schenectady. For these winter was the fitting season. The greater hardships and the difficulty of subsistence were more than made up for by the security against surprise when there was no foliage to cover an ambush. One such expedition was set on foot in the winter of 1695 against Albany. But it was intercepted by a force of Indians and dispersed with loss. A few fled to Albany and were there taken prisoners; none returned to Canada.[2]

Such raids across the frontier by the Indian allies of each Power made up the whole sum of hostilities till

<small>Raid against Albany.</small>

[1] Colden, p. 193.   [2] *Ib.*

the Peace of Ryswick. The French had failed in their main object, in their purpose of detaching the Five Nations. But the struggle had inflicted a heavy blow on the prosperity of New York. The population on her north-west frontier had lessened instead of increasing. Albany, as the great mart for the Upper Hudson, for the trade in furs and in all kinds of produce, should have been a rapidly growing settlement. Instead, its population dwindled during the ten years which followed the Revolution. In 1689 it had over six hundred and sixty male adult inhabitants. In 1698 they were reduced to three hundred and eighty-two.[1] Moreover, if we may believe Fletcher, men were leaving the colony to avoid military service and heavy taxation, and taking refuge in Pennsylvania and Connecticut.[2]

Injury to New York by the war.

Though Fletcher's Indian policy—or one should perhaps rather say that of his advisers—was well conceived and showed intelligence, yet its failure in detail was in all likelihood largely due to his own misdeeds. We are told that he appropriated the money which should have been spent on military stores, and that he drew pay calculated on fictitious muster rolls.[3] His successor found Schenectady and Albany, in his own words, 'so weak and ridiculous that they look liker pounds to impound cattle than forts,' that at Schenectady gateless, while the garrisons had hardly clothes enough for decency.[4]

Fletcher's corrupt administration.

[1] This is stated by Bellomont in a despatch in the N. Y. Docs. vol. iv. p. 337.

[2] Fletcher to Lords of Trade, October 2, 1693.

[3] N. Y. Docs. vol. iv. pp. 434, 512. Col. State Papers, 1622, 611. There is a further statement of Fletcher's misdeeds in a letter addressed by De Lancy, afterwards Chief Justice of New York, to some correspondent in England. This is in the Col. State Papers, 1692. It is too obviously an *ex parte* statement to be trustworthy. De Lancy is printed Delanoy, an obvious error.

[4] N. Y. Docs. vol. iv. pp. 687, 752.

In another way Fletcher's policy was fatally opposed to the needs of the colony. More than one colonial politician pointed out to the English Government the importance of having along the frontier a class of military yeomen who might be self-supporting, and at the same time available for defensive warfare. To create such a class was no easy matter. But Fletcher's policy actually went far to make the existence of such a class impossible. He rewarded his political supporters with large grants of land, and thus by creating a small body of monopolists set up a fatal obstacle to the increase of freeholders. There appear to have been eight of these great tracts, or, as Fletcher's successor calls them, palatinates. Two were revoked by the Assembly, not so much as it would seem because they were specially injurious, but because the grantees, Colonel Bayard and Dellius, a Calvinist minister, were hostile to the party then in power. The grants seem, too, to have been somewhat tainted by the fact that they were made by Fletcher after he was superseded. Dellius's grant, moreover, was a direct encroachment on the Indian allies. By negotiation with the Mohawks he professed to have obtained a quasi-title extending over about three hundred and forty square miles.[1]

Large land grants.

There can be little doubt that Fletcher's consent to these grants was the reward for political support. There is the very strongest presumption that he did not confine himself to such guarded and indirect forms of corruption. Of his dealings with pirates I have spoken elsewhere.[2] The specific

Fletcher's other corrupt dealings.

---

[1] For the revocation of these grants see Acts of Assembly, p. 26. Dellius's dealings with the Indians are told in a memorial in the N. Y. Docs. vol. v. p. 10. The documents contain several references to these grants Cf. Smith, p. 134.

[2] *Puritan Colonies*, vol. ii. p. 433.

charge that he received ten thousand pounds from Kidd may be untrue. But it is clear that the Board of Trade, a body in no ways prejudiced, and with access to much evidence that would have moral, though perhaps not legal, weight, believed Fletcher guilty of corruption. It is said that his dishonest dealings were not confined to pirates, but that he, the members of the Council, and the custom-house officials were all in league with smugglers.[1] An argument adduced by Bellomont in confirmation of this charge assuredly has weight. The trade of New York, he says, has doubled itself in ten years. But during that time the customs instead of increasing were actually much lessened. Of the goods imported not more than two-thirds he believed paid duty, and so universal and complete was the corruption that a wealthy offender if prosecuted was certain of acquittal.[2] The evil practices of a set of officials playing into one another's hands are always hard to track. But the very line of defence taken up by Fletcher's defenders, who were in all likelihood his accomplices, raises a prejudice against them. They had the impudence to say that since he had been in office only one pirate had sailed from the colony.[3] Such an unblushing lie makes the whole evidence of the witnesses worthless.

It must be remembered, too, that Fletcher enjoyed the support of an Assembly who had every motive for befriending him and making the best of his conduct. It was by his support that the victorious faction were holding down their still vindictive opponents, the supporters of Leisler. Thus, after the opening squabble over the Endowment Act, the relations between Fletcher and the Assembly were uniformly friendly. They were indeed suspicious enough

Fletcher's alliance with the Assembly.

[1] N. Y. Docs. vol. iv. pp. 303, 317. [2] Ib. pp. 303, 518.
[3] Ib. p. 620.

of malpractices to set on foot an inquiry into the conduct of the Receiver-General, but there is no trace of any wish to extend the investigation to the more important offender.

Nothing illustrates more strongly that characteristic of New York history, the predominance of personal motives over clearly defined party issues, than the disputes which raged over the conduct of Fletcher. We find Bayard and Heathcote, men of respectable character, signing a declaration testifying to the good conduct and public services of Fletcher.[1] On the other hand we have a letter or memorandum written by De Lancy, a leading New York merchant and a prominent member of the Assembly, in which Fletcher is charged with the grossest corruption. He will do nothing without a bribe, he pockets the soldiers' pay, he connives at piracy, he intimidates voters, and packs the Assembly by giving fraudulent qualifications. It is said that at Albany he tried to turn an election by closing the gates and so excluding wealthy merchants who lived outside. Then he is induced by bribes to admit them. Our faith in De Lancy as a witness, however, is somewhat shaken when we find him belittling what was undoubtedly the best feature in Fletcher's policy, and saying that the name of Cayenguirago, or 'the Swift Arrow,' bestowed on Fletcher by the Indians was not given in recognition of his speed and certainty in war, but was 'a droll upon the vainglory of the man, being a sarcastical pun on the name of Fletcher. De Lancy must have reckoned on the credulity of his correspondent, if he was to believe that the Iroquois Indians knew the derivation of Fletcher's name.[2]

I have spoken elsewhere of the character of Fletcher's successor, Bellomont, and of the acts by which

[1] Col. State Papers, 1696–7, 696–7, 217. [2] See p. 308, n. 3.

he is best remembered in history. By a most unhappy administrative blunder, the cause of which is nowhere explained, Fletcher was superseded in 1695, and Bellomont did not reach the colony till the spring of 1698. Thus for more than two years the colony was left in the hands of a faction who had none of the real responsibility of power, and who had every temptation to make the most of the short time left them.

Interregnum between Fletcher and Bellomont.

With all Bellomont's administrative capacity and moral good qualities one may doubt how far he was suited to play the peculiarly difficult part assigned to him. Plainly he was a man who always struck right at one main object, heedless of side issues. He found the colony in the hands of a corrupt faction, against whom he had personally good grounds for resentment. Without hesitation or inquiry he threw himself into the arms of their opponents, compromising his dignity and weakening his efficiency by appearing at the very outset of his career as a party leader.

Bellomont's policy.

The inevitable effect of this was at once to bring Bellomont into an attitude of hostility towards his Council. His opening speech to the Assembly was a plain denunciation of his predecessor.[1] Under any circumstances one may reasonably doubt whether such a proceeding was calculated to beget a respect for authority. Moreover, the proceedings of Fletcher and his alleged accomplices were at present *sub judice*. Yet Bellomont did not hesitate to tell the Assembly that the Acts of Trade had been violated by the connivance of those who were bound to enforce them, and with a distinct allusion to his predecessor to announce that he would neither embezzle the public money himself nor suffer such dishonesty in others.

[1] The speech is given in Smith, p. 130.

We are told that the Assembly was not able to carry through any business.¹ It is not unlikely that the Leislerite party, though still in a minority, were strong enough when backed by the encouragement of the Governor to obstruct the proceedings of their opponents.

The election of 1699.

The election of the next Assembly early in 1699 showed the state to which parties had come. The dominant faction endeavoured to keep their majority by promising an abolition of customs.² This was not only a popular cry, it was calculated to injure Bellomont by stopping the resources of government. Thus it might even so far discredit him as to bring about his recall. So far one may well believe Bellomont's charges. It may be true, too, that there was an element of Jacobitism in the opposition, and that they objected to the late Revolution being called the happy Revolution.³ Leisler's claim, a wholly unfounded one, to represent the Whig Government may have driven his opponents into some such attitude; though, on the other hand, it may well be that they merely refused to approve of what had been done in their own colony in the name of the Whig party. One may believe, too, the somewhat ludicrous story told by Bellomont, that in Queen's County, where two-thirds of the voters were of Fletcher's party, they professed themselves Quakers in order to avoid taking the necessary oaths, and then signalized their new profession by a drunken riot.

But we have a right to become suspicious when Bellomont reports that the candidates put forward by the so-called anti-Dutch party were generally Dutchmen who could hardly speak English. Indeed, it is

---

[1] Smith (p. 131) says, 'The house, though unanimous in a hearty address of thanks to the Governor for his speech, could scarce agree upon anything else.'

[2] Bellomont in N. Y. Docs. vol. iv. p. 507.

[3] This is stated in the same despatch.

clear that Bellomont was that most dangerous witness, a conscientious and public-spirited partisan, quite unconscious of his own partisanship. One would ask, too, for some better evidence before one believes that the Clerk of the Council was a man who had fled from England in disgrace, and the Clerk of the Assembly a convicted coin clipper.[1] It is singular that the charge of inability to speak English was also brought by Bellomont's enemies against the candidates whom their opponents put forward. It would seem as if knowledge of English had become a test of a certain standard of education and social culture.[2]

Complaints as to the conduct of the election were not confined to the Governor and his supporters. The other side averred that Bellomont so arranged the times and places for polling that in some cases electors who had four votes could give only one.[3] The mere fact of this charge being brought confirms what everything seems to make probable, that the party which supported Fletcher and opposed Bellomont drew its main strength from a wealthy oligarchy. It was the predecessor and ancestor of the party in New York who at a later day broke the unity of that resistance which the colonies offered to the unjust demands of the mother country.

It was also said that Bellomont gave an additional member to Albany, and called into existence a fresh constituency in Orange County, with but twenty freeholders.[4] The result was the return of one Abraham Gouverneur, the ancestor of a house well known in the political history of New York. He had been Leisler's secretary, and had married the widow of Millborne, and seems thus to have stepped into the position of the recognised leader of the now victorious party. It is

---

[1] All these charges are in the same despatch.
[2] N. Y. Docs. vol. iv. p. 620.   [3] Ib.   [4] Ib.

said, and that by a witness with no prejudices to bias him, that Gouverneur by his energetic action and influence over the house suppressed all attempts to investigate the conduct of the elections.[1]

Whatever were the means employed, the result was the return of a house in which the Leislerite party had a majority. If, indeed, we may believe their opponents, out of the twenty-one members returned, fourteen were Dutch. The result was a series of measures designed to reverse the policy of the previous house. Fletcher's land grants to Bayard and Dellius were annulled. An Act was passed indemnifying those who had been excepted from the general pardon granted in 1691. Another, in which we may probably trace Gouverneur's direct influence, restored Millborne's estate.[2] The turn of public feeling was shown by the fact that the corpses of Leisler and Millborne were taken up and reburied with religious solemnities.[3]

Victory of the Leislerites.

It was characteristic of Bellomont's impatient determination to establish his ascendancy that he at once removed ten of the Council whom he thought likely to be hostile, and substituted six of his own way of thinking.[4] Among those struck off was Bayard. Setting aside all question of fairness, such a proceeding was unwise strategy. No party will gain by the attempt entirely to exclude the more reputable and responsible among its opponents from public life, or by such sudden and wholesale attempts to silence them. Nor did Bellomont's success even secure him against immediate difficulties. On financial matters, indeed, the dominant party dealt with him as liberally as their predecessors had dealt with Fletcher. They voted a fixed revenue for six years, and imposed

Changes in the Council made by Bellomont.

---
[1] Smith, p. 133. [2] Acts of Assembly.
[3] N. Y. Docs. vol. iv. pp. 523, 620; Smith, p. 105.
[4] N. Y. Docs. vol. iv. p. 620.

no fresh restraints on the expenditure of it. That is in itself no small proof of the prosperous condition of the colony.[1]

But on other administrative questions the Governor soon found himself at variance with the Assembly. His instructions authorised him to create courts of justice. The principal legal authorities, the Chief Justice, Colonel Smith, whose union of military and judicial dignity suggests the American of later days, and the Attorney-General, Graham, advised that the exercise of this power by the Crown or its representative was unconstitutional. Bellomont gave way, and a bill for the same purpose was drafted in Council and sent down to the House of Representatives. They introduced amendments which, in Bellomont's opinion, conflicted with the laws of England, and when the bill was returned he refused his assent.[2]

Bellomont's disputes with the Assembly.

The main dispute, however, arose out of the question of defending the frontier. The peace of Ryswick was far from relieving the English colonists from all anxiety in that quarter. It freed them from the actual dread of invasion, from the chance of such a fate as had befallen the men of Schenectady. But it was plain that the officials of New France merely looked on the peace as a truce, that they had no intention of relaxing their attempts to secure their hold over the debateable land as one may call it, and the tribes who occupied it. Frontenac, indeed, died in the year in which peace was made. His successor, De Callières, was far less of a soldier. He seems to have had no love of a military policy for its own sake. His aim was rather to develope the resources of Canada as it was than to extend the boundaries of the colony westward. But for either policy the Iroquois

French policy towards the Five Nations.

[1] N. Y. Docs. vol. iv. pp. 507, 620.
[2] See Bellomont's own statement, N. Y. Docs. vol. iv. p. 515.

alliance was needed. Moreover a renewal of hostilities between England and France might at any time lay Canada open to the danger of invasion. If the Five Nations could be detached from England that danger would be greatly lessened; if they were won over to an alliance with France it would be at an end. The honest determination of the English Government to carry through the treaty of Ryswick, and to enforce its provisions on the Indian allies, was turned against England. An instruction was given to Bellomont that if it were necessary he should co-operate with the ruler of Canada in forcing the Five Nations to respect the peace. A letter from Bellomont explaining this to De Callières was shown to the Indian chiefs as a proof that they were betrayed by their old allies. Appeals were made to their vanity; they were taunted with listening to the diplomatic overtures of Schuyler, overtures which were represented as commands.[1] De Callières was so far successful that he induced the Five Nations to send representatives to Quebec. There a treaty was signed.[2]

The fact that certain of her allies had made an independent peace with France was not in itself a matter of danger to England nor an evidence of disrespect. The real danger lay in the uses to which the French were sure to put the ground which they had won. Even in times of peace their policy was sure to be one of covert aggression. The policy of patiently undermining the colonial power of England would never be abandoned. It was certain that the country of the newly acquired allies would be used as a base from which missionaries and traders might spread French influence among the three tribes who had so far withstood diplomacy. Thus the peace did nothing to release the Governor of New York from the

[1] Colden, p. 199.   [2] N. Y. Docs. vol. ix. p. 708.

obligation of constant watchfulness, of persistent and studied efforts to win back the tribes who had yielded, and to secure those who might be wavering.

In the spring of 1699 two commissioners and an interpreter were sent to Onondaga to confer with the Five Nations. At every turn they are met with evidence of French influence. The Senecas stayed away altogether. The Cayugas for a while avoided all intercourse with the English on the transparently frivolous pretext that they were busy hunting for wood-pigeons. After some rather vague negotiation it was agreed that five sachems, one from each of the confederated tribes, should visit Albany.[1]

<small>Commissioners sent to Onondaga.</small>

Whatever errors there might be in Bellomont's policy he might be trusted to follow up the opportunity thus offered. We find him approaching the matter with characteristic directness and energy. The Five Nations were to be regarded as English subjects, their land as English territory. Colonel Nanfan, Bellomont's lieutenant, was sent on an embassy to Quebec, with instructions to demand the surrender of Mohawk prisoners and to warn the Governor of Canada against any encroachment on English, which no doubt meant Mohawk, soil.[2] An Act was also passed by the Assembly making it a capital crime for any Popish priest to enter the colony, a measure avowedly aimed at the missionaries from Canada.[3]

<small>Bellomont's Canadian policy.</small>

Another measure designed was the building of a fort in the Onondaga country, that is, the district which is now Vermont. An Act was passed ordering this to be done at the cost of the colony, and under the control of commissioners appointed by the Assembly. Bellomont expressed his disapproval of the

<small>The Onondaga fort.[4]</small>

[1] N. Y. Docs. vol. iv. pp. 558-78. [2] N. Y. Docs. vol. iv. p. 578.
[3] Acts of Assembly, p. 42. [4] N. Y. Docs. vol. iv. p. 713.

Act, but with unwonted moderation forbore to veto it, thinking that such a proceeding might alarm and discourage the Indian allies. He evidently trusted that the Crown would use its veto, and in all likelihood employed his own influence to bring about that result. The matter was taken out of the hands of the Assembly, and undertaken by officers directly appointed by the Crown. The difficulty was a characteristic one. On the one hand it was undoubtedly necessary that all military operations should form part of a united schem. The task of checking French aggression could not be left to the discretion of any individual colony. On the other hand it could be hardly expected that any colony would throw itself into the contest zealously or contribute liberally unless it had some voice in the conduct of the struggle.

Another incident illustrates the difficulties which beset Bellomont in his anti-French policy. The English colonies were far better suited for horse-breeding than Canada. Horses were of great service not for cavalry purposes, but for the conveying of stores, and it was important that the English colonies should retain this natural advantage. Nevertheless horses were sold from New York to Canada, and Bellomont was accused by his enemies of conniving at the trade. In a despatch to the Lords of Trade Bellomont indignantly denied this, declaring that he had done his best by proclamation to check the traffic, but that in spite of his attempts no fewer than fifty brood mares had been sold into Canada. There will be no checking such malpractices till the English Government adopts a more liberal policy, and employs more efficient law officers.[1]

Bellomont clearly saw that a merely passive policy would not suffice. We must not only exclude the French missionaries, but we must counteract their

[1] N. Y. Docs. vol. iv. pp. 646-7.

efforts by rival missions. This, it will be remembered, was the policy advocated by Dongan. Unfortunately there was one fatal obstacle, the lack of real missionary zeal among the English settlers. Bellomont himself points out the difficulty in a spirit of apology rather than condemnation. He himself, he says, had found an Indian conference an unpleasant business, shut up with fifty chiefs all stinking of tobacco, bear's grease and rum.[1] 'How,' he asks, 'can one expect missionaries to spend their lives among men who never wash their hands or cooking-dishes, and who eat the flesh of bears and dogs?'[2]

<small>Lack of missionary enterprise.</small>

When one reads that, and thinks of those French missions where such hardships were luxury, of priests and Recollect fathers going with calm, unboasting courage to the certainty of tortures which taxed the seasoned courage and brute-like endurance of the savage, one is constrained to admit with shame that the superior ascendancy of France was not wholly due to crafty diplomacy or unscrupulous use of force.

The most capable and strenuous of all Bellomont's advisers on Indian policy was Livingstone. In 1700 he was sent on a mission to the Mohawks. He, like Nelson, was a conspicuous advocate of what might be called in language borrowed from a closely similar situation a forward policy.

His views are to be found in a report addressed to Bellomont,[3] and in a letter written shortly after to the Board of Trade.[4] He states that two-thirds of the Iroquois confederacy were now within French territory, supplied by the French with clothes and taught by the priests. If the English are to check this they must have continuous and secure communication with the Iroquois country. For this purpose there ought to be

[1] N. Y. Docs. vol. iv. p. 714.
[2] Ib. p. 717.
[3] Ib. p. 645.
[4] Ib. p. 870.

a fort within a day's march of Schenectady. Like Lodwyck and Nelson, Livingstone urges the need for an irregular force on the frontier answering to the French *coureurs de bois*. These are to form part of an organized scheme of frontier defence. There is to be a standing force of four hundred men in the colony. Every two years half these are to be disbanded and replaced by fresh troops from England. Those discharged are to be settled on the frontier with grants of land, and are to form garrisons for a chain of forts round Albany. Continuous connexion is to be kept up between these forts by the bushrangers ' moving every day round the frontier garrisons, as is the motion of the pendulum of a clock.'

The French fort at Oswego, or as it was then called Cadaraquie, must be destroyed. The King ought to acquire the territory of the Iroquois by purchase from them, and then re-establish them there as his tenants. Livingstone also mentions that those Indians who were in the French interest were cutting off the English allies by poison. This is repeated in a public document of the following year, with the added detail that the Jesuits supply the poison and that one of their converts, a squaw, administers it.[1] It would also seem that the very same charge was being brought by the French allies against the English.[2]

The transfer of territory suggested by Livingstone was almost immediately carried out, though there is no evidence that it was done in deference to his advice. In 1701 the sachems of the Five Nations executed a deed signed with their respective totems making over the territory, a tract of eight hundred miles, to the King of England. The deed is extant, or at least was so far on in the nineteenth century.[3] Unhappily no chronicle or

[1] N. Y. Docs. vol. iv. p. 689.   [2] Parkman's *Count Frontenac*, p. 439.
[3] It is printed with facsimiles of the totems used as signatures in the New York Documents, vol. iv. p. 708. The publication of these documents began in 1853.

official records tells us the means whereby it was obtained. Its chief, probably its only, value lay in the fact that it might always be used as a bar to any territorial claim over the Iroquois country made by France.

One can hardly say that Bellomont's career as Governor was a successful one. Yet his death after two years of office was beyond doubt a calamity to the colony. Disposed as the colony was to those rapid oscillations of policy which are the almost certain accompaniment of two parties bitterly opposed and equally balanced, continuity of administration was that which gave the best hope of improvement; and even a worse governor than Bellomont would have been a heavy loss, looking to the character of his successor. The advent of Lord Cornbury to office may be said definitely to mark that evil and unhappy state of things when a colonial governorship was enough of a prize to tempt an incompetent and worthless placeman. The legitimate emoluments might not be great, but the position now brought influence. Even used fairly it brought patronage, and if corruptly used, the post might become, as the example of Fletcher showed, a valuable prize. And while the possible gain had increased in value, the drawbacks attending it had lessened. In this way the very increase of material prosperity which had befallen the colony was a detriment. Hitherto the hardships, the monotony, the dreariness of colonial banishment repelled men of high stations and luxurious tastes. Now America had become a place where a dissolute courtier with a train of greedy followers might find life endurable.

Bellomont dies, and is succeeded by Lord Cornbury.

In the two colonies in which Cornbury held office, in New York and in New Jersey, things were such that a capable and efficient governor might have failed to find favour. In each the hostile feeling which separated parties in the mother country was

Character of Cornbury.

reflected, intensified, as is usually the case, by the smallness of the field on which it was displayed. In such a state of things no public man could escape abuse. But the case against Cornbury does not rest on the evidence of his enemies in the colony. The most effective condemnation of him is to be found in his own writings. There are passages in his correspondence with those who opposed him which are like a travesty of the style of a hack pamphleteer. These outbursts of violence enable one to believe what one would otherwise set down as partisan calumnies: the tales of Cornbury's grotesque want of personal dignity, of his appearing in public dressed in woman's clothes, and the like.[1]

In other respects Cornbury's character was to that of his father, the second Lord Clarendon, much what the father's had been to that of the founder of the house. The Churchmanship of Edward Hyde, like that of his first royal master, may have been narrow, but it was reverential and dignified. The Churchmanship of his son and successor was that of a staunch political partisan with whom Anglicanism is an accepted article in the party creed. Cornbury's Church principle seems to have had no influence over his conduct, save by making him the bitter enemy and, as far as might be, the persecutor of Nonconformists, when there was no political necessity to palliate such an attitude. The immense wealth of the first earl showed that he did not rise above the practices, common to all public men of that generation, which in his day made official life so lucrative. The son clung to power by subterfuges and compromises which would have shocked his father. But he was not, like his successor, venal in a manner and to an extent which outraged the morality of his own age.

[1] Morris, then a rising politician, complains that business is hindered by Cornbury dressing up as a woman, and 'putting a stop to all business while he is pleasing himself with that peculiar but detestable maggot.' N. Y. Docs. vol. v. p. 38.

Cornbury's entry on public life was characteristic. In the Revolution of 1668 he was the willing, one may even say the zealous, instrument of a treason, of which the details had been so carefully pre-arranged that no intelligence was needed in the perpetrator. Four years later, Young, the fraudulent discloser of an imaginary Jacobite plot, deemed Cornbury of sufficient importance to select him, with Marlborough, Sprat and Sancroft, as the alleged conspirators. His services to William such as they were, probably still more his close kinship to the royal family, gave him a hold on the favour of the Crown. That such claims should have been rewarded by the governorship of an important province is a melancholy instance of the colonial policy which the opening century brought with it.

The choice of a governor was not the only error for which the advisers of the Crown were responsible. As in the case of Bellomont's appointment, they so managed matters that an interregnum of more than a year occurred during which the governorship was vacant. During the last year that Bellomont held office the support given by him to the Leislerite party had effectually kept down their opponents. His death, however, at once gave the signal for a renewal of hostilities. Unfortunately the Lieutenant-Governor, Colonel Nanfan, was absent from the colony. A dispute at once arose. In such a case how was the executive power, normally vested in the Governor or his deputy, to be exercised? The right was claimed for himself by Smith, the President of the Council a member of the party opposed to Bellomont. On the other hand the Leislerite majority in the Council

Interregnum between Bellomont and Cornbury.[1]

[1] There is a lack of official documents during this period, and we are compelled to rely mainly on the guidance of Smith. There is no appearance of partisanship in his account. His leanings were on the whole towards the Leislerite party, but he does not palliate the misdeeds of Nanfan, and he is conspicuously fair to Livingstone.

contended that executive power was vested in the whole body, that is virtually in themselves. Among the supporters of Smith were Schuyler and Livingstone. The latter was, like Schuyler, a member of a wealthy house at Albany. His position and connexion had given him an interest in the dealings of the English with the Five Nations. He seems to have possessed the same energy and resolution as Schuyler, with wider views and greater powers of expression. In spite of his anti-Leislerite sympathies he held under Bellomont the post of Secretary for Indian affairs, and his despatches are, as we have seen, among the ablest of the many official documents which deal with the attitude of the colony towards Canada and the Five Nations. Nothing could illustrate more strongly the evil influence of that factious spirit which had established its hold on the colony than the attempt which was now made to drive Livingstone altogether out of public life.

The temporary difficulty was settled by the return of Nanfan. He, acting probably on the analogy of a dissolution of Parliament following the demise of the Crown, dismissed the Assembly. A violent party conflict ensued; the Leislerites retained their majority and elected Gouverneur as Speaker. An attempt to dispute that choice on the ground that Gouverneur was an alien was defeated and brought heavy retaliation. The house resolved that no person could be eligible as a representative except for the county in which he dwelt. On this ground eight elections were annulled, all as it would seem of the anti-Leislerite party. This goes far to throw light on the composition of the two parties. The Leislerites drew their main strength from the country districts, their opponents from the New York and Albany merchants, who formed an oligarchy of wealth and to some extent of family.

Meanwhile the party which had triumphed in the elections was gaining important advantage in another quarter. The Lords of Trade had approved the act of attainder against Leisler and Millborne. The younger Leisler, who seems to have inherited his father's persistent energy, appealed to the Crown against this decision. He also represented that his father had expended four thousand pounds in advancing the cause of the Revolution. He succeeded in getting a hearing of the King. The attainder was reversed, and an instruction sent to Bellomont ordering him to bring Leisler's case before the Assembly in the hopes that they would give him relief.

Leisler's attainder reversed.

Party spirit overpowered the strong antipathy which a colonial legislature naturally has to such dictation. A measure was passed raising a sum of money to satisfy the debts of the government, among them a thousand pounds due to Leisler.[1]

The effect of Leisler's embassy to England did not end there. We may be sure that the knowledge that they could reckon on the approval and support of the Crown confirmed the Leislerites in their uncompromising policy towards their opponents. Livingstone was charged with a refusal to account for public moneys, and also with having solicited the Five Nations for a commission to act as their agent with the English Government. If Livingstone's own account be true he was withheld from answering the first charge by the conduct of the Lieutenant-Governor and other officials, who seized his books and papers. Livingstone may not have been wholly clean-handed; few public men of that day were. Indeed it was one of the worst evils of the political morality of that day that in such

Attack on Livingstone.[2]

---

[1] Smith, pp. 139, 140. He gives the text of the King's letter to Bellomont.

[2] *Ib.* p. 139.

matters there was so wide a gap between the letter of the law and the conventional standard of right and wrong. There was hardly a public man who had not at some time put himself within danger of the law, and against whom party malevolence could not find a weapon. But the whole after-career of Livingstone fully justifies us in the belief that the present charge was simply used as a weapon to strike down a political opponent. The alleged intrigue with the Indians was a matter, from its nature, hardly susceptible of proof. The Assembly endeavoured to put Livingstone himself on oath. This he refused. Thereupon the Assembly petitioned the Crown through Nanfan to remove Livingstone from his post. That does not appear to have been done. But in all likelihood the removal of Livingstone from the Council was virtually a suspension of his functions as Secretary for Indian affairs.

The Leislerite party, however, were not to have the ear of the Government unchallenged. Bayard and a number of those who thought with him drafted petitions to the Crown, to Parliament, and to the new Governor. The chief features of their case were set forth in the petition to Parliament. This at once grappled with the main point on which the whole case of Leisler's representatives rested. They had sought to perpetuate the contention which Leisler had in his lifetime advanced, that he had been the representative of a party acting on behalf of the Prince of Orange, and that his losses and his sufferings had been undergone in the cause of the Revolution. The petition pointed out that his action had involved him in no expense as he had not to encounter any resistance, and that he had attacked many who were loyal supporters of the Prince of Orange. They furthermore charged the Assembly with exercising corrupt

Bayard and his supporters petition Parliament.[1]

[1] Smith, pp. 141-3.

influence over the Lieutenant-Governor and the Chief Justice.

Nanfan at once replied to this declaration of war. He did not, however, at first strike at Bayard who was apparently the moving spirit, but at Hutchins, a tavern-keeper and an alderman of New York, at whose house Bayard and his supporters had held their meetings and drafted their addresses. Bayard and three of his chief followers at once took up the cause of their ally, protesting by a written address to Nanfan against his arrest and demanding his release. In the Assembly which met after the execution of Leisler an Act had been passed making it high treason to endeavour by force of arms or otherwise to disturb the peace of their Majesties' Government in the colony. There can be no doubt that the Act was designed by the enemies of Leisler then in power as a measure for effectually silencing their defeated opponents. We may well believe, too, that the greater part of the colony was in a frame of mind when it would assent to anything which had the superficial appearance of securing peace, and which at the same time implied a condemnation of the usurper from whose power they had just escaped. In more tranquil times every thoughtful man would have shrunk from leaving on the Statute Book an enactment so vague in its provisions, and so easily used as a weapon of oppression by any party in power. Under this Act Bayard was now arrested and put on

Trial of Bayard.[1]

---

[1] Our knowledge of the proceedings against Bayard is mostly derived from the necessarily *ex parte* statements made in writing by himself and his son. These are confirmed by a memorial drawn up on Bayard's behalf by Henry Adderly and Charles Lodwick (the latter a London merchant) and by them submitted to the Lords of Trade. There is not enough known of these men to enable us to judge of the value of their evidence. We have also an anonymous paper entitled 'Abstract of letters from New York, dated May 1702, relative to the proceedings of Mr. Atwood, Chief Justice, and of the Assembly there.' The trial itself is in the State Trials, vol. xiv.

trial. It would have been but natural for Nanfan to postpone such important business till the arrival of his new superior. On the other hand he hurried on proceedings, and Bayard was convicted of high treason.

The specific charges brought against him were, firstly, that he and others had drawn up addresses to Cornbury as the incoming Governor, to the King, and to the Houses of Parliament, setting forth certain grievances, especially as it would seem the appointment of 'the hottest and ignorantest of the people to places of trust.' He was further charged with having incited the soldiers to mutiny. The last charge appears to have been wholly unfounded. The other does not appear to have been anything but a legitimate use of political criticism. Nevertheless Bayard and his chief supporter, Hutchins, were found guilty and sentenced to death, with all the horrors incident to an execution for high treason.

One can hardly suppose that Nanfan ever contemplated the actual execution of Bayard. In all likelihood he and his supporters only aimed at silencing and intimidating an opponent. It is said, too, that his object was a corrupt one, and that he used the advantage he had gained to attempt to extort a heavy bribe from Bayard as the price of a pardon. Be that as it may, it is certain that Nanfan's conduct by involving the judicial and executive powers in a party conflict could not fail to bring government into discredit, to shatter the one influence which might counterbalance the spirit of faction which was rending the colony asunder.

As far as the evidence now accessible goes there is nothing to show that Cornbury was in any way pledged to one party among the colonists rather than another. But it is probable that there was a closer connexion between parties in the colony and parties in the mother country than appears on record.

<small>Expected attitude of Cornbury.</small>

The chief motive over and above personal gain which seems to have urged Cornbury was an unintelligent adhesion to Anglicanism, or one should perhaps rather say a factious hatred of Nonconformity. In all likelihood the main supporters of the Church were to be found among the wealthy New York merchants, while Nonconformity had its chief hold on the country districts. This may in part explain what is undoubtedly a fact, the certainty which seemed to prevail that Cornbury would reverse the policy of his predecessor and ally himself with the party of Bayard and Livingstone. So strong was this conviction that Atwood, the Chief Justice, and the Attorney-General, Weaver, both of whom had supported Nanfan, fled to Virginia. That they should have thought it necessary for safety to conceal themselves under feigned names raises a strong presumption of their guilt. Cornbury's hostility alone need not have reduced them to such a strait unless they were conscious that their official conduct would not bear investigation.[1]

Partisan as Cornbury was from the outset, in one respect his partisanship took a form which made for the best interests of the colony. As with Fletcher, the one creditable feature of his administration was his attitude towards the Indians. In that matter the wealthy merchants of New York and Albany were the men who might be relied on to adopt the policy which was best for the whole body of colonies, and best in the long run for New York itself. To them the security of the Indian trade was a matter of vital importance, their estates could bear the temporary strain of taxes for defence, and they were comparatively free from that narrow provincial jealousy which hindered any united and organized policy.

Cornbury's Indian policy.

In May 1702 Cornbury reached his province. One

[1] Smith, p. 145.

of his first acts was to receive a deputation from the Five Nations at Albany. It is clear that the recent surrender of territory was not regarded by them as in any way injurious or humiliating. They expressed their satisfaction at having a ruler among them of the royal house, and they testified the loyalty appropriate to their new position by singing a dirge over the late king.[1]

Cornbury and the Five Nations.

The despatches sent home by Cornbury in his first year show that he was fully alive to the need for guarding against French violence and counteracting French intrigue. He complains that Bellomont had left the frontier and defences in a deplorable condition, the forts broken down, the guns honeycombed, the men ill-clad and ill-shod. There is withal, he says, a public debt of eight or ten thousand pounds. Some of the blame for this may justly rest with Bellomont. But the guilt lay far more with Fletcher and those other offenders, whether officials or private persons, whose malpractices had crippled the revenue and absorbed Bellomont's time and energies. Cornbury also mentions a somewhat improbable rumour that the French Admiral Iberville had been taking soundings in New York harbour,[2] and that the Onondagas had received two French priests.[3] It is clear from other and perhaps better evidence that the peace of Ryswick had not checked the aggressive action of France. If the wisdom of Cornbury's advisers inspired his reports of the evil, we can see his own folly in the light-hearted confidence with which he proposes the

Undefended state of the frontier.

[1] N. Y. Docs. vol. iv. pp. 980, 986.
[2] *Ib.* p. 1057. I can find no confirmation of this. Iberville had a scheme which he submitted to the French Government for seizing Boston. But this was to be done by a land expedition Parkman's *Half Century of Conflict*, vol. i. p. 3.
[3] N. Y. Docs. vol. iv. p. 1069.

remedy. The French, he thinks, can be driven out of Canada by a well-officered force of fifteen hundred men and eight fourth-rate frigates.[1]

Cornbury's account of the deplorable condition of the frontier defences is borne out in a report from Colonel Quarry.[2] He had been Governor of South Carolina, and was now a Councillor in New York. He is said to have held the same office simultaneously in four other colonies.[3] Practically he was acting as in some sort an agent for the English Government, with a general commission to observe and report. The employment of such men might be a necessity, but it is easy to see how in many ways it must have injured the relations between the colonies and the mother country. Such men would be looked on as spies. Their policy would always be one of consolidation; they would be indifferent to those local prejudices which kept the colonies apart, fully alive to the military and administrative evils resulting from separation. The very fact that such men were the advocates of intercolonial union would tend to harden the colonists in their prejudices against it.

Quarry and Livingstone might support Cornbury's views as to the need of prompt action against Canada. We might be quite sure that they were too sensible and well-informed to share his delusions as to the cost of such policy. The more practicable part of his proposal, that of missionary efforts among the Five Nations, was furthered in a different quarter. Chamberlayne, the

Chamberlayne and the Society for the Propagation of the Gospel.[4]

---

[1] N. Y. Docs. vol. iv. p. 977.

[2] Quarry's report is in the N. Y. Docs. vol. iv. p. 1052. The editor of the New Jersey Archives, a collection of which I shall have occasion to speak later, gives an account of Quarry in a note, vol. ii. p. 280.

[3] The colonies were New Jersey, Pennsylvania, Maryland, and Virginia. This is stated in a footnote to the New York Historical Documents, v. 199.

[4] This is in the N. Y. Docs. vol. iv. p. 1077.

Secretary to the Society for the Propagation of the Gospel, was urging on the Lords of Trade the need of such missions. He no doubt looked firstly to spiritual results; but he saw that he could appeal effectively to temporal motives, and he points out that the matter is one which concerns the State as well as the Church.

It is true that Cornbury saw the danger ahead and endeavoured to impress English statesmen with a sense of it. In that one has exhausted all that can be said in his praise. The needful conditions of a successful policy against New France were that the government should be financially strong, and that the colonists should co-operate readily and eagerly. Cornbury's corruption kept the government poor; his arbitrary and impatient temper, the zealous partisanship with which he threw himself into the conflicts of the colony, made it odious.

<small>Cornbury's financial misdeeds.</small>

As we have already seen, the financial system of the colony contained no effective check on a corrupt Governor. When once a sum of money had been voted by the Assembly, and deposited in the public treasury, he could draw it out by his own warrant. The Assembly could punish maladministration by refusing to grant supplies, they could not exercise any direct control over the expenditure of money once granted.

It was soon manifest that this system was no restraint on such a Governor as Cornbury. At the very time that he was calling the attention of the authorities at home to the exposed condition of New York on the seaward side, he was believed to have appropriated to his own use fifteen hundred pounds, raised by the Assembly for the purpose of strengthening the defences of the harbour.[1] There is nothing in Cornbury's character to make the charge improbable. If it were exaggerated, even if it were unfounded, the

[1] Smith, p. 155.

existence of the suspicion was almost as bad as its truth. The evil lay not so much in the particular act, as in the system which made it impossible to detect and check such acts.

The Assembly which was elected upon Cornbury's accession to power was one in which the anti-Leislerite party had a majority. One of the representatives for the city of New York was Philip French, who had supported Bayard in the recent dispute, and had been outlawed by Nanfan.[1] The Speaker was Nicolls who, in the days of Fletcher, had been set down as the accomplice of the Governor in his worst actions.[2] In all likelihood the knowledge that the house was under the influence of strong party feelings, and that some of its chief members were men whose acts could ill bear investigation, emboldened Cornbury in his rapacity. For a year his demands on the exchequer were granted as it would seem without any demur. But the alleged malversation of the money designed for harbour defences seems to have been too much for the forbearance of the Assembly. A clause had been inserted in the Act voting the money, which specified that it should be employed for the defence of the harbour and for no other purpose.[3] But it was clear that with a Governor like Cornbury some more effective check was needed, and the house in June 1703 demanded the appointment of a treasurer, whose warrant should be necessary for the expenditure of public funds.[4]

No attention as it would seem was paid to this proposal, and in the following year the Assembly appointed a committee to investigate the public accounts. The result was a complete breach between the Governor

Cornbury's dealings with the Assembly.

---

[1] Smith, p. 144.
[2] If we may believe Bellomont (N. Y. Docs. vol. iv. p. 507), Nicolls was a go-between for Fletcher and the pirates.
[3] Smith, p. 152.   [4] Ib.

and the Assembly. The committee reported that nearly a thousand pounds of public money was not accounted for. Cornbury retaliated by an assertion of principles which, if put forward by a man of weightier character and more serious purpose, would have been a denial to the colonists of the common rights of English subjects. 'I know,' said the Governor, 'of no right that you have as an Assembly, but such as the Queen is pleased to allow you.' The Assembly might be permitted of royal favour to inquire into the state of the public finances; if they found anything wrong, then they might complain to the Governor, depending on his good will for redress.

Disputes between the Governor and the Assembly.[1]

The Assembly was between two cross fires: it had no hold on popular good will, and it was forfeiting the favour of the Governor. It had, however, independence enough to resist the monstrous claims put forward by Cornbury. It refused to impose an excise suggested by him. The result was an empty treasury, and the officials of the house left without salaries. The Assembly, furthermore, refused to pass a money bill in the amended form in which it was sent down to them by the Council. Matters were at a dead-lock, and Cornbury dissolved the Assembly.

The new Assembly at once showed a very different spirit from its predecessor. Two thousand five hundred pounds had been raised since Cornbury's arrival for purposes of defence, all, or nearly all, of which had been misappropriated. Though the Governor had specially dwelt on the need for fortifying the harbour, and though his appeal for funds to be so used had been liberally met, yet nothing had been done, and a French privateer had actually sailed in unmolested. Accordingly the new Assembly, while raising

A fresh Assembly.[2]

[1] Smith, p. 153. He quotes Cornbury's actual words, as recorded.
[2] Cornbury in Documents, vol. iv. p. 1145. Smith, p. 155.

three thousand pounds for purposes of defence, took the money out of the control of the Governor, and demanded that it should be placed in the hands of a treasurer appointed by themselves. Cornbury acceded to this, saving his dignity by asserting that the money formed no part of the ordinary revenue, and by stipulating that the treasurer should be accountable not to the Assembly alone, but also to himself and the Council.

The right of the tax-payers through their representatives to control taxation, the right of all citizens to choose their own method of worship unhindered by the civil power, these were the vital points round which the political battles of England raged during the seventeenth century. Both reproduced themselves faithfully in the field of New York politics. Never has the Church of England in that colony been more unfortunate in the character of her political allies than in the reign of Anne. The Churchmanship of the house of Hyde had through three generations steadily deteriorated, till in Cornbury it had become a mere factious antipathy to Nonconformists. At the very outset of his colonial career he contrived to entangle himself in an ecclesiastical dispute. We have seen how the settlement, if it may be so called, arrived at in 1693 had left the relations between the Episcopal Church and the other denominations existing in the colony undefined and full of possibilities of conflict. There had been at Jamaica, twelve miles from Long Island, in the time of Fletcher a battle between Churchmen and Nonconformists for the possession of a house of worship. Each congregation claimed it. We have no account of the dispute by an unbiassed witness, and no means of knowing what measure of justice there was in the respective claims of the two parties. It is, however, very certain that both sides

Ecclesiastical dispute at Jamaica.[1]

[1] Our only authority for this business is Smith, pp. 146-8.

carried on the battle violently, and with a total lack of dignity and decorum. It is said, with every probability, that Fletcher used his official power unfairly on behalf of the Episcopalians. Cornbury chose Jamaica as his country residence. He, too, is charged with having played the partisan, and that in a singularly mean and ungracious fashion. It is said that he borrowed for his own use the house of the Presbyterian minister, and then put the Episcopalians in possession both of that and of the glebe. Be that as it may, it is clear that he bore a part in the contest, and that his rancour against the Nonconformist party in the colony was thereby confirmed and defined.

The quarrel at Jamaica was a purely local one. But the bigotry of Cornbury brought on a further dispute which raised general and important questions of law. As we have seen, Episcopalians, members of the Established Dutch Church and French Huguenots had all places of worship in the city of New York recognised by the legislature. There were also in the north-eastern part of the colony, among the settlements formed from New England, places of Presbyterian worship. It is not certain, but it would seem probable that these places were licensed by the Governor. But the English Presbyterians had no place of worship in the city, and were in the habit of meeting in a private house. This seemed to Cornbury to give an opening for a blow at Nonconformity. In 1703 two Presbyterian ministers landed, one apparently a Scotchman or an Ulsterman, Francis M'Kemie, the other John Hampton, probably an Englishman. Both had preached in Maryland and Virginia, and had there complied with

The trial of M'Kemie.[1]

---

[1] There is a very full account of M'Kemie's trial in a pamphlet published originally in 1707, and reprinted in the fourth volume of Force's *Tracts*. The writer does not sign his name, but entitles himself 'A learner of law and a lover of liberty.'

the conditions prescribed for Nonconformist preachers by the Act of Toleration. Cornbury, hearing that M'Kemie intended to preach in the Dutch Presbyterian church, forbade him. He so far acknowledged Cornbury's jurisdiction in the matter as to abstain, and instead to preach in a private house. We do not hear of the same prohibition being applied in the case of Hampton, but subsequent proceedings imply that it was. He preached in the regular Presbyterian chapel at New Town, a village on the coast of Coney Island opposite the north-western portion of New York. Both M'Kemie and Hampton were arrested, and prosecuted by the legal officers of the colony on two counts, for having preached in violation of the provisions of the Toleration Act and also in defiance of the Governor's instructions. The charge against Hampton was thrown out by the grand jury, either through the connivance of the prosecutors, or because the evidence of his having preached, or having been prohibited, was defective in fact. M'Kemie on his arrest had pleaded that he had virtually satisfied the requirements of the Act of Toleration by his compliance in Virginia and Maryland. The validity of that plea in law was doubtful, but the matter was really unimportant, since it seems to have been generally accepted that the penal laws did not extend to the colonies. The real question then turned on Cornbury's right to prohibit. The law officers claimed it as a constitutional right, inherent in the first instance in the Sovereign, and then delegated by special instruction to Cornbury. The jury held that neither point was made good, and M'Kemie was acquitted, though not before his law expenses had mounted up to over eighty pounds.

The strictly legal aspect of the case is really of minor importance. The right of the Crown to interfere in such a matter was assuredly one which could not easily be made good either by precedent or principle. The clause in Cornbury's instructions on which the prosecution relied was at least doubtful. It ran thus: 'You are not to permit any minister coming from England to preach in your government without a certificate from the Bishop of London, nor any other minister coming from any other part or place without first obtaining leave of you, as Governor.' It was plausibly argued by M'Kemie's counsel that minister here meant clergyman of the Church of England. It must do so in the first clause since otherwise it would be meaningless to require a certificate from the Bishop of London, and if in the first clause, then also in the second. It may certainly be said that if this was not the necessary interpretation it was a reasonable one, and that the prisoners were entitled to the most favourable interpretation. But in real truth the question was not one of law, but of equity and policy. The Crown might have the constitutional right to prohibit a Nonconformist preacher. But no one could doubt that such a right even if it ever existed had by disuse fallen into abeyance, and that the attempt to revive it was an act of injustice. The letter of Cornbury's instructions might have authorized him to act as he acted. But there was no doubt that the exercise of that power was left to his discretion, and there was equally little doubt how the discretion of a discreet man would have guided him. To silence one isolated Presbyterian preacher had not even the merit of being part of a consistent policy for extirpating Dissent. It was an irritating act of capricious tyranny, which could do nothing but exasperate.

Yet it must be admitted that there was more excuse for this special error of Cornbury than there was for many of his official misdeeds. The situation was singularly complicated and calculated to mislead anyone unfamiliar with the peculiar state of things subsisting in New York. There was something strangely anomalous in a system which, while it gave the Bishop of London a certain control over every church in the colony, yet did not give any exclusive privileges to the Episcopalian Church. Cornbury's fault lay not so much in his accepting the claims made by that Church, as in the arbitrary and unscrupulous fashion in which he strove to support them.

It was characteristic of Cornbury's recklessness, and of his incapacity to gauge opinion or to look forward, that he should have involved himself in this quarrel at the very time when he was otherwise losing whatever hold he had once had on popular good will, and when it was needful for his own purposes to preserve every shred of influence which still remained to him. Later in the same year a fresh Assembly was elected. That the anti-Leislerite party still had the upper hand may be inferred from the election of Nicolls as Speaker. Yet the attitude of the Assembly towards Cornbury was wholly changed. They plainly saw that the Governor could not be trusted with the expenditure of public money, and that his discretion in that matter must be fenced in with strict safeguards. Instead of, as usual, voting a sum of money for gifts to the Indian allies, the house required the Governor to draw up a schedule of such presents, and of their prices. They should then be provided.[1]

The Assembly opposes Cornbury.

Cornbury's misconduct had done more than call out mere isolated resistance to separate acts of corruption. It led the representatives of the people to make a formal declaration of what their constitutional rights were. A Committee was appointed to inquire into public grievances. It laid before the house a series of resolutions, declaring what were these

A Committee of grievances appointed.

[1] Smith, p. 145*.

rights of the colonists.[1] It was not in every case set forth that Cornbury had specifically violated these rights, but that charge was implied in the resolution.

The conduct of the Governor in taking the appointment of coroners out of the hands of the freeholders, in creating a Court of Equity without the approval of the Assembly, of imposing heavy port dues, and of compelling prisoners, even when acquitted, to pay law fees, is censured. But by far the most important resolution was one declaring that to levy any money from the inhabitants of the colony on any pretence without the consent of the Assembly was 'a grievance and a violation of the people's property.' In that was foreshadowed the whole policy of resistance to the Stamp Act and the tea tax.

In another matter, too, we may trace in these resolutions the first risings of the distant storm. In *Restraints on colonial industry.* more than one of Cornbury's despatches he warns the Government that the colonists are beginning to manufacture, and that unless their progress was watched they would soon be clothing themselves independently of the mother country.[2] It was in all likelihood in anticipation of the policy suggested by Cornbury, and in protest against it, that the Committee declared that 'any tax on imported or exported goods, or any clog or hindrance on traffic or commerce, is found by experience to be the expulsion of many and the impoverishing of the rest of the planters, freeholders and inhabitants of the colony, and of most pernicious consequence, which if continued will unavoidably prove the ruin of the colony.'

Thus New York may fairly claim to have been the first colony which plainly claimed the right of self-

---

[1] Smith. The resolutions are given *verbatim*.
[2] N. Y. Docs. vol. iv. p. 1151 ; vol. v. p. 55.

taxation, and which protested against being sacrificed to the commerce of the mother country.

Cornbury's personal extravagance and his open and glaring misappropriation of public money put him at the mercy of the Assembly. So far from making any head against their opposition or questioning any of their claims, he had to acknowledge with gratitude their liberality in paying for him a debt of two hundred and fifty pounds, incurred as it would seem on the public behalf, but for which he had become himself liable. Moreover, his private debts left him at the mercy of his creditors.[1] In New Jersey his career was equally discreditable. There indeed, as we shall see, he had met with far more bitter and consistent opposition, and had in consequence had fuller opportunities of showing the shallowness of his brain and the violence of his temper, his utter inability to play the part either of an intelligent administrator or a dignified figure-head. The advisers of the Crown might at ordinary times be culpably indifferent to the character of their colonial officials, but there were now reasons which forced upon them special vigilance. For seven years the colonies of England and France had escaped being dragged into the conflict in which the parent countries were engaged. That no doubt was largely due to the cautious policy of De Callières and his successor, De Vaudreuil. They saw that France had more to lose than to gain by hurrying on a conflict, that she was steadily gaining ground by the labours of her missionary envoys and her teachers. Moreover, the resources of France were too heavily taxed to make her rulers eager to extend the field of war. English statesmen, on the other hand, shrank from a struggle which would at once stir up a host of administrative difficulties. But in 1708 united action against Canada was

Cornbury recalled.

[1] Smith, p. 146*.

determined upon as part of the foreign policy of the country. It was hopeless to make any such attempt without the hearty co-operation of the colonies, and New York was the one on which the success or failure of the attempt must mainly turn. It would be dangerous to make the attempt with an unpopular Governor there, hopeless with one as incapable as Cornbury. He was accordingly recalled early in 1708, and the governorship conferred on Lord Lovelace.

For an English nobleman to make all the needful preparations for taking up his abode beyond the Atlantic was no light matter in those days, and the result was the almost inevitable occurrence of a dangerous interregnum between two governors. We have seen how it operated before the arrival of Bellomont and after his death. In each case a dominant faction seized the opportunity, and used its short-lived tenure of power either to glut itself with public spoils or permanently to incapacitate its opponents. But Cornbury's administration had brought with it one indirect good. The need for united resistance had abated the spirit of faction. The men whom Leisler's followers denounced as the servile tools of arbitrary power had now been making common cause with their opponents in an emphatic declaration of popular rights. Thus in the six months which intervened between the appointment of Lovelace and his arrival we hear of no rekindling of the old party quarrel.

The new Governor was a remote kinsman of that genial, energetic and public-spirited man who had nevertheless, by a certain lack of administrative foresight and definiteness of purpose, brought his career in New York to such a disastrous end. The second Governor Lovelace seems to have resembled the first in personal attractiveness. There is the same outspoken frankness in all his public utterances. Yet it is difficult to think that one whose only

<small>Appointment of Lord Lovelace.</small>

experience of public life had been gained as a cornet in the Life Guards could have long proved equal to a task which sorely embarrassed the far-sighted and self-restrained statesman who succeeded him. A chill, caught apparently on his arrival in crossing Brooklyn ferry, brought on an illness which ended fatally before Lovelace had been six months in the colony. Cornbury's successor was almost sure to be popular by contrast. Given winning manners and intelligence enough to avoid any conspicuous blunder, and he would live in tradition as a colonial Marcellus.

Yet in spite of the eulogies which followed his early death and the friendly tone of his dealings with the Assembly, his popularity did not disarm the fears of the Representatives or make them forget the lessons which they had learnt under Cornbury. On Lovelace's arrival in April 1709 a new Assembly was elected. Since Nicolls kept his post as Speaker we may assume that the character of the house was little changed. Lovelace's demand that the public accounts should be investigated, so that it might be made clear to the world in what condition he took over the finances of the colony, was virtually a censure of his predecessor, and as such could not but be welcome to the Assembly. After some discussion a revenue of two thousand pounds was voted. Of this, sixteen hundred was to form the Governor's salary, the rest was strictly and specifically apportioned for the supply of the frontier forts with certain necessaries and for the payment of public officials. But the Assembly now for the first time limited the grant of revenue to a single year.[1] It is certain that the cordial relations between Lovelace and the Assembly would not have survived this attempt to obtain entire control over the public expenditure.

Dealings of the Assembly with Lovelace.

[1] Smith, p. 150.

On the news of Lovelace's death reaching England the governorship was conferred on Colonel Robert Hunter. The singular good fortune which presided over Lovelace's career did not extend to his successor. No governor could have reached his province under conditions less favourable to popularity, more likely to make his task an arduous one. The interregnum between Lovelace's death and the arrival of his successor was occupied with that disastrous attempt against Canada which ended in the ineffectual march to Wood Creek. New York was the one colony which threw itself into the attempt with hearty enthusiasm. On that colony fell the whole burden of building boats for crossing the lake to the number of a hundred, of providing land transport, and of maintaining the Indian force of auxiliaries. This alone meant keeping six hundred armed men in the field, and maintaining at Albany a thousand more non-combatants who were dependent on them. To effect all this the public credit had to be pledged for more than twenty thousand pounds.[1] The inability of the English fleet to co-operate was no doubt due to the turn of events in Europe, and could hardly be imputed as blame to the Government. But the colonists, threatened, taxed and disappointed, could not be expected to make due allowance for that.

After the failure of the expedition the colonists resolved to lay their grievances before the Government at home. An address was drafted to the Crown in the name of the Lieutenant-Governor, the Council, and Assembly, setting forth the perils to which the colony was exposed from the French alliance with the Indians. The document is noteworthy for the clearness with which it sets forth that danger which for the next half-century ever loomed greater and greater in the eyes of English statesmen. 'It is well known that

[1] Smith, p. 143.

they can go by water from Quebec to Montreal. From thence they can do the like through rivers and lakes at the back of all your Majesty's plantations as far as Carolina.'[1] For the conveyance of this address a suitable messenger at once offered himself. The whole conduct of the Indian alliance seems to have been in the hands of Peter Schuyler. We read how he kept open house at Albany, entertaining any chiefs of the Five Nations who might be there, and how he thus built up an influence over them equal to that which the French Jesuits exercised among their savage allies.[2] He had laboured, not unsuccessfully, to persuade the chiefs of the confederacy to break their treaty of neutrality with Canada. Among the Senecas the influence of a French missionary, Joncaire, was too strong for Schuyler.[3] With the other four tribes he succeeded, and a Mohawk contingent took part in the expedition of 1711. But the real value of the alliance did not lie so much in their co-operation in any one organized attack on Canada, as in the sense of insecurity and the need for constant watchfulness which their hostility imposed on the French.

After the failure of the scheme for invasion Schuyler decided, apparently on his own responsibility, to take *Schuyler takes Five Iroquois chiefs to England.* five of the allied chiefs to England in the hopes of bringing home to the Indians the greatness of the country which they served, and of impressing vividly on English public men the importance of the alliance. Almost a century had passed since any American savage had made a public appearance in London. These visitors had neither the same novelty nor the same romance attaching to them as Pocahontas.

[1] Smith, p. 145*. For the actual text of the address see Appendix II.
[2] Smith, p. 144*.
[3] The neutrality of the Senecas and the action of the other four Nations is stated in a despatch from De Ramesay, Governor of Montreal, to Vaudreuil, October 1709. N. Y. Col. Docs. vol. ix. p. 839.

Yet their presence seems to have made something the same stir in fashionable society. They were followed in the streets by a staring crowd, and their pictures formed the latest novelty of the print shop. They were presented to the Queen, and as the Court was then in mourning for Prince George, the savage costume was reduced by the aid of a professed theatrical dresser into some conformity with the occasion.

The visit to Court was not a mere pageant. The chiefs through their interpreter made a short speech declaring the attitude of the confederacy to the two great European Powers. Savages though the Five Nations might be, there was always an honest and vigorous directness about their diplomatic declarations. They never hesitated to declare plainly where the obligations of friendship ended and those of self-interest began. They now told the Queen that, unless she took such measures as to protect their hunting grounds against French encroachment, they must either leave their country or stand neutral.[1]

One can hardly suppose that the gracious reception of the Indian chiefs counted for anything in the American policy of England. It may have had some slight value among the savages themselves and among the colonists interested. They may have felt that the Mohawk alliance was being more definitely and vividly forced under the notice of English public men. In England itself the incident would in all likelihood have faded from public memory if chance had not given it a certain literary immortality. The Indian kings furnished Addison with the ground for perhaps the first of those apologues in which a foreign visitor is the imaginary vehicle for criticisms on manners and institutions.[2]

In June 1710, probably before Schuyler and his

---

[1] The visit is very fully described by Smith, pp. 145-6.
[2] The 50th *Spectator* by Addison.

companions had returned, Hunter reached his government. His character is one of those which tempt one to think that a certain change must have come over the minds and tempers of Scotchmen. The Scotchman of the seventeenth century was, like his modern descendant, clear-sighted, pertinacious and self-reliant. But he seems to have had in him more of the gifts of the courtier and the soldier of fortune, more moral flexibility, a greater capacity for compliance and compromise. That this should be so is but natural. The Scotch character as we know it now has been produced by the training of a society where more than anywhere home ties and home discipline have paramount force. The well-born Scotchman of an earlier day was far more exposed to foreign influences than his English contemporary. He might have kinsmen in the service of half a dozen foreign courts. There were constantly recurring opportunities for intercourse with the French nobility. Calvinism had not yet worked itself into the moral texture of the national character; where it influenced the wealthy and well-born it more often did so by way of repulsion than of attraction.

Character of Hunter.

There was no lack of energy about Hunter, nothing that can be fairly called insincerity, and no reluctance to fight when a point could best be carried by fighting. But it is clear that he owed his success in no small measure to winning manners, to patience, and to the tact which never seeks nor creates a difficulty. Started in life as an apothecary's apprentice, he had taken to the sea. His good looks, helped by his other gifts, gained him a rich wife of high birth. Attaching himself to the Whig party he became intimate with Addison and Swift, and it is no small testimony to the attractiveness of his character that his personal friendship for the latter outlived the severance of their political alliance.[1]

[1] See Swift's letter of March 10, 1713.

Hunter's actual career as a colonial administrator began in New York. His connection with the colonies, however, dated from 1707. In that year he had been appointed Lieutenant-Governor of Virginia, but on his way to the colony was captured by a French privateer, and for some time kept prisoner.[1]

Three months intervened between Hunter's arrival and the meeting of the Assembly. A portion of that time was spent by him in a journey to Albany and in conference there with the chiefs of the Five Nations, in which the existing alliance was renewed and confirmed.[2] While at Albany, Hunter received overtures from New England asking him to employ the Mohawk allies in operations against the tribes who were harassing the frontier of Massachusetts. Hunter might well think that if such operations were to be undertaken at all they should form part of a connected scheme approved of by the Government at home. Private alliances, as one might call them, between colonies for isolated warfare were a form of common action more likely to embarrass than to help the mother country. A New York historian tells us that Hunter's refusal was looked upon by the New Englanders as a grievance,[3] but the feeling was not wide-spread enough nor lasting enough to have found any record in New England history.

Hunter visits Albany.

In September the Assembly met. Hunter's somewhat conventional disclaimer of any party preferences and his exhortation to the House to keep out of party contentions met with formal approval. But it soon became manifest that there was no real

Lewis Morris.[4]

---

[1] See Colonial Papers. [2] Smith, p. 163. [3] Ib. p. 164.

[4] Our knowledge of Lewis Morris is largely derived from his own letters and official writings. These are collected in the New Jersey Historical Society's Publications. Smith, who might in a sense be called his contemporary, tells us a good deal of his early life. He will come before us again in New Jersey. There are many references to him in the archives of

abatement of party strife. A conspicuous figure had of late appeared in the field of New York politics. Lewis Morris was a cadet of a rich New York house. He had spent a vagrant and adventurous youth. But if his career had been one of prodigality, he had neither impaired his capacity nor as it would seem seriously lowered his reputation. He made his entry into colonial politics in New Jersey, bearing a prominent and not always dignified part in the battles there which attended the extinction of proprietary government. Political success seems to have brought a sobering sense of responsibility. For forty years he held a leading place in colonial history, and our knowledge of the history of the middle colonies is in no small measure due to his official writings.

In the very first year of Hunter's governorship the violence of Morris's language in debate led to his expulsion from the Assembly.[1] Possibly by an exceptionally ready and acute perception of character, more probably by good fortune, Hunter saw that Morris would be a formidable enemy and could be a serviceable ally, and succeeded in enlisting him as a supporter of Government.[2]

This personal dispute was soon followed by a constitutional one, turning on a perpetually recurring point of difficulty. The Assembly sent up a money bill in which certain payments were specified, while it was also ordered that they should be made through an official appointed by the Representatives. The Council introduced amendments intended to give the Governor a wide discretion in

<small>Dispute between the Council and the Representatives.</small>

---

that colony. Mr. Tyler, in the second volume of his *History of American Literature* (vol. ii. p. 210), gives a short sketch of Morris. He deals with him more as a political writer than as a practical politician, and, as is sometimes the case with Mr. Tyler, he is a little inclined to exaggerate the intellectual and literary merits of the person with whom he deals.

[1] Smith, p. 161. [2] *Ib.* p. 165.

dealing with the money. The Assembly refused to pass the bill so amended, and the dead-lock was only relieved by an adjournment.¹

In this dispute Hunter appears to have allowed the Council to fight his battle for him. But when the house met he laid down their duty in such matters in language which plainly showed that he did not apply his Whig doctrines to the conduct of a colonial legislature. He distinctly denied the Assembly the right to exercise any control over official salaries. He indeed made a somewhat ingenious attempt to represent this as kindness to the subjects. The Queen took upon herself the responsibility of fixing official salaries, and relieved the colonists from all temptation to make presents to the Governor.² But we may doubt whether the Assembly were beguiled by this somewhat obvious sophism, especially when it was followed by the declaration that to give money for the support of government and to dispose of it at their own pleasure was the same thing as giving none, and that the Queen was the sole judge of the merits of her servants.

<small>Dispute between Hunter and the Assembly about salaries and fees.</small>

This was not the only matter in dispute. The Assembly further resolved that Hunter's conduct in 'erecting a Court of Chancery without consent in general Assembly is contrary to law, without precedent, and of dangerous consequence to the liberty and property of the subjects.' They also declared that the right to fix fees was vested not in the Governor, but in the Assembly. These grievances were set forth in a memorial to the Board of Trade. The answer was that the Governor as the representative of the Crown had the right to create courts of law. The question of fees and salaries was passed over.³

¹ Smith, p. 166. ² Hunter's speech is given by Smith, p. 167.
³ N. Y. Docs. vol. v. p. 359. Smith, p. 175.

The practical effect was that the Assembly, unwilling to do what the Governor asked, were content to do nothing. Their adjournment had been the act of the Governor, when he was residing out of the colony at the seat of government for his other province, New Jersey. This, the Assembly held, invalidated his action and their existence, and they dissolved.[1]

Next year a fresh house was elected, composed of much the same members. On the question of official salaries they were as far from compliance as ever. They made amends, however, by throwing themselves zealously into the scheme for an invasion of Canada. Hunter had no difficulty in persuading them to enlist troops. Ten thousand pounds was to be raised by a loan, to be paid off in five years by a property tax, and commodities were to be supplied to the army at fixed rates.[2]

On no colony did the disastrous and discreditable failure of the Canadian expedition bear so heavily as on New York. None had made such sacrifices, and to them as to no other the very existence of New France was a standing threat. Nothing could have occurred more certain to enhance the difficulties of Hunter's position. When the Assembly met in 1711 there was no side issue by which the contest over official salaries could be diverted or delayed. As before, the point of form on which the dispute turned was the right of the Council to amend a money bill. The discussion brought out into broad light two conflicting theories, which had been vaguely working in the minds of the opposed parties. The Council claimed to be a branch of the legislature, having equal rights and powers with the House of Representatives. Each was called into existence by the mere grace of the Crown. The power of each, therefore, was held by the same tenure and subject to the same limits.

[1] Smith, p. 168. [2] *Ib.* p. 170.

The Representatives drew a distinction. The Council were not analogous in constitution to the House of Representatives. They were not like an upper chamber, representing a certain rank or estate. They existed simply by the pleasure of the Sovereign. But the control of the Assembly over the revenue was not a right conferred by the Sovereign. It was a natural and inherent right, proceeding from the fact that they represented the people, and that the people could not justly be divested of their property without their own consent. The Council had appealed to the opinion of the Lords of Trade. They, it was said, could see no reason for denying the Council the right to amend money bills. Their inability, the Representatives pointed out, to see such reasons did not prove that none existed.[1]

The difficulty was one of those ultimate ones which can only be settled by an avowed compromise or an appeal to force. In such questions there is no common tribunal which both parties acknowledge, no law and no precedent which they recognise as binding. In form the dispute may be one as to the interpretation of what the constitution is. In reality the question is what the constitution ought to be.

The necessities of the Governor's position enabled the Representatives to achieve a victory on at least one point. He was obliged to allow them to pass in their own form, and without accepting any amendment from the Council, the vote for his salary, thus abandoning the very ground which in his opening speech he had so strongly taken up. It is to be noticed that both now and afterwards the form of the vote was not so much money, but so much plate—that is, no doubt, bullion. This was in all likelihood intended to mark

[1] Smith, p. 173. In his account of all these disputes Smith has the great merit of usually giving the actual resolutions passed and speeches made in their original form.

emphatically the fact that the vote was not simply a confirmation of the grant made by the Government in England.¹

Hunter soon found himself engaged in another dispute with the Assembly. In conformity with his instructions he constituted a Court of Chancery, in which he was himself to discharge the office of chancellor. The Representatives thereupon voted that to establish such a court without their consent was contrary to law and precedent, and dangerous to liberty and property, and that it was illegal to levy fees without their approval.²

<small>Dispute about the establishment of a Court of Chancery.</small>

Here, again, the dispute went to the very root of the question, what ought to be the relations between the Assembly and the representatives of the Crown? Hunter did not really bring the difficulty nearer solution by producing the opinion of the Lords of Trade in his favour.

The proceedings of the next year were almost a repetition of those of 1711. Again the Assembly, in spite of Hunter's expostulations, backed by the opinion of the Lords of Trade, refused to accept money bills as amended, and again Hunter was compelled to accept a sum specially voted in bullion instead of a regular salary.³

In various ways did circumstances seem conspiring to make the Governor's task a hopeless one. The terms of the peace of Utrecht were far from giving satisfaction to the inhabitants of New York. It did, indeed, decide one important point, that the territory of the Five Nations was to be regarded as English soil, and that any aggression in that quarter would be considered an act of hostility to England. To secure that territory as a guard to the frontier of

<small>The treaty of Utrecht.</small>

---

¹ Smith, p. 174. It may possibly have been due to the fluctuation in the value of paper-money. ² *Ib.* p. 175. ³ *Ib.* p. 175.

the English settlements was something gained, even though the treaty did not exclude, as indeed it was hardly possible for any restrictions to exclude, the operations of Jesuit envoys.

But it is seldom that the terms of a treaty leave no room for conflicting interpretations. A question im-mediately arose as to the limits of the Mohawk territory. Did it extend north of the St. Lawrence? The principle of the peace of Utrecht was the *status quo ante*. There was to be mutual restitution of all possessions taken during the war. The colonists contended that under this clause the French were bound to evacuate Fort Frontenac. It had been abandoned by the French garrison in 1688, when the Five Nations made their raid on Prairie de la Madeleine. It is needless to say that the savages did not follow up the attack by anything that could be called occupation. They simply contented themselves with injury to the works, and the fort remained an empty ruin till it was re-established by Frontenac in 1695. There is no doubt that the existence of the fort was a serious threat to the Five Nations, and therefore to the English. On the other hand the French might with perfect fairness urge that it was a needful defensive work. And there is little room for doubt on the legal view of the question. It could not be held with any show of reason that a mere Indian raid could constitute territorial occupation. If Schenectady had remained vacant for a time after the massacre of 1688, would the English have admitted that it was during that time French territory by right of conquest? But a sober and impartial interpretation of treaties is hardly to be looked for in people as deeply interested as were the colonists. To them and their savage allies, Fort Frontenac was a standing menace, and the tone in which a New York historian, writing some forty years later, speaks of the matter shows that the

Dispute about Fort Frontenac.

surrender of the claim by the English Government rankled in the minds of the colonists.[1]

Jealousy of the home Government meant practically jealousy of Hunter. Nor was this the only administrative difficulty which beset his path. He must have seen plainly that his chief hope of support lay among the wealthy merchants and landholders. Yet to his great credit Hunter was at this very time sending home advice which, if adopted, could hardly fail to alienate one of those classes, or one should perhaps rather say that class, for as things then stood in New York they were in a great measure identified. Hunter saw that the economical progress of the colony was not a little hindered by landholders nominally occupying tracts of land far too large for them to cultivate, and thereby excluding settlers who would have turned the soil to account. To meet this he proposed the strict enforcement of a quit-rent of half-a-crown for every hundred acres, which, small though it sounds, would, he believed, act as a check on the existing evil.[2]

Hunter's land policy.

Moreover, in 1712, a misfortune befell the colony, not one indeed for which government was really responsible. Yet public calamities, even if they are not expressly laid to the charge of a government, never fail to bring upon it ill-will. And in this matter, as in others, Hunter showed that his courtesy and compliance did not withhold him from braving unpopularity for the sake of principle.

The negro plot.

The industrial system of New York did not suffer it to be a slave State in the same sense as the tobacco-growing colonies of the South. While in South Carolina the negroes were actually a majority of the population, in New York they did not form one-

Slavery in New York.

---

[1] Smith, p. 182.
[2] See his despatch of November 14, 1710, in N. Y. Docs. vol. v. p. 180.

sixth.[1] The Southern plantations offered a better market to the importer, and not more than a hundred negroes on an average were brought into the colony in a year.[2]

Yet, as far as we can judge from the statute book, the negro in New York was viewed with just as much apprehension as in Virginia or Maryland. All trade with slaves was forbidden.[3] Not more than three might meet together except on their master's business,[4] and a free negro might not entertain his countrymen who were still in slavery.[5] No negro could be accepted as a valid witness against a white man.[6] Nor was the negro if accused of crime entitled to the same civil rights as the superior race. Upon arrest he might be summarily tried before a jury of five freeholders, summoned by three magistrates, nor might the prisoner challenge his jurors. His master might indeed claim for him an ordinary jury of twelve, but must pay the jurors himself.[7] Special provision, too, was made lest the tenderness of a master should make his slaves a source of danger or expense to the community. The negro might be set free, but the process was fenced in with precautions. The master who gave a slave his liberty must bind himself under a penalty of two hundred pounds to furnish him also with an allowance of twenty pounds a year, lest he should become chargeable to the State. If the master died, his executors must make the same undertaking; if they did not, the manumission became void.[8] The conversion of negroes was encouraged, but, as in the South, an Act was passed declaring that baptism did not carry with it any claim to freedom.[9]

---

[1] I have discussed the whole question of population, white and black, in an Appendix to the volume which accompanies this, entitled *The Colonies under the House of Hanover*.

[2] *Ib.* Cornbury in N. Y. Docs. vol. v. p. 55.
[3] Acts of Assembly, p. 81.   [4] *Ib.*   [5] *Ib.*
[6] *Ib.* p. 46.   [7] *Ib.* p. 81.   [8] *Ib.*   [9] *Ib.* p. 65.

The whole tenour of the legislation about slaves in New York shows a greater degree of suspicion than was entertained in the Southern colonies. It seems at first sight strange that where they were fewest they should be viewed with most dread. Yet this is not hard to understand. The society of the South was a society in which slavery was one of the chief economical features. With the system naturally grew up appropriate safeguards. Every planter had a direct and personal interest in keeping his own slaves in check, and nearly every well-to-do man was a planter. Thus there came into existence a complete system of control and discipline. Every plantation was a little despotism in itself. In New York, on the other hand, slavery was but one form of industry co-existing with others. The colony was not broken up into a number of separate jurisdictions, each with a head who was distinctly responsible for its safety. Nor was this all. The economical condition of the colony had called into existence a distinct and extensive class of free negroes. In the old days of Dutch rule the West India Company had made it easy for their slaves to obtain freedom. Their position, indeed, was not unlike that of the indented servants in the English colonies to the South. After a certain period of service to the Company the negroes become free, paying a fixed sum in dues. Thus an American traveller, writing in 1679, tells us that there was on Long Island a large population of free negroes, the emancipated slaves of the West India Company.[1] At the same time their status was so far servile that their children apparently remained slaves.[2] It is easy to see how this would tend to increase the danger to be feared from the presence of slaves. The spectacle of a free

[1] This is stated in the travels of the Labadists, Dankers and Sluyter, p. 136.
[2] See Appendix III.

black population near him would at once incite the negro to discontent, and furnish him with the means of doing harm. Thus it might well be that the smaller negro population of New York was more a source of danger and apprehension than that of Virginia or Maryland. There was, too, always the fear that negroes might escape to the French. So strongly was this felt that an Act was passed in 1705 under which any fugitive slave found forty miles north of Albany might be put to death, his owner receiving compensation.[1]

In 1712 there was an armed outbreak of negroes in the city of New York.[2] A house was set on fire, and in the confusion which followed nine white inhabitants were put to death and more wounded. The soldiers were called out, and the rioters were dispersed and fled into the open country. There they were without difficulty captured. Six saved themselves from certain punishment by suicide. Of the remaining twenty-seven all save one were executed. Some more fortunate than their fellows were hanged, others burnt, one broken on the wheel. It is clear from the tone of Hunter's despatch reporting it that, while he had no sentimental horror of needful severity, he was anxious to check punishment, and was not carried away by the panic which pervaded the colony. 'There has been much blood shed already, I am afraid too much,' were the words in which he commented on the matter to Popple, the Secretary to the Board of Trade.[3]

Punishment of the conspirators.

While Hunter was meeting these administrative difficulties he was exposed to attack in another quarter. By order of Government he had taken out with him upwards of two thousand of those inhabitants of the

[1] Acts of Assembly, p. 60.
[2] The discovery of the plot and the various punishments of the offenders are told in Hunter's despatch of June 23, 1712. N. Y. Docs. vol. v. p. 341.
[3] N. Y. Docs. vol. v. p. 371.

Palatinate who had been rendered homeless by the cruelty of the French King and his councillors. These exiles were to be settled on the upper waters of the Hudson, and to be employed in making pitch and felling ship-timber for the English navy. Cornbury, to whom his successor was hateful, probably as a Whig, accused Hunter of wasting public money in the maintenance of the Palatines, as they were called, and of playing into Livingstone's hands in the choice of a site for their settlement. Instead of receiving supplies as they did from Government they might have been self-supporting. Livingstone, Cornbury says, had a corn mill and a brewery near the site chosen, and the increase of settlers there was a direct source of profit to him. There may have been some foundation for this last charge. But, even if it were true, one can hardly blame Hunter, new to the colony, if he took the counsel of a man whom he must have known to be a capable adviser and a good public servant. The other charge can be easily disposed of. If the Palatines were to be purveyors for the English navy, they must be freed from the task of finding their own supplies.

The Palatines.[1]

Dissatisfaction with the home Government for the terms of peace was not the only ill consequence which the war left behind. In 1714 the condition of the public finances was such that the Assembly had to apply itself in real earnest to the task of making a schedule of its debts. The whole amount was found to be nearly twenty-eight thousand pounds.[2] This was met by issuing bills of credit. The extremity of the case and the need for gaining the zealous support of the colonists forced Hunter to yield in part the point which he had hitherto contested. The bills of credit were

Financial difficulties.

---

[1] All the documents with reference to the Palatines are to be found in the New York Historical Documents, vol. v.

[2] To be exact, £27,600. Acts of Assembly, p. 96.

placed in the hands of a treasurer appointed by the Assembly, to be paid out by him according to the instructions of that body.[1] The maintained prosperity of the colony under this heavy burden is as strong a proof as could be found of its resources, of the stability of its commerce and industry.

It is easier to understand the difficulties of Hunter's situation than to trace the precise steps by which he overcame them. We may be sure that his success was largely due to that conciliatory spirit shown in dealings with individuals which leave little trace in public records. At the same time there was no surrender either by Hunter or by the Assembly of the main constitutional points for which they contended. The Representatives persisted in their demands that all revenue should be paid into the hands of a colonial Treasurer appointed by themselves. It is clear, however, that on this point there was an undercurrent of opposition to the dominant party among the Representatives. A number of the chief New York merchants drew up a memorial to the Lords of Trade protesting against the claim of the Assembly to be supreme in matters of taxation.[2]

Further disputes between the Governor and the Assembly.

Neither the tactical skill of Hunter nor the action of his allies among the colonists could do more than postpone the contest. The contention that in all matters of internal finance the Assembly should be supreme and the colonists independent was, under whatever form, the vital question at issue down to the separation from England. But the fact that the difficulty was postponed, not overcome, hardly makes Hunter's work less valuable. If the conditions of the case made perfect and enduring harmony impossible, it was no small matter to secure temporary agreement. Such agreement was a needful

General effect of Hunter's policy.

[1] Acts of Assembly, p. 124.   [2] N. Y. Docs. vol. v. pp. 522, 539.

condition of success in that coming struggle with France on which turned the whole future of the English race in America.

The support of men like Morris and Livingstone, no doubt, had its full share in strengthening Hunter's hands. It was in all likelihood the voice of a few such partisans which, in 1719, set forth the Governor's virtues in an official address. Hunter had announced to the Assembly that he had obtained leave of absence and would visit England. He had at the same time spoken with enthusiasm of the state of the colony, where 'the very name of party or faction seems to be forgotten,' and of the existing Assembly as having set an example to be followed by all its successors.

In reply, the address of the Assembly described Hunter as having 'played the part of a prudent magistrate and an affectionate parent.' No future governor could earn higher praise than to be likened to him.[1]

---

[1] These proceedings are given in full by Smith, pp. 187-9.

CHAPTER VII.

SETTLEMENT OF NEW JERSEY.[1]

OF the religious movements which England in the seventeenth century brought forth, three have left abiding traces in colonial history. We have already seen Congregationalism at work as a constructive

[1] The materials for the early history of New Jersey are abundant in quantity and, on the whole, satisfactory in kind. The archives of the colony from the date of the first grant to Berkeley and Carteret are published in a series consisting of ten volumes, edited by Mr. Whitehead under the authority of the State government. Many of these documents are in our Record Office, some in America. Mr. Whitehead has also published two useful monographs, entitled *East Jersey under the Proprietary Governments*, and *Contributions to East Jersey History*. The best history of the colony is still that by Samuel Smith, written in 1765. It is a sober, business-like work, showing a careful study of original documents. Some of these are embodied in the text, and do not, apparently, exist elsewhere. There is also a valuable collection of documents, published about 1750, edited by Aaron Leaming and Jacob Spicer.

As the Proprietorship of the colony, or rather of the two provinces into which it was divided, passed at an early stage into the hands of what one may call a-joint stock company, there was a strong inducement to stimulate emigration by descriptions of the county. The result was a number of small books, or rather pamphlets, much like those published in the early days of the Virginia Company. They set forth the material resources of the country, describe the progress hitherto made in colonization, and give practical advice to intending emigrants. It is needless to say that they are apt to give a somewhat highly coloured feature of the advantages open to settlers. Three of them deserve special notice: George Scot of Pitlochie's *Model of the Government of the Province of East New Jersey in America*, 1685; Thomas Budd's *Good Order established in Pennsylvania and New Jersey in America*, 1685; Gabriel Thomas's *Historical and Geographical Account of the Province and County of Pennsylvania and New Jersey*, 1698. Fenwick's proceedings are described in an excellent little monograph by R. S. Johnson, published in 1839. Several original documents are incorporated with it.

power; we have seen the Baptist and the Quaker coming in as dissentients and disturbers. Each of those sects also took part in the task of colonization. But the method in which each worked was widely different. The Baptist, denied a share in the corporate life of New England, fashioned for himself in Rhode Island a community in some measure modelled on that which had cast him out. He was at once the opponent and the imitator of New England Puritanism. There was no direct community of action between the Quakerism which disturbed Boston and the Quakerism which founded New Jersey and Pennsylvania. The Baptist came to New England because in many respects he was in harmony with Puritanism. The Quaker went thither, as he went to Turkey, because there was spiritual darkness to be cleared away; New England was to him not a possible home, but a mission field. Nor can we speak of Quakerism as a colonizing force as we can of Puritanism. It is true that Quakers became colonists because, like Puritans, they wanted a home free from the control of a State Church, free from what they deemed the corruptions of the Old World. But their religion did not of its very self suggest, one might almost say enforce, certain political forms. The Congregational system suggested and strengthened an appropriate political system. Quakerism had of its very nature no such creative power. Its strength lay in its assertion that mental and spiritual life is not to be found in forms. Its weakness lay in denying that such forms might be needful conditions of stability. In a Puritan community the legislator was sure to find the spiritual teacher at his side, jealously watching his work, eager to co-operate wherever his principles allowed him to approve. There the civil power was looked upon as a needful agent in creating the highest spiritual life. With the Quaker it was an alien influence, only needful because men had not risen to a perception of spiritual truth.

There is a faint and distorted element of truth, and no more, in the view which represents Fox as a puzzle-headed fanatic, whose theological doctrines and moral teaching were made fit for decent society by educated men like Penn.[1] Such a view evades criticism, because it turns on arguments to which canons of criticism are hardly applicable. It is difficult to see how anyone can study the writings and lives of Fox and his companion, Burrows, without tracing in them the great spiritual truths which found more definite form and more articulate, though not more emphatic, utterance in later Quakerism. But this at least is true: the Quakerism of Fox and Burrows was so full of the elements of social and political disruption, so averse to compromise, that a community based on it was an impossibility. Penn and those who acted with him so modified their creed that it could enter largely into the political life of a society which still fell short of their ideal standard. Yet even then Quakerism had no elements in it which blended with the political life of the community. Therein lay its great difference from Puritanism. Puritanism actually gained in force and intensity from union with the political life of New England, because its ecclesiastical forms at once allied themselves with political forms, because its moral discipline at once seized on the civil power as its instrument. It waned not because it was impeded by union with the civil power, but because it could not satisfy the mental and spiritual wants of continued generations. Quakerism, on the other hand, was no more than a motive which

[1] That is the view expressed by Lord Macaulay. A hearty admirer of the great Whig historian need not hesitate to admit that he was wholly out of sympathy with a manifestation of spiritual enthusiasm, such as that of the Quakers, and that where he was so out of sympathy, his critical faculties were apt to fail him.

impelled men to choose a common home. It did not inform and animate their corporate life, and it was thus ever liable to be thrust into the background by temporal and secular needs.

At the same time if these considerations made the ultimate course of Quaker colonization less effective, they made the initial steps more easy. The Congregational Puritan could act with no allies but those who accepted his doctrinal creed, his ecclesiastical system, and those political principles which had become inseparably connected with that creed and that system. The individual Quaker might find it hard to adapt himself to an organized community. But Quakerism as a whole did not demand certain specified forms of civil or religious life. It could not dominate life as Puritanism did; it could far more easily influence and modify it.

We are wont when Quaker colonization is mentioned to think exclusively of Pennsylvania. But its influence extended to the whole territory between the Hudson and the Susquehanna. Pennsylvania was hardly more truly a Quaker colony than West New Jersey. The personal influence of Penn has indeed given it a more prominent place in the history of the sect. But in neither case was the colony set aside by its founder as an exclusive home for those of his own faith. And if it be said that in New Jersey the Quaker did but enter into an inheritance which others had prepared for him, the same is in a measure true of Pennsylvania. There the Quaker proprietor found the nucleus of a population already in possession, and their presence was a permanent influence in the life of the colony. If then we deal, as for convenience we may, with a group of Quaker colonies, New Jersey ranks first among them in time. I have already described the process by which Carteret and Berkeley acquired a portion of the territory which conquest had vested in the Duke of York, and I have sketched the system on which at the outset they organized their colony.

It so happened that the very epoch at which New Jersey was thrown open to English settlers witnessed a movement of emigration from New England. I have already described how Newark was founded by those resolute citizens of New Haven who could not brook being swallowed up by Connecticut.[1] Elizabethtown was peopled by another band of emigrants from the north-east. Of them we know less than we do of the Newark settlers. Some came from Jamaica on Long Island,[2] some in all likelihood from New England. That this was so may be assumed almost with certainty from one of their first acts. In the very year following the first occupation, portions of the territory of Elizabethtown were detached to form two hamlets, Woodbridge and Piscataqua.[3] Both were New England names, and their retention illustrates the persistency with which the inhabitants of a New England village clung to the traditions of their home. Two other settlements were created on the mainland near Staten Island, by the names of Middletown and Shrewsbury. There was beside a Dutch settlement at Bergen,[4] and there is reason to think that there were beside scattered relics of Dutch and Swedish settlements which were incorporated with New England immigrants.

The first colonization of New Jersey.

To all this tide of colonization Carteret and Berkeley contributed nothing. Even their claim of territorial sovereignty was imperfectly recognised.

---

[1] See the *Puritan Colonies*, vol. ii. p. 162.

[2] In the formal grant of territory from Nicolls two of the grantees are described as of Jamaica, N. J. Archives, vol. i. p. 18.

[3] Whitehead, *Contributions*, pp. 354-401.

[4] Mr. Whitehead in a note to *East Jersey* (p. 17) brings together various documents which seem conclusively to show the continuous existence of the Dutch settlement at Bergen.

Within four months of the grant to Carteret the inhabitants of Elizabethtown, with the approval of the Governor, purchased a title to the soil from the Indians and secured a confirmation of it by Nicolls.[1] In the following year Nicolls made a grant of land to the settlers of Middletown and Shrewsbury. Nor did he limit this to territorial rights. He also gave them certain rights of internal jurisdiction, and a guarantee against being taxed against their will for the maintenance of clergy.[2] Such an assertion and acknowledgement of a certain sovereignty still vested in the Duke of York could not fail to bring about conflict between the original Proprietor and his grantees. For the present, however, the settlers by an illogical compromise took the oath of fidelity required by the Proprietors of New Jersey.[3]

Dealings of the Proprietors with the existing settlements.

For two years after the arrival of Philip Carteret the various townships maintained a separate existence, with no common bond save the vague and slight one of their allegiance to the Proprietors. Such political life as they enjoyed lay in those municipal institutions which they had brought with them as part of their New England training. One would gladly know something more of that life than has come down to us. It would be of no little interest to mark the compact, well-organised system of the Puritan township passing into new territory beyond the bounds of New England. One, and only one, such trace can we find. The records of Newark tell us that the settlers started on their

---

[1] The Indian grant and Nicolls's confirmation of it are given in full in the New Jersey Archives, vol. i. pp. 14–19. In the following century certain disaffected persons in New Jersey produced a document, dated 1666, by which Philip Carteret gave permission to the settlers to purchase from the Indians 'what quantity of land you shall think convenient.'

[2] The patent as confirmed by Carteret in 1672 is given in the Archives, vol. i. p. 88.

[3] N. J. Archives, vol. i. pp. 48–51.

corporate life with a declaration that they would
'endeavour the carrying out of spiritual concernments,
as also civil and town affairs,' and that to this end none
should enjoy civic rights who was not a member of a
church congregation.[1] New Haven had kept to the
last to the rigid and impracticable severity of her
founders, and she bequeathed it to the colonies which
arose out of her downfall. We shall hardly err in
believing that the material success of New Jersey was
due to this solid and organized foundation. The settlers whom Carteret brought out during 1667 and 1668
fell into place as recruits to a disciplined force. As the
basis of the colony were men inured to the hardships of
forest life, duly tempered alike in body and mind, and
trained in the needful kinds of mechanical skill.

Yet this very cohesion and self-reliance which made
New Jersey materially prosperous could not fail to
bring with them political difficulties. The
situation was one to which the history of
English colonization had no parallel. Where
proprietary government existed as in Maryland
and in Maine, and during the short life of the Company
in Virginia, the authority of the Proprietor and the life
of the settlement had a common origin. In the case of
New York, there was the actual transfer of a sovereignty
which had been already fully accepted. The colony
handed over to the Duke of York had been ground into
uniformity by the harsh and repressing sway of the
Company. But the Proprietors of New Jersey were
called on to exercise their authority over a body of
townships which had each an independent civic existence. So far as the various members of the colony
had any community of feeling, it rested on their past
connexion with New England, a connexion which was

Difficulties between the colonists and the Proprietors.

[1] Whitehead, *E. Jersey*, p. 40.

sure to hinder the ready acceptance of the proprietary authority.

The first attempt to bind the colony together for legislative work revealed these difficulties. The townships had their own meetings. Even more, Middletown and Shrewsbury would seem to have taken common action, and in 1667 to have held a joint meeting, at which certain laws were passed.[1]

Such a proceeding made it almost impossible that the system of a common legislature designed by the Proprietors could work smoothly. Local meetings would secure for the settlers all that they needed; the General Assembly was rather the badge of a domination which they regarded with disfavour. There was no motive to outweigh the cost and inconvenience of attendance.

For three years Carteret made no attempt to call together an Assembly. It is not unlikely that the action of Middletown and Shrewsbury made him feel the necessity for such a course. In May 1668 the Assembly met at Elizabethtown. Its proceedings plainly show how largely its members were imbued with the spirit of New England Puritanism. Thus swearing, drunkenness and fornication were all made penal, any person tippling or walking abroad after nine at night was to be punished at the discretion of the magistrate, and the child over sixteen who should curse or smite a parent was to be put to death. An Act was also passed in the true New England spirit of protective legislation, forbidding imprudent marriages. It is somewhat remarkable that the stealing of mankind was made a capital offence. In all likelihood this meant merely the kidnapping of free men, and did

The First General Assembly.[2]

[1] Whitehead, *E. Jersey*, p. 61.
[2] Carteret's proclamation calling the Assembly is in the Archives, vol. i. p. 56. The proceedings of the Assembly are in Leaming and Spicer, p. 78.

not in any way limit slavery or the employment of indented servants. Some light is thrown on the condition of the colony by other enactments. Every male over sixteen was to provide himself with a serviceable gun and ammunition. Rates might be paid in commodities estimated at a fixed value. Each township was to have a brand for its own live stock, and all sales of horses were to be registered. We may assume that there was enough intercourse between the townships to make it needful to provide for travellers, since every town was bound to keep an ordinary. One enactment shows that the province was still in that condition when public office is looked on as a burden rather than a privilege, since all deputies absenting themselves were fined four shillings for each day of absence.

This attempt to enforce attendance seems to have been but imperfectly successful, since after a session of four days several members objected to a longer absence from their homes, and the meeting broke up.[1] Part of the proceedings of the Assembly was the levy of a rate for public expenses. This Middletown and Shewsbury refused to pay. There is no record of the ground for their refusal.[2]

When the Assembly again met in November the same spirit prevailed. The elected Representatives from Middletown and Shrewsbury refused to take the oath of allegiance and fidelity except with certain reservations.[3] It is clear that in this matter they were representing the temper of their constituents. In March 1669 the Governor found it necessary to issue an order that no inhabitant of Middletown or Shrewsbury should hold any office or have the right of voting unless he took the oath of allegiance to the King and fidelity to the Proprietors.[4] At the same time we find a reference in the

---

[1] Leaming and Spicer, 84. [2] *Ib.* 89. [3] *Ib.* 85.
[4] N. J. Archives, vol. i. p. 59.

archives to a certain paper reprinted by the inhabitants of Middletown in opposition to the laws.[1] This was not all. The Representatives of those other districts which accepted the authority of the Proprietors quarrelled with the system whereby they and the Council sat in separate chambers. It was impossible, they said, to work together smoothly, and after a short session they dissolved.[2]

So far, though there had been occasional disaffection, the real force which was certain to kindle active hostility between the Proprietors and the settlers had not come into play. Under the Concessions no quit-rents were to be levied for the first five years. It was very certain that when they were called for they would be withheld. The settlers in establishing themselves had bought the soil from the Indians, whom they regarded as the equitable owners, and by their agreements with Nicolls they had satisfied the claims of the Crown. They might well resent the intrusion of a body in whose demands they could trace nothing of moral right. The first recorded symptom of the coming storm was the claim set up by the townsmen of Woodbridge to admit as freemen incomers who had not taken out patents for their land. They were formally admonished by the Governor that no one could hold land, enjoy any office, nor have a vote at the town meeting unless he accepted the authority of the Proprietors.[3]

Difficulties between the Proprietors and the settlers.

In the following year discontent grew into open defiance of authority. Under the Concessions sent out by the Proprietors it was specially provided that there should be at the beginning of every year an Assembly.

[1] N. J. Archives, vol. i. p. 61.
[2] Leaming and Spicer, p. 90.
[3] Carteret's letter is in the Archives, vol. i. p. 63. It is addressed to 'Mr. John Pike, Justice of Peace and President of the Court at Woodbridge, his assistants, and to all other the well-affected persons of that Corporation or whom it may concern.'

Philip Carteret however omitted to summon one. Thereupon five of the seven towns—Elizabethtown, Newark, Woodbridge, Piscataqua and Bergen—elected Representatives who met in session at Elizabethtown. It was further provided by the Concessions that if the Governor should absent himself from an Assembly, it should be competent for the deputies to elect a president. The elected Representatives interpreted this to mean, not that the Assembly might supply itself with a chairman, but that it might by its vote supersede the Governor. Acting on this theory they chose James Carteret, a disreputable young cadet of the Proprietor's house, who was on his way to Carolina. Without knowing more of the details of the matter than have come down to us, it is impossible to speak with any confidence as to the equity of the case. The settlers had undoubtedly at the very outset a grievance in seeing the title which they had, as they thought, acquired from Nicolls overridden. On the other hand their choice of James Carteret did them little credit. But it is at least clear that they sought redress in a sober, constitutional fashion, limiting themselves to certain definite claims.

[Marginal note: Rebellion under James Carteret.[1]]

Philip Carteret issued a proclamation commanding the deputies of the five towns to make submission, and return to their allegiance. He then fled to England to obtain support from the Proprietors.

If the Assembly had thought to profit themselves by putting a Carteret at the head of a movement they were deceived. The Proprietors showed no hesitation in supporting their Governor. James Carteret was ordered to resume his journey to Carolina, and the Proprietors sent the Governor back, fortified with two documents.[2]

[1] Our knowledge of this business is derived mainly from Philip Carteret's proclamation. N.J. Archives, vol. i. p. 89. The Labadists give a bad report of James Carteret.

[2] Both are in the New Jersey Archives, vol. i. pp. 99-103.

One was a declaration that no land grants made by Philip Carteret could be upset or revoked, and that no patent from Nicolls or from anyone but the Proprietors had any validity. The malcontents were to be proceeded against according to Philip Carteret's declaration unless they forthwith petitioned for the remission of their punishment. Together with this was sent a document, avowedly a declaration of the true meaning of the Concessions, that is to say, of the conditions which the Proprietors had made with the settlers, in reality an alteration of them in more than one important point. The power of appointing ministers of religion, a power which the original Concessions vested in the Assembly, was now transferred to the Governor and Council. Formerly the Governor was bound to summon a General Assembly at the beginning of every year; now he was left free to summon it, and to dissolve it at his discretion. The right to grant land and to admit freemen was transferred from the Assembly to the Governor and Council. It was also decided that the Governor and Council should continue to sit as a second chamber. It was further ordered that no one could be a freeman— that is vote for Representatives in the Assembly—who did not hold land under a patent from the Proprietors. This was in defiance of an article in the Concessions, which expressly granted the freedom of the colony to all who would take an oath of allegiance to the King and fidelity to the Proprietors. It is true that the same clause reserved to the Proprietors the right of changing this condition, but no such change was to affect any interests already existing. This encroachment on the Concessions was practically identical with the declaration that the patents granted by Nicolls were null and void, and those who held them must take out fresh patents from the Proprietors.

The result was, at least for the time being, a victory

for the Proprietors. It is noteworthy that Middletown and Shrewsbury had in the original attack made on the Governor stood aloof from all the other towns. There was nothing in their origin to account for this. It must have been due to some unrecorded personal influence. They were rewarded by a grant of special privileges which placed them on a different footing from the rest of the colony.[1] The patent granted them by Nicolls was confirmed in full. Thus the Proprietors in the case of these townships abandoned all territorial rights. They were invested with supreme jurisdiction in all cases under ten pounds ; in all civil and military appointments the freeholders were to nominate two from whom the Governor was to choose, and no compulsory rate was to be levied in either township for the maintenance of a minister of religion.

Special privileges granted to Middletown and Shrewsbury.

In 1673 the invading Dutch force met with no more forcible opposition from the English settlers of New Jersey than they did from their countrymen on the Hudson. John Berry had been left by Philip Carteret to act as Deputy in his absence.[2] If he had any purpose of resistance it was at once frustrated by the action of the deputies. As soon as the news came that New York was occupied, the deputies of four towns—Elizabethtown, Newark, Woodbridge, and Piscataqua—sent a petition desiring to be heard in the matter of a surrender, and specially asking that till then no audience should be granted to Berry.[3] As in the previous year the men of Middletown and Shrews-

The Dutch reconquest.

---

[1] See Appendix IV.

[2] Berry's commission does not seem to be extant. He is frequently referred to as Deputy-Governor.

[3] This application is recorded in the Minutes of the Council of New Netherlands, N. Y. Docs. vol. ii. This and all the other passages bearing on the dealings of the Council with New Jersey are given also in the New Jersey Archives, vol. i. pp. 122-51.

bury showed themselves more loyal to the Proprietors and took no part in the petition. The Dutch settlers of Bergen also stood aloof, probably taking the view that their allegiance would be accepted as a thing of course, without special surrender. The petition was favourably received; the four townships were to send delegates to treat with the Dutch authorities, and warning was sent to the other settlers to do the same on pain of attack. The threat was effective and delegates from six English settlements attended. Their surrender was received on the same terms that had been granted to the English settlers in New Netherlands. Government was to be carried on thus: each town was to name six men for the office of Schepen, and of those six the Dutch Governor and his Council were to choose three. Delegates from all the towns were to nominate two men, one of whom was to be named as Schout. A Secretary was to be chosen in the same fashion. The latter office was bestowed on that Samuel Hopkins who had contributed so largely to the success of the Dutch enterprise.[1] Bergen, of special favour, was allowed to choose its own Schepens, together with a single officer to act both as Schout and Secretary.

In September the Council of New Netherlands issued an order which practically defined the constitution of New Jersey in its altered form.[2] As in New Netherlands, the Reformed religion as accepted by the Synod of Dort was to be maintained throughout the colony. Civil and criminal jurisdiction was to be vested in the first instance in the Schepens of each township: in important cases or on appeal, in the Schout and the Schepens of the whole colony. In all civil cases over two hundred and forty florins there was a further appeal to the Governor and Council. The townsmen had in the first

The Dutch Council fixes the constitution of New Jersey.

---

[1] *V.s.* p. 173.   [2] N. J. Archives, vol. i. pp. 135-7.

instance had a share in the nomination of their Schepens. This was not to be so in future. The Schout and Schepens before retiring from office were to draw up a list. From this and from the retiring officers the Supreme Council were to nominate the new officers. Thus the whole jurisdiction, civil and criminal, was vested in what would become more and more an irresponsible oligarchy. The power of this body, subdivided into smaller local oligarchies, was to override the old power of the townships. In each district the laying out of highways, the allotment of ground, the observance of the Sabbath, the erection of schools and churches—in short all that in the free New England township was left to the town meeting was here transferred to the Schepens. Nor was anything said of a general legislative assembly, while the Governor and Council reserved to themselves the right to publish ordinances which should have the full force of laws.

That there was no implied reservation of power vested in the people and exercised by their representa-
<small>Assembly at Elizabethtown.</small> tives is clear, since in November the Schout and Schepens met at Elizabethtown under the title of an Assembly,[1] but there is nothing to show what were its proceedings.

We have already seen how New Netherlands was won back for England, how that acquisition brought <small>Recovery of the colony by the Proprietors.</small> with it the transfer of the dependencies on the Delaware, and with what craft Carteret contrived that his own territorial privileges should be restored to him unimpaired. Early in 1674 Philip Carteret reappeared in the colony. It may well be that the harsh and ungenial prospect opened by Dutch rule had cleared away any feeling of dissatisfaction against the Proprietors which had existed. The

[1] Mr. Whitehead gives an extract from the Albany Records showing the existence of this body.

instructions issued to Philip Carteret were practically a reaffirmation of the ground taken by the Proprietors in their dispute with the colonists three years before.[1] No one was to have the rights of a freeman unless he held land under a patent from the Proprietors. The patents granted by Nicolls were to be null and void. But the Proprietors with wise moderation granted to all who held under such patents five hundred acres of land in such places as should not prejudice any other inhabitants. The same moderation was shown towards those who had supported James Carteret. It was only required that they should formally sue pardon from the Governor, and indemnify any private persons who had sustained loss by the outbreak. It is plain that the freeholders as represented by the Assembly met the Proprietors in a like spirit of conciliation. An Act was passed annulling all contracts which had been made for revolutionary purposes, and prohibiting the use of any language which could revive differences.[2]

In the next year came the transfer of which I have already spoken from Carteret's partner Berkeley to Bylling. Bylling, as we have seen, was in difficulties, and it is said that the sale was an act of charity on the part of Berkeley.[3] It is more likely that the charity came in elsewhere. With Bylling were associated three prosperous members of his sect, one of them William Penn. It has always been the practice of the Quaker brotherhood to rescue insolvent members of their own sect, and in all likelihood this, Penn's first, step in the direction of colonization was taken with that motive. Be that as it may, by a deed dated February 10, 1674, Bylling's interest was vested in Penn, Gawain Lawrie, and Nicolas Lucas.[4] Fenwick

Transfer of land to Penn and his partners.

[1] The instructions are printed in full in the Archives, vol. i. pp. 167-75.
[2] Leaming and Spicer, p. 110.
[3] This is stated in the travels of the Labadists, p. 241.
[4] Smith, p. 79.

retained an interest of one-tenth, which, making worse the existing complication, he appears to have encumbered by a mortgage, or sale, involving a further subdivision.[1]

The only one of the new firm, as we may call them, who took any immediate action was Fenwick. Issuing highly coloured accounts of a country of which in reality he knew nothing,[2] he soon gathered a band of Quaker emigrants. But before sailing he was arrested, and though he succeeded in getting free he lost his title-deeds, a loss which brought trouble with it later.[3]

Fenwick's proceedings.

In 1675 Fenwick sailed from London. To keep wholly clear of the existing province under Carteret he pitched on the west side of the peninsula for the site of his settlement, and in the autumn landed on the northeast bank of the Delaware, nearly opposite the site of the Swedish colony at Newcastle. The folly against which Nicolls had vainly remonstrated, of separating the settlements on the Delaware from those on the Hudson by the creation of an intermediate province, was now fully seen. Fenwick appears to have known nothing of the condition of the country to which he was coming. He made his grants of land from an imperfect map, and partitioned out to his settlers swamps and woods as though they had been habitable territory. Owing to this and the loss of the title-deeds, the settlers were unable to identify the tracts which they had bought.[4]

A body of emigrants united by merely commercial motives and the ties of worldly interest would inevitably have fallen to pieces. But it is plain that Fenwick's followers, or at least a party among them, were bound together by the same strong sense of corporate aims which animated a New England

Settlements at Salem and Cohansick.

---

[1] Archives, vol. i. p. 233. All that is clear is that Fenwick parted with a share of his interest, and still retained a certain share.
[2] Travels of the Labadists, p. 242.   [3] Ib.   [4] Ib.

community. Some fell away, settling as it would seem in other colonies.[1] The rest, however, accepted and did their best to remedy the defects of their position. A fresh survey of land was ordered and two towns were laid out, each with its tract of common granted to it by Fenwick.[2] One, Cohansick, seems to have been no more than a scattered rural township; the other, Salem, was a village methodically laid out, with its street down the middle and on either side houses, each with its sixteen-acre enclosure.[3]

Although the Duke, by his grant to Berkeley and Carteret, had divested himself of all control over the territory, yet there seem to have been settlers there who regarded themselves as attached to the government at Newcastle and who resented Fenwick's intrusion. According to their statement he had turned out peaceful inhabitants and destroyed their buildings. The matter was brought before Cantwell, the Sheriff at Newcastle, and was promptly reported to Andros.[4] Andros was at this very time reorganizing the government on the Delaware, and creating two subordinate courts at Upland and Hoarkill, under the jurisdiction of Newcastle. To take Fenwick in hand fell in naturally with this policy. Accordingly Collier, the newly appointed military Commander at Newcastle, was specially instructed to arrest Fenwick and send him to New York.[5] Collier appears to have modified his instructions and to have contented himself with a 'friendly and civil letter,' in which he requested Fenwick to come to Newcastle. Fenwick, obstinate with the combined obstinacy of a Quaker and an old Ironsides, refused to come. Collier then visited him in person. Fenwick refused to accept

[Marginal notes: Difficulties with the existing settlers and with Andros.]

[1] Agreement between Fenwick and the colonists quoted by Johnson, p. 16.
[2] *Ib.* p. 17. [3] *Ib.* [4] Brodhead. vol. i. p. 302.
[5] The letter from Andros to Collier is in the Archives, vol. i. p. 189.

any orders unless they came direct from the King or the Duke of York, and, having succeeded in thrusting Collier from the house, finished the colloquy through a hole in the door. Collier reported the matter to the four magistrates who formed his Council. With their approval he issued an order for the arrest of Fenwick, who was sent prisoner to New York.[1] His inability to produce the originals of his documents told against him, and he was fined forty pounds and for some time kept in custody, but was finally released on pledging himself, if we may believe Andros, to exercise no authority in New Jersey.[2]

This dispute is not unimportant since it undoubtedly did much to determine the attitude which Andros adopted in all his dealings with the settlements on the Delaware. The crude and ill-considered enterprise of Fenwick was soon followed by more methodical and judicious attempts. The division of the territory was a necessary step before it could be turned to account. The formation of the country suggested the severing of it into two portions, each with its own river frontage. The south-west bank of the Hudson and the north-west bank of the Delaware were each well fitted to be the home of a community living in part by agriculture, in part by trade. But between the two there was no real and integral connexion. A pathless wilderness severed them; there could be no communication for trade, for common political action, nor for defence. If either was to be united with any other territory, the north-eastern half belonged naturally

Division of the province.

[1] All these proceedings are described in the Minutes of a Court held at Newcastle, Archives, vol. i. p. 190. Fenwick's own side of the story is told in a document, drawn up by himself, called *A Remonstrance and Declaration* (published by Johnson), pp. 37, &c.

[2] The proceedings at New York against Fenwick are all in the New York Documents, vol. xii., and have been reprinted in the New Jersey Archives, vol. i. pp. 235-9.

to New York, the south-western to the little dependency which had its head-quarters at Newcastle. If the whole territory had been under the direct control of the Crown it is possible that the growing sense of the necessity for colonial unity, both for purposes of defence and for purposes of trade, would have hindered any scheme for division. But Berkeley and Carteret were certain to deal with their territory on purely commercial grounds, and on those grounds a definite apportionment of territory to Bylling and his partners was expedient. Accordingly, some two months after Fenwick's arrival at Salem, an agreement was drawn up by which the province was divided into two moieties, whereof the western, that on the Delaware, was assigned to Penn and his partners, while the eastern was retained by Carteret.[1] As a mere division of a landed estate the arrangement was complete, and there could be no doubt that so far its main purpose was a good one. But it wholly failed to solve an important difficulty, which as time showed could not be ignored. It conveyed to Penn and his partners all such rights over the western portion of the province as Carteret and Berkeley had received from the Duke. But the extent of those rights was not specified, and it is difficult to think that the omission was accidental. Nothing in the deed showed whether the Duke's grant to Carteret was merely territorial, or whether it carried with it political sovereignty. Yet at this very time Philip Carteret was engaged in a dispute with the Duke of York's collector of customs, Dyer.[2] We can hardly suppose that Penn and his partners did not know that fact. If they knew it in all likelihood they saw the difficulty ahead, and avoided instead of facing it.

[1] The deed of division is in the Archives, vol. i. p. 205.

[2] A letter from Werden, the Duke of York's Secretary, to Andros, August 31, 1676, refers to Dyer's 'late bickering with Captain Carteret.' N. Y. Docs. vol. iii. p. 240.

In the summer of 1676 the partners sent out commissioners to represent them in the colony. The designs of the new Proprietors may be learnt from their instructions to their commissioners,[1] from a letter to their intending settlers,[2] and from an agreement drawn up with them and signed by each party.[3] The commissioners, three in number, were to represent the Proprietors, and to act as an executive government for the colony till such a time as a representative Assembly should be set on foot. The commissioners were to hold office for a year and then to be reappointed. Should the Proprietors neglect to appoint, the right devolved on the freeholders. It is not easy to understand the precise details of the land system intended. Apparently the commissioners were to choose sites for townships, taking care to satisfy by purchase any claim which the natives might have. Each township was to be divided into a hundred spaces. These were to be assigned by lot to the various Proprietors and then sold to the settlers. In fact it was the duty of the commissioners, first to secure an equitable partition of the soil among the Proprietors, and then a satisfactory distribution of it among the freeholders. It is plain that the Proprietors considered that Fenwick in establishing himself, and so getting first choice of land, had encroached on the rights of his colleagues. Accordingly in portioning out the territory the ground already occupied by his grantees was to be included, but the actual occupants were not to be disturbed. If when the lots were cast the ground occupied by them fell to any other Proprietor, the occupying holder was to retain his land, and the Proprietor was to receive an equivalent out of Fenwick's lot. Fixed quantities of land were to be assigned to

Policy of Penn and his associates.

---

[1] New Jersey Archives, vol. i. p. 219.   [2] *Ib.* p. 231.
[3] *Ib.* p. 241.

all persons approved by the Proprietors, and emigrating at their own cost. Those who went out in the first year (1677) were to receive seventy acres, with seventy more for every able-bodied male servant, and fifty for every woman or inferior man-servant. In the next year these quantities were to be reduced to fifty and thirty acres, in the following year to forty and twenty. For such land a quit-rent was to be paid of a penny an acre if the land was within a township, otherwise a halfpenny. But if any tenant failed adequately to occupy his land—that is to settle it with a servant to every hundred acres—the holding was to revert to the Proprietors for twenty years.[1]

Besides these provisions for dealing with the land, thirty-two articles were drawn up defining the constitution of the colony. The first set forth that the constitution there described was to be unalterable, and that the Assembly was to have no power to make any laws at variance with it. This was confirmed by the second, which prescribed that any person designedly, wilfully, or maliciously moving anything which should subvert or contradict the fundamental constitution was to be treated as a traitor.

Articles of constitution.

It is needless to point out the futility of such a provision. There must in every community be some sovereign body which has among its other powers the power to annul any law. It is certain, too, that when the time comes if men wish the constitution altered they will alter it, if not avowedly, by raising questions of interpretation. Such a declaration is only valuable as an emphatic way of saying that those who have fashioned the constitution wish it to be permanent. The constitution went on to enact that no person should suffer in any way for his religious faith or his form of worship, that there should be trial by jury, and that the liberty of

[1] It would seem that after twenty years the interest of the original tenant was to revive.

the subject should be secured by provisions analogous to those of the *Habeas Corpus* Act.

Special provision was made for avoiding any hostility with the Indians. No land was to be taken up till the commissioners had satisfied themselves that the claims of the native occupants had been fully satisfied, and all cases between a native and an Englishman were to be tried by a mixed jury. The Proprietors expressly renounced all right of taxation. No impost of any kind might be imposed except with the approval of the Assembly. Till that should come into existence the direct consent of the people themselves was required.

The existence of a representative Assembly was to be postponed till the formation of local divisions. When the surveying and allotment of the holdings were complete there would be a hundred townships, or as they were to be called proprietorships. Each of these was to return a member. The Assembly thus composed was to be the supreme legislative body, but its powers were, as we have just seen, to be limited by the immutable character of the fundamental constitutions. The Assembly was to elect ten commissioners, to act as the Executive Council of the Province. Judges and other officials were to be chosen by the Assembly, justices and constables by the people, probably acting in their different districts, though this is not expressed.

There is in this constitution something, though far less, of the same elaborate and fantastic character as there is in the first constitution of Carolina. It is an attempt to construct an ideal community with little regard to the peculiar needs and condition of the country. Especially was it an error to require a hundred members for the Assembly.

In the same year the foundation of the new province was laid by a settlement on an eastern tributary of the Delaware above Salem. The settlers came in two

bodies, one from London, one from Yorkshire, each
with certain territorial rights acquired by purchase from
Penn and his co-Proprietors. Each occupied
one side of the stream, but the whole formed
a united township, named after the Yorkshire
town Bridlington.[1] This soon passed into the colloquial
form of the original, Burlington.[2] Fenwick's settlement
remained for the present a detached community,
managing its own affairs. There were thus three
separate governments existing in New Jersey: the
eastern colony, under Carteret, with Elizabethtown for
its capital, and the two detached settlements at Burlington and Salem. The principal incident in the history
of each at this stage was a feud with Andros. Each
turned on the same point: the contention of Andros
that the Duke in parting with the soil of New Jersey
had retained some sort of fiscal authority over the
inhabitants.

Foundation of Burlington.

In the case of Fenwick the dispute was reopened
in 1678. In the spring of that year he called a meeting
of the settlers at Salem, and demanded from
them an oath or declaration of fidelity, and at
the same time appointed officials.[3] It is clear
that there were about Salem some isolated settlers,
squatters as we should call them, not connected with
Fenwick, who hitherto so far as they acknowledged
any jurisdiction belonged to Newcastle.[4] They do
not seem themselves to have raised any objection to
Fenwick's proceedings. But Cantwell attended the
meeting and, as it would seem, on their behalf protested

Fresh dispute between Andros and Fenwick.

---

[1] Smith, ch. vi. He quotes letters from the original settlers, and refers to other documents.

[2] Burlington is used in 1683. N. J. Archives, vol. i. p. 428.

[3] This is stated in the depositions of Cantwell and three other witnesses given in the N. Y. Docs. vol. xii. p. 592.

[4] This is implied in Fenwick's proclamation mentioned below. The proclamation is in the New Jersey Archives, vol. i. p. 277.

against Fenwick's claim of jurisdiction.[1] Fenwick replied by issuing a paper ordering all settlers in and about Salem to acknowledge his rights as landlord, and it is said that he also forbade them to pay any dues at Newcastle.[2]

This was reported at New York, and Fenwick was immediately summoned to attend there, on the ground that he had violated the conditions on which he was set free.[3] Fenwick on this occasion showed himself more tractable than before. He presented himself at New York. There his case was submitted to the Supreme Court, who decided against him.[4] The result was that Salem was for the time being incorporated with Newcastle. A local government of a simple kind was established. Six of the inhabitants were appointed by Andros to act as 'overseers, select men or commissioners under the authority of the court at Newcastle.'[5]

To Penn and his partners the question was one of overwhelming importance. If the claim of Andros to exercise authority over Salem was allowed, it must be on the ground that the grant of New Jersey carried with it no political rights. If that were so the whole scheme of forming a colony must fall to the ground. It was very certain that Penn and his friends would not have troubled themselves to acquire the territory if they were to be simply a company of landholders under the political sovereignty of the Duke. It was very certain, too, that their claims would be pushed with perseverance and dexterity.

Position of Penn and his partners.

It was no doubt fortunate for the Quaker Proprietors that the settlements in the eastern half of the province had gained a secure foothold. Philip

---

[1] Cantwell's deposition.   [2] *Ib.*
[3] N. Y. Docs. vol. xii. p. 595.   [4] *Ib.* pp. 597–600.   [5] *Ib.* p. 610.

Carteret and his companions had in fact been acting as pioneers for the Quaker colonists. To annul political rights which rested on a prescription of thirteen years would have been a manifest violation of equity. Yet any attempt to incorporate the western half of the colony with Newcastle must carry with it as a logical consequence the incorporation of the eastern half with New York.

Having regard no doubt to these considerations Andros made no attempt to enforce, or even to raise, a general claim of sovereignty over the settlers at Burlington. There was, however, a claim which he might make, less serious, yet enough to strike a heavy blow at the prosperity of the new colony. It might be urged that, though the Duke of York had abandoned all political authority over the territory of New Jersey, he still kept certain fiscal rights. This claim, too, might be put forward with a show of equity, since a colony set free to frame its own system of import duties might be a most formidable rival to its neighbours in the paths of commerce. If the ports on the Delaware were set free from customs, they were certain to draw away the trade of New York. Andros at once saw this danger, and issued an order that all vessels landing goods within the territory of Penn and his partners should pay the same duties as if they had landed their cargoes at New York. This was not only the assertion of a dangerous right, but also the exercise of it in a peculiarly irksome form. For the duty was to be levied not only on goods imported and exported for purposes of trade, but also on the landing of such goods as were needful for stocking the colony. The Quaker partners at once saw the importance of the issue raised and responded to the challenge. We can hardly err in assigning to the hand of Penn the remonstrance which they put forward.

Dispute about customs.

The document is one of the most remarkable in colonial history. Hitherto, in all the disputes between the New England colonies and the home Government, the colonists had limited themselves to strictly legal grounds. They had invariably pleaded the letter of their charters, and had declined to touch on general questions of what one may fairly call imperial policy. Penn held firmly to his legal right as transmitted to him through Carteret. The conveyance made by the Duke to Carteret and Berkeley expressly gave power of government, and what the Duke conveyed to Carteret they had handed on intact to Penn and his partners. 'Was it likely,' Penn urged, 'that they would have gone to all the labour and cost of establishing a colony if it had been otherwise?' Who would leave a prosperous country and settle in a wilderness unless he were at least assured of the fruit of his own labour, free from the possibility of arbitrary taxation?

Penn's remonstrance.[1]

The argument waxes bolder as it advances. If the partners had not bought the right to be independent of control from without, what had they bought? Not the right to the soil itself, for that was vested in the natives and was not the Duke's to sell. Then, with an anticipation of the ground taken up by the colonists a hundred years later, Penn argues that the grant to the Duke, on which he based his claim, was limited by a reference to the laws and government of England. But those laws expressly protected the subject against the levy of any tax save by his own consent.

Penn then passes from the declaration of the strictly legal aspect of the case to those considerations of equity and good policy which make it to the interest of the Duke to forbear, and of the Crown to enforce such forbearance. The duty is not merely one upon

[1] The remonstrance is given in full in Smith, p. 117.

goods imported for the purpose of trade. It will fall also on the stock which is absolutely needful for the settlement of a new colony. Thus to adopt a system by which any external power could levy duties on the colonists was to cut up the roots of commercial prosperity. 'There can be no trade without a people; there will be no people where there is no encouragement, nor can there be any encouragement where people have not greater privileges by going than staying; for if their condition be not meliorated they will never forgo the comfort of their kindred they must leave behind them, nor forsake their native country, run the hazard of the seas, nor, lastly, expose themselves to the wants and difficulties of a wilderness; but, on the contrary, if they have less privileges there than at home 'tis in every way to worst themselves to go.'

Penn points out, too, that the claim is an unlimited one. If it is admitted 'what security have we of anything we possess? We can call nothing our own, but are tenants-at-will not only for the soil, but for all our own personal estates.' 'This is to transplant not from good to better, but from good to bad; this sort of conduct has destroyed governments, but never raised one to any true greatness, nor ever will in the Duke's territories, while so many countries equally good in soil and air are surrounded with greater freedom and security.'

We seem to hear the pleading of Adams and Franklin. Moreover, Penn's arguments show a conception of colonial policy clearer and more advanced than anything with which we have yet met.

Yet, on the other hand, the ground taken by Andros asserted a principle which could not safely be put aside. It was needful that there should be for the whole body of colonies some uniform fiscal system. To impress that on men's minds was indeed one of the main results of the conquest of New Netherlands and the acquisition of the adjoining territory. In two ways, by making some common system of defence necessary and some common system of revenue possible, that conquest was the first step towards colonial unity.

In all likelihood Penn's position, and the favour with which he was regarded by the royal family, did more for him and his partners than the justice of his reasoning. In August 1680 the question was referred to Sir William Jones, the Attorney-General. He gave it as his opinion that inasmuch as the grant to Berkeley and Carteret had contained no reservation of any profit, nor even of any jurisdiction, the Duke's claim as made by Andros was not binding in law.[1]

Legal opinions in favour of Penn.

Before the end of the year the question was finally set at rest. A fresh grant was made by the Duke of York conveying to Bylling and his heirs and assigns, for a nominal quit-rent, the territory purchased from Carteret.[2] With the land was conveyed all such political rights as the King's grant had conferred on the Duke. The document embodied a practical compromise which gave the Quaker Proprietors all that they asked for, but it did not acknowledge the justice of their case. The Duke granted the very thing which, according to their contention, he had before alienated.

The matter compromised by a fresh grant.

To the present grantees it was a matter of indifference which view was accepted, whether the Duke surrendered his claim as invalid or extinguished it by a fresh grant. But otherwise there was a very great difference between the two views. Sir George Carteret had died early in 1680. The grant to Bylling was an implicit denial of the title

Altered position of the East Jersey Proprietors.

[1] This opinion is in the N. Y. Docs. vol. iii. p. 284.
[2] N. J. Archives, vol. i. p. 324.

enjoyed by Carteret's heirs. Recent doings in East Jersey showed that they had real grounds for apprehension. In West Jersey the attack, as we have seen, began with the demand to levy customs. The vigorous action of Penn kept it from reaching a further stage. In East Jersey the strife had a like beginning, but ran a different course.

For some years after the foundation of the eastern colony under Philip Carteret the question of customs remained in abeyance since there was no port. But about 1677 vessels began to land at Elizabethtown, and the Governor had exercised the right of clearing them there without reference to New York.[1] Elizabethtown was a more dangerous rival to the commerce of New York than the settlements on the Delaware could be. It is clear, too, that the Assembly of the colony was determined to contest any claim that might be made by the Governor of New York to levy custom duties. A sum of one hundred and fifty pounds was raised by rate, and kept as a reserve fund, to indemnify any ship-owner that might suffer by the action of the authorities of New York.[2] Andros not improbably thought that the death of Sir George Carteret offered a favourable opening for enforcing the claims of his master. In the spring of that year (1680) he wrote a letter to Philip Carteret forbidding him to exercise any jurisdiction over the King's subjects on the ground that it would be an encroachment on the Duke's authority. He also claimed the right to establish a fort on the coast of New Jersey and to erect beacons, on the plea that these works were for the benefit of all the King's subjects.[3] Whatever justice there might be in Andros's case as far as customs were

Andros attempts to levy customs in East Jersey.

---

[1] See Mr. Whitehead's (*E. Jersey*) note, p. 82. He quotes a proclamation by Carteret and a statement made in 1698 by Graham, Attorney-General of New York, to Bellomont. N. Y. Docs. vol. iv. p. 382.

[2] Leaming and Spicer, p. 131.   [3] N. J. Archives, vol. i. p. 292.

concerned, his general contention was manifestly extravagant. He was disputing a title which for fifteen years had been uncontested, and on the strength of which men had conveyed themselves, their goods, and households to a home in the wilderness.

Carteret answered in a temperate letter.[1] He had consulted his council and the chief settlers. They bore him out in the view that the Duke's grant, the letter of the King, and the prescription of undisputed possession all justified him in refusing to accept the authority of Andros. He was willing, however, to refer the matter to the King. In the meantime, if force was used, he would meet it with force.

One expression in Carteret's answer is noteworthy. He was acting, he said, with the most eminent though not numerous part of the country. This awakens a suspicion than Andros was relying on the help of a party within the colony who were disloyal to Carteret. Later events showed plainly that the spirit of disaffection roused by James Carteret was not extinct. Those who had been his partisans had no ground for cleaving to Andros, but they were ready to make common cause with anyone in opposition to the Proprietors and their Deputy.

Andros had not the fairness or courtesy to wait for Carteret's answer. Relying in all likelihood on his adherents within the colony, he issued a proclamation forbidding not only Carteret, but all acting under him, to exercise any jurisdiction.[2] For the present Andros confirmed the existing constables in their office. Presently he would take further order in accordance with the terms of his commission. In other words, New Jersey was to be dealt with as forming a dependency of New York.

Carteret now abandoned the somewhat submissive

[1] N. J. Archives, vol. i. p. 294.   [2] Ib. p. 293.

attitude which he had hitherto taken up. He admonished Andros to abstain from any disturbance, and notified him that if any such took place he should appeal to the King.[1] At the same time he took measures as if against a foe from whom he anticipated invasion. He appointed a deputy to succeed him in case of accident,[2] and raised an armed force of a hundred and fifty men to act as a body-guard.[3] A summons had been issued for the calling of a General Assembly. This was now revoked, which makes one think the Governor feared the influence of Andros over the people.[4]

Carteret in nowise exaggerated the danger. In April Andros set sail for New Jersey. It is hardly likely that he set forth with any definite purpose of using violence, since he was attended only by his official staff, and a few volunteers carrying no arms save swords. This seems to have allayed Carteret's suspicions, and though Andros met more than one armed party, no resistance was offered. Having reached Elizabethtown, Andros read aloud the Duke of York's title to the whole province. This, as Carteret reasonably urged, 'signified little to the purpose,' since it was no part of the Proprietors' case to question the Duke's original title. Some discussion followed, but Andros turned a deaf ear to all remonstrance, and was content to silence his opponents by vague threats. He then returned to his vessel and set sail for New York.

Andros visits Elizabethtown.[5]

[1] N. J. Archives, vol. i. p. 297.   [2] *Ib.* p. 295.
[3] Carteret's letter to the Proprietor, July 9, 1680, N. J. Archives, vol. i. p. 314.
[4] Carteret's letter to Andros as above.
[5] There are two accounts of Andros's visit published in the New Jersey Archives, vol. i. pp. 299-302 and pp. 304-6, taken from manuscripts at Albany. They appear to have been written by members of Andros's staff. We have also Carteret's own account in the letter of July 9, referred to above.

The next incident reads like some story of mediæval violence. Carteret lived, not in Elizabethtown, but in a detached dwelling-place. Three weeks after Andros's departure, in the night a party from New York, having corrupted one of Carteret's servants, gained access to this house. The Governor was dragged out of bed, thrown half-naked into a boat, and hurried off as a prisoner to New York. There he was kept for five weeks awaiting his trial. In New Jersey the hostility of an important party to Carteret had smoothed the path for Andros. In New York we may well believe that the unpopularity of the Duke's deputy stood his enemy in good stead. Carteret was put on his trial on the count of having exercised illegal authority. The jury acquitted him, and in spite of repeated charges from Andros and refusals to accept their verdict they stood firm. Nevertheless they appended to their verdict the somewhat illogical addition that if Carteret returned to New Jersey he should give security not to assume any authority or jurisdiction, civil or military. If this authority was illegal it is not easy to see on what grounds he was acquitted.

Arrest of Carteret.[1]

Meanwhile the settlers in East Jersey were taking advantage of the existing state of things to throw off the yoke of the Proprietors. In June Andros revisited the colony. His purpose was avowedly peaceful, since he was accompanied by his wife and her train of gentlewomen.[2] He had already issued writs for the election of an Assembly. Each township returned two Deputies.

Andros revisits Elizabethtown and summons an Assembly.

---

[1] Our knowledge of this business is derived partly from Dankers and Sluyter, p. 345, partly from Carteret's own account, contained in two letters, one to a certain Coustier of whom we know nothing else, one to Captain Bollen, the Secretary of West New Jersey. The incident seems, not unnaturally, to have made a great impression on the Labadist travellers, and is told by them very vividly.

[2] The Labadists, p. 346.

The proceedings of the Assembly opened in a curiously illogical fashion. The Deputies presented an address to Andros, expressing their wish, or rather their demand, that the privileges granted them in the concessions from Berkeley and Carteret should remain unimpaired. Thus, in the very moment of repudiating the authority of the Proprietors, they acknowledged the validity of past acts done by that authority.

It is impossible to say what relations Andros believed to exist between the Duke of York and the New Jersey settlers, or how he wished to arrange those relations. Probably he had himself no clear idea on the subject. He submitted to the Assembly that code of laws drawn up after the conquest of New Netherlands known as the Duke's laws, and he gave the members to understand that the Court of Assizes on Long Island was now to be the supreme tribunal for the colony. In other words New Jersey was to be, like the settlement on the west bank of the Delaware, a dependency of New York. Yet it is very certain that the Assembly would never have accepted that view, nor does Andros seem in practice to have put any restraint on their exercise of legislative power.

Meanwhile Penn and his partners in fighting their own battle were also fighting that of Carteret. The grant from the Duke to Bylling was followed six weeks later by one to the young Sir George Carteret, the grandson and heir of the original proprietor, bestowing on him also full territorial and political rights.[1] This grant fully reestablished the authority of Philip Carteret, and the recall of Andros early in 1681 left the Governor free to assert that authority without danger of molestation. In March 1681 he issued a proclamation warning the inhabitants of the province that the supremacy of

Further disputes between Carteret and the settlers.

---

[1] This grant is in the N. J. Archives, vol. i. p. 337.

the Proprietors was again in force, that all acts done by Andros were invalid, and that no courts which he had constituted had any legal power.[1] Later in the year Brockholls, that incompetent deputy whom Andros had left in his stead, called in question the authority of Carteret.[2] It was easy to meet that by producing the Duke's grant and Carteret's own commission. But the attack made by Andros had brought about troubles not to be got over so lightly. There was, as we have seen, among the settlers an anti-proprietary party. The leaders of that party were shrewd enough to see danger in the recent grant to the Proprietors. It might be said that while the grant conferred future authority on the Proprietors, it annulled the authority which they had claimed in the past, and would enable them to disclaim their past obligations. It is plain that those who opposed the Proprietors were the ruling party in the Assembly. On October 17 the Deputies met. Their very first proceeding was to pass a resolution asking the Governor and Council whether they were to consider the late grant as the foundation of government.[3] The question was an embarrassing one. To admit it was to admit that Andros had been right and Carteret wrong. To deny it might reopen questions which it was far more convenient for the Governor and his party to let rest. It will be remembered that in 1672 Carteret, acting for the Proprietors, had made certain modifications in the Concessions. If he fell back on the Concessions as the basis of his authority, it might be needful to revoke these later changes. A sense of this difficulty was clearly

[1] N. J. Archives, vol. i. p. 346.
[2] He writes to Carteret (July 26, 1681) that he has received certain papers from him, but can 'find no power thereby for you to act in or assume the government of New Jersey.' N. J. Archives, vol. i p. 352.
[3] This and all the other documents which make up the history of this dispute are in the New Jersey Archives, vol. i. pp. 354-65.

disclosed in the petulant tone of the answer. The original grant on which the Concessions were based was, Carteret said, the foundation of government. Only 'the seed sown by Sir Edmund Andros could have bid men raise such questions; let them leave such disputes, and fall upon something for the good of the province.'

The Deputies had now cleared the ground for an obvious and effective line of attack. They passed a resolution declaring that the changes introduced in 1672 were a violation of the Concessions. The lack of temper which the Council had shown in their first answer became more and more manifest as the dispute went on. The Deputies were reminded that they alone did not form the Assembly, and they were told that, though they might, as they said, have read and weighed the documents in dispute, they had failed to understand them. On one point, however, the Council had the best of the dispute. They bade their opponents remember that the payment of quit-rents was part of the original constitution. If the Proprietors had broken their compact, so in that matter had the settlers. The difficulty was increased by the arrangement, on which at an earlier day the Governor and Council had insisted, whereby the Council and the Deputies sat as two separate chambers. Proposals were made for a conference, but it is clear that neither side was in earnest in asking for it, nor was there any such wish for agreement as could make it useful. After a fortnight of profitless bickering the Governor dissolved the Assembly. The Deputies protested against the proceedings as unconstitutional, but do not seem to have made any attempt to prolong their session.

Throughout the history of the proprietary colonies, every dispute between a Proprietor and his settlers was almost certain to end in favour of the latter. The

THE PROPRIETARY SYSTEM. 399

one exception was New York, and New York was proprietary only in name. There no doubt the authority of the Proprietor was really felt. But it was so mainly because the Proprietor had the supremacy of the Crown at his back, and also because the position of New York gave it exceptional importance. It was the key of the military position, and the Crown had a direct interest in the security and stability of the government. But in every other case the Proprietor was certain to be fighting at odds. Where resistance to arbitrary government may involve material loss, the suspension of works in which capital is invested, the waste of that time which is the equivalent of capital, there the members of a prosperous society may acquiesce in much bad government before they risk a breach of the peace. But in a colony beginning its life none of these restraints exist. And when it came to the ultimate resort, to force, what resources had the Proprietor? He had no armed force of his own wherewith to overawe his colonists. He must depend on the help of the Crown, and what motive had the Crown for supporting him? Even in its dealings with its own colonies, we shall see the sovereign and his advisers ever slow and reluctant to push matters to extremities. There was little chance that they would show a vigour in the cause of others which they failed to show in their own.

Thus the Proprietor was virtually at the mercy of his colonists. If the political arrangements which he enforced were convenient to the settlers, or not so objectionable to them as to be worth a dispute, they would be accepted with more or less good will. If the quit-rents charged fairly represented what one may call the monopoly value of the soil, they would be paid, probably with more or less grumbling. Those, it may safely be said, were the limits within which proprietary

Working of the proprietary system.

authority could be exercised. The Proprietor inevitably sinks into the position of a titular sovereign who does not govern, and a rent-charger.

There was indeed one exception to this, one really valuable office which the Proprietor might discharge. He might be at the foundation of a colony what one may call the superintending capitalist. He could to some extent select the emigrants, survey the soil, decide the apportionment of land, and be responsible for the needful outfit and supply of live stock. We have seen in Plymouth how a colony suffered from the lack of some one person responsible for these things, who at the same time had an interest in the permanent welfare of the colony, how it thereby fell into the hands of a body of money-lenders who had no sympathy with the wants and objects of the colony. On the other hand, in Maryland and Carolina the difficulties attending the foundation of a colony had been successfully overcome by the action of a Proprietor or body of Proprietors. We may even say that Massachusetts was in a measure an instance of success achieved in the same fashion.

A proprietary government, however, can hardly fulfil these conditions, unless there be on the part of the Proprietor a desire for the success of the colony apart from personal gain. The most successful proprietary colonies were those where leading members of some sect were building up a home for their brethren in the faith. No such motive had been at work upon the proprietorship of Carteret and Berkeley. It was working successfully in that part of their territory which they had sold to Penn and his partners. To Sir George Carteret no doubt the position of a colonial Proprietor had attractions. It conveyed dignity, and it might be a useful piece to play in his game of political ambition. But to his heirs the colony was nothing but a troublesome property. Accordingly

Transfer of Carteret's proprietorship.

early in 1682 they disposed of their territorial and other rights, it is said by auction.[1] No stronger illustration could be found of the inconveniences of the proprietary system, or the possibilities of abuse which attached to it as it existed. Carrying with it as it did the right of appointing officials and of granting or withholding political rights, it should have been regarded as a trusteeship, only to be vested in trustworthy and competent persons. The government of each colony was a link in a chain on which the whole security and welfare of the empire depended. That it should have been put up for sale in open market shows how far the Crown and its advisers were from any distinct and comprehensive scheme of colonial administration.

There was, too, another serious objection to such an arrangement. To give a man proprietary rights over a vacant territory which was to be peopled under his own supervision, and in some measure at his own cost, was a very different thing from giving him proprietary rights over a settled province, which had already put on all the forms of political life. In the former case settlers came at their own risk and of their own free choice. Some community of feeling and interest between them and the Proprietor might safely be presumed. But here a body of colonists were made over to a new sovereign without the possibility of their expressing consent or disapproval. The principle, it is to be observed, was one wholly new in the history of the proprietary colonies. The nearest approach to it before was the settlement of Middletown and Shrewsbury simultaneously with the original grant of New Jersey to Berkeley and Carteret. That, however, was an accident, not the result of set purpose, and it might fairly be said that the emigrants risked such a con-

[1] *E. Jersey*, p. 103. Mr. Whitehead states this but does not give his authority.

tingency by settling on the strength of an uncertain title. There was at all events no reason for confirming and extending the precedent. A Colonial Proprietorship should have been regarded not as an ordinary landed estate, but as a trusteeship or office. If circumstances made it impossible or inexpedient for the Proprietor to continue his trust, his proper course was not transfer but resignation. If the Crown had insisted on that principle, New Jersey would have escaped years of bickering and confusion. But in truth the mischief began when the Duke of York was allowed to carve his grant into provinces and to dispose of them at his pleasure.

In the present case the best security against evil lay in this, that the purchase was from a mercantile point of view an unattractive one. No one was likely to become a purchaser unless he had some interest in the colony, and some designs for its future other than those of a land speculator. The purchasers were a body of partners of whom Penn was the chief.[1] That was in itself some guarantee for the safety of the settlers and the good government of the province. It might, moreover, be a step towards uniting the whole territory between the Hudson and the Delaware, either by bringing it under a single government, or if not, at least by securing a certain community of origin, usage, and principle among all the settlers.

<small>Purchase of East New Jersey by Penn and others.</small>

The basis of this Proprietary Company was soon extended by the addition of twelve fresh partners. Among them was that corrupt and discreditable politician the Earl of Perth. With him were associated three Scotchmen of a far worthier type, Gawain Lawrie, who

---

[1] For the deed of transfer see N. J. Archives, vol. i. p. 366. I have called it a purchase. It was really the purchase of a leasehold at a peppercorn rent.

already had a share in West Jersey, Barclay of Ury, the soldier of fortune who had bowed his neck to the peaceful yoke of George Fox, and his brother John Barclay. The presence of these men among the partners was possibly the cause, more probably the symptom, of a new movement in colonial life. So far Scotland had no part in the task of colonization, nor are there frequent traces even of isolated Scotchmen figuring as colonists. But a great wave of social and economical change was now passing over that kingdom. Scotland had not—indeed, the day was far distant when she could have—the resources needful to make her a colonizing nation. Her children had not the needful training in trade or industry. Moreover, with the contracted and exclusive principles of commerce which then prevailed, every colony was dependent for its markets on the parent nation. The trade and the shipping of Scotland could not maintain dependencies in prosperity. Yet Scotland was beginning to feel the need of colonies as a vent for her surplus population. A poor soil and petty industries had long been unequal to the task of furnishing a livelihood for all whom the country produced. 'The Scot abroad' had found in mercenary soldiership that career which the Englishman or the Hollander found in the New World. With the cessation of the great continental wars that resource had failed. Even if Scotch commerce could have expanded, family pride would have withheld the cadets of landed houses from profiting thereby. Moreover, the country was just awakening to a sense of the inadequacy of its resources. There is nothing to prove the Scotchman of 1680 was worse off than his grandfather. But such writings as those of Fletcher of Saltoun show that one of those waves of thought was passing over Scotland, in which a country suddenly awakens to evils which it has long endured tranquilly.

There was too, as was shown a little later by the tragedy of Darien, a certain desire to prove that any path which Scotland's old rival and oppressor had trodden successfully she too could tread. It needed but a slight impulse to turn these newly awakened wants and aspirations into the channel of American colonization. One argument which was used by the Scotch advocates of colonization to allay the doubts of their countrymen is worth special notice. It was urged that the colonists would lose their national independence and become English subjects. The advocate for colonization points out that this will really be a gain, since they will then share in the benefits of the Navigation Act.[1] The use of that argument throws light on the motives which twenty-four years later led to the passing of the Act of Union.

The appointment of Barclay as Governor would seem designed to conciliate the two classes on whom the future of the colony was to depend, the Quakers and the Scotch. Apparently it was the weight of his name rather than his actual ability which was valued. The terms of his commission authorized him to discharge his duties by deputy.[3] This he did, and there is nothing to show that he even so much as set foot on the soil of America. His choice fell on Thomas Rudyard, a London attorney, who, though not himself a Quaker, had been of service to Penn when under prosecution in 1670.[4]

Robert Barclay appointed Governor of East Jersey.[2]

In theory the new Proprietors were but stepping into the position occupied by Carteret, a position of

---

[1] *A Brief Account of the Province of East New Jersey*, published by the Scots Proprietors. Reprinted in *New York Historical Magazine*, 2nd series, vol. i.

[2] Barclay's commission does not seem to be extant, but it is referred to in the Fundamental Constitutions to be mentioned hereafter.

[3] This is stated in the Fundamental Constitutions.

[4] For Rudyard's commission see N. J. Archives, vol. i. p. 376.

territorial possession and political sovereignty, subject only to the rights inherent in the Crown. But, as we have seen, the view that the Duke of York had by his original grant divested himself of all rights, though asserted when it could be useful, was not consistently held. Men evidently felt that he had a certain undefined supremacy which must be taken into account at each fresh transfer of territory. Early in 1683 the new partners obtained from the Duke a grant making over to them, for payment of a fixed sum not specified in the grant, and for a small annual quit-rent, all his rights not only over the soil, but also of jurisdiction and government.[1]

Attitude of the Proprietors towards the Duke of York.

Rudyard's first proceeding was to call an Assembly. Their measures were in themselves of some importance, and are of interest as showing that the Assembly did not regard its powers as provisional or anticipate any interference from the new proprietary. The colony was divided into four counties. Laws were passed regulating the relations of servant and master. No indented white servant was to serve for more than four years, unless under seventeen. In that case he was to serve till he was twenty-one. He might not be transported out of the colony against his will, and at the end of his term he was to have from his master an axe, a hoe and seven bushels of corn. Injury to limb by the master was to be indemnified by the servant being set at liberty, and the infliction of unmerciful chastisement was to be punished at the discretion of the magistrate. Though this protection only extended to white servants, yet something was done for the negro slave by an enactment securing him sufficiency of food and clothes. At the same time the rights of masters were protected

Proceedings of the Assembly.[2]

---

[1] N. J. Archives, vol. i. p. 383.
[2] Leaming and Spicer, pp. 229-53

since it was penal to receive a runaway slave as an apprentice. Other enactments show traces either of the original Puritanism of the settlers or of later Quakerism. A large consolidating Act which summed up previous legislation made it penal to afflict the widow or fatherless. This attempt to enforce a vague precept of morality was thoroughly characteristic of New England legislation. A general prohibition of Sabbath-breaking was explained and amplified by specific enactments. No work was to be done on that day, there was to be no drinking at ordinaries, no riding save of necessity, no going abroad save for sober and religious exercise. As in New England, the drinking of healths was penal. Acting, sword-playing, games, masques, revels, bull-baitings and cock-fightings were not explicitly forbidden, but were to be 'discouraged' by the judges and courts. Here again we have an absence of precision and a confusion of the spheres of law and morality, thoroughly characteristic of New England.

In 1683 Rudyard was superseded, not apparently for any offence or shortcoming, but to be replaced by a deputy, Lawrie, who was himself one of the original twelve purchasers, and who more fully understood and entered into the schemes of the Proprietors. He was charged with the task of carrying out what his colleagues regarded as a thorough-going and valuable scheme of constitutional reform. Instead of being content with the system of representation in use which fifteen years of practice had done something to perfect, and with which at least the settlers were familiar, they drafted a brand-new constitution. It began by defining the position of the Governor. He was to be resident and was to hold office for three years. Fears seem to have been enter-

The New Fundamental Constitution.[1]

[1] N. J. Archives, vol. i. pp. 395-410.

tained that the Governor might seek to continue his office beyond the statutory time or to make it hereditary. Any person furthering the reappointment of the Governor or the appointment of his son was to be reputed a public enemy.

The Assembly, or as it was called the Great Council, was to consist of the twenty-four Proprietors, acting personally or by proxy, and a hundred and forty-four delegates chosen by the freemen. For the present, however, in consideration of the smallness of the colony the elected representatives were to be seventy-two. It is hard to imagine anything more grotesquely complicated and unpractical than the method of election prescribed, and the qualifications imposed on representatives. 'For the full preventing of all indirect means the election shall be after this manner: the names of all the persons qualified in each county shall be put on equal pieces of parchment, and prepared by the Sheriff and his clerk the day before, and at the day of election shall be put in a box and fifty shall be taken out by a boy under ten years of age; those fifty shall be put into the box again, and the first five-and-twenty then taken out shall be capable to be chosen for that time, the other five-and-twenty shall by plurality of votes name (of the aforesaid twenty-five) twelve if there be three to be chosen, and eight if there be two to stand for it; these nominators first solemnly declaring before the Sheriff that they shall not name any known to them to be guilty for the time, or to have been guilty for a year before, of adultery, whoredom, drunkenness, or any such immorality, or who is insolent or a fool, and then out of the twelve or eight so nominated, three or two shall be taken by the ballot as aforesaid.'

The Assembly thus composed was to meet every year. Every motion must be carried not by a simple majority, but by two-thirds. The Proprietors and the elected representatives were to sit together, but were to act so far separately that nothing could be carried without the consent of half the Proprietors. Under this system one may doubt which would be more troublesome, to elect the legislature or to obtain any results from it when elected.

There was to be also an executive committee, consisting of the Proprietors and of twelve others chosen by ballot from among the elected representatives. This was to be divided into three sub-committees, whose provinces of action were thus assigned to them. One was 'for the public policy and to look to manners, education and arts,' one 'for trade and management of the public treasury,' one 'for plantations and regulating of all things.'

There was also to be a war department. This part of the public policy was much complicated by the views of the Quaker section of the colony. To prevent the colony from being prejudiced by their peculiar principles it was provided that they should, by a process described in very complex and cumbrous terms, be excluded from all deliberations on military questions. Their consciences were to be protected by a provision that they need not contribute to any funds raised for purposes of war. That, however, was made somewhat illusory, since in that case they were to contribute a proportionately larger sum to other public purposes.

The landed system was as fantastic and unpractical as the rest. Its general principle was to allow the subdivision of the proprietary interest within certain limits. Each Proprietor might alienate three-fourths of his share of land without prejudice to his political rights. If, however, he failed to retain one-fourth, his rights came to an end. But where a proprietorship was held by coheirs they might elect a representative to act for them. Otherwise, the original Proprietor was to be replaced by some one who held the fourth of an original share. This qualification, however, might be reduced to five thousand acres, or if necessary even below.

On the other hand, increase of territory was guarded against as much as diminution, since no one might, by purchase, amass into his own hands more than one original proprietary share.

For the rest, trial by jury was provided for, no persons professing a belief in God were to be in any way molested for their opinions, and a simple declaration of belief in Christianity was to be the only qualification required for office.

It is clear that the Proprietors were beset by no doubts or fears as to the merits of this scheme. Nor had they any doubts that the settlers would, when once they understood it, hail it as a vast improvement on the clumsy and commonplace constitution under which they lived. But they do seem to have felt that to force the scheme on reluctant settlers might be attended with difficulties, that it would be in some sort a breach of those obligations to which they had succeeded. Accordingly, Lawrie is not to put the new constitution in force at once, but to explain to the settlers its advantages, 'how much it exceeds their former commissions,' and so with the approval of the Assembly to secure its acceptance. Meanwhile the Proprietors exercised their power of vetoing, or at least of refusing to confirm, the Acts passed by the Assembly in the previous year, avowedly on the ground that the new constitution would render them needless. At the same time they suggested that whatever deficiencies there might be in that system could be supplemented from the common law of England without special legislation.[1]

[1] See the Instruction to Lawrie in N. J. Archives, vol. i. pp. 426-34.

Lawrie was not long in discovering that the new system was not accepted as eagerly as the Proprietors had expected. They then changed their ground and declared that the constitution was not intended to apply to the old settlers, but only to those who should come out after the late purchase of the province. In other words they proposed to set up, side by side in the same province, two systems of government, each applying to a separate section of the population. The old settlers, however, might be admitted as a special act of grace to the benefit of the new constitution on certain conditions. They must submit to a resurvey of their lands and an inquiry into the validity of their title. They must pay up all arrears of quit-rent, and must pass an Act providing the revenue needed for the purposes of government.[1]

A compromise adopted.

As in Carolina, usage proved too strong for theory. Lawrie does not seem to have made any serious attempt to enforce the new constitution. Assemblies met annually, and the Great Council with its complicated ballots was even less of a reality than the landgraves and caciques of Locke's imagination.

Meanwhile strenuous attempts were being made to carry out one part of the Proprietors' scheme in the erection of a great seaport town. So important did the Proprietors consider this that it formed the subject of a special set of instructions issued to Lawrie.[2] Twenty-four houses were to be built, one for each Proprietor, and when these were finished, a house for the Governor. Markets and wharfs, too, were to be laid out. The site for the town was to be divided into one hundred and fifty lots. The purchaser of each was bound to build a house on

Establishment of a town at Perth Amboy.

---

[1] Additional Revisions to Constitution in Archives, vol. i. p. 443.
[2] N. J. Archives, vol. i. p. 434.

it, on pain of forfeiting his claim, and was to hold with it three acres of upland. The town was to retain the Indian name of the site, Ambo, soon modified into Amboy, with the prefix Perth in honour of the chief Proprietor.

Meanwhile Lawrie and others were doing all in their power to stimulate interest and confidence in the colony among those at home.[1] We are reminded of the early days of Virginian colonization as we read the glowing accounts of the resources of the country and of the prosperity of the settlement, sent home by Lawrie and his associates. Thanks to a good climate and soil, to the pacific temper of the natives and to the absence of any serious interruption or hindrance from those in authority, the course of New Jersey had doubtless been one of unbroken material prosperity. We may well believe that Lawrie hardly exaggerated when he wrote that there was ' not a poor body in the province, nor one that wants.'

Material condition of the colony.

His report, however, is something more than a mere eulogy. It contains in a short compass the best account that we have of the visible and material condition of the colony, and also of the mental and moral state of the settlers. There are a few stone houses, but most are of wood. The towns are not compactly built, but are straggling rural communities like many of those in New England. Between the houses are large vacant spaces, and the sheep feed where the streets should be. Most of the towns are, as in Maryland and Virginia, on the banks of streams where small vessels can land goods. There are no large Proprietors; a planter with ten servants and thirty cows is exceptionally wealthy. The most abundant stock are horses; these breed wild through the country. Wages are high; a workman can earn two shillings or half-a-crown a day. That

[1] Lawrie's Report with others is to be found in Scot's *Model*.

being so, it is hardly surprising to learn from another writer that they are a careless and unfrugal people.[1] They have already fallen away from the traditions of New England Puritanism. There is not in all East Jersey a minister of religion who has not some secular calling; there is no regular public provision for schooling, but something is done by the voluntary efforts of the settlers.

Other witnesses, not assuredly accustomed to a high standard of luxury, show a less favourable picture of the material condition of the colony. They tell us of the comfortless houses, built of ill-fitting logs, of the hard fare of the indented servants, living on maize-bread and water. They also mention the impoverishment of the colony by reason of the trade restrictions imposed by the Government of New York. Burlington, the chief town, has shrunk to a settlement of fifty wooden houses.[2]

While the transfer of East Jersey from Carteret's heirs to the new body of Proprietors did not bring with it those constitutional changes which were designed, we must not regard it as an unimportant measure. It was a step towards the consolidation of the whole body of colonies. Though the two Jerseys and Pennsylvania were not connected by any political bond, yet they were now exposed to influences which fitted them to work together at a future day. Each was largely influenced by Quakerism. Each came under the personal influence of one man, William Penn. The records of each state show a certain identity of principle guiding legislation. The colonists were drawn from the same sources; we may in fact say that from 1680 onwards the three provinces were fed by one common stream of emigration.

Effect of the change of proprietary.

---

[1] Letter from Johnstone of Spotswoode, in the *Model*, p. 299.
[2] The Labadists, pp. 173-227.

If the new Proprietors had erred in thinking that they could suddenly impose on the colonists a new system of government, constructed without regard to its existing condition, they at least deserve the credit of having soon drawn back from an untenable position. They saw that no good administrative results could attend the action of a body living in England and endeavouring to manage the affairs of the colony. Accordingly in 1684 the authority of the whole body of Proprietors was vested in a resident committee.[1] Their approval was to give temporary validity to laws, and thus the legislature was freed from the inconvenience of referring all its measures to a non-resident body. They were furthermore entrusted with the duty of maintaining the territorial rights of the Proprietors, acting, in fact, as the resident agents of an absentee Proprietor. The political authority of the Proprietors was short-lived, and even while it lasted ineffectual. But by this system of delegation they saved their territorial rights, and administered them with better effect.

The Proprietors represented by a resident committee.

Meanwhile the glowing pictures of colonial prosperity drawn by Lawrie and his friends were doing little to attract colonists. The contrast between the reluctance of the Scotch to support New Jersey and the success with which the Darien scheme appealed to them illustrates the national character as it then was. The Darien scheme was exclusive and military. It appealed to the patriot and to the soldier of fortune. There was little attraction in the prospect of being absorbed into a community of English farmers and tradesmen.

Lack of enthusiasm in Scotland.

Such emigration as there was from Scotland was hardly the result of voluntary choice. Among those who took a leading part in pressing the claims of New

[1] Leaming and Spicer, p. 195.

Jersey on his countrymen was George Scot of Pitlochie. He was a wealthy laird in Midlothian, who had three times been heavily fined and imprisoned for persistent attendance at conventicles and for harbouring a Nonconformist minister. It was during his third imprisonment that the change of proprietorship in New Jersey seemed to offer a refuge for persecuted Covenanters. The presence of Perth among the Proprietors, Royalist and High Churchman though he was, was no obstacle to such a scheme. His tenets, political and religious, were but a matter of convenience. Covenanters in Scotland were obnoxious to him as interfering with a system of government in which he was personally interested. He assuredly would not have thought of sacrificing to the demands of religious uniformity anything which could help the material prosperity of the colony. Nor was his presence, and that of others who may have thought with him, likely to stand in the way of Scot's projects. The Proprietors of East Jersey, as we have already seen, included men of widely different views in politics and religion, Kingsmen and Commonwealthmen, Churchmen and Quakers. Nothing is more noteworthy in the history of Scotland during the seventeenth century than the ease with which men of widely different views and principles could form temporary combinations. The men who plotted for Argyle and Monmouth and murdered Sharp in the interests of the Covenant were ready at a later day to plot against William, and to support James and Dundee for the same end.

Another peculiarity of Scotland at that time no doubt made Scot's task an easier one. Predial servi-

(margin note: Scot of Pitlochie.[1])

[1] The main, one may indeed say the only, authority for Scot's proceedings is Wodrow. His partisan bias makes him a dangerous witness, but here one sees no special reason why it should have misled him. For Scot's own writing see the introductory note to this chapter.

tude was still a recognised institution in Scotland. In the English plantations the class of indented servants was mainly recruited by professional kidnappers, or from men exempted from the gallows. But the Scotch labourer who voluntarily sold himself for a term of service was not sinking below the level commonly occupied in his own country by a collier or saltworker.

Accordingly Scot asked and obtained leave from the Privy Council to transport with him a company of men like himself undergoing imprisonment for their religious practices. But it was specially provided that he should not take advantage of this to remove any prisoners of importance, since none might go who had real estate of more than a hundred pounds annual value. The whole company collected amounted to two hundred. A contemporary chronicle not likely to be unfavourable to Scot accused him of 'tampering with' some of the prisoners, by promising them their liberty in New Jersey on a payment of five pounds.[1] This is denounced as 'making merchandise of the suffering people of God.' As far as we can see, Scot asked for nothing but a very moderate recompense for the necessary cost of outfit and transport.

The voyage was disastrous: violent sickness broke out, and Scot with seventy of his followers perished. Among the tragedies of the voyage was the death of Scot's daughter, Euphemia, newly married to a young Scotchman of a noted Covenanting house, John Johnstone, destined to play a leading part in the history of New Jersey. The Presbyterian chronicler of whom I have just spoken tells us that the ship's captain made an attempt to land them in Virginia, there to be sold as slaves, and was only thwarted by weather which forced him to his original destination. One is tempted to class this with the legend which brought the *Mayflower* to

[1] Wodrow.

Plymouth not of set purpose, but as the result of Dutch malevolence and the captain's treachery.

This, though the most extensive, was not the only immigration into New Jersey, brought about by the political and ecclesiastical troubles of Scotland. After the extinction of Argyle's rebellion his brother, Neil Campbell, already one of the Proprietors, visited the colony, followed by many of the defeated party, and was appointed Governor.[1] Campbell's stay in the colony was a short one. Within half a year he resigned his post, and named Andrew Hamilton as his successor, an appointment confirmed by the trustees.[2]

<small>Lord Neil Campbell.</small>

Andrew Hamilton was, as his name suggests, of Scotch extraction. He himself was established as a merchant in London. His connexion with colonial politics lasted for some years, and he showed himself throughout a capable administrator, with clear and sound views of colonial policy; but in his present post he had little opportunity of displaying his fitness for office.

<small>Andrew Hamilton.</small>

The removal of Andros had as far as outward appearances went re-established peace between New York and New Jersey. But there were underlying causes of jealousy and enmity which went far deeper than the personal feeling of any one official. New Jersey was a perpetual menace to the commercial prosperity of her neighbour. Unless the New York officials could exercise their authority over the settlers to the west of the Hudson it was wholly impossible for them to check smuggling in their own territory. Moreover that which the Proprietors of New Jersey made the chief aim, the establishment of a prosperous sea-port at Perth Amboy, was fraught with

<small>Jealousy felt by the New York settlers.</small>

---

[1] Whitehead, *E. Jersey*, p. 117. Mr. Whitehead says he was 'Deputy-Governor.' He was 'Deputy' only in the sense of representing the Proprietors.

[2] N. J. Archives, vol. i. p. 541.

danger to New York. By granting more advantageous terms to merchants, the Proprietors could draw off the stream of trade and emigration to their own colony. For New York was not like a New England town, where the settlers were bound to the spot by ties other than those of self-interest and stronger. The New York traders and householders now felt the reality of the danger. If we may believe a memorial sent by the Mayor of New York to the Proprietors' Secretary, by 1685 the city had lost a third of its trade, and there was a manifest falling off in inhabitants and in buildings.[1]

Thus, outrageous as had been the form of Andros's proceedings, there was some justification for the feeling which prompted them. There was no danger of their being imitated by a man so sagacious and self-restrained as Dongan. His relations with the rulers of New Jersey were ostensibly friendly. But he was in reality just as urgent for reunion as any of his predecessors. Early in 1684 we find him sending home a memorial in which the Proprietor is urged to reannex New Jersey, and thus prevent the ruin of New York.[2] The New Jersey Proprietors at once addressed an angry remonstrance to Dongan.[3] He received it courteously and with a soft answer, but none the less persisted in his advice to his master.[4]

Dealings of Dongan with New Jersey.

The general dispute was embittered by a conflict of claims for a piece of territory. Staten Island, lying in the very mouth of the Hudson, might well seem to each colony an invaluable possession. Without the control of it the trade neither of New York nor of Perth Amboy could be effectually secured against smugglers. The island had since the very first establishment of New Jersey formed matter of debate. It was originally occupied under the Dutch West India Com-

Contest for Staten Island.

---

[1] This memorial is in the N. J. Archives, vol. i. p. 491.
[2] N. Y. Docs. vol. iii. pp. 348-56. [3] *Ib.* p. 348. [4] *Ib.* pp. 353-6.

E E

pany, and thus formed part of New Netherlands. As such it passed in the natural course to New York. Berkeley and Carteret, however, put forward such claims to it as forming part of their grant that the Duke thought it well in 1668 to get a formal acknowledgement of his right.[1] Philip Carteret himself had apparently already acknowledged the validity of this claim by buying the island as a private estate from the Duke's representatives.[2] Next year Nicolls's successor Lovelace confirmed his patron's right by a purchase of the soil from the natives. After the treaty of Westminster the territory reverted to the Duke, and was made by Andros into a separate jurisdiction under a ranger. That office was held by John Palmer, at a later day a conspicuous and not very creditable figure in the history both of New York and New England.[3] No attempt was made for eleven years to challenge the title or to detach Staten Island from New York. But in 1681 Carteret's widow revived the claim. The new title created by the grant of September 1680 furnished a pretext, but in all likelihood Lady Carteret built her hopes of success on the recall of Andros and the disfavour which had fallen upon the Duke. Accordingly, in July 1681, Philip Carteret wrote to Brockholls, the Deputy-Governor of New York, demanding in peremptory terms the surrender of Staten Island, as being included in the recent grant.[4] At the same time a notice was sent to the settlers on the island forbidding them in any way to acknowledge the jurisdiction of New York.

Brockholls met the demand with a plain refusal,

[1] Maverick, in a letter to Winthrop (February 24, 1669), says 'Staten Island is adjudged to belong to New York.' *Mass. Hist. Coll.* 4th series, vol. vii. p. 315.

[2] Brodhead, vol. ii. p. 149.

[3] *Ib.* p. 166. Mr. Brodhead quotes the actual text of the conveyance.

[4] Carteret's letter and the other documents to which I refer are in the N. J. Archives, vol. i. pp. 349-52.

whereupon Carteret announced his intention of appealing to the Government at home, and laying before them Brockholls's 'uncivil' letter.

Philip Carteret's claim dealt with political sovereignty over the island. At the same time Lady Carteret, the widow of Sir George, who had died in 1680, was advancing a territorial claim on her own account. That could easily be met. Even if Staten Island had been Carteret's to dispose of, such territorial interest as he had in New Jersey was disposed of by a will which took it all out of the hands of his widow. If any claim could be set up, it must be made not by her, but by the legatees. Both Philip Carteret and Lady Carteret seem to have quietly accepted defeat. When in 1683, under the short-lived system of representative government introduced by Dongan, New York was divided into electoral counties, Staten Island was incorporated with one of them.

In the same year East Jersey under the new Proprietors was also divided into counties. No attempt was made to include Staten Island. This might have been taken for an acknowledgement that the claim was at an end. But in 1685 Perth and his partners without any pretext reopened the matter. Dongan might well be indignant when he learnt that papers were being distributed among the settlers in the island bidding them accept the jurisdiction of New Jersey,[1] nor can we wonder that he should have pressed upon his patron the necessity of resuming his grant and annexing New Jersey to New York.[2]

At the same time Dongan addressed Perth as representing the Proprietors of New Jersey, clearly and forcibly setting forth the justice of the Duke's claim to

[1] This is stated in Dongan's letter to Perth. It is in the N. Y. Docs. vol. iii. p. 353.
[2] *Ib.* pp. 354–6.

the island and the impolicy of combating that claim, and pointing out that it was as well not to force the Duke to extremities. It was better to surrender Staten Island than to run the risk of some curtailment of territory on the mainland.

The firm front shown by Dongan answered its purpose, and the claim of New Jersey to Staten Island was quietly allowed to drop.

The question was one of far more practical importance than many of the barren disputes about territory which embittered the relations between colony and colony. Staten Island contained two hundred families. It commanded the mouth of the Hudson, and might at any time become the key to the navigation of the river.

The various elements of division and discord from which East New Jersey had been suffering were happily absent in the Western province. Proprietors and settlers were a homogeneous body. There were no inhabitants already established with their own traditions and usages, and it was therefore easy for the Proprietors to mould the colony to their own wishes. Moreover they had the wisdom to steer clear of those elaborate fantasies with which the Eastern Proprietors encumbered themselves. The first representative Assembly met in 1681.[1] It at once passed a set of resolutions defining the principles of the constitution. These were practically a repetition and acceptance of the concession. There was to be an Assembly elected every year. Their concurrence was necessary for all purposes of legislation, finance, or foreign policy. Nor could the Assembly itself impose any tax to last beyond the period of its own life. There was to be full liberty of belief and worship, and no religious disabilities were to exist.

State of West Jersey.

While it was provided as by the Concessions that

[1] Laws of W. Jersey.

all public lands should be laid out by commissioners appointed by the Assembly, certain general principles were now set forth on which these commissioners should act. No one person was to have more than a certain amount of river frontage, and the settlements were to be as far as possible continuous. Moreover, to promote the growth of a town at Burlington, it was enacted that any land there left for six months unoccupied and unemployed should revert to the community and be apportioned by the Land Commissioners. Two years later this last provision was extended further, and it was enacted that no one should have land allotted to him at Burlington unless he gave security to build a house there.

The proceedings of 1681 showed the perfect unanimity of feeling which existed between Proprietors and settlers. This was further confirmed in 1683. The Assembly of that year took upon itself to investigate and decide the question whether this purchase was of land or of Government—in other words, what was the position of the Proprietors. Their unanimous decision was that the Proprietors had acquired not merely the soil but also political rights.[1] This action of the Assembly was in itself a proof that it regarded itself not merely as the mouthpiece of the commonalty, but also of the Proprietors. For a third party, having no judicial status, to pronounce judgment on the relations between the Proprietors and the Crown would have been absurd. The vote of the Assembly was virtually a declaration by the Proprietors themselves claiming certain rights.

Harmony between the Proprietors and the settlers.

In the same year the Assembly modified that provision in the Fundamental Concessions which aimed at making them unalterable.[2] While however it claimed for its successors the right to make changes, it jealously fenced in that right. It could only be exercised by a

[1] Laws of W. Jersey, p. 468.   [2] *Ib.*

majority of six-sevenths, and it could not be extended to what was regarded as the specially vital portions of the system. The laws which were to be exempt from this change were those which provided for liberty of conscience, for the security of property, for the annual meeting of the Assembly, for trial by jury, and that which required every verdict to be based on the evidence of two witnesses.

The Concessions of West Jersey differed not a little from those of the Eastern colony in their practical, businesslike character. But they differed even more widely in the general principles on which they rested. The East Jersey constitution was a system forced upon the settlers from outside, in disregard of their wishes and in defiance of their existing institutions. The West Jersey constitution was almost as much the work of the settlers themselves as of the Proprietors.

There was a possible element of discord in the independent attitude of Fenwick. His position, however, was now materially changed. The grant of territory to Penn in 1681 detached the little dependency on the Delaware from New York, and incorporated it with the new province of Pennsylvania. There was now no choice for Salem but incorporation with Pennsylvania or West Jersey. In 1682 Fenwick made over his territorial rights to Penn and his partners, whose jurisdiction was thereby effectively established over the whole of West Jersey.[1]

<small>Fenwick's province incorporated.</small>

The moderation and the conciliatory temper of the Proprietors did not wholly avert disputes. The settlers claimed the right to elect their own Governor. The Proprietors had at the outset invested Bylling with that office. He discharged his duties by a deputy, Samuel Jennings. In 1683 the Assembly, apparently

---

[1] The deed of transfer was printed for the first time in the N. J. Archives, vol. i. p. 370.

without any communication with Bylling or the other Proprietors, elected Jennings as Governor. Bylling re-
Dispute about the governor- ship.[1] fused to approve of the appointment, and the Assembly thereupon sent Jennings and another representative to England to confer with the Proprietors. At the same time they in some measure prejudged the question by appointing one Thomas Oliver Deputy-Governor. According to Quaker usage the matter was referred to the arbitration of a Committee of Friends. Their decision was in favour of the Proprietors, and when Bylling nominated one John Skene as Deputy-Governor, the Assembly acquiesced.

The inclusion of West Jersey was really no essential part of the scheme of consolidation suggested by
New Jersey forms part of the con- solidated territory under Andros. Dongan and adopted by James. West Jersey belonged as distinctly to what one may call the Delaware Bay group of settlements as did East Jersey to those on the Hudson. But neither the Duke of York nor his advisers were likely to understand the different position of the two halves of the province. If the policy of resumption of charters and consolidation of government could be justified at all, assuredly it might be in the case of East Jersey. That colony was a standing menace to the commercial prosperity of New York, its independence made any effective system of revenue impossible, and the recent conduct of its government in the matter of Staten Island showed that it might be a greedy and unscrupulous competitor for territory. The Eastern province dragged down the Western in its inevitable fall. The one thing that might have saved either or both was the personal influence of Penn at Court. But since he had become a

---

[1] This account is borrowed from Mr. Whitehead's chapter on New Jersey in the *Memorial History*, vol. iii. His statements are based on two contemporary pamphlets. I have failed to find these either in the British Museum or in the Bodleian Library.

separate colonial Proprietor with a province of his own, his interest in New Jersey had practically vanished. There are no extant documents to show precisely how the desire of James II. to consolidate the American colonies was brought before the Proprietors of New Jersey. But in the summer of 1687 we find the Proprietors of the Eastern province laying before the Crown a representation evidently meant as a protest against the intended annexation to New York.[1] They point out that they are not in the position of Proprietors who have received a free grant from the Crown. They have invested a large sum in the province, and to interfere with their proprietary rights is to deprive them of all hope of return. The question of customs was dealt with somewhat superficially and disingenuously. It might be true, the protest urged, that if the duties imposed at the New Jersey ports were lower than those at New York, ships would land at the former and so trade would be drawn off. But if the scale of customs in New Jersey was so raised as to equalize it with that at New York, the only effect would be to enable other ports to undersell them both. To this it might fairly be answered that there was a certain fixed amount of trade which must go to the Hudson, and that New York and East Jersey were the only possible rivals who could compete for it.

Then came a proposal which showed that the Proprietors attached little value to their political rights in themselves. What they really dreaded was not the loss of sovereignty, but such a transfer as should make their province a dependency of New York, and so put her at the mercy of her commercial rival. Accordingly they petitioned not to retain their charter, but that the whole of New Jersey, East and West, should be united

[1] N. J. Archives, vol. i. p. 535. It is headed 'Representation of the case of the province of East Jersey, with their proposals.'

in a single colony. Let New York have no authority over the customs and no appellate jurisdiction, but let New Jersey be under the direct control of the Crown. Let the King show his respect for the interest of the Proprietors by appointing one of them Governor. The great number of them would give him an ample choice.

There is nothing to show how this document was received, and for some time we hear no more in the way of either threat or protest. But a document is extant which shows that the Proprietors had found resistance useless. In April 1688 they drew up a short statement setting forth that as the King desired ' for several weighty reasons of State' to resume the government of the colony they made a full surrender of authority.[1]

Proposed surrender of authority by the Proprietors.

If the records of the surrender of East Jersey are scanty, that of the Western province has left no traces. We only know that both were included in the commission issued to Andros in March 1688,[2] that in the following August he visited first Elizabethtown and then Burlington, and that at both places he asserted his authority and was favourably received.[3] It is easy to see why the transfer was so quietly accepted. There was no interference with local institutions, and as long as that was so it was a matter of indifference to the settlers where the titular sovereignty resided. The territorial rights of the Proprietors were respected. And though the change as made was not exactly that which the East Jersey Proprietors had asked for, yet it was still further from that which they had dreaded. The real danger in the eyes of the Proprietors was incorporation with New York. Give the New York Assembly any sort of

Surrender of both provinces to Andros.

[1] N. J. Archives, vol. ii. p. 26.
[2] The commission to Andros is in the N. Y. Docs. vol. iii. pp. 537-42.
[3] Andros to the Lords of Trade, N. Y. Docs. vol. iii. p. 554.

authority, and commercial jealousy might check the tide of emigration into New Jersey and make the territory worthless. But now New York was only one of a group of united dependencies, invested with no superiority and no jurisdiction over her neighbours.

In the case of West Jersey the matter was probably simplified by the death of Bylling, which, as far as can be now learnt, happened early in 1687. His share passed into the hands of one Daniel Coxe, who bears the title of doctor, though there is nothing to show in what faculty. His intentions are set forth in a long letter addressed to the whole body of Proprietors.[1]

<small>Daniel Coxe.</small>

With somewhat grotesque pomposity he disclaims the intention of 'arrogating to himself any absolute despotic power.' Nevertheless, it is the opinion of 'all intelligent disinterested persons' that the Government of England, by Sovereign and Parliament, is the best of constitutions. Since New Jersey is fortunate enough to have a government modelled on that, Coxe will not attempt any change, but will duly fall into his place as a constitutional monarch. There may be some doubt whether Bylling's consent to the Fundamental Concessions was really binding on him, as at the time he gave it he was not yet invested with full authority. Coxe, however, will waive his strict rights and accept the constitutions as they stand. There is a grotesque contrast between the profession and the reality. As a matter of fact the only position that Coxe occupied was that for a few years of the chief partner in a firm of absentee landlords. There is nothing to show that his acquiescence in the surrender of New Jersey was ever asked for, even as a matter of form.

It is probable that New Jersey owed something to the troubles of the northern colonies. To cope with

---

[1] N. J. Archives, vol. ii. p. 4. In this letter, written September 1687, Coxe uses the words 'after Mr. Bylling's decease.'

the stubborn will of New England was a task which left Andros no leisure for asserting the commercial supremacy of New York. He had maltreated Carteret and enraged the Proprietors of New Jersey, not from any sympathy with New York merchants, but from that unintelligent and mechanical fidelity to his master which was among his more creditable characteristics. Now his object was to organize an effective government for the whole body of colonies, and to provide for their security against the French and their Indian allies. To subjugate New England, to extirpate her peculiar usages, and as far as might be her exclusive tone of political thought, was a needful step to that end. New Jersey offered no such hindrance, and no such process was there needed. Thus it need be no matter of surprise that the authority of Andros was accepted by the New Jersey settlers with content and even cordiality.

Policy of Andros towards New Jersey.

As the establishment of Andros's authority failed to disturb the course of New Jersey history, so was it with his overthrow. As far as we can learn from the records, or one should rather say from the total absence of records, William and his advisers felt that the settlers might safely be left to their own devices. This neglect was no doubt in some measure due to the fact that Hamilton, returning to England with many official documents, was captured by a French privateer and was probably thus deprived of his papers.[1] Thus the Proprietors were almost cut off from communication with their colony through any recognised and trustworthy channel. The only authentic record of the action of the Proprietors during these

The revolution in New Jersey.

---

[1] Hamilton's capture is stated by Mr. Whitehead in the *Memorial History*. I have been unable to find an authority for the statement. Smith does not mention it, but his information on this period is so imperfect that his silence proves nothing.

years of their connexion with the colony is a statement made seven years later by the Proprietors of East Jersey when charged by the settlers with having neglected the interests of the colony. They had appointed, they say, as Governors, first John Tatham, himself a Proprietor, then Joseph Dudley.[1] But neither was accepted by the settlers. What attempt was made in either case to enforce authority, and what was the nature of the resistance, are matters on which there is no evidence. But one can hardly err in thinking that during these years neither colony had a central government. One is forced to believe that the organization of the township sufficed for all the purposes of administration and control. We may, at least, safely say that the training in self-government which the settlers had brought with them from New England stood between them and anarchy. Nor can we withhold something of the same praise from those religious principles which had moulded the life of the late founded settlements in New Jersey. Quaker politics have their weak and ignoble side; of that side the later history of the American colonies will show us more than enough. But Quakerism has never failed to supply in moral sanctions an adequate substitute for the grosser forms of legal restraint, just as she provides an equitable substitute for civil litigation. Four such years as passed over New Jersey between 1688 and 1692 would in all likelihood have left Maryland or Virginia in anarchy.

Meanwhile a change had come over the position of the Proprietors in West Jersey which removed an element of discord, and working in conjunction with other influences wholly altered the political condition of

[1] This is stated in a Memorial from the Proprietors to the Lords of Trade in answer to charges brought against them by the inhabitants, October 9, 1700. N. J. Archives, vol. ii. p. 349.

the colony. Coxe transferred his whole interest and rights, territorial and political, to a company of fifty shareholders.[1] The events of the revolution had made a practical severance between the Proprietors and the colonists. The new body of Proprietors made no serious attempt to revive or confirm their political authority. They sank contentedly into the position of absentee landlords, and their authority gained durability by curtailment. The existence of a proprietary company exercising political power would have been a serious hindrance even to that very moderate amount of centralization which the Crown required in its colonies. If the Proprietors had endeavoured to maintain their original position they would in all likelihood have lost all. Their territorial rights escaped because they were not encumbered by untenable political claims.

Formation of a new proprietary.

At the same time the Proprietors wisely strengthened their position as landowners by forming a machinery specially designed to uphold that portion of their rights. They were constituted a joint-stock company. There was to be a capital made up of sixteen hundred shares, each ten pounds. The land of the province was not to be divided among the shareholders, but was to be a joint estate administered for the benefit of the company. The administration of this estate was to be vested in a committee annually elected. Every shareholder holding ten or more shares was to vote for this committee, having one vote for every ten shares. No one, however, might in any case have more than ten votes. No person might be elected to this committee who had not twenty shares. The company was to enjoy the right of nominating the Governor and Deputy-Governor, and also all officials directly connected with trade. But beyond that it was

[1] The transfer by Coxe and the constitution of the new proprietary are both in the N. J. Archives, vol. ii. pp. 41-81.

to exercise no control over legislation and no authority over the colonists.

Nor can we doubt that the example of the West Jersey Proprietors influenced the sister body. That there was a general community of action and a recognition of like principles was shown by the appointment of Andrew Hamilton in 1692 as the Governor of both colonies.[1] Hamilton was one of the first public men who clearly saw and expressed the need for some system of colonial union. His views on that point at once brought him into conflict with the settlers. Thus in the autumn of 1696 we find him writing to Fletcher lamenting the obstinacy and the narrow views of his Assemblies.[2] They cannot be made to believe or understand the danger to which Albany is exposed. The very prosperity of the colony increases the difficulty, since it makes them more reluctant to leave their homes and employments. So strong is the aversion of the settlers to military service that some have fled to the southern colonies to avoid it. The younger and more adventurous, for whom it would naturally have had more attractions, are drawn off to join the crews of smugglers and pirates.

Hamilton appointed Governor of both colonies.

In the next year Hamilton's official career was for a while interrupted in a somewhat singular fashion. An Act was passed in 1696 for preventing frauds upon the revenues in the colonies.[3] Among the provisions of the Act was one to the effect that all Colonial Governors must be born Englishmen. The Proprietors imagined that as Hamilton was by birth a Scotchman his appointment was invalid, or at

Hamilton superseded.

---

[1] Hamilton's commission for West Jersey and his instructions from the Proprietors of East Jersey, both dated April 9, 1692, are in the Archives, vol. ii. pp. 84–8. I cannot find his commission for East Jersey.

[2] N. J. Archives, vol. ii. p. 115.

[3] 7 and 8 William III. c. 22.

least might be so regarded, and accordingly it was cancelled.¹ In all likelihood this interpretation found more ready acceptance since there was, especially among the East Jersey Proprietors, a party who disapproved of Hamilton's conduct.²

This party succeeded not only in ousting Hamilton, but in replacing him with a partisan of their own, Jeremiah Bass. He had already acted as agent for the West Jersey Society. His supporters seem to have belonged mainly to that colony, but at the same time he had influence enough among the Eastern Proprietors to get himself appointed to the governorship of their province. The events that followed showed plainly the need for some system of united control which should take in New York and New Jersey. Bellomont was engaged in his campaign against the pirates, and it was above all needful that he should have a free hand in all dealings with suspected vessels. Smuggling and piracy on the American coast were at least first cousins, and Bellomont at once found himself thwarted by the old jealousy of the East Jersey settlers on the subject of customs.

Bass appointed Governor.

The wavering and undecided policy of the Crown and its advisers had indeed left that question in a tangled state. As we have seen, the chief law officer of the Crown had in 1680 declared that the Duke of York had as Proprietor of New York no control over the customs of New Jersey.³ In 1687 an Order in Council declared it legal for vessels to load and unload at Perth Amboy.⁴ But this was limited by the provision that the Receiver-General of Customs at New York should either in person or by

Difficulty with New York about customs.

---

¹ The Proprietors to Hamilton, N. J. Archives, vol. ii. p. 176.
² What we know about Bass is almost entirely derived from the Archives.
³ *V.s.* p. 391.   ⁴ N. J. Archives, vol. i. p. 540.

deputy levy tolls at Perth Amboy on the same scale as that adopted in his own colony. The New Jersey traders were simply relieved from the inconvenience of having to clear their vessels at New York, but were not allowed any commercial advantage over their neighbour.

But in 1696 the Commissioners of Customs in England appointed by their own authority a collector for Perth Amboy, thereby encroaching on the privileges which nine years before had been conferred on the collector at New York.[1] This, however, was not accepted as a settlement of the question. In the autumn of 1697 the Lords of Trade reopened the whole question by challenging the right of the New Jersey Proprietors to create a free port. The question was submitted to the law officers of the Crown. Their opinion was a flat contradiction of that given in the previous reign. It declared that the original grant to the Duke of York did not invest him with any right to create ports or to exempt any colonists from the operation of the revenue Acts, and that no power could be in the subsequent grantees which were not conferred by the original deed.[2] Fortified by this opinion the Lords of Trade obtained an order from the King in Council prohibiting the importation of any goods into the Hudson without their paying customs at New York.[3] This was followed by instructions of the same tenor to Bellomont.[4]

A test case soon presented itself. In November 1698, six months after Bellomont's arrival, he learnt that a vessel, the *Hester*, was at Perth Amboy loading for a voyage to Madeira. Bellomont thereupon sent an armed force, variously estimated as from thirty to sixty men, to support his collector in

The case of the *Hester*.

[1] N. Y. Archives, vol. ii. p. 130.   [2] *Ib.* pp. 136, 177.
[3] *Ib.* p. 200.   [4] *Ib.* p. 201.

levying his dues. The crew resisted, and an affray followed. No lives seem to have been lost, but some sailors were wounded.[1] Bass seems to have so played his part in this affair as to offend all parties. He refused to support Bellomont's authority, and incurred his displeasure as an aider and abettor of smugglers.[2] At the same time when the New Jersey settlers warned him of the intended attack, and offered to back him in resisting it, he refused to act. They averred, too, that after the vessel was taken the captors heaped insults on the Governor, which he tamely received with words of good will and offers of meat and drink.[3] It is possible to put a better construction on Bass's conduct. He may have believed that Bellomont's claim was illegal and so refused to support it, yet he may have thought that it was not a case for meeting force with force. Finally the vessel was taken to New York, and there under Bellomont's authority sold at auction.

Bellomont's assertion of authority was the signal for more paper warfare. The New Jersey Proprietors at once petitioned the King, asking that either Perth Amboy should be made a port, or that at least the matter should be settled by the trial of a test case at Westminster.[4] At the same time they laid a memorial before the Lords of Trade.[5] In this they went over all the well-worn ground of the original right to levy customs vested in Carteret and Berkeley. They also urged various practical reasons, showing that the commerce of East Jersey would be

Demands of the New Jersey Proprietors.

[1] The facts of the capture are stated by Bellomont in a despatch to the Lords of Trade, N. Y. Docs. vol. iv. p. 438; and in a petition from Bass to Parliament, N. J. Archives, vol. ii. p. 311.
[2] Bellomont's despatch.
[3] This side of the case is stated in a petition from the freeholders in the towns of East Jersey addressed to the Proprietors. N. J. Archives, vol. ii. p. 273.
[4] *Ib.* p. 255.
[5] *Ib.* p. 259.

greatly hindered if vessels coming or going thence had to touch at New York. That, however, was no argument against the proposal to have a separate collector at Perth Amboy acting under orders from New York. Finally they repeated the proposal to bring the matter to a trial in Westminster Hall. This they pointed out would at least put them right with their settlers. The colonists who were the parties mainly interested would then know who was really responsible for refusing their demands. Otherwise they might deem that they had been betrayed and their interests surrendered by the Proprietors.

The case came to trial in the form of a civil action brought against Bellomont by those who had been losers by the seizure of the *Hester*. The Court found for the plaintiff with substantial damages, and the commercial independence of Perth Amboy was established.[1]

Judicial settlement.

Meanwhile the colony was torn asunder with conflicting claims and interests. The Scotch settlers were numerous enough to be of weight. The proclamation by which the King's subjects were forbidden to give any assistance to the settlers of New Caledonia seemed specially intended to restrain Scotch settlers already established in America, and thus in New Jersey, as in Great Britain, Darien was a watchword of strife. Quakers were strengthened in their opposition to authority by the sympathy of their brethren in Philadelphia. Many citizens of no mean standing were almost openly in league with smugglers and pirates. The Elizabethtown settlers were reviving their old claim to a title derived from Nicolls and wholly independent of the Proprietors. It is plain, too,

Disunited state of the colony.

---

[1] The result of the trial is stated in a despatch from Bellomont to the Lords of the Treasury, N. Y. Docs. vol. iv. p. 777. As might be expected, he complains of the damages as excessive.

that while there was in no party any cordial sympathy with the Proprietors, there was not any sort of positive agreement among their opponents. The colony was in fact broken up into jealous factions. It is the tendency of representative government to cause all political opinions to crystallize into certain definite forms, and to marshal men in bodies where the more exact shades of opinion disappear, and where convictions are roughly stretched or cut down to fit a party standard. But this at least carries with it one compensation. It saves a community from being torn to pieces by petty groups, it makes parties manageable and responsible by dividing them into certain well-defined and opposed bodies.

So it now was in New Jersey. Out of this conflict and chaos there gradually emerge two definite parties, and the political history of the colony is more and more the history of their opposition. So far as we can clearly trace the lines on which they were organized, the one was the party of the large landed Proprietors, the other that of the small freeholders. On the one side were the chief Scotch settlers in East Jersey, forming an oligarchy of birth and in some measure of wealth, and allied with them the leading Quakers, forming an oligarchy of religion. The support of the Proprietors was chiefly thrown into that scale, but there was a section, those who had brought about the election of Bass, who were opposed to the main body of their order.

<small>Division into parties.</small>

The main hindrance to the success of this party was the incompetence and irresolution of Bass himself. On the other hand his opponents were held together by that able tactician who, as we have seen, at a later day became conspicuous in the field of New York politics, Lewis Morris. At first his position among parties in New Jersey was that of a free lance, distinguishing himself mainly by trenchant

<small>Position of Morris.</small>

attacks on Bass and his supporters, couched in language calculated to bring contempt on the whole proprietary authority. But either conviction, or an estimate of the probable result of the contest, attracted him to the side of the Scotch party. We soon find him taking his place in colonial politics as the ally, and afterwards as the successor, of Hamilton, at the head of those who represented the interests of the large landholders.

By 1699 the disaffection against Bass had become such that he found it impossible to carry through the Assembly an Act for levying a sum of money needful for purposes of government.[1] Next year he and his Council endeavoured to smooth the passing of the Act by certain amendments, but it again failed, and the strife became so fierce that the Assembly broke up, the majority of the members departing and not leaving a quorum to carry on business.[2] Nor were his opponents content with such constitutional resistance. When the Supreme Court met at Perth Amboy, under the presidency of Bass, Morris appeared and challenged their right to sit. For this he was arrested and imprisoned for contempt of court. A riotous mob of his partisans soon gathered together, attacked the jail and freed Morris.[3]

Opposition to Bass.

In West Jersey Bass fared even worse. The magistrates at Burlington were beset and refused admission to the Court House by a mob strangely described as ‘a riotous number of Quakers.’ Bass thereupon himself

[1] This is stated in a letter from Morris to the Lords of Trade, N. J. Archives, vol. ii. p. 398. Morris was a partisan, but he would hardly have dared to misrepresent what must have been a matter of notoriety.

[2] *Ib.*

[3] The records of Morris's arrest and the subsequent riot are in the New Jersey Archives, vol. iii. pp. 479-82. They were forwarded to the Lords of Trade ten years later by the opponents of Morris as part of their case.

visited the place. He found the insurgents gathered together in un-Quakerly guise with colours, drums and arms. The arrival of the Governor seems, however, to have quelled the riot. The disaffected laid aside their firearms and, after certain threats of using their bludgeons, allowed Bass access to the Court House.[1]

Disturbance in West Jersey.

In 1699 the question as to Hamilton's qualification was reopened. Though avowedly a point of legal interpretation, it is plain that the question was fought out on party lines. Hamilton was the candidate of that influential Scotch party in the colony from whom a large part, though not the whole, of the opposition to Bass had proceeded. This party so far prevailed that Bass was superseded, and Hamilton reappointed to the governorship of both provinces.[2] There was, however, a sufficient section of the East Jersey Proprietors hostile to Hamilton to get that part of his commission rescinded, and one Andrew Bowne appointed.[3] Bowne's appointment does not seem to have been recognised as valid, and it only had the effect of putting an additional difficulty in Hamilton's way. On his arrival he found himself confronted with an opposition, who refused to recognise his authority on the ground that his appointment was only the act of the Proprietors and had not been sanctioned by the Crown.[4]

Further dispute about the governorship.

It is plain that those who supported Hamilton relied largely on the help of Morris. It is clear that his conspicuous and somewhat discreditable appearance

---

[1] This is stated in a memorial from Bass's partisans in West Jersey, N. J. Archives, vol. ii. p. 380. I do not find any contradiction.

[2] N. J. Archives, vol. ii. p. 301.

[3] Bowne's commission does not seem to be extant. But his appointment is mentioned in a letter from the Council of East Jersey to the Proprietors, June 18, 1701. N. J. Archives, vol. ii. p. 385.

[4] This is stated in a petition from Hamilton himself and his Council to the King. N. J. Archives, vol. ii. p. 369.

as a party leader had not destroyed his influence, since we are told by a contemporary that Hamilton, in placing Morris on the Council and appointing him Chief Justice, looked on him as the only man that could make the colony submit.[1] His opening exploit as an administrator hardly justified Hamilton's confidence. Hearing, as it would seem, that certain men in Monmouth County were showing some symptoms of disaffection, Morris ordered the sheriff to make some arrests.[2] The sheriff came back with a broken head. Thereupon Hamilton raised a force of forty or fifty men and marched towards the scene of the disturbance. He was met by a hundred and seventy men unarmed. Hamilton thereupon withdrew. Meanwhile the Councillors residing in the disaffected districts were disclaiming any responsibility for the Governor's action. Threats were heard that Hamilton, Morris, and their chief supporter John Leonard would be arrested and held prisoners till the King's pleasure was known. Rumours, too, were circulated that men in office had been drinking Jacobite toasts, and that the King's government could not be secure without a change.

Disturbances in Monmouth County.

The events of the next year revealed a more probable and less creditable cause of disaffection. A pirate named Butterworth, said to be one of Kidd's crew, was put on his trial at Middletown. An armed force beset the Court, rescued the prisoner, and, to ensure his safe escape, seized the judges and the law officers and kept them for four days as prisoners.

Riot at Middletown.[3]

---

[1] Letter from Bowne and Hartshorne (probably to one of the Proprietors), July 23, 1700. N. J. Archives, vol. ii. p. 327.

[2] Our knowledge of these affairs is derived from the letter of Bowne and Hartshorne, just quoted, and from a letter, of which the signature is lost, addressed to Bass at the same date. N. J. Archives, vol. ii. p. 329.

[3] The record of these proceedings by the Clerk of the Court at Monmouth is in the New Jersey Archives, vol. ii. p. 362. Cf. the Petition of the Governor and Council to the King, *ib.* p. 371.

In West Jersey matters were better. Yet there Hamilton seems to have ruled rather as the head of a victorious party than as an impartial peace-maker.[1] He relied for his support on the same party, mainly Quakers, who had rebelled against Bass. According to their opponents they were numerically in a minority, but made amends by their greater energy and better organization. It was alleged, too, that they traded on the superstitions and on the peace principles of the settlers generally by persuading them that if their opponents regained power, they would introduce an endowed clergy and a standing militia. If we may believe the memorial which set forth these grievances, the Quaker party was supported by the Proprietors. The petitioners accordingly ended their remonstrance by a request that the proprietary government might be dissolved, and that they might be placed under the direct authority of the Crown. This was soon followed by a numerously signed memorial from the inhabitants of East Jersey, praying that if the Proprietors failed to appoint in the place of Hamilton a Governor who should be approved by the King, they should be united into one colony with West Jersey, and placed under the direct control of the Crown.[2]

Hamilton in West Jersey.

There was little likelihood that the Proprietors would feel any inclination to hold out against this proposal. Two years before the Proprietors of East Jersey had made overtures to the Crown for a surrender.[3] Their proposal involved the abandonment of all political sovereignty, but the retention of their territorial rights. The colony was to be annexed to New York. At the same time the well-being of the settlers, and consequently the com-

Proposals for the surrender of the proprietorship.

---

[1] The case against Hamilton is set forth in an address from the inhabitants of West Jersey to the Crown. N. J. Archives, vol. ii. p. 380.

[2] N. J. Archives, vol. ii. p. 394.

[3] Memorial of the Proprietors, *ib.* p. 294.

mercial prosperity of the colony, were to be protected by certain specified provisions maintaining existing rights. Perth Amboy was still to be a port independent of New York. The inhabitants were to have the right of trading freely with the natives. The colony was to have its own separate law courts. There was to be a joint legislature, in both branches of which, the Council and the House of Representatives, New Jersey was to have its proportionate share.

There is nothing to show what befell this proposal, whether it ever came before any authoritative body in England, and if so what was its fate. But in 1701 a fresh proposal was made, this time by the Proprietors of both colonies.[1] They did not as before propose annexation to New York, but a consolidation of the two colonies into a single government under the Crown. There was a further important difference. In 1699 the Proprietors of East Jersey offered up their political rights as a sacrifice, hoping thereby to retain their position as landholders. Now they took higher ground. The document proposing the surrender was accompanied by a private letter from Morris to Popple, the Secretary to the Lords of Trade.[2] In this the motives and policy of the Proprietors are clearly explained, and by the light of this commentary we must read their proposals. The Proprietors set forth that the planters had lately broached the theory, vesting the right to the soil in the natives and denying the claims of the Crown, and consequently all rights derived by grant from the Crown. The Proprietors accordingly proposed, as one of the articles of surrender, that the Crown shall declare all titles to land resting on purchase from the Indians null and void till confirmed by the Proprietors, and that no one but the Proprietors shall have such right of purchase. As Morris points out, they would induce the

[1] N. J. Archives, vol. ii. p. 404.   [2] *Ib.* p. 412.

Crown to secure for them a right which they were not strong enough to secure for themselves. The settlers were to retain the same right of trading with the natives as in New York or in any other Crown colony. Perth Amboy, Burlington and Cohanzey were to be independent ports, each with its own customs officers. There was to be a joint Assembly, sitting alternately at Perth Amboy and Burlington. A provision was inserted as to the composition of the Assembly manifestly intended for the benefit of the class with whom the Proprietors were most closely connected, and adverse to the general body of settlers. No man might vote for a representative unless he had a freehold estate of a hundred acres, and no man might sit in the Assembly without a freehold estate of a thousand acres. The religious rights of the settlers were to be protected by a clause making all Nonconformists capable of holding office, and by the substitution of a declaration for an oath. Finally, the Proprietors were to be allowed to nominate the first Governor. The last stipulation was confirmed by a petition signed by sixteen Proprietors, asking the King to confirm Hamilton's appointment till the surrender was effected. The retention of Hamilton was, Morris points out, of importance to the Proprietors in two ways. He could be trusted to look after their interests, and the fact of their being allowed to retain a Governor of their own choice would impress the settlers with the belief that the claims of the Proprietors were approved by the Crown. The appointment or rejection of Hamilton had in fact become a test question between the Proprietors and their opponents.

The proposal at once called out a remonstrance from the anti-proprietary party, of whom Bass was the mouthpiece. Within four weeks a memorial from Bass was presented to the Lords of Trade.[1] He had not seen

[1] N. J. Archives, vol. ii. p. 418.

the proposed articles of surrender and therefore could not criticize them in detail. But he denied the right of the Proprietors to make any such surrender. Those who made it were only a portion of the whole proprietary body. They could only surrender their own rights, not those of their colleagues. The original grant to the Duke of York was a personal trust and could not be assigned: it gave the Duke authority to govern the province as a whole, not to cut it up in three.

Attitude of Bass.

There was no doubt great force in this argument, but unluckily it came thirty-seven years too late. It was an excellent argument against the original grant to Berkeley and Carteret. It was an excellent argument against the system whereby the Crown allowed sovereignty to become a mere incident of territorial possession, equally capable of transfer. But it wholly failed to bear on the case in hand or to carry the stress which Bass laid upon it. So far from making against the surrender, it tended to show that the surrender was the only means of repairing a wrong.

That was the view of the case which presented itself to the Lords of Trade. They declined to express an opinion as to the validity of the Proprietors' title, and therefore as to their competence to make a surrender. But on the ground of general policy, for the prevention of disorder within the colony and for the military security of the English possessions, it was expedient that it should be under the control of the Crown. Accordingly they recommended that the King should accept the proposal of the Proprietors, and should, by his instructions to the new Governor, determine the constitution of the colony.

Opinions of the Lords of Trade.[1]

With all parties substantially agreed there could be only one result. The proposal to unite New Jersey

---

[1] Their Memorial is in the Archives, vol. ii. p. 420.

with New York was abandoned, possibly through the representations of Hamilton, who pointed out that in a mixed representative Assembly the smaller colony would be swamped. The death of King William caused some slight delay, but in April 1702 a deed was formally executed by the Proprietors of each province acting jointly, whereby they transferred their whole sovereignty to the Crown.[1]

The proprietorship transferred to the Crown.

[1] N. J. Archives, vol. ii. p. 452.

CHAPTER VIII.

NEW JERSEY A CROWN COLONY.

WE have already seen what was the extent and character of the territory which thus passed under the direct dominion of the Crown. The Eastern and Western halves of the peninsula were connected by a single road of some fifty or sixty miles in length.[1] On the Eastern coast were seven townships, on the West three. None, except perhaps Perth Amboy, were in the ordinary sense towns. Each was a scattered collection of farmsteads, with at one or more points a more closely set nucleus of houses.[2] The Indian fur trade was the staple of the colony; we hear nothing of the exportation of corn or horned stock; horses however were numerous and were shipped to the West Indies.[3] There can be no doubt that a considerable portion of the trade of the colony lay in the purchase of cargoes brought in by pirates, which could be landed more safely in New Jersey than in such ports as Boston or New York. We read of saw-mills,[4] ironworks[5] and copper mines, and tanning was an industry

Condition of the colony.

---

[1] Whitehead, *Contributions*, p. 268.
[2] This is clear from a memorial addressed by Lewis Morris in 1690 to the Bishop of London, published in the collection of the New Jersey Historical Society.
[3] Budd, p. 39 ; Gabriel Thorne, p. 25.
[4] Lawrie in the *Model*, p. 292.
[5] Budd, p. 38, with note in the reprint of 1902.

of sufficient importance to be made the subject of special legislation.¹

As in most of the colonies the want of coined money was a difficulty which disturbed the legislature, and rates were especially enacted at which commodities might be taken in payment of public dues.² One attempt to remedy the lack of a currency deserves notice. One of the most enterprising of the early settlers, Budd, to whom we owe much of our knowledge of the early history of the colony, bestirred himself to supply the want of a circulating medium by that device which has so often appealed to speculative imaginations. Anticipating by a few years Chamberlain's proposal, he would have allowed all landholders to issue notes on the security of their estate.³ Budd eagerly points out how such a measure will give the whole soil of the colony an immediate commercial value, by making it the basis of credit and an equivalent of capital. Happily for the well-being of the colony Budd did not find listeners ready to turn his theory into practical experiment.

Want of money.

The New Jersey settlers almost wholly escaped one set of difficulties that beset the infancy of most of our colonies. There was not between the Hudson and the Chesapeake any compact or formidable Indian power. The horrors of savage warfare were to the New Jersey settlers but a name. Thus in neither colony do we find any stringent prohibition of trade with the natives. In East Jersey indeed in the early days, when its inhabitants were little more than a few scattered bands of New England emigrants, haunted by memories of Pequod and Mohican wars, we find an Act prohibiting the sale of arms and ammunition to the Indians.⁴ Nor might any smith mend a gun for a native.

Dealings with Indians.

---

¹ Leaming and Spicer, p. 112.   ² *Ib.* p. 78.
³ Budd, pp. 49-51.   ⁴ Leaming and Spicer.

There would seem to have been at this time special apprehension, since it was also ordered that each town should have a fortified guard-house.[1] Two years later the Act prohibiting the sale of arms and ammunition was repealed.[2]

The sale of drink to the natives was also a subject of legislation. In 1677 an attempt was made to control without absolutely prohibiting it.[3] The publican who sold it was to 'take effectual care to prevent disturbance.' But two years later all sale of drink to natives was prohibited under penalty of flogging.[4] This was re-enacted in 1692,[5] and like enactments were passed in the Western province.[6] The existence of negro slaves is shown by the fact that they were in more than one instance included in this prohibition.[7]

It was no doubt largely due to the absence of any external pressure from the savage that the New Jersey township became, as we have seen, a loose, straggling community. The same cause also co-operated with the large Quaker element in the population to disincline the inhabitants for military service, and to make New Jersey, like Pennsylvania, a dangerously weak link in the English chain of defence. In New Jersey we see a community largely of Puritan origin, some members of it at the outset deeply imbued with the exclusive spirit of New England, gradually under the influence of climate and natural conditions drifting into a mode of life akin in some degree to that of Maryland or Virginia. The emigrant from the shores of New Haven could safely isolate himself amid the pastures by the Hudson. Close corporate union became no longer a necessity, and as a consequence close spiritual union ceased. Education suffered as

State of education.

[1] Leaming and Spicer, p. 86.
[2] *Ib.* p. 125.
[3] *Ib.*
[4] *Ib.* p. 133.
[5] *Ib.* p. 316.
[6] Laws of West Jersey, p. 435.
[7] *Ib.* p. 512.

well as religion. An Act passed in East Jersey in 1693 authorized each township to levy a school rate.¹ But two years later another Act expressly declared that this had failed from the fact that the towns had no definite centre. The legislature sought to remedy the evil by creating a committee of three responsible school managers in each town.²

We have a very full and vivid picture of the religious condition of the colony extant. In 1690 Lewis Morris sent a memorial to the Bishop of London describing the spiritual needs of his fellow-citizens.³ Morris, even in more mature and sober years, had the temper of an advocate and a partisan. He was avowedly hostile to a large section of the settlers, and it would be rash to take his statements as sober historical evidence. But after all possible deduction they describe a state of things singular in a colony whose original root was in New England Puritanism, and which had been replenished by Quakers and Covenanters. The colony presented in the fullest degree an example of that 'polypiety' so hateful to Puritan New England. Elizabethtown and Newark kept their original Presbyterianism, with a slight admixture of Anglicans, Baptists and Quakers. At Piscataway there was a Baptist church, at Freehold one of Scotch Presbyterians, and at Perth Amboy one of Anglicans, but in each place about half the inhabitants were of no church and, Morris suggests, of no religion. At Aquednek and Bergen there were Dutch Calvinists and Swedish Lutherans who had settled there before the English occupation. Middletown, though largely peopled from New England, had no place of worship. There, as elsewhere, Sunday was commonly spent in racing, fighting and drinking at taverns.

Religious condition of the colony.

¹ Leaming and Spicer, p. 328. ² *Ib.* p. 358.
³ See above, p. 480.

Shrewsbury had a small Quaker congregation, but was otherwise in the same plight. About 1689 an attempt was made to carry a measure for endowment of the clergy, but it was frustrated by the joint action of Quakers and Baptists, and an attempt to revive the scheme was successfully opposed by Bass, himself a Baptist. If we may believe Morris, such religion as did exist among the colonists was to be found among the older settlers, those who had come either from the mother country or from New England. The younger generation, brought up under no restraining influences of religion or of schooling, and released by the natural advantages of soil and climate from severe labour, had drifted into godlessness and debauchery. Vague charges of this sort against a community are always to be received with doubt, and Morris no doubt had in him much of the advocate. But, on the other hand, he had nothing of the Puritan about him, and if the stories of his own youth be true is not likely to have had an exacting standard of morals.

Of West Jersey he tells us less. There Quakerism was distinctly the dominant creed, numbering as it did in its fold a third of the inhabitants, among whom were all the wealthiest and most influential men. Beyond them were, Morris tells us, 'a mere hotchpotch of religions.'

The attempt of Hamilton's friends to secure his appointment as Governor failed. It would assuredly have been an unwise act if the Queen had at the very outset identified the supremacy of the Crown with an act which could have been regarded as a party victory. But it was hardly more unfortunate that her choice should have fallen upon Cornbury, then Governor of New York. The affairs of New Jersey alone would have been task enough for an abler man, and it would have been well to avoid anything which

Cornbury appointed Governor.

seemed to treat the province as in any way dependent on her jealous and arrogant neighbour. And even if the task had not been beset by these difficulties, Cornbury was wholly unfitted for it by his personal faults.

The new constitution of the colony was fully determined by Cornbury's commission and instructions.[1] In the skeleton of the constitution there was no change. It conformed to the ordinary model, made up of Governor, Council, and House of Representatives. The difference lay in the increased precision and definiteness which was given to the constitution. Hitherto the rights of the Governor and the distribution of powers among the various members of the body politic had been matter of usage. There was indeed, as we have seen, in each colony an elaborate paper constitution, but the very completeness at which it aimed made it a dead letter.

The new constitution.

The new constitution provided for the supremacy of the Crown by giving the Sovereign a veto on all legislation, and by authorizing the Governor to impose not only on all members of the Assembly, but also on all citizens as far as he thought fit, the oaths now substituted for those of supremacy and allegiance. The Governor had also an independent veto on legislation, he had the custody of the great seal and the power of pardon. No money could be spent out of the public funds without the Governor's warrant, and he had the power in conjunction with his Council to appoint fairs and markets, and to constitute ports. He had also power to suspend Councillors, referring their case to the Crown, and to nominate them provisionally so as to bring the Council up to the necessary number of seven. It was also provided by the instructions, though not by

[1] Cornbury's commission is in the New Jersey Archives, vol. ii. p. 489, and his instructions at p. 506. They come under a hundred and three heads, and occupy thirty pages of small octavo of a rather large type.

G G

the commission, that Cornbury was to propose to the Queen the names of twelve Councillors, six from each province, and to suggest names to fill any vacancy that might occur. Three of the Council might form a quorum, but unless on some special emergency the Governor was not to sit with less than five.

An Assembly was to be summoned immediately on Cornbury's arrival. It was to consist of twenty-four members, half for each province. Two were to be chosen by Perth Amboy, two by Burlington. Except in the case of these places there was to be no representative of township or shire, but the whole body of electors in each province were to choose ten members. There was to be a property qualification, a thousand acres of freehold for members and one hundred for electors. There can be no doubt that these qualifications were allowed as a concession to the Proprietors, or rather to that party among the Proprietors who stood by the great landholders. The practical result was to give a solid foothold to the party headed formerly by Hamilton and now by Morris, a party which under a less exclusive franchise would have been hopelessly outnumbered. All Acts passed by the Assembly were to be forwarded to England, if possible within three months. Cornbury was also instructed on his arrival to send home a statement of all enactments in force.

There was no clause expressly giving the right of taxation to the Assembly. But it is implied in an instruction to Cornbury that all money raised by the Assembly is to be formally appropriated to the public use of the government, and that in voting any money, the purpose to which it is to be applied shall be clearly specified and the approval of the Crown asked. The control of the Assembly over the public purse is even more fully implied in an instruction to Cornbury to

' propose with the Assembly, and use his utmost endeavours with them,' that an Act be passed to raise a revenue for the purposes of government, and especially for a competent salary to the Governor and other officials.

Judges, executive officers, and justices of the peace are to be nominated by the Governor, but are not to be removable except with the approval of the Crown. Jurisdiction in cases of piracy had already been vested in Cornbury as Governor of New York. He may also, in time of war and with the approval of his Council, put in force and administer martial law. In all cases of over a hundred pounds value there is to be an appeal from the local courts to the Governor in Council, and in cases of twice that value a further appeal to the Sovereign in Council.

Supreme military and naval power within the colony is vested in the Governor. But it is to be noticed that, while there is no restriction imposed on his military authority, it is provided that his jurisdiction shall not extend to any of the King's ships, even though they may be within a harbour or river of the province. In other words, the militia under Lord Cornbury was the recognised army of the colony, but naval operations were to be carried on by the King's ships. It was a special instruction to Cornbury to put the militia on an efficient footing, and to induce the Assembly to pass an effective mutiny Act. He was also to 'dispose them' to make a reasonable contribution, either in men or money, to the defence of New York.

In ecclesiastical matters the commission and the instructions show singular ignorance of the condition of the colony. The commission authorizes Cornbury to present to all ecclesiastical benefices. So, too, the instructions provided that the Book of Common Prayer should be read on Sundays and holy days throughout the whole colony, and the Sacrament administered according to the rites of the Church of England. A competent endowment, a house and a glebe were to be secured to the minister of each orthodox church, and no one was to be preferred to any benefice without a certificate of orthodoxy and good character from the Bishop of London. It would have been easy to twist this into an engine of tyranny against the Nonconformists, who formed at the very least nineteen-twentieths of the whole population. Yet it is clear that the framers of the instruction had not the slightest intention of its being so used. The advisers of the Crown appear to have thought that the colony had something like a parochial system with endowed churches. As we have seen, such religion as there was lay entirely among sects who had resented any attempt at State control.

That there was no wish to interfere with freedom of thought or worship is manifest, for it is expressly provided that all except Papists shall enjoy liberty of conscience. The rights of Quakers were specially secured by an instruction that for all public purposes, whether judicial or administrative, a declaration should be allowed instead of an oath. Freedom of speech, however, was so far restricted that nothing was to be printed without leave from the Governor.

In various ways provision was made for the well-being, or supposed well-being, of the colony. Harbours were to be selected. Titles to land were to be revised and confirmed. Workhouses were to be built for the aged and indigent. Stringent measures were to be taken against smuggling, and full statistical reports of the condition of the colony were to be sent home.

One clause has a melancholy interest. It has often been made matter of reproach against England that of set purpose, and by deliberate and persistent policy, she fastened on her colonies the curse of negro slavery. In the case of New Jersey the charge cannot be denied. The instruction stated that the Queen was desirous that the colonies should have a constant and sufficient supply of merchantable negroes at moderate rates. The Royal African Company should be urged to send such a supply. In return payment must be prompt, and all private trading with Africa must be kept in check.

Yet in this the English Government only acted on what any set of statesmen in that day would have reckoned sound and benevolent principles. And it must be said in extenuation that if Cornbury's instructions furthered the slave trade, they aimed at abating the worst evils of slavery. The conversion of negroes and Indians was to be specially proposed to the Council and Assembly as an object of public policy. Cornbury was to endeavour to secure the passing of a law which should restrain inhuman severity against slaves by making it a penal offence to maim one, and a capital crime wilfully to put one to death.

To enforce a somewhat elaborate system of administration on a community which had grown up virtually independent of external control was a dangerous experiment. Whatever hopes of success it might have had must have been frustrated when it was entrusted to such an one as Cornbury. He was not altogether wanting in intelligence. But his levity and contentiousness, his lack of all solid judgment and of all respect for the feelings and wishes of those with whom he had to deal, were faults worse in such a position than actual stupidity.

Difficulties of Cornbury's position.

In one respect his path was cleared for him. The death of Hamilton, just before Cornbury's arrival, removed one whose presence in the colony, exciting, as it would have excited, the hopes of a party, and stirring up recollections of strife, could not have failed to prove a stumbling-block in the path of the new Governor.[1]

Yet even as it was there were abundant elements for conflict, and in some measure they were set in action by the change. Every party felt that its chance of success depended on the position which it could now gain for itself.

In August 1703 Cornbury visited his new province. Almost his first proceeding, as told frankly enough by himself, illustrated his extraordinary levity and his lack of all sense of official responsibility. He proceeded to administer an oath to the Councillors. Three being Quakers declined the oath. Cornbury thereupon referred to his instructions. From the way in which he tells of the matter one would suppose that he had not read them before: it is at least perfectly certain that he had no real knowledge of their contents. He found that it was necessary to administer an oath to all persons in a position of trust or authority. It was, however, pointed out that there was a clause specially exempting Quakers. Unless Cornbury does himself great injustice these were two successive discoveries of which before he knew nothing. He adds in his report that the ground assigned for this toleration, the paucity of inhabitants fit to sit as Councillors, was wholly unfounded.

Cornbury falls out with the Quakers.[2]

After appointing sheriffs and justices of the peace, and examining the composition of the law courts, Cornbury issued writs for the election of an Assembly. The unsatisfactory nature of the franchise and of the distribution of seats as determined by Cornbury's instructions at once made itself felt. The

Election of an Assembly.

---

[1] The Council announced to Cornbury on his arrival that Hamilton had died on April 26, 1703.

[2] See Cornbury's despatch to the Lords of Trade, Sept. 9, 1703. N. J. Archives, vol. iii. p. 1.

qualification which made it essential both to electors and candidates to be landholders, unsuitable as may be easily supposed, excluded many who were well fitted to vote or to sit without insuring any merit in those whom it admitted. As might have been foreseen, the remote country townships were swamped by Perth Amboy and Burlington. In the latter case, indeed, it is said that the energy and electioneering skill of the Quakers enabled them, though a minority, to get all the representation in their own hands.[1] It was also said, and it would seem with a fair show of truth, that in East Jersey the unscrupulous action of the returning officer, a Scotchman named Gordon, enabled Hamilton's party to carry the elections in defiance of a large majority.[2]

Amid a cloud of conflicting testimony, darkened by abuse and recrimination, this at least stands out clear. *Proceedings of the Assembly.*[3] The new Assembly set before it as its main object to secure the territorial rights of the Proprietors. A bill was brought in and passed affirming the title of the Proprietors not merely to the province of New Jersey, but also to Staten Island, which had been judicially declared to belong to New York. The Assembly also, in affirming the title of the Proprietors, decided against the claims of those who held under grants from Nicolls. They passed a bill assigning all royalties within the colony to the Proprietors.

[1] For all these statements I have relied on the not very trustworthy evidence of Cornbury. But his statement is probable in itself, and one cannot see any motive for misrepresentation. His despatch on the subject to the Lords of Trade, dated Jan. 14, 1704, is in the New Jersey Archives, vol. iii. p. 28.

[2] This is stated by Colonel Quarry, of whom I have spoken before, in a letter to the Lords of Trade, Dec. 20, 1703. N. J. Archives, vol. iii. p. 13.

[3] Our knowledge of the proceedings of this Assembly is derived from Quarry's despatch. He may err in his estimate of motives, but he can hardly be mistaken about plain facts, nor would he have been guilty of misstatement where contradiction was easy.

They also exempted all unimproved lands from taxation, thus laying all public burdens on the smaller landholders. To give the Governor a motive for assenting to this, they adopted a device of Parliamentary procedure, and tacked to it a money bill granting a revenue of a thousand pounds. Cornbury, however, refused his assent to this and to nearly the whole of their legislation, and nothing was passed but a short bill forbidding any purchase of land from the Indians.

If Cornbury had been a man of any judgment or character there is little doubt that he might have now Dispute in the Assembly. established his own authority on a secure footing, and might have taught the great body of settlers to look on the English Crown as a friendly and protecting power. The Assembly was, beyond all doubt, acting in the interests of the Proprietors regardless of the general body of settlers. Nor had they even the advantage of representing the Proprietors as a whole, for at this very time a fierce dispute was going on within the proprietary body. There were certain members of it who considered themselves aggrieved by the manner in which the lands had been divided. Their agent, Sonmans, was in the Council, and the other Proprietors were endeavouring to have him excluded as a bankrupt and man of bad character.[1] The nature of the strife was fairly described by a shrewd observer. That section of the Proprietors, he says, who swayed the Assembly were endeavouring to substitute for joint proprietorship, individual proprietorship favourable to themselves.[2]

The defeated party saw that their only chance was a dissolution and a fresh election. At first they sought to induce Cornbury to dissolve, by a message sent

[1] The memorial petitioning for the removal of Sonmans is in the New Jersey Archives, vol. iii. p. 35. It is not dated, but was received January 27, 1704.

[2] Quarry's despatch quoted above. N. J. Archives, vol. iii. p. 18.

through Quarry, hinting that a different Assembly might deal with him more liberally in the matter of salary. **Intrigues in the Assembly.** They found, however, that Cornbury wanted something more certain and tangible than this prospective advantage. Accordingly, as it was said with every show of truth, they raised a fund and bribed the Governor to dissolve the Assembly.[1]

The intrigue, if there was one, was clumsy and ineffectual, and the dominant party came back with a majority in the new Assembly. The majority, however, was brought down to a narrow one.

It was now an open battle between the supporters of the Proprietors and the general body of freeholders with Cornbury's influence at their back. It is **Disqualification of members.** plain that parties in the Assembly were closely balanced, and that two or three votes would be enough to turn the scale. Two members of the Governor's Council protested against the return of three Representatives as not possessing the needful qualification in land.[2] The question, according to the precedent of elective petitions, was referred to the Assembly. They found in favour of the Representatives. The Governor then claimed that not only must the house, but also he himself, be satisfied. This, as his opponents pointed out, was practically a claim to veto any election.

The suspension of these members gave the enemies of the Proprietors the upper hand, and it is plain that they used their power harshly. Parties, in fact, were in that unwholesome state when each uses any temporary superiority not merely to carry out its own policy, but

---

[1] Various documents substantiating this charge are to be found in the third volume of the Archives.

[2] On the question of the qualification of the three members both parties were agreed as to the facts. These are set forth by Cornbury's opponents in a Remonstrance sent to him, May 8, 1707 (N. J. Archives, vol. iii. pp. 174-80), and admitted in Cornbury's answer (*ib.* pp. 180-98). These two documents are my authority for what followed.

to perpetuate its ascendancy and permanently cripple its opponents. Three measures in particular are mentioned, and though the statement comes from one of the oppressed party, and is no doubt coloured by prejudice, yet there can be little doubt that it is in substance well founded.[1]

A revenue of two thousand a year was granted to the Governor. It was supposed that the bulk of this would be raised by a rate on uncultivated lands. This was in itself a violation of Lord Cornbury's instructions, and, if the Proprietors were right in their contention that those instructions were deliberately intended as terms of surrender, it was a breach of faith. It appears, however, to have recoiled on the heads of those who designed it, since the unoccupied lands were quite insufficient for the purpose, and the tax fell with crushing weight on the bulk of the settlers.

<small>Oppressive acts of the majority.</small>

In passing a militia Act it was provided that the Quakers might compound for a money payment. These payments, we are told, were unfairly assessed, and when enforced, the necessary distraints were carried out harshly and inequitably. It is also alleged that the officials appointed to lay out the highways deliberately used their powers to inflict wanton damage on the defeated party.

A more legitimate measure was a bill for altering the qualification of voters and representatives. Here, again, the Proprietors contended that the existing qualification was inserted as one of the conditions on which they consented to the surrender. As a matter of equity and expediency one may question whether the Proprietors were a fit body to determine such a question once for all, and one assuredly cannot blame

[1] All these proceedings are set forth in a letter written by Lewis Morris to the Secretary of State, Feb. 9, 1708. The letter gives a very clear account of the state of parties in the colony and of their proceedings. N. J. Archives, vol. iii. p. 274.

the settlers for doing their utmost to secure a change. The existing qualification was not only unjust to those whom it excluded; it is clear that it did not a little to cripple the efficiency of the legislative machine. It was in all likelihood due to this that when Cornbury had adjourned the Assembly to meet at Burlington in May 1705, he found it impossible to carry on business owing to the absence of members.[1] An adjournment of five months to Perth Amboy did not wholly mend matters.[2] This illustrates what indeed might have been plain enough to the authorities in England, that Burlington and the rest of West Jersey would have been far better attached to Pennsylvania.

Before the proceedings of the Assembly could be sent to England for confirmation, the object at which they aimed had been practically effected. An instruction from the Queen, acting by the advice of the Lords of Trade, altered the whole system of representation.[3] Each province, the Eastern and the Western, was no longer to return ten members in a lump, but the Eastern half was to have two members for each of the five counties, the Western two for each of the four and two for the township of Salem. The qualifications were also modified. A property qualification was retained, but it was no longer to be exclusively in land. Personal estate of five pounds was to be now taken as equivalent to real estate of ten acres.

Change in the franchise.

On two important points the Lords of Trade showed no inclination to encourage Cornbury. He was admonished to be content with a revenue of fifteen hundred pounds for his first year and one thousand for subsequent years. He was also cautioned against interfering in any question of the qualification of members for Assembly.

Action of the English Government.

[1] N. J. Archives, vol. iii. p. 104.   [2] *Ib.* p. 112.
[3] Lords of Trade to Cornbury, April 20, 1705. N. J. Archives, vol. iii. p. 96.

Almost immediately after this the Lords of Trade received Cornbury's report of the state of affairs in the colony, together with the draft of the Acts passed by the Assembly. Their reception of it showed an honest wish to deal fairly and impartially with the parties at strife.[1] It was plainly declared that the surrender by the Proprietors was unconditional, that whatever concession was made to them was made as an act of grace. At the same time Cornbury was admonished as to his future conduct in terms which were a severe censure on his past. The qualification of individual members was a question for the Assembly, not for the Governor. He had removed Morris from the Council; he was instructed to replace him. As things stood, the sums levied as a commutation for service in the militia were to be spent at the Governor's discretion. This manifest abuse was checked. Henceforth they were to be paid to the Receiver-General for the colony, and to be applied to purposes specified in the Act under which they were levied.

Cornbury, too, had compelled the Proprietors for the Western province to deliver over their official papers to Bass, and they had in consequence been carried out of the colony. They were now to be restored and the proceeding not to be repeated.

Reports, too, had reached the Lords that Cornbury had commissioned unfit persons as militia officers and justices of the peace. They do not go into the question, and neither accept nor disbelieve the charge. But the Governor is cautioned to exercise due care in such matters. Such a reprimand was practically a condemnation.

It was now plain to Cornbury that the field of New

---

[1] Lords of Trade to Cornbury, Feb. 14, 1706, N. J. Archives, p. 124. There is also (p. 117) a memorandum in which the views of the Board on each special charge brought against Cornbury are given.

Jersey politics was one in which there was little hope of personal profit, and as soon as he saw that his in-
<small>Cornbury ceases to interest himself in the colony.</small> terest in the colony ceased. He was not, like Randolph, a harsh and aggressive administrator, with a definite theory of colonial government, and with at the same time a certain sense of satisfaction in thwarting the wishes of the colonists. Cornbury was, as far as one can see, simply corrupt. Every cause and every party was simply measured by the power of filling his pockets. One other motive did indeed colour his language and feelings, though it hardly affected his policy. He had inherited so much of the religious principles of his ancestors as taught him to dislike Nonconformists as factious, underbred dogs. He had just enough of the conventional Churchmanship of the eighteenth century to despise Quakers as enthusiasts, and quite enough of the profligate to hate them as kill-joys.

During the whole of 1706 Cornbury does not seem to have set foot in New Jersey. The death of his wife
<small>The Assembly of 1707.</small> furnished an excuse, perhaps a reason, for his absence. In March 1707 he called an Assembly. The change in the franchise does not seem to have altered the character of this body, nor to have detached it from the interest of the Proprietors. Nor was the proprietary party one whit more inclined to deal in friendly fashion with the Governor. It would seem during the interval to have become more influential and better organized, and it enjoyed the advantage of having two efficient leaders in Morris and Samuel Jennings. Cornbury had endeavoured to weaken the influence of the latter by placing him on the Council. But, much to the annoyance of his opponents, he declined the appointment, preferring to sit as a member of the elected body.[1]

[1] Cornbury to the Lords of Trade, June 7, 1707. N. Y. Docs, vol. v. pp. 234-9. As Cornbury puts it, the true reason why he (Jennings) desired to be dismissed from the Council was that he might be chosen into

Morris was in a somewhat similar position. Cornbury had been instructed by the Government at home to replace him on the Council. This the Governor offered to do if Morris would make proper submission.[1] Morris no doubt felt that he was in a far stronger position as an elected member, excluded from the Council by the arbitrary will of the Governor. The first proceeding of the Assembly was, in Cornbury's language, 'to set up a committee of grievances and spend a whole month in finding out grievances which nobody in the province had ever heard of before,' 'imaginary grievances, the produce of Mr. Morris's peevish brain.'[2] How far his description is just may be judged from a petition which the Assembly presented to the Crown and a remonstrance to the Governor. In these two their complaints are set forth with statesmanlike clearness, force, and self-restraint.[3]

The main charges fall under two heads: the levying of illegal dues, and the hindrance and added cost of public business owing to the absence of the Governor. Prisoners are compelled to pay court fees even when the grand jury fail to find a true bill against them. Official fees have been fixed not by the whole Assembly, but by the Governor in Council. The Governor has granted patents to carriers between Burlington and Perth Amboy, and has prohibited all persons not so licensed from carrying goods for hire. Owing to the Governor's long absence from the colony, offenders committed for trial have remained in prison untried.

Grievances of the Assembly.

There are also other grievances: there is only one office for the probate of wills, that at Burlington, and

---

the Assembly, where he knew he could oppose the Queen's service more effectually than he could do in the Council.

[1] Cornbury as above.   [2] *Ib.*
[3] For the remonstrance and Cornbury's answer, *v. s.* pp. 458, *n.* 1, and 463.

consequently all settlers living in the Eastern province have to resort thither for business. The records of the Eastern province have been entrusted to Sonmans, the agent of a section of the Proprietors, a man living out of the colony. Finally, the remonstrants recall the case of the three excluded members, and the story of the bribes offered to Cornbury to bring about the dissolution of the Assembly.

Cornbury's answer illustrates his character and temper as a ruler, and his fitness for administering a colony largely peopled by Quakers. He begins by declaring that the real calamity of the province is 'the dangerous and abominable doctrines of those who under the pretended names of Christians have dared to deny the very essence and being of the Saviour of the world.' The document as a whole was worthy of this exordium, its arguments throughout overlaid by diffuse rhetoric and vague countercharges. The charge of having dissolved the Assembly from corrupt motives, a charge supported by abundant testimony, was met by a bare denial. One specimen may serve to illustrate the spirit in which Cornbury was prepared to meet the complaints and to consider the need of the settlers. He admits that the absence of a probate office compelled them to visit New York. But what hardship is that journey to Quakers who never complain of travelling several hundred miles to one of their meetings, 'where continual contrivances are carried on for the undermining the government both in Church and State'?

Cornbury's answer.

On one or two detailed points Cornbury was undoubtedly able to show that the remonstrants were in the wrong. In fixing the scale of fees with the aid of his Council, instead of leaving it to the Assembly, he was only carrying out the letter of his instructions. To license public carriers was hardly the same thing as creating a monopoly, at least in any bad sense.

Not content with acting on the defensive, Cornbury endeavoured to bring countercharges against the Assembly. They had given a man into custody, they had expelled a member for refusing to take an oath, they had arbitrarily discharged a prisoner, and had appointed their clerk out of their own body, contrary to law.

This called out an exceedingly vigorous rejoinder. Each of the acts alleged against the Assembly was <small>Rejoinder of the Assembly.[1]</small> shown to be in accordance either with positive law or with Parliamentary precedent. The charges of having interfered in the question of members' qualifications were insisted upon and brought out more fully. On one point Cornbury's argument is disposed of with no little controversial neatness. He pleaded that the absence of a registration office at Perth Amboy was no hardship, since wherever the Governor was there was the office. The office then might be in the West Indies or in England, and the case of the settlers would be far worse than they had imagined.

Next year another Assembly met. They chose as Speaker one Gordon known to be hostile to <small>The Assembly of 1708.[2]</small> the Governor. At the same time the tone of their communications with Cornbury was on both sides less acrimonious. Yet the Assembly practically took the same ground as their predecessors. Most of the grievances, they say, still remain unredressed. They continue, too, to find some fresh ones; the law officers of the Crown are in the habit of instituting frivolous prosecutions and intimidating the advocates who appear for the prisoners. Most of the

[1] Published in the New Jersey Archives, vol. iii. pp. 242–67. It is also in Smith's History.

[2] The Journal of the Assembly is in the New Jersey Archives, vol. iii. pp. 291–3. It was sent home by the Lieutenant-Governor and Council to the Lords of Trade, with a remonstrance against the proceedings recorded in it.

legal business of the colony is carried on at Perth Amboy and Burlington, to the inconvenience of those who live elsewhere.

Morris acting as the authorized agent of the Assembly wrote a letter to the Secretary of State giving a very clear and forcible, though no doubt an *ex parte*, description of the state of things in the colony.[1] If we may believe this, the opposite party had not weakened their hold on popular favour by their ill-judged financial policy. To conciliate Cornbury and secure his support they had voted him a revenue of two thousand a year for two years. They had, however, so arranged that the money should all be raised in one year, hoping, so Morris says, that the rate would fall mainly on the wealthy landowners. But they were wrong in their calculation. The wealthy men were able to bear the strain. It really fell heavily on the small Proprietors, many of whom it brought near bankruptcy.

<small>Account of matters by Morris.</small>

In its denunciations of Cornbury the letter went beyond the ordinary decencies of official correspondence. He puts a stop to all public business that he may please himself 'with that peculiar, but detestable maggot of dressing in woman's clothes.' He is a 'wretch who by the whole conduct of his life here has evinced that he has no regard to honour and virtue.' That such language should have been pardoned, that it should have been no bar to the success of Morris in public life, says much for his capacity, something, too, for the forbearance of those whom he addressed, while it is also an indication of a somewhat low standard in such matters.

Morris's letter was followed about three months later by a counter-declaration from the Council. It was alleged at a later day that signatures were obtained by deceit, that the document was drafted by those who

[1] This is the letter, which I mentioned at p. 458, n. 1.

were specially the adherents of Cornbury and never made the subject of open deliberation in Council; that some who would have withheld their signatures were told that it was a document duly drafted by a majority of the Council and thus induced to sign.² The document was in truth no more than a vague denunciation of Jennings, Morris, and their allies as disturbers of the public peace.

[Sidenote: Answer of the Council.¹]

The best practical proof that Cornbury's opponents had in the main justice on their side is to be found in the action of the Lords of Trade. They had before them a full account of the grievances of each party. Before an answer could come Cornbury's official career was at an end. But the instructions given to his successor Lovelace are practically a judgment on the main points at issue, and on almost every one the Board found against Cornbury. They specially recommend, in accordance with the opinion of the remonstrants, that all money levied under the militia Act should be paid to the Receiver-General, and employed not at the discretion of the Governor, but for purposes specified in the Act. The papers belonging to the Proprietors should not have been handed to Bass and carried out of the colony. Prisoners against whom the grand jury do not find a true bill are not liable for any fees. The Lords approve of the proposal to establish a probate office in each division of the colony. The patent for carriers is a violation of the Statute against Monopolies. No fees are lawful unless warranted by prescription or established by the legislature.

[Sidenote: Lovelace's instructions.³]

---

¹ N. J. Archives, vol. iii. p. 287.

² This is stated in an address from the Assembly to Hunter, Lovelace's successor. N. J. Archives, vol. iv. p. 24.

³ The instructions given to Lovelace were up to a certain point identical with those given to Cornbury. So much of them as was different is in the New Jersey Archives, vol. iii. pp. 316–23.

Jennings and Morris could not have asked for a more complete justification of their complaints, and the tribunal which gave it was one which was not likely to lean towards the side of disaffected colonists or to be eager to condemn a Governor who had special claims on the favour of the Crown.

The dispute between Cornbury and the New Jersey Assembly is of greater importance than on the face seems to attach to it. It marked the rise of a new spirit in colonial politics. There had before been resistance to the English Government on the part of Massachusetts, but the action of that colony was largely due to influences whose power was by this time spent. It was not the general spirit of constitutional resistance to arbitrary government, it was the determination of an exclusive oligarchy to withstand any encroachment on its rule. Between the New Englanders who fought Andros and Randolph and the New Englanders who fought Hutchinson and Bernard a great gulf is set. The old crust of Puritan exclusiveness had broken up. Mather and Danforth deemed themselves the champions of a chosen people. Otis and Adams deemed themselves the spokesmen of doctrines common to and needful for all mankind. But in the resistance of the New Jersey politicians to Cornbury we see a forecast on a small scale of the great struggle sixty years later. There is in Cornbury the same dull obstinacy, the same narrowness of view that we see in Gage and Dunmore.

Importance of the dispute between Cornbury and the Assembly.

Like George III. and too many of George's Ministers, Cornbury deals with the question as though it were a mere legal controversy. It is enough for him if he can answer his opponents on side issues. He wholly fails to see that the very fact of their being dissatisfied and disaffected is in itself of importance.

The parallel, too, holds good on the other side. In

Morris and Jennings, as in the Revolutionary leaders, there is the same mixture of public spirit and lawyer-like adroitness. They are patriots after a fashion, but there runs through their patriotism a leaven of ungenerousness and unscrupulousness. And it was this very mixture of qualities which made the weakness and the strength of the American Revolution. The national cause was perpetually being endangered by the selfishness and pettiness of its own supporters, their narrow views and incapacity for self-sacrifice. On the other hand it was strong in that it rested on motives obvious enough and wide enough to appeal to every man who had taxes to pay.

In two important respects the earlier movement differed from the later. In each, the motive force was given by a class with many of the prejudices and feelings of an oligarchy. But though the leaders of the American Revolution, with a few exceptions, were not men of wide sympathies, yet the movement soon extended itself. There may have been a lack of generous enthusiasm and of readiness for self-sacrifice in the spirit with which the rank and file followed their leaders, but unquestionably the voice of the whole commonalty was on the side of those leaders. In New Jersey it would rather seem as if the opposition to Cornbury was confined to the well-to-do and to those who had the leisure and the means to take some active part in political life.

There was yet another difference. When we compare the colonial policy of Queen Anne's advisers with that of George III. and his Ministers, the comparison is all to the advantage of the former. Among those who were personally responsible for the policy adopted towards New Jersey, Dartmouth and Stamford are the only ones whose names have gained any place in history. Neither of them was in anything more than the second rank of public life. Yet they and the less known men associated with them showed an anxiety to enter into the views of the colonists, and a readiness to redress grievances, which we look for in vain in Grenville and Townshend and their followers.

The career of Cornbury's successor, Lovelace, was cut short by death before his personal character could make itself felt either for good or evil. In New Jersey, as in New York, his praise and the laments over him probably reflect the conventional voice of official flattery. The chief feature of his short term of office was the persistency with which those who had supported Cornbury strove to discredit Morris, and exclude him from office. It says a good deal for the caution and sobriety of his later conduct that his enemies should have been forced to rake up the old charges of misconduct when Bass was Governor ten years before.

It is clear that at the time of Lovelace's death the anti-proprietary party were in the ascendancy in the Assembly. Thus the Council and the dominant party among the Representatives were at one, and they at once used their ascendancy to strike a series of blows at their opponents. It was, however, necessary to secure the compliance of the Lieutenant-Governor, Ingoldsby. This was done by bribing him at the expense of Lady Lovelace, the widow and inheritress of the late Governor. Lovelace's salary of eight hundred pounds had been voted before his death. Unfortunately the Act had prescribed that the warrant for the money must be signed by the Governor in Council, and did not provide for the possibility of a vacancy. There could be no doubt that the claim of Lady Lovelace to the money was an equitable

Inter-regnum between Lovelace and Hunter.[1]

---

[1] All the proceedings of this time are fully described in a despatch from Hunter to the Lords of Trade, May 7, 1711. N. Y. Docs. vol. v. p. 199.

one. But instead of rectifying their omission by providing that the warrant might be signed by the Deputy Governor, the Assembly treated the vote as null and void, and voted six hundred pounds out of the eight hundred to Ingoldsby, in addition to his existing salary. The Council themselves, if we may believe the evidence of Lovelace's successor, had their share in the spoil, since by a private agreement between them and Ingoldsby a portion of the money was set aside to buy each Councillor a silver cup.[1]

The majority of the Assembly then struck a blow intended permanently to weaken their opponents. A precedent was set which had its parallel in New England, which at a later day became an accepted principle in American politics and has had far-reaching results. It was enacted that no person should be returned to the Assembly who was not a resident within the colony. Among the wealthier planters there were a certain number who had their principal houses in New York, chiefly, it is said, to give their children better schooling than New Jersey could offer. Among these were Morris and one of his chief allies, John Johnstone. The mere possession of property without local knowledge or local interest may be a bad title to political power. But that this was not the case with Morris is sufficiently proved out of the mouths of his enemies. He could not be at once an absentee and a dangerous intriguer.

Another Act limited the right of impounding cattle to cases where they had been actually found breaking fences. In the same spirit an earlier Act for restraining stray swine was now repealed. Both these Acts, it is said, were aimed at the larger and wealthier landholders. Most of the enclosed and well-cultivated land was in

---

[1] Hunter as above. N. J. Archives, vol. iv. p. 66.

their hands, and they were the chief sufferers by the incursions of stray animals.[1]

Another Act shows the traces of what we have not seen before, local jealousy between the Eastern and Western divisions of the province. The instructions given by the Queen to Lovelace provided that the Assembly should sit alternately at Perth Amboy and Burlington. The dominant party, it is clear, belonged mainly to the Western province, and they endeavoured in their own interest and that of the electors who supported them to fix the Assembly permanently at Burlington.[2]

The appointment of Lovelace's successor, Hunter, Hunter appointed Governor. at once changed the balance of parties. Appointed by the great Whig Ministry, Hunter almost inevitably approached his task in something of the spirit of a partisan. There was not indeed any exact coincidence between the lines which divided parties at home and those which divided them in the colony. But though there was not identity there was likeness. In the colony we have on the one side an oligarchy of large landholders and wealthy merchants, clinging firmly to certain forms of constitutional government; on the other side we have the official party, resting hitherto on the arbitrary authority of the Governor and the Council, at the same time claiming as against their opponents to be the friends of the people. The likeness to English Tories and Whigs was strengthened by the fact that the party of Hunter's allies, Morris and Johnstone, was also the party of the Quakers and Presbyterians.

Hunter from the outset made no attempt to ignore this state of things, nor to carry on the administration Hunter's attitude towards parties in the colony. of the colony above or independent of parties. In New Jersey, as in New York, he at once reversed Cornbury's policy and threw in his lot with the party of Morris. He formed for himself

[1] N. J. Archives, vol. iv. p. 69.   [2] *Ib.* p. 67.

what his opponents called a Cabinet Council [1]—that is, a small knot of favoured advisers within the Council itself, of whom Morris was one. His policy was in all likelihood the best that could have been adopted in the interests of the colony. When parties have once been thoroughly established in a community it is a hopeless attempt to govern on any but a party system. There may be an acknowledged truce, a temporary suspension of party hostilities in the face of some special danger. But the attempt to form an executive which shall be independent of party ties, while party feeling exists, is almost certain to be a failure. It was probably well for New Jersey that Hunter was no idealist, but a party politician, not unscrupulous, but fully capable of entering into party politics, and using their recognised and legitimate arts. In all likelihood his Whiggery predisposed him in the first instance towards the party of Morris. Yet we cannot doubt that any clear-sighted and public-spirited man starting without bias would have been drawn that way. Morris may not have been a very high-principled man—a vein of arrogance and self-seeking runs through his whole career; but he was at least a capable man, and if he was a self-seeker, it was at the bidding of ambition, not of avarice. He and his associates are accused of acting in the interests of a class, but no charge of personal corruption is brought against them. On the other side it is clear that Bass was a weak man, and Sonmans a vicious one. The charge of having supported Ingoldsby from corrupt motives was never even contradicted, and men who upheld Cornbury can have had no sense of official decorum and personal dignity.

Hunter at once succeeded in weakening his op-

---

[1] This expression is used in a letter sent to Dockwra in England from the colony in July 1711. The writer of the letter is unknown. N. J. Archives, vol. iv. p. 119

ponents in the Council by detaching Quarry from their party.[1] He had, as we have seen, been sent out by the Lords of Trade to observe and report on the state of things in the American colonies, and his word was therefore sure to carry weight with the English Government.

Unfortunately for the colony, parties were, as we have seen, in that evenly balanced condition when each Sandford is tempted to use every moment of superiority expelled to crush and cripple the other, when each is from the Assembly. compelled in self-defence to think more of strengthening and perpetuating its power than of using it. In the Assembly returned in 1711, the year after Hunter's arrival, the Whigs, as we may call them, had recovered their ascendancy.[2] Among the members was one Sandford. He was also a member of the Council, and as such had signed the address sent to the Queen in 1707, in which Cornbury and his Council made an attack upon the Assembly. The Proprietors, or at least that majority of them who were favourable to Morris, had petitioned the Queen to remove Sandford together with certain others of the same way of thinking from the Council.[3] This was not complied with, and when on Hunter's appointment a fresh list of Councillors was drawn up, Sandford's name appeared in it. But the first despatch sent home by Hunter pressed for the removal of the other Councillors to whom objection had been made. A seat on the Council and one in the Assembly plainly could not be held by the same man. Sandford either preferring the latter, or more probably anticipating expulsion, stood for the Assembly and was elected. The house thereupon passed a general resolution that

[1] See Quarry's letter to John Pulteney, one of the Lords of Trade. N. J. Archives, vol. iv. p. 6.

[2] This is plain from the address of the Assembly to Hunter, N. J. Archives, vol. iv. p. 24, and from the letter to Dockwra, quoted above.

[3] N. J. Archives, vol. iii. p. 497. The other Councillors whose removal was asked for were—Cox, Mompesson, Townly, Sonmans and Pinhorn.

no person who had signed the address was fit to be a member. At the same time they gave Sandford the opportunity of apologizing. This he refused to do and accordingly was expelled. His constituency re-elected him, but the Assembly stood firm and he was excluded.[1] The drama of the Middlesex election, at least in its earlier scenes, was anticipated in the sphere of colonial politics.

The dominant party in the Assembly followed up this by an attack on their opponents contained in an address to Hunter. Severe as it was, it offered a complete contrast to the document to which it was opposed alike in its definiteness and in the method with which the charges were arranged. We are again reminded of the documents in which the aggrieved colonists pleaded their case fifty years later, by the persistency with which Morris and his associates disclaim any disaffection towards the mother country, and discriminate between Cornbury and the Sovereign whom he unworthily represents.

<small>Address by Morris and his party to Hunter.[2]</small>

The conflict between the Assembly and the Council had the effect of paralysing legislation. Of the Acts sent up by the House of Representatives to the Council, every one was either rejected, or sent back so loaded with amendments as to be unacceptable to the lower House.[3] Two, indeed, of the Acts dealt with matters in which the Representatives must have known beforehand that they were at variance with the Council. Though in the case of elected Representatives a declaration was allowed instead of an oath, in legal proceedings an oath was required. This excluded Quakers from serving on juries, and in many

<small>The Council veto the Acts of the Assembly.</small>

---

[1] Letter to Dockwra, as above.
[2] The address is in the Archives, vol. iv. pp. 24-48.
[3] For this dispute see Hunter's despatch of May 7, 1711. N. Y. Docs. vol. v. pp. 199-212.

cases from obtaining redress. The Assembly now sought to remedy this by an Act substituting a declaration in all cases. Another measure obnoxious to the Council was a proposal to extend the English law of bankruptcy to the colony. This, it was urged, would invalidate such titles to land as rested on purchase from Fenwick and Bylling, since both had become bankrupts. It is absurd to suppose that there could have been any difficulty in securing all existing titles by a special enactment. With far better reason, the advocates of the measure pointed out that the absence of a bankruptcy law would make the colony a refuge for disreputable debtors.

In opposing this Act the Council were combating not only the Representatives, but also the Lords of Trade. Hunter's instruction had specially referred to such a law as desirable. He vainly pointed out to the Council that by their action they were opposing the judgment alike of the Queen's advisers and the Representatives of the people, and he plainly hinted that the personal interests of Councillors were the real cause of rejection and would be recognised as such.

If the Council had singled out these Acts for opposition, they might have been looked on as confining themselves to a policy constitutionally legitimate, though certainly barren and probably unwise. But their opposition to every Act sent up to them by the Representatives was a plain avowal of their intention to hinder public business if they were denied their own way.

There, however, their success ended. From that time onward the persistent determination of Hunter and the Assembly prevailed. There is nothing in the records of the colony to show precisely the causes to which the change was due. The Council seems to have been weakened by the death of one or two members, and Hunter was quite astute

Triumph of the Whig party.

enough as a political tactician to find means for disuniting and crippling his assailants. The overthrow of the Whig Ministry did indeed give hopes to Hunter's opponents of his overthrow, and of a reversal of policy in England. The parallel between the politics of the mother country and those of the colony became more marked indeed as time goes on. Hunter reports the formation of a Jacobite party under a nonjuring clergyman, Talbot.[1] He denounces an opponent, Mr. Vesey, as 'a sour Jacobite,' and likens him to a Sacheverell.[2] And we find one of the worst features of English politics reproducing itself in the apprehensions of outrage. Just as Swift believes that the Mohocks were political assassins, bent on waylaying him and other Tory leaders, just as he detects a Whig plot to blow up Harley with an infernal machine,[3] so Willocks, a strenuous partisan of Hunter, mentions vague rumours of a purpose to burn down the Quaker places of worship and dwelling-houses at the time of an election.[4]

To the great body of the American colonies the accession of the House of Hanover was a matter of little direct importance. New Jersey was an exception. There beyond a doubt it finally turned the scale in favour of Hunter and Morris and their allies, and overthrew the last hopes of their opponents. Not indeed that the strife altogether ceased; the Tories made a last desperate attempt to deprive the Quakers of their civil rights by a forced and palpably unfair interpretation of an Act of the English Parliament. That Act, passed in 1713, provided that a declaration should be accepted

---

[1] N. J. Archives, vol. iv. p. 209. Talbot and his real or supposed Jacobitism will come before us again.
[2] *Ib.* vol. iv. p. 219.
[3] See the forty-third and forty-fifth letters in the journal to Stella.
[4] N. J. Archives, vol. iv. p. 302.

from a Quaker for all civil purposes instead of an oath.[1] This, however, was not to extend to the colonies, and a clause was specially added to the effect that no Quaker should by virtue of this Act be qualified to hold office there. The opponents of the Quakers contended that this clause was intended as a positive disqualification, that under it the Quakers in the colonies were not merely to enjoy no fresh rights, but were to forfeit those which they already enjoyed. In other words, the very Act which was designed to improve the condition of the Quakers was to put a large and important body of them in a worse position than before. This contention, however, was overruled by the Lords of Trade.[2]

So, too, Hunter was still harassed by petty complaints against his administrative proceedings. One may serve as a specimen. He has invaded the freeholds of private men by cutting down their timber, and he has burnt and destroyed titles to land. Hunter gives a full account of what is meant by each charge, and his explanation was allowed to go unchallenged.[3] He had to provide a certain number of flat-bottomed boats for the expedition of 1711 against Canada. For these some short, crooked timbers were required. Hunter accordingly, on his own responsibility, ordered them to be cut on some waste land, 'where,' as he says, 'they might have remained uncut till the end of the world,' giving notice at the same time that he would indemnify anyone whose property was injured. He explains that he had exposed himself to the other charge by protecting an unfortunate native chief against a trader who, in defiance of the law, had made him drunk and swindled him out of his land.

[1] I shall deal with this Act more fully in connexion with Pennsylvania. [2] N. J. Archives, vol. iv. pp. 342-5.

[3] Hunter's answer to these charges is given in a letter to Ambrose Philips, agent in England for New York, July 27, 1717. N. J. Archives, vol. iv. pp. 312-24.

These, however, were but the ineffectual railings of a beaten faction. The report which Hunter sent home in 1714 shows that the majority in the Assembly was able to apply itself to the work of practical legislation, and that changes either in the composition of the Council or in the temper of its members made it no longer a hindrance. Acts were passed simplifying legal procedure, and making it easier to establish a title to land. In one important respect the policy declared by the English Crown in Hunter's instructions was reversed: a duty was laid on imported negroes with a view to encourage the influx of white servants.

To have brought to a successful issue the affairs of an obscure colony on the Atlantic sea-board is to the great Whig Ministry of Queen Anne's reign but a trifle of added praise. Yet their work there was thoroughly useful and honourable, and wholly worthy of their traditions. It may well be that Hunter's conduct as a Governor was not faultless, that there were elements of truth in the attacks upon him, that he was guilty in special instances of administrative errors, and even of administrative injustice. But if we look at his career as a whole we may truly say that he, almost alone among colonial Governors of his age, had, though beset by many adverse influences, set on foot a system which left the Crown in full possession of every right that it could justly claim, and at the same time satisfied every reasonable aspiration towards self-government.

CHAPTER IX.

THE FOUNDATION OF PENNSYLVANIA.[1]

Absence of biographical interest in American history.
IN studying the history of the American colonies we are at once struck with a certain lack of biographical interest, with the absence of conspicuous figures who have towered above their fellow-men, and stamped their own personal influence on the community. New England in its early days is in some measure an exception to this. There, indeed, Calvinism, which in theory annihilated the will of the individual, but in practice gave it intenser force by identifying it with the Divine purpose, Puritan discipline, which crushed weak natures but braced and stimulated strong ones, had produced men of some real greatness such as Bradford and Winthrop, men of at least marked

[1] Our chief authorities for the early history of Pennsylvania are:
1. The Colonial State Papers.
2. The Pennsylvania Archives, Philadelphia, 1852–6.
3. Colonial Records, Philadelphia, 1852.
4. Proud's *History of Pennsylvania*, Philadelphia, 1797.
Proud has preserved several original documents of value, not accessible elsewhere. He is a sound, laborious writer, one of the best of the early colonial historians.
Shepherd's *History of Proprietary Government in Pennsylvania* (1891) is an exceedingly valuable work, based on unpublished documents.
There are several lives of Penn, but none of them throw much fresh light on the history of the colony. Decidedly the best in that respect is Mr. Fisher's *The True William Penn*, Philadelphia, 1900. Mr. Fisher has written two other books on Pennsylvania: *The Making of Pennsylvania*, 1896, and *Pennsylvania Colony and Commonwealth*, 1897. The former is the best account that I know of the various waves of emigration which together made up Pennsylvania. In both books Mr. Fisher is at times somewhat dogmatic in tone.

character such as Endicott and Dudley. Yet even there we feel that the biographical interest which attaches to particular men is swallowed up in the collective interest which attaches to the corporate growth of the whole community. And if we except that short era when Puritanism informed and dominated New England, almost to the exclusion of every other motive, there is scarcely an exception to this tendency. Everywhere among the colonies the life of the community is far more interesting than the life of any man in it. There is no disparagement in this. It is rather praise to say that a community is better and stronger than its best and strongest men. For that means that a community has in its institutions, its faith, and its corporate morality, guarantees for its well-being of which it cannot be robbed by chance. But it is a state of things likely to mislead historians, above all to mislead contemporary and partial chroniclers. The absence of real greatness tempts them to manufacture an image of greatness out of materials in which it has no existence. They seize greedily on a figure endowed with attributes faintly resembling heroism, and he becomes under their hands a hero.

This has been in some measure the case with the founder of Pennsylvania. Only blinded partisanship can withhold from Penn the praise of being a good man. We may even go further and say that he had in him elements of real greatness. Benevolence, disinterestedness, the power of self-sacrifice, a rare capacity for understanding and loving things spiritual and for dealing effectively with things temporal—these qualities, joined to the conspicuous success of the colony to which he gave his name, and which was in some measure the creation of his judgement, all amply explain the reputation which attaches to the name of William Penn. Yet we can hardly say

Character of Penn.

that as a colonial statesman Penn was great, or that his work in America brought out the best qualities of his mind or character. When we analyse that work with care, much of the traditional glory that attaches to it fades away.

It is needless to go again over the oft-told tale of Penn's early days. When we read of one who is alternately a fanatical enthusiast denouncing the conventional standard of social life, and crying aloud for a far more rigid observance of religious and moral precepts, or a fashionable fine gentleman, mixing freely with the lax and corrupt society into which he was born, one of two explanations at once suggests itself. Either he is seeking to serve God and Mammon, craftily building up a reputation in pious circles, without forfeiting worldly pleasures or worldly advantages; or it may be said that he is an unstable enthusiast, drawn hither or thither as emotions leading him towards God or emotions leading him towards pleasure gained the upper hand. Either explanation is at variance with the whole tenour of Penn's life. If a man of his astute perception, gifted with rare fascination of manner and keen insight into character, had played a double game he would have played it to better purpose. Nowhere do his writings breathe anything of the spirit of passion; his morality was far-sighted and self-restrained. To charge a man with inconsistency is often but a convenient way of confessing the limitations of our own view, our inability to understand how features of character usually separated may in exceptional cases be conjoined. The more one studies Penn's writings the more one sees the singular catholicity of his mind, his power of recognising what was good in all men, his real indifference to all external marks whether of creed or station. Thus it was that Penn's character and his formal creed were thoroughly at one, that he out-

Quakered those who were recognised as the founders of his sect. Fox admitted formally and in theory that the divine spirit dwelt within every man. In practice he would have found it hard to recognise its presence in the squire who committed Quakers to gaol or the priest who served in a steeplehouse. In Penn the formal principles of his creed worked in harmony with a kindly and sympathetic temper. He was by nature the friend of all men, be their condition what it might, and his innate simplicity and independence saved him alike from servility in dealing with the rich or patronage towards the poor.

Penn may, indeed, justly claim that praise which is often claimed with no truth for earlier Nonconformists, of being in the true sense of the word tolerant. He is the follower of Jeremy Taylor, the forerunner of John Mill. As fully as either does he recognise that a dogmatic creed has no value in it unless it be the root of active morality; that human tests can measure only the morality, and that a mere formal compliance with any particular creed, such as can be exacted by tests, is valueless. 'That man cannot be said to have any religion that takes it by another man's choice, not his own.'[1] 'The way of force makes instead of an honest dissenter but a hypocritical conformist, than whom nothing is more detestable to God and man.'[2]

It is clear that his attitude was made easy to him by the fact that he himself was indifferent to dogma, that religion was for him not a philosophy but a moral code. He protests against the attempt to overlay religious teaching with metaphysical propositions; it is quite clear that he could not in the least enter into the feelings of those with whom the difference between

---

[1] The Great Case of Liberty of Conscience. Penn's Works (ed. 1726), vol. i. p. 451.
[2] Ib. p. 457.

Athanasius and Arius, between Arminian and Calvinist is vital. Penn indeed fully anticipates the eighteenth century doctrine, 'He can't be wrong whose life is in the right.' It is hardly needful to point out how that view overlooks the fact that dogma may be itself an influence towards the formation of character. And it also overlooks this, that the spiritual life of the individual and of the society do not stand on precisely the same footing. Dogmatic articles of faith, embodying the convictions of some and outraging those of none, may be valuable as a basis for outward agreement.

As it was with Penn in spiritual so was it in secular matters. There, too, he would have fully admitted, 'whate'er is best administered is best.' The religious and the political side of his teaching had each their dangers, dangers specially felt in the position which Penn occupied. Through all the errors, and even the atrocities, of which New England dogmatists were guilty, there ran a conviction that a new society is beset by peculiar perils, and that external unity capable of being enforced by positive law is the only safeguard. And in civil matters we shall constantly see how the relations between Penn and his colonists were impaired by his indifference to specified rules and fixed terms of agreement. He could not understand that a general reliance on the goodness of his intentions was not a sufficient guarantee for his colonists. It is not enough that a system of government is well administered. It must contain in itself some security for the continuance of good administration, over and above the good will of the individual ruler. Penn's inability to see that fully explains his toleration of James II., one may even say his sympathy with him. James, like Penn, distinctly recognised that a ruler had moral obligations which he must fulfil though his view of those obligations was far cruder and meaner. Both men failed to see that the subject reasonably demanded something more certain and and more lasting than the good will of the individual ruler.

The conditions of the time were such as might naturally encourage Penn to believe in the possibility of a colony where all creeds might find a common home. The system of rigidity and the system of laxity had each been tried, and the victory might well seem to be on the side of the latter. Massachusetts was in troubled water. New Haven, the very type of the sectarian colony, was blotted out, absorbed in her more liberal neighbour Connecticut. In Maryland, Independents and Quakers seemed to be entering into the inheritance prepared by a Roman Catholic founder. The conquest of New Netherlands transferred to English dominion a colony in which, despite the efforts of some among its rulers, the principle of religious equality had firmly established itself. Nor did the effect of the conquest end there. It placed at the disposal of the English nation a large territory on which to try the experiment of colonization, religious in character, yet non-sectarian. The time assuredly had not come—one may doubt whether it will come till human nature is widely changed—when that experiment could be made successfully. Penn was endeavouring to found a colony which should rest on Quakerism as its main foundation, yet which should not be sectarian. His position was not unlike that of Roger Williams. And if all Baptists had been as tolerant as Williams, all Quakers as undogmatic as Penn, the experiment might well have succeeded. As it was, both in Pennsylvania and New Jersey, there was enough nominal toleration to bring sects together, hardly enough of the real spirit of toleration to enable them to live together peaceably. Yet when we look back on Massachusetts we feel that the bickerings of Quakers in

Penn's schemes of colonization.

New Jersey and Pennsylvania were in many ways better than the uncontrolled domination of Puritanism.

It was in all likelihood the desire to try the experiment of State-building with a freer hand than he could have as one of the part Proprietors of New Jersey that urged Penn to sue for an independent grant. He was able to ask it as something more than a favour. Sixteen thousand pounds was due from the Crown to his father's estate. The conquest of New Netherlands had put the Crown in a position to pay the debt. The annihilation of the Dutch title was a consequence of that conquest. Thus Charles II. was in a position to claim sovereignty over the whole territory between Connecticut and Maryland. The grant to the Duke of York absorbed only a portion of that; it left the southwest bank of the Delaware and all the upper valley of the Susquehanna, and the soil watered by its tributaries. This accordingly was handed over to Penn.[1]

The formal boundaries of the new province were as follows : The Delaware was to be the eastern boundary and the north-east corner was to be the point where that river intersects the forty-third degree of latitude; a northern frontier of five degrees of longitude extended to the edge of Lake Erie, thence the line ran due south through the wilderness. The southern boundary was the point where complication arose, and the question was one of moment not only to Penn and his settlers, but to his neighbours. It determined, what was yet an open question, the boundary of the Duke of York's province, and it altered that of Maryland. As we have seen, the grant to the Duke of York gave him no territory west of the Delaware. That portion of the soil conquered from New Netherlands was in a strangely undefined condition. It was claimed

Limits of Penn's grant.

---

[1] The charter, wherein the grant is set forth, is given in full by Proud, vol. i. pp. 171–87.

by Maryland. *De jure* it either belonged to that colony or was a waif, placed by right of conquest in direct dependence on the Crown. *De facto*, as we have seen, it was an outlying dependency, under the Governor of New York, but separate from that colony. No attempt had been made to define the limits of this jurisdiction. But Penn's charter now fixed them, and in doing so fixed the boundary of Maryland. But this was done in such ambiguous language as to leave a loophole for future dispute. The new province was to be bounded ' on the south by a circle drawn at twelve miles' distance from Newcastle northward and westward into the beginning of the fortieth degree of northern latitude; and then by a straight line westward.' There was, however, one objection to this boundary: a radius of twelve miles from Newcastle would not at any point reach the fortieth degree of latitude. Accordingly Penn claimed, and finally, though not without years of dispute, succeeded in establishing, the right to draw his southern boundary from a point twelve miles due west of Newcastle. This line fell south of that originally assigned to Maryland as its northern frontier, and thus transferred, at least in theory, from Lord Baltimore to Penn a belt of land nearly three hundred miles long and fifteen miles wide. It is to be noticed, too, that while this document assumed the existence of a territory attached to Newcastle, there had never been any attempt to define the limits of that territory. Moreover the apportionment of the west bank of the Delaware between Penn and the Duke of York was purely arbitrary. Of the land occupied by the Swedes, a portion was retained for the Duke, a part handed over to Penn. The latter included Upland, a small rural township, of which the nucleus was Swedish, but which had been strengthened by an influx of English settlers. Thus Penn's grant, like that to Berkeley and Carteret, but even more distinctly, was a grant not of vacant territory, but of jurisdiction over an existing settlement.

There were certain important differences between this and any earlier proprietary grant. It resembled the grants to Lord Baltimore and to the Duke of York in vesting the soil of the colony in the Proprietor, and requiring from him a nominal acknowledgement and the reservation of a quit-rent. But in two important points it differed. Those who drafted the earlier documents had been content with a general provision of allegiance to the Crown and conformity to the laws of England. This charter prescribed certain definite forms of control. All laws enacted within the colony were to be sent home for approval. The King might then within six months veto them. But by a singularly ill-judged arrangement five years might elapse between the passing of a law and the transmission of it. For that time the colonists might be living under conditions which would only be temporary. The patent also provided that while Penn might constitute ports, and with the consent of the inhabitants levy customs, this was not to hinder the enforcement of the general revenue laws of the kingdom, nor the right of the revenue officers to visit such ports. As a further security a novel provision was introduced. The Proprietor must always have an agent living in or near London. His place of abode must always be notified to the Privy Council. If the Proprietors should at any time be held to have violated the Navigation laws, the agent was to be summoned and was to give an explanation. If this were not satisfactory, the Proprietor was to make good any damage sustained by the Crown. If he failed to do this, his grant was to be forfeited pending payment.

<small>Provisions of the charter.</small>

Another special feature of the charter was that it made some attempt to prescribe the relations which should exist between the Proprietors and the settlers. The Proprietor was empowered to pass laws 'for raising money for public uses, or for any other end appertaining either unto the public state and peace, or safety of' the colony, with the approval and assent of the freemen or their deputies. If this did not make it absolutely clear that such assent was necessary, that was further declared by a clause allowing the Proprietor in case of emergency to pass ordinances which, however, should not affect life or property.

A clause was also inserted by which the Crown renounced for itself all right of taxation. But the very same clause expressly declared that Parliament had that right. No tax might be levied but with the consent of the Proprietors, or Governor or Assembly, or by Act of Parliament in England. The question of the right of Parliament to tax a colony was assuredly not a question to be settled by mere precedent or by the will of Charles II. and his counsellors. One can only say that there was nothing in the Pennsylvania charter which protected the colonists against the exercise of such a right. The Proprietor was, as usual in such cases, the supreme fountain of justice. He had the right to establish courts, and to appoint judges and magistrates. Only he might not pardon treason or murder, but grant a respite till the pleasure of the Crown should be known. One provision, and one only, was made on behalf of religion. Twenty of the inhabitants might by a signed requisition to the Bishop of London have a licensed preacher allotted to them. It is not unlikely that the insertion of this clause was due to Penn's personal friendship with Compton. It was also by Compton's advice that Penn settled the claims of the natives to the land by purchase from them.[1] The proceeding, however, was too much in consonance

[1] Penn to Lords of Trade, Col. Papers, August 6, 1683.

with Penn's own temper and principles to have needed the intervention of any adviser.

As we have seen, the grant included territory already inhabited. Accordingly the King, following the course adopted in the case of the second grant to Berkeley and Carteret, issued a declaration commanding all persons within the limits of the patent to obey the Proprietor.

According to Penn's own story his modesty would *Penn's intentions as a colonizer.* have avoided associating his name with that of the new colony. The King, however, insisted, out of respect to the memory of the Admiral, and Penn yielded.

It is plain that Penn had no intention of making his colony specially a refuge for those of his own religion. Quakers no doubt would be welcome. But the colony was to fulfil Penn's ideal, not by its creed, but by its conformity with his moral standard, by applying the principles of primitive Christianity to its dealings whether with civilized men or savages, by the spectacle of a harmony unbroken by any divisions resting upon dogma.

This was clearly shown by the Address in which Penn invited settlers, and in the first document in which he set forth the principles on which he would deal with his colony. He issued a general account of the character of the territory, and published appended to it a copy of his patent.[1] Land might be had on three conditions. Emigrants might acquire the fee-simple of their land, subject to a quit-rent, by payment of two pounds for a hundred acres, the renewed quit-rent being one shilling for every such parcel. Or those who were content to come as annual tenants might do so at a payment of a shilling an acre. As in most

[1] Proud gives the substance of these conditions. As he does not publish the text, the probability is that he could not discover it.

colonies a portion of land (fifty acres) was to be allotted to every intended servant when his time was out.

We must take in conjunction with this another document which appeared immediately afterwards, and which one would suppose might have better been incorporated with it. By these so-called conditions or concessions, the method of land tenure was more fully prescribed. There was no restraint on the amount of land which might be held by a single Proprietor. But it was provided that no one might have a continuous estate of more than a thousand acres unless he parcelled it into farms of that extent, each occupied by a family. Any landholder who failed to occupy his ground within three years after obtaining his grant might be dispossessed with compensation. Regard was shown to two industries which might become important by a clause providing that no more than four-fifths of any ground was to be cleared; the rest was to be left woodland, so that there might be no lack of oaks for shipping or mulberries for feeding silkworms. Yet it is not easy to see how this provision was to be turned to account without some rather elaborate system of public forestry.

The concessions.[1]

Special and just honour has always been paid to Penn for his scrupulous regard for the rights of the natives, and for the success with which he enforced such regard on his followers, and succeeded in embodying it as a part of their traditional policy. All goods sold to them were to be tested by public assayers. Every provision of the penal law was to apply as fully to the protection of the Indian as of the white man, and all differences were to be tried by a mixed jury. In the last provision there may have been little practical wisdom, but it at least

Policy towards the natives.

[1] These are printed by Proud in an appendix to his second volume.

strongly shows how the equality of all men was with Penn no mere doctrinal tenet of the schools.

Penn's charter was signed in March 1681, and by October a party of emigrants were ready to sail.[1] The colonists were not venturing to an unknown land. The climate, soil, and the general conditions of life-industry closely resembled those already in existence in New Jersey. The emigrants found the natives friendly, the woods teeming with game and the streams with fish. The leader of the expedition, William Markham, could write home to his wife, ' If a country life be liked by any it might be here.'[2]

The first emigration.

The patent had done no more than suggest the skeleton of a constitution. There was already extant in the colony a local government sufficient for the wants of a small and simple community. As we have seen, a court sat at Upland, acknowledging the jurisdiction of the Governor of New York. That court was continued as the judicial tribunal. A council of nine of the chief settlers, with Markham as Deputy-Governor at the head, served as the executive.[3]

Constitutional arrangements.

Meanwhile Penn was fashioning a system of government suited to the wants of a larger and more scattered community. His conduct in this showed that he belonged to a rare class, that he was a philanthropist who was willing to help men according to their wishes, not according to his own. He did not start with a constitution and then invite settlers. He got together the material for his colony, and then framed a constitution in conjunction with those who were to live under it. Beside consulting those

Penn's frame of government.

[1] Proud, vol. i. p. 193.
[2] *Pennsylvania Magazine of History,* vol. vi.
[3] Hazard's *Annals of Pennsylvania,* pp. 37, 51.
[4] The draft of this instrument is published by Proud in an appendix, vol. ii. pp. 5-20.

who had formed his colony, Penn took the advice of the chief legal authority, Sir William Jones, the Attorney-General. We read, too, with some surprise, that he consulted one who was in private life a dissolute courtier, in public at best an adroit diplomatist, Henry Sidney.[1]

Penn's own view about constitutional and political forms made it all the easier for him to accept and adopt suggestions. That view is very clearly set forth in some remarks which Penn prefixed to the draft of the new constitution. 'There is,' he says, 'hardly one frame of government in the world so ill-designed by its first founders, that in good hands would not do well enough, and history tells us the best in ill ones can do nothing that is great and good.' 'Let men be good and the government cannot be bad; if it be ill they will cure it.' He wholly overlooks the fact that neither men nor governments are divided by a hard-and-fast line into good and bad; he assumes that the individual and the state are each in a fixed condition, forgetting that in each at its best there are evil tendencies which act and react on one another.

Penn's practical sagacity did not wholly save him from the error which seemed inevitably to beset colonial Proprietors in the task of grafting a constitution. He made his government unnecessarily complex. The government was to be nominally after the regular pattern, consisting of three members: the Governor, the Council, and the House of Representatives. But in Pennsylvania, alone among all the colonies outside New England, both houses were to be chosen by the whole commonalty. The Council was to consist of seventy-

---

[1] Penn's adviser may have been Henry's brother Algernon. The evidence on the point does not seem to me conclusive. It is shortly discussed, and the original authorities referred to, in the *Memorial History*, vol. iii. p. 506.

two, twenty-four chosen each year. The lower chamber was, in the first instance, to consist of the whole body of freemen. The meaning of this, plainly, was that the first acceptance and ratification of the constitution should be the direct act of the whole body of freemen. So far the Council was really an upper chamber with the essential qualification of such a body in that it differed essentially in its structure from the lower chamber. But after the first year the lower chamber was no longer to be a primary body, but to consist of two hundred elected deputies. This number might be increased till it reached five hundred. Several obvious objections to this constitution at once suggest themselves. It is easy to see what hopelessly unwieldy bodies would be two chambers of seventy-two and five hundred, or even two hundred, respectively. It would be wholly impossible for the colony for many a day to supply that number of men capable of public service and willing to undertake it. The Council, too, was wholly unfitted by its size for the discharge of executive functions. An almost inevitable result would be the informal creation of a small body within the Council, possessing no recognized constitution nor power, but monopolizing those portions of public business which require despatch, secrecy, or frequent communication. A closer examination of Penn's work to some extent removes these difficulties, but in doing so it discloses others, not less serious.

The size of the lower house was not as material as it seems, for it is plain that Penn did not design his Assembly to be a legislative body. That is clearly implied in the clause which provides for the holding of Assemblies 'to the end that all laws prepared by the Governor and Provincial Council aforesaid may yet have the more full concurrence of the freemen of the province.' The Council elected by the freemen was to legislate, the larger representative body was only to accept and ratify. Thus we must not judge the constitution of Pennsylvania by the analogy of other colonies. We are tempted to look at it as though it consisted of a council answering to the ordinary council in its functions, but chosen by the people, and a lower house also of representatives. It would be more true to say that there was to be no council in the sense in which one existed elsewhere. The so-called Council answered to the ordinary legislative Assembly. Below that there was to be a body at first primary, afterwards representative, which had nothing analogous to it elsewhere, and which was to exist merely for the purpose of reaffirming the approval of the whole body of settlers of that which had been enacted by their representatives. It is difficult to see what useful function this last body was really to serve, or what inducement the settlers would have to make it a working reality. It is always difficult in a new country where no class enjoys leisure, and where a political career has no rewards to offer, to induce men to leave their business and attend to public affairs. But it would be indeed hopeless to expect such attendance in the members of a body so entirely subordinate in its rights and duties.

And if Penn's constitution erred there in excess, it also erred elsewhere in defect. The so-called Council might be well fitted for a legislative body, but it was far too large for executive purposes. An attempt was made to get over this by breaking it up into four committees. The various functions assigned to these bodies are more easily enumerated than analysed or translated. The first was to be 'a committee of plantations to situate and settle cities, ports, market-towns and highways, and to hear and decide all suits and controversies relating to plantations.' The second was to be 'a committee of justice and safety to secure the peace of the province and punish the maladministration of those who subvert justice, to the prejudice of the public or private interest.' The third was to be 'a committee of trade and treasury who shall regulate all trade and commerce according to law, encourage manufacture and country growth, and defray the public charge of the province.' The fourth was to be 'a committee of manners and education and arts, that all wicked and scandalous living may be prevented, and that youth may be successively trained up in virtue and useful knowledge and arts.' It is obvious on the face of it that the functions of the first committee would perpetually clash with those of the second and third, that in fact there was no real distinction between their provinces.

It is to be noticed, too, that although the Council was chosen by the whole body of settlers, yet it was not so chosen as to make it a certain and effective representative of popular wishes. One-third of the members were to be chosen each year. In other words, that portion of the legislative body which was most in touch with popular opinion was to be within the legislature itself the least influential. For it is obvious that when a new element, and that a minority, is added to an existing body it is powerless against the predominant feeling of those already in office. Its members are hindered by feeling themselves unfamiliar with the forms and traditions of business; they soon become assimilated to the body into which they have been elected. Thus the system of partial election is specially ill fitted for enabling the electors to make their wishes known and felt, for giving them direct and efficient control over the legislature. The fact, too, that at a time when public feeling ran high, when there might be a demand for important legislative changes, one-third of the community had the right of election which was denied to the rest, could not fail to call out ill-feeling. The right which was withheld from the electors was at the same time brought near them. Moreover a clause was inserted providing that no outgoing member should be eligible for re-election for seven years. This would in itself go far to cripple the efficiency of the Council, to prevent continuity of principle and tradition, or that formation of organized parties under acknowledged leaders which is essential to the efficiency of a representative body. It might, too, seriously limit the electors in their choice of representatives, and by weakening the Council it would strengthen the hands of the Governor in any attempt to encroach on their functions. Penn's system appeared to vest all government in the commonalty. In reality popular representation would have been far better secured, with a nominated Council and a House of Representatives, the latter all elected together at stated intervals with a short tenure of office.

There was, too, a lack of practical sense in the declaration that this fundamental frame of government could only be altered by the consent of the Proprietor and six-sevenths of the Assembly. Such limitations of power may be of use in mere matters of formal procedure. It may be well, for example, to limit the power of suddenly reversing a motion or bringing one forward without notice; it may be well to prohibit absolutely the revival of a proposal within a certain time of its rejection. Such restraints are in reality declarations of a very emphatic opinion that a particular course is undesirable; the restraints which they impose are seldom irksome; if they were so in any special instance they would no doubt be set aside by the vote of a majority. But this was an attempt to enable one-seventh of the community on a point of vital importance to defy the wishes and opinion of the remaining six-sevenths, and such an attempt is by its very nature foredoomed to failure.

A wiser part of the frame of government was the declaration that no theist should be molested for his religion, or compelled to attend or support any form of worship of which he did not approve. A clause of some importance was that which provided that all elections were to be by ballot, though in both houses of the legislature voting was to be open. The appointment of law officers was vested jointly in the Proprietors and the freemen. The latter, acting through their deputies, or the Assembly were to nominate two candidates for each office, of whom the Governor was to appoint one.

There was always a possibility that the Duke of York might assert a claim of conquest over Penn's territory. This danger was disposed of by a deed from the Duke relinquishing any such claim.[1] This was followed by a far more important concession. The territory assigned to Penn laboured under one serious—indeed almost fatal—drawback, a want of sea-board. Not merely had he no harbour, but the navigation of the estuary was, on the west bank, in the hands of the New Jersey Proprietors, on the east, in those of the Duke. The outlying dependency of scattered settlements grouped round Newcastle was useless as a part of New York, but it would be of inestimable value to Penn. Accordingly by a wise arrangement, the whole bank of the river as far as the Hoarkills, and to a breadth of twelve miles, was made over to Penn.[2] It would have made the arrangement more complete and more satisfactory if the boundary between the territory and Maryland had been at once authoritatively defined.

Further grant of territory by the Duke of York.

[1] The deed is given by Proud in a note, vol. i. p. 200.
[2] The concession is cited in an Act of the Pennsylvania Assembly. This also is given by Proud, vol. ii. p. 202.

The line was, in fact, an arbitrary one, and it was almost certain that the Proprietor of Maryland would make some protest. It would have been far better if the King had at once anticipated the difficulty instead of leaving it to be disputed over by the Proprietors.

In 1682 Penn himself set sail for his colony, with three ships freighted with settlers.[1] He was preceded *The Welsh settlers.* by a band of emigrants from a country which as yet had borne little or no part in the task of colonization. Almost every great wave of religious enthusiasm has made itself felt with full force in Wales. The emotional nature of the race, and their accessibility to all those external influences through which religion works, ensure a ready access for any new creed looked at on its devotional side ; their mental subtlety makes them approach it with interest in its doctrinal and metaphysical aspect. The Church of England had not yet learnt the great lesson of adapting herself to the wants of a Welsh-speaking people. On the other hand there is nothing to show that any of the forms of Dissent had laid hold on the affections of a people to whom a barren worship and an austere morality were uncongenial. The teaching of the first Quaker missionaries took root and bore fruit among the Welsh, and Fox could report that ' a precious seed the Lord hath thereaways, and a great people in those parts is since gathered to the Lord Jesus Christ, to sit down under His free teaching, and have suffered much for Him.'[2]

If the Welsh had shown no inclination to bear a hand in the work of colonization, it was from no inherent unfitness for the task, but from lack of opportunity and necessity. The Welshman has in a high

[1] Penn's departure is mentioned in the *London Gazette* of September 4, 1682. I owe my knowledge of this fact to the Narrative and Critical History.

[2] Fox's *Journal*, vol. i. p. 378 (ed. 1891).

degree that versatility which is specially needful in a colonist. But the obstacle of language would naturally withhold isolated settlers, or even small societies; and Wales too was then an underpeopled and a prosperous country, and was regarded by her children with an intensely tenacious patriotism which disinclined them to exile. But the loyalty of the Welsh Quakers to their new ties was too strong for this, and a large body of settlers, in all likelihood some four hundred households, took part in the emigration of 1682.

They had, however, no intention of being absorbed in the general community of English settlers. A territory was marked off for them. That peculiar arrangement by which much civil and judicial business was left to be managed by the community as organized for religious purposes, enabled them to be in a great measure a self-governing community. Like the Puritan settlers of New England, they named their new townships after the homes which they had left. Such names as Uwchlan, Tredyffren, Whiteland, Newtown, Haverford, Radnor, and Merion told plainly the nationality of their first civilized inhabitants, and showed that the counties of Pembrokeshire, Montgomeryshire and Radnorshire had contributed to the stream of emigration.

Penn first landed at Newcastle. It is clear that it was his original purpose to deal with this as a separate territory, since he promised the settlers there to hold a legislative Assembly. At the same time he told them that their constitutional rights were to be the same as those of the settlers in Pennsylvania.[1] The ease with which this amalgamation was effected is a remarkable contrast to the difficulties which beset every attempt at consolidation in New England. Neither for good nor evil had the middle colonies any

Newcastle incorporated

[1] Proud, vol. i. p. 205.

share in that intense and isolating spirit of local patriotism which marked Puritan New England.

The foundation of a city, to be the capital of his province, was, as we shall see, a leading feature in Penn's schemes. For the present he made Upland the centre of government, changing its name to Chester, at the request, it is said, of a friend and companion, Pearson, who came from that city.[2] There the earliest Pennsylvanian Assembly met. One of the first proceedings was to pass an Act incorporating the three counties recently made over by the Duke of York. It is clear that the Assembly was not intended to be in the ordinary sense a legislative body. A constitution and a code were to be submitted to it, to be accepted, ratified, and possibly altered in detail. The code had, no doubt, been drawn up by Penn, together with the frame of government in England. This explains what is otherwise hardly intelligible, the great size of the Assembly as designed by Penn. Such a body would be ill fitted for the work of making laws. But if the real work of constructive legislation was done by the Proprietor with a small circle of confidential advisers, then the size of the Assembly was rather an advantage. When all that is required is an expression of assent and confidence, a large body is as effective as a small one. It is probably more likely to accept measures without discussion. One may doubt whether such a system was likely to satisfy Englishmen who kept their hereditary liking and capacity for self-government, a liking which had never grown less by transportation beyond the Atlantic.

The first Assembly.[1]

That the work of drafting the laws to be enacted had been done in advance by the Proprietor and his advisers may be almost assumed for certain from the short time taken up by their deliberations. A session

[1] Proud, vol. i. p. 206.   [2] Clarkson, vol. i. p. 332.

of three days sufficed to pass a code of sixty articles, known as the Great Body of Laws. The work was, no doubt, made easier by the fact that many of the heads only repeated and expanded what had been already set forth in the code drawn up a year earlier by Penn. Yet there was enough new matter to have furnished far more than a three days' sitting, and it is almost certain that the Assembly can only have ratified, and here and there amplified and amended, a code already submitted to them.

The clauses in Penn's code which secured the more important spiritual and civil rights of the subject were re-enacted. The provision whereby all theists were to enjoy freedom of worship and belief was brought into greater prominence. No tax was to be levied save by the Governor and the Assembly. Not only, as we have seen, were the offences of Indians to be tried by a mixed jury, but any purchase of land from the Indians was void, and the buyer was to forfeit one hundred pounds. One provision illustrates the view of political duties which may be expected in a new country. Anyone elected to the Assembly and neglecting to attend was to be fined five shillings a day for such absence. No person might leave the colony without thirty days' notice, and no unknown person might travel without a pass from a magistrate or a certificate from some authority representing his country. No servant might be taken for a debt. This was not, as might be thought, a humane protection of the servant; it was for the benefit of the master, 'that the means of livelihood may not be taken from him.' We are reminded of the provision in Magna Charta exempting the necessary tools of the husbandman from seizure.

The same conditions of land tenure were prescribed as have been already mentioned. Various Acts were

---

[1] Printed in Hazard's *Annals*, p. 619, &c.

passed designed to further and protect husbandry. All cornfields were to be fenced five feet high. To encourage the breeding of live stock no heifer, calf, nor ewe lamb was to be killed. As in New Jersey, no stallion under thirteen and a half hands might run in the public pasture. There were to be three public ferries, and each county was bound to build bridges, ten feet wide, with a rail. Certain restraints were imposed on the disposition of land. No testator might leave more than one-third of his real estate away from his family, nor might he make any settlement extending beyond fifty years. All children were to be taught reading, writing and a trade. Parents neglecting this were liable to a fine of five pounds. One clause in which the Assembly followed, but expanded, the legislation submitted to them is almost verbally identical with the law of New Jersey, and reminds us of the close connexion between the two colonies. It forbade 'riotous practices, such as prizes, stage plays, masques, revels, bull-baitings and cock fights,' under a penalty of ten days' imprisonment, while half that penalty was imposed on those guilty of 'dealing with cards, dice, lotteries, or any such enticing, vain and evil sport.'[1]

It is clear that this code is to be taken in conjunction with the *Conditions* and *Concessions*, as making up the system of law under which the colonists were to live, supplemented as in every colony by the application of the Common Law of England in cases not otherwise provided for.

Penn's next step was to lay the foundations of a capital city for his province. As a rule cities, like constitutions, grow and are not made. Events in their course generally make a better choice of a site than the wit of man can make. It is a strong evidence of Penn's practical turn of mind that he

[1] Compare the law of New Jersey in Leaming and Spicer, p. 233.

should at once have chosen a site, marked out by nature as the best one for his province, and proving its fitness by the fact that no rival ever contested its ascendancy.

<small>Penn's treaty with the Indians.</small> In 1683 took place that event which more than any other in the early history of Pennsylvania has secured a hold on popular tradition. Markham, acting on Penn's behalf, had already confirmed Penn's title to the soil by a purchase from the Indians.[1] Penn had also in June 1682 written a letter from London, somewhat strangely addressed to the 'Emperor of Canada.' It begins with the characteristic words, 'The great God that made thee and me and all the world incline our hearts to love justice.' Penn goes on to say that the King of England, ' who is a great Prince,' has granted them a large county in America. He is bringing out 'just, plain, and honest people, who neither make war, nor dread war,' and he is establishing a Company of Traders who will deal with the natives on fair and reasonable terms.[2] Even if the letter is not authentic, it is thoroughly representative of Penn's temper and attitude towards the natives.

Penn, with instinctive perception of the savage character, saw that it would be well to impress the natives by some special ceremonial. On June 23 he met the chiefs of the Delaware at Shackamaxon, on a spot now included in the city of Philadelphia.

Tradition and the legitimate pride with which Penn's brethren have treasured his memory have woven round his simple description of the scene a mass of picturesque details. The very dress which he is supposed to have worn was long treasured as a sacred relic in a Quaker household.[3] What we learn as authentic from Penn himself is that he unfolded to the assembled chiefs his

---

[1] See Penn's letter of August 1681, given by Proud, vol. i. p. 195.
[2] The letters are in the Archives, vol. vii. appendix.
[3] Clarkson, vol. i. p. 340.

general purpose of that friendship which ought to exist between all the children of one Divine Father. His purchase of land, he explained to them, was not to lead to any exercise of superior authority.[1] They were still to enjoy for their own purposes any portions of it which might be unoccupied. It was in fact not such a transfer as should dispossess the previous occupants. It was only to give the new comers common rights in the soil. He also explained to the Indians that all disputes between the two peoples were to be settled by joint tribunals.

Though tradition may have erred in some of the details with which it has embellished this scene, it has assuredly not overrated its importance.

It is impossible not to see in Penn's attitude towards the Indians an evidence of the depth and sincerity of his religious conviction. The light indwelling in all men was not with him a conventional doctrine of the schools, but a guiding principle of action. Yet in his Indian policy he bequeathed to his successors a legacy in which good and evil, justice and weakness, were mingled. In its steadfast policy of fair dealing with the natives, Pennsylvania was an honourable exception to the rest of the English colonies. An optimistic conviction that justice and humanity were by themselves all that was needed in determining the attitude of the white man to the Indian was responsible for many errors and tragedies, and that conviction was a legacy bequeathed to the colony by its founder.

[1] All that is authentic in the account of this conference by later historians is derived from Penn's own letters. He describes it in his letter to the Society of Friends mentioned below (p. 507), and again somewhat more fully in a document found in a public office at Harrisburgh. This is endorsed, 'Minutes of the Indian Conference in relation to the Great Treaty made with William Penn at the Big Tree Shackamaxon, on the 14th of the tenth month 1682.' Bowdoin, *History of Friends in America*, vol. ii. p. 62.

The first Assembly was hardly intended as an ordinary meeting for purposes of legislation and government. It was rather of the nature of a special convention met to accept and ratify the constitution as prescribed by Penn. This, indeed, was implied in the clause which made the Assembly of the first year a primary one, while those which succeeded it were to be of the ordinary representative pattern. Accordingly, another Assembly was summoned early in 1683. The result of their labours was practically the remodelling of the constitution. Time had not yet revealed all the defects inherent in the charter granted by Penn to his colonists. But one very practical difficulty of a kind likely to impress ordinary men had at once made itself felt. The colonists protested that it was impossible to furnish the necessary number of members, either for the Council or the Assembly. Accordingly, they returned but three Councillors and nine Representatives for each county.

<small>The second Assembly.[1]</small>

Whether this failure showed Penn the need for remodelling his constitution, or whether, as it was put to the test of practice, its other defects became manifest, does not appear. But Penn's opening words to the Representatives seem to imply that changes had been suggested. They petitioned that the failure of the electors to comply with the requirements of the charter might not invalidate their rights. Penn replied that they might amend, alter, or add for the public good. If, like most founders of commonwealths, he erred somewhat in overrating his own prescience, in endeavouring to fashion an ideal constitution without waiting for the teaching of events, in this instance at least he made ample amends by his readiness to abandon an untenable position.

[1] Proud, vol. i. p. 235.

Penn and his colonists seem to have thought that it was wiser policy to construct a fresh instrument than to piece and patch the old charter. When he offered the alternative of the old charter or a new one, the unanimous demand was for the latter. Accordingly, a joint committee of the two houses was set to work, with general instructions to frame the required instrument.

The new charter.[1]

The result of their labours was the issue of a new charter. This removed the most obvious blot on the earlier charter, the feature which had been most productive of immediate inconvenience. The numbers of both houses were reduced. The charter only required for the present eighteen members for the Council and thirty-six for the Assembly. These might be ultimately expanded to the original limits of seventy-two and two hundred. The cumbrous arrangement of breaking up the Council into committees was abandoned. But a very significant clause was introduced, providing that 'one-third of the provincial Council, residing with the Governor from time to time, shall with the Governor have the care of the management of public affairs relating to the peace, justice, treasury and improvement of the province and territories, and to the good education of youth and sobriety of the manners of the inhabitants therein as aforesaid.' This was practically the creation of a Council in the generally recognised sense of the word.

At the same time there was no vital change in the system of legislation. Measures were to be introduced by the Council. The power of the Assembly was, indeed, somewhat strengthened by a clause providing that their approval of any new law must be carried by a majority of two-thirds. This in a somewhat cumbrous fashion increased the power of the popular Repre-

[1] Printed in Proud, vol. ii. p. 21.

sentatives to resist encroachments by the Governor or the Council. It did not give the popular Representatives any power in the way of constructive legislation, and it greatly increased the chance of a deadlock in administration. It might deter the Governor and Council from bringing forward unpopular measures; it in no way compelled them to bring forward popular ones. In the matter of the appointment of officials and in the provisions for secrecy of voting the provisions of the old charter were left intact.

One practical advantage there was no doubt in the formal introduction and acceptance of a new charter. The incorporation of Delaware was subsequent to the passing of the old charter. The application of the charter, therefore, to those three counties was implied, not expressed, and future complications might be avoided if a new charter were accepted by the whole united colony.

One matter of discussion, and in some measure of dispute, was the appointment of public officers. Was it to be vested in the Governor or in the Assembly? The first clause in the new charter vested the appointment of all officers in the Assembly. It was agreed, however, that this should be suspended during the life of the Proprietor, and that his power of appointment should not be curtailed.

A letter which Penn sent home this summer is, perhaps, the most important document in the history of the colony.[1] Hackneyed though it is by constant quotation, its interest is neither exhausted nor impaired. It is of double interest.

Penn's account of the colony.

It is the description of a new country, its resources and its inhabitants, by a singularly acute observer, detached from all prejudices likely to impair his judge-

[1] The letter is addressed to the Society of Friends. Proud prints it in full, vol. vi. pp. 246–64.

ment. It also shows us the hopes and expectations that guided Penn in his works as a constructive statesman.

In his description of the country Penn shows himself equally alive to its picturesqueness and attractiveness as an abode and to its material resources. He dwells on the rich woodland flowers, from which even the best-stored London gardens might borrow something. March brings with it cold, but not, as in England, accompanied by north-east winds and 'foul thick black weather,' but dry frost, with a sky as clear as summer. The woods abound in wild-fowl, and the soil is naturally productive. There are wild vines. These he hopes may with care be improved into yielding wine. He will not, however, rely on that but will import vines. Between the two he hopes to make as good wine as any European country of the same latitude can yield. Live stock, too, of every sort is increasing; two cargoes of horses have already been exported to Barbadoes. Unfounded stories of scarcity have reached England. 'The greatest hardship we have suffered hath been salt meat.'

Penn's account of the natives is of peculiar interest. It is pervaded by a pathetic optimism. First and almost alone among European travellers, he writes of the Indians not as a people on a wholly lower level, but as having opinions to be respected and institutions to be seriously studied and respected. He dwells throughout on the happier side of their life and the better side of their character. Penn's conception of the equality of man leads him in the track followed by Rousseau. He finds true happiness and true wisdom in the woods. If the savages are 'ignorant of our pleasures, they are also free from our pains. They are not disquieted with bills of lading and exchange, nor perplexed with chancery suits and

Penn's description of the natives.

exchequer reckonings. We sweat and toil to live; their pleasure feeds them; I mean their hunting, fishing and fowling, and their table is spread everywhere.' Their one source of unhappiness is that which civilized men have brought among them, drink.

He dwells on their hospitality and their mirthfulness in ordinary life. 'The most merry creatures that live, they feast and dance perpetually,' yet he is not less struck with their gravity in all public matters. At a conference not a man is seen to whisper and smile. He has 'never seen more natural sagacity without the help (I was going to say the spoil) of tradition. It is admirable to consider how powerful the Kings are, and yet how they move by the breath of their people.' His enthusiasm extends to all details. He dwells on the personal comeliness of the natives. Their features may find a prototype in ancient Rome, their complexion in modern Italy. No European language 'hath words of more sweetness or greatness or accent or emphasis.' A list of place-names quoted 'have grandeur in them.' With the taste not uncommon among Biblical students for strange ethnological speculations, Penn endeavours to trace back the stock of the natives to the Jews.

Penn's indifference to dogma, to the introduction of any metaphysical element into religion, enables him to enter into the theology of the Indians with a sympathy far beyond the reach of the ordinary missionary. He does not see dark superstitions to be extirpated. Rather he would tell the natives in the spirit of St. Paul that he had to declare to them the God whom they ignorantly worshipped. 'Without the help of metaphysics,' they have arrived at the two essential articles of faith, belief in God and in a future life.

Of the civilized inhabitants already in the country

Penn tells us no more than we already know. But we learn something of the progress of his favourite project, the formation of a capital city. Philadelphia has already four-score houses, with merchants and craftsmen following their vocations as fast as they can.

<small>Progress of Philadelphia.</small>

It was inevitable from the outset that Penn's grant should bring him into conflict with the Proprietor of Maryland. Of all the disputes which had their origin in the slipshod dealings of the Crown with American territory, that was the bitterest and the most prolonged. It can be more conveniently dealt with, not now, but as a detached episode belonging to a later phase of our subject.

<small>Dispute with Maryland.</small>

In 1684 Penn left his colony. The years which followed were years of trouble and disappointment to Penn himself, years of anarchy in the colony. Penn's friendship with James brought him into discredit with those who would naturally have been his political allies. The old charge of Jesuitry was revived. A letter from Sir William Popple, the Secretary to the Lords of Trade, shows that the accusation was influencing those who had to deal with Penn in his character of a colonial Proprietor.[1] Penn's reply is a thoroughly characteristic exposition of his doctrine of toleration. He plainly denies the charge of being a Papist, and in more than in one detail proves its utter absurdity. But he shows as plainly that the charge of belonging to any particular school of Christianity or holding any set of dogmas is one which he esteems but lightly. 'As if,' he says, 'a mistake about an obscure proposition of faith were a greater evil than the breach of an undoubted precept. Such a religion the devils themselves are not without; for they have

<small>Penn defends himself against the charge of Popery.</small>

---

[1] Popple's letter and Penn's answer are both given in full by Proud, vol. i. pp. 314-32.

both faith and knowledge: but their faith doth not work by love, nor their knowledge by obedience.' And one may almost say that the whole doctrine of toleration is summed up when Penn says, of liberty of conscience, 'I ever understood that to be the natural right of all men, and that he that had a religion without it his religion were none of his own.' Unhappily Penn failed to see that to many men such an attitude was incomprehensible. That toleration was compatible with earnestness was a conviction so deeply rooted in his own mind that he could not even imagine others in honesty holding a contrary belief. Confident in the stability of his own religious convictions, he could not in the least comprehend how they could become suspected in the eyes of others.

The same inability to understand the views, possibly too limited, and the suspicions, possibly unreasonable, of his fellow-men was telling against Penn in his secular career. Discontent was showing itself among the colonists. Although Penn had refused to alienate the Indian trade, yet he had allowed a body to come into existence with certain restricted rights of trade and with the right to acquire land. Their President, Nicholas Moore, was also Chief Justice, a somewhat undesirable combination of offices. He incurred the displeasure of the Representatives, and was by them impeached before the Council. After two refusals to appear, he was provisionally deprived of all his public offices. Whether he made submission and was acquitted does not appear, nor is there any evidence that he was restored to the office of Chief Justice. But in the following year he was appointed by the Proprietor one of the Commissioners to administer the colony in his absence.[1] The spirit in which Penn met the complaints of his settlers was characteristic. He writes to some of

[1] Proud, vol. i. pp. 295-9.

his principal followers exhorting them to concord. 'Be not so governmentish, so noisy and open in your dissatisfactions.' In other words, leave the forms of government to be settled for you by a well-meaning ruler who knows what you really want.

One inherent defect of the constitution at once showed itself. The Committee of the Council nomi-
<small>Establishment of a small Privy Council.[1]</small> nated by the Proprietor was found too large for practical work. In 1686 he cut it down to a Council of Five, or one might rather say he superseded the Council by an appointment of that number, by the title of Commissioners of State. Penn's instructions to these Commissioners are trenchantly despotic. Three of them are to form a quorum, and may exercise the power delegated to them by the Proprietor of vetoing the amending laws. If the Council are negligent in their attendance they are to be dissolved. No conference is to be held between the two chambers; each is to be kept strictly to its own functions, the Council to proposing laws, the Lower House to accepting or rejecting them. Furthermore the Council was to abrogate all laws passed since Penn's departure, and to pass them afresh amended by the Council in conjunction with a new Assembly.

The Council are also instructed to maintain the decisions of the law courts by 'turning their severe brow upon all the troublesome and vexatious, more especially trifling appeals.' No Stuart king, no minister of the school of Strafford, could have given instructions more despotic in tone, more calculated to uproot constitutional liberty. A constitution containing in it many elements of arbitrary government was to be so administered as to deprive it of all those influences which made for freedom. Such conduct in one like

---

[1] Penn's instructions to these five Commissioners are contained in a letter of December 1, 1686, printed by Proud, vol. i. p. 305.

Penn, a man of real and even intense benevolence, no self-seeker, in many respects humble and distrustful of his own judgement, should make us often pause before we condemn the moral principles of those whose political action we justly reprobate.

One matter of complaint in Penn's instructions to his Councillors is 'the most slothful and dishonourable attendance of the Council.' We see other traces of this lack of public spirit and indifference to public duties. In 1684 the Assembly found it necessary to require that at least one Representative from each county should attend under pain of a fine of one pound for every day's absence.[1] The same temper showed itself in the neglect of judicial duties. An Act was passed imposing a fine of thirty shillings on justices and ten shillings on jurors who should fail to attend County Courts.[2] To curtail still further the political action of the general body of citizens, and to vest power practically in a little oligarchy nominated by the Proprietor, was assuredly not the way to cure this, or to inspire the settlers with an interest in public affairs, or a sense of public responsibility.

Lack of activity in public life.

The scanty records of the legislation of this time throw little light on the life of the colony. An Act limiting the rate of interest to eight per cent. shows that the colony suffered from that lack of money which was such an economical hindrance alike in the mercantile commonwealths of New England and the slave plantations of the south.[3]

Legislative measures.

It may also be taken probably, though less certainly, as evidence of the growing prosperity of the colony, or one should perhaps rather say of its increasing commercial enterprise. Borrowers are of two classes, those who borrow to meet unproductive expenditure and

[1] Laws, p. 167. [2] *Ib.* p. 176. [3] *Ib.* p. 180.

those who use their credit to extend their business beyond the limits of their available capital. The usages and traditions of the Quaker colony made it certain that there would be no borrowers of the first class to need what is considered the protection of the State. If men sought to borrow it shows that the trade of the colony held out prospects, which tempted traders to strain their credit to what seemed dangerous lengths.

Another Act passed about this time illustrates that unpractical optimism which not infrequently appeared in Penn's constructive policy. It prohibited paid lawyers, by providing that no one should plead in court till he had made a formal declaration that he had not and would not receive any reward.[1]

Act against lawyers.

By 1685 Philadelphia contained over three hundred and fifty houses, and as a consequence the value of town lots had risen in some cases it is said as much as four thousand per cent.[2] There is also indirect evidence of the rapid growth of the colony in a letter from Penn, where he speaks of the number of drinking houses and of the looseness that is committed in the caves.[3] It is plain that settlers, pressing in faster than houses could be built for them, took up their abodes, like the dwellers by the Loire, in caves on the bank of the Delaware. It is easy to see how the colony was peculiarly exposed to the risk of moral disorder. In common with New York and New Jersey, it lacked the restraints which operated on their northern and southern neighbours. New Hampshire was protected by its poverty and unattractiveness, and in all the other northern colonies the system of exclusive churches operated as a process of selection, and tended to make every individual citizen in some measure responsible

Growth of the colony, and consequent moral decline.

---

[1] Records, vol. i. p. 172.
[2] This is stated in the *Memorial History*, vol. v. p. 493. See Appendix V.
[3] The letter is published by Proud, vol. i. p. 296.

for the corporate morality of the whole society. In the southern colonies all public life was in the hands of an oligarchy, with no doubt the failings, but also some of the redeeming virtues, of an oligarchy. Anarchy below was repressed by the system of servitude. Nor were the southern colonies exposed to those temptations and dangers which the Greek philosopher dreaded for his model state in the coming and going of a crowd of traders and sailors. But the Quaker colonies, New York and in a great measure Rhode Island, were exposed to those temptations and dangers with no counteracting influence. There men were neither restrained by the ecclesiastical machinery and the exacting corporate morality of New England, nor by the semi-feudal system of the southern plantations.

Another measure shows that the possibility of danger from the Indians was wholly forgotten. An attempt was made to repeal the Act which prohibited the sale of drink to the natives.[1] This sense of security was for a moment dispelled. During the year 1688 a rumour reached the colonists, set on foot as it would seem by two mischief-making or foolish squaws in New Jersey, that the Indians were about to invade Pennsylvania and massacre the settlers.[2] The report soon gathered substance and definiteness. Three families, it was said, had actually been cut off. In many colonies such a panic would have led to a wild outburst of retaliation. That it was not so was largely due to the principles which Penn and the Quaker teachers associated with him had impressed on the colonists. A peaceful embassy was sent to the Indian head chief. Himself old and crippled, he was surrounded by an armed force of five hundred warriors. If any evil designs had been entertained this show of boldness and confidence on the part of the settlers at

[1] Laws, p. 169.   [2] Proud, vol. i. p. 336.

once put an end to them. Kindly words were exchanged, and the friendship which Penn had laboured to build up suffered no hurt.

In 1688 Lloyd whom Penn had left as his deputy resigned. Penn appointed in his stead one John Blackwell, who was not a Quaker. At a later day Penn apologized for this appointment, pleading that no Friend would take the post. Yet it is clear that at the time of the appointment Penn felt satisfied with it, and not as it would seem without good reason. Blackwell was in Penn's judgement 'a grave, sober, wise man, I suppose independent in judgement.' He was well connected, having married a daughter of General Lambert, and he had been in the paymasters' department of the Commonwealth army.[1] In a later letter, after Blackwell had disappointed the hopes formed of him, Penn describes him as 'being in England and Ireland of great repute for integrity, ability and virtue.' Yet in this same letter Penn manifestly admits that the appointment had been a failure, owing in part to the 'peevishness' which Blackwell had shown to the Quakers.[2] The instructions given to Blackwell are curiously illustrative of the weaker side of Penn's character as a statesman.[3] They are pervaded by vagueness, by general declarations of principles, of which everyone would accept the propriety and almost everyone dispute the application. Blackwell is instructed 'to be careful that speedy, as well as thorough and impartial, justice be done ; and virtue in all cherished and vice punished ; that feuds

Penn's instructions to his deputy Blackwell.

[1] 'Treasurer to the Commonwealth's army in England, Scotland and Ireland,' are Penn's actual words. The letter is quoted by Clarkson, vol. ii. p. 40.
[2] This letter is given by Proud in a note, vol. i. p. 340. It is here that Penn states that he could not find one of his own denomination to take the post. It will be seen hereafter what this peevishness in all likelihood was.
[3] These are given by Proud, vol. i. p. 339.

between persuasions or nations or countries be suppressed and extinguished if any be ; and if none, that by a good conduct they may be prevented.' In other words, Blackwell is, by some mysterious process not specified, to create a morally perfect community. The provinces of law and morality are confused by instructions 'that the widow and orphan and absent may be particularly regarded in their rights,' and that Blackwell is to 'rule the meek meekly, and those that will not be ruled, rule with authority.'

Even instructions that sound more definite are tinged by the same fault. Blackwell is to support the commissioners of property where people are unruly in their settlements, or ' comply not with reasonable obligations.' Sheriffs and Clerks of the Peace are not to impose on the people, and 'magistrates are to live peaceably and soberly, for I could not endure one loose or litigious person in authority.' Penn fails to see that he is throughout using terms which in all likelihood the settlers and his representative will interpret each in his own fashion. The whole document, indeed, illustrates that tendency of Penn's mind which made toleration seem to him so simple a matter, intolerance so incomprehensible. He evidently thought that there was a broad ground of moral truth on which all men might agree, disregarding theological differences. He forgot that while men may agree on the abstract doctrines of morality, any attempt to apply these doctrines to details of practice would be sure to reveal differences just as real as those which separate theologians.

Meanwhile that spirit of theological discord which Penn so dreaded, and which he believed himself to George Keith. have exorcised, was making itself felt among the settlers. The dispute as recorded seems to have been from the outset personal. But in theological, as in political, quarrels the personal element readily comes to the front, and becomes not only the most prominent but to many the most important feature in the contest. Earlier differences in which that personal element is absent are forgotten. As it has come down to us, the dispute was mainly due to the independence and pugnacity of one man, George Keith.

Keith was, with the possible exception of Penn, the most cultivated and brilliant of all the early Quakers. He was born about 1640, and graduated as a Master of Arts at Aberdeen. He was a born fighter, and it was probably rather opposition to authority than any positive adherence to the essential principles of Quakerism which led him to join the brotherhood.

In 1689 Keith went to Philadelphia. There he soon created scandal by holding, though not, as it would seem, very openly advocating, the doctrine of transmigration of souls. He also quarrelled with Penn's deputy, with Lloyd, and with another influential man, Stockdale. They retaliated by charging Keith with heresy. A large section, including it is said a majority of elders, took his part. Finally, however, the magistrates, with probably an intuitive feeling that Keith's attitude and temper were subversive of Quaker principles, had him tried for heresy by a tribunal specially appointed for that end.

As the result, Keith was inhibited from teaching. Nevertheless, he and a number of followers held to their principles, calling themselves Christian Quakers. In some respects his attitude seems to have been an application of Quaker doctrine too severely logical to be practical. He denounced the magistrates for helping the friendly Indians against their enemies by supplying them with arms and ammunition, and for employing force against privateers. He also denounced slavery.

Mixed with these moral protests were personal attacks on Lloyd.

In 1694 Keith left Pennsylvania for England. There he held his ground for five years as the head of a congregation nominally Quaker, but bitterly opposed to the recognised Quaker practice and teaching. In 1700 he abandoned this position and received episcopal ordination. Two years later he returned to America, employed by the Society for the Propagation of the Gospel, and acting as a strenuous and proselytizing representative of the Church of England.[1]

At the same time that Keith was disturbing the religious peace of the colony, it was being harassed by a series of secular disputes. In 1689, one Samuel Richardson, a member of the Council, was expelled by a vote of that body for having used unbecoming language about the Governor. The right of the Council to take this step became the subject of much such a dispute as raged over the expulsion of Wilkes.[2] This was followed by a dispute prophetic of many future ones. There was an alarm of an Indian attack. Blackwell contended that the control of the militia was vested in the Governor, as it is in England in the Crown. To this some objected on the grounds that their conscience forbade them to approve of any use of force. One member of the Assembly, Dr. Hues, boldly defied public opinion, and proposed that every man should provide himself with arms and ammunition. Apparently, however, the danger passed over without the difference of opinions coming to a head.[3]

A dispute which followed had more definite and abiding consequences. Lloyd the President of the

[1] There is a full account of Keith in the *Dictionary of National Biography*. His writings, mostly controversial, are numerous, often acute, but somewhat verbose.

[2] Records, vol. i. p. 188.

[3] For this dispute see Records, vol. i. pp. 299-307.

Council, and Blackwell, the Governor, seem to have been respectively the heads of the Quaker and the non-Quaker parties. Blackwell endeavoured in the first instance to deprive Lloyd of the custody of the great seal, and then to invalidate his election as a Councillor. Lloyd, backed by the Quakers, held his ground on both points.[1] Blackwell thereupon left the colony, but as it would seem without formally resigning his post as Governor. Before departing he read certain instructions which he had received from Penn. The Assembly was to choose three, out of whom Penn would appoint one Deputy-Governor. Pending the arrival of his commission that one of the three who had received most votes was to act provisionally as Governor. At the same time that Blackwell reported this instruction, he apologized for his own 'ignorance and weakness,' and acknowledged his deserved unpopularity.[2]

Dispute between the province and the territories.

The Assembly then reappointed Lloyd Deputy-Governor, as it would seem without authority from the Proprietors, and without any acknowledgement that necessity had driven them to an irregular step. The immediate result of this was a rupture between the two sections of the colony, between the three counties of the original royal grant and those afterwards acquired from the Duke of York.[3]

There is little to show what determined the attitude taken up by the two parties. It may well be that some personal question which has left no trace in the records entered into it. Visibly and externally the main ground was the appointment of judges. The inhabitants of the lower province seem to have thought that in this matter their due rights were overlooked. Their demand apparently was the not unreasonable one that

---

[1] Laws, p. 520.   [2] Records, vol. i. p. 312.
[3] See Penn's letter, 29 iv. 1682, in Proud, vol. i. p. 357.

a separate commission should be made out for each portion of the colony. Each commission should contain the names of all the judges in the colony, but in that for the upper half one of the judges appointed for that district should have precedence, and so for the lower half. Lloyd and those members of the Council who represented the wishes of the upper province resisted this concession. Six of the Councillors from that district met and, taking upon themselves the functions of the Council, appointed six judges for their own counties.[1]

It is hardly to be expected that Penn, living in England, harassed by private anxieties and hunted down as a Jacobite spy, could give much profitable attention to the affairs of his colony, least of all to a dispute involving probably complex personal issues. His belief, too, that forms were all much the same, that there was always in the citizens a fund of good sense and moderation which would keep matters straight, now led him to suggest a way out of the difficulty. He suggested the adoption of one among three alternative schemes of government. The executive power might be vested in the Deputy-Governor, in the Council, or in a Committee of Five. The Upper Counties were in favour of a Deputy-Governor. The Lower however, or at least seven Representatives who claimed to speak in their name, objected.[2] They should prefer government by five Commissioners; they would accept that by the Council. But they wholly objected to the cost of a Deputy-Governor, and to a scheme which would vest all power in the hands of one person. In all likelihood their objection lay in the certainty that a

[1] The demand of the six Councillors for the territories is given in the Archives.
Their action is condemned in a declaration drawn up by Lloyd and the Councillors for the province. This is given in Proud, vol. i. p. 352.

[2] This declaration is given in Proud, vol. i. p. 355.

Deputy-Governor would be chosen from the Upper Counties. They further stipulated that if the Government were vested in the Council, the representatives of the lower half should have a veto in all appointments of officials within their own district.

None of these terms of agreement were acceptable to the inhabitants of the Upper Counties. A compromise was then effected, introducing a novel and peculiar arrangement. There was to be one representative Assembly legislating for the whole colony, but two executives, one for the Upper, the other for the Lower province.

Pennsylvania included in Fletcher's commission. It was but natural that every adherent of the fallen house should be looked on with suspicion as a probable malcontent and a possible spy. There seems to have been some delay in the proclamation of the new Sovereigns,[1] which may have given rise to a suspicion that there was a Jacobite tendency in the colony. By 1692 the tide of Whig feeling was running with such force against Penn as to bring with it the loss of his privileges as a Proprietor. The mode of his deprivation was altogether peculiar. There was no formal revocation of his charter. But while his charter was left intact, Fletcher, the Governor of New York, received a commission extending his authority to Pennsylvania. The only announcement of the extent and nature of the change was that implied in this commission to Fletcher.[2] This set forth that by great neglects and miscarriages, and the absence of the Proprietor, Pennsylvania had fallen into great confusion, and that it was therefore necessary that 'we (the King) should take the government into our own hands.'

At the same time the system of government was

[1] Records, vol. i. p. 302.
[2] For Fletcher's commission see Col. Papers, 1696–7, 2296.

modified. There was still to be a Council and an Assembly of Representatives. But the Council was to be nominated by Fletcher. It was to consist of twelve, and three were to be a *quorum*. The only change in the system of administration was beyond doubt an improvement. All laws were to be transmitted within three months of their passing, and the approval or dissent of the Crown was to be declared at once.[1]

Penn did not suffer this encroachment on his rights to pass unchallenged. In December 1692 we find him writing to Fletcher in a tone of vigorous remonstrance. There is little of Quakerly submissiveness in the opening words, ' I caution thee that I am an Englishman.' Pennsylvania, the soil and the government, have been ' dearly purchased ' by him. There have been no judicial proceedings against him. The abrogation of his rights can only be due to misinformation given to the Board of Trade. ' I hope therefore thou wilt tread softly, and with caution in this matter.'[2]

Penn's remonstrance.

About the same time we find Penn writing to a friend in Pennsylvania in a more moderate and diplomatic strain :

' The bearer will inform you of the transfer of Pennsylvania to the Governor of New York during the war and my absence. Insist upon your Patent with wisdom and moderation but steady integrity. You will obey the Crown of England speaking the language and voice of the law, which this is not, but *sic volo, sic jubeo*, due doubtless to misadvice of your neighbours that the French will make their way into the colonies through you. Set forth the falsehood of it by your singular situation on land and sea, your hazards, charges, labours — that the government was your

[1] Colonial State Papers, 1692, 2296.
[2] *Ib.* December 5, 1692.

motive more than land, that you were a people who could have lived at home, and went there not upon motives of guilt or poverty, and that it will ruin the Colony which brings more customs to the Crown than revenue to the colonial government.' 'Friends will deliver your representations to the Lords of Trade or the King in Council, if you protest against any proceedings of the Governor of New York upon this arbitrary commission and excessive anxiety as to the French.'[1]

In 1693 Fletcher reached Philadelphia, and was apparently well received by the settlers.[2] The tranquillity with which they accepted the change shows that with all Penn's benevolence and public spirit he had not succeeded in inspiring his colonists as a whole with reverence or affection. It illustrates perhaps more strongly the absence among the Pennsylvanians of that tenacious respect for the forms of law which existed so intensely in New England. The colonists were liable to two incompatible sets of claims, both existing as far as one can see in legal force: the claims of the Proprietor as authorized by his charter, the claims of the Crown as implied in the commission to Fletcher. The Assembly of a New England colony would at once have seen the difficulties of the situation. The Pennsylvanian settlers can hardly be said to have questioned the legality of this procedure. All that they did was to endeavour while acquiescing to secure from Fletcher, as a matter of favour, the rights which Penn had granted to them. They petitioned that in summoning an Assembly all the forms required by the charter should be observed, and that all laws hitherto passed

Fletcher visits Philadelphia and asserts his authority.

[1] Colonial State Papers, 1689-90, 2668. The letter was probably sent to the Board of Trade by Fletcher.
[2] *Ib.* 1693, 397, iii.

should be still in force.[1] They also in the preamble to this second request declared that it had pleased the King and Queen in the Proprietor's absence to supply his place by the appointment of Fletcher. This half-hearted effort to turn the flank of the attack was wholly without effect. Fletcher showed no corresponding wish to shirk the real difficulties of the case or to take refuge in diplomatic courtesies.[2] He plainly told the Assembly that 'their desires were grounded on great mistakes.' The King, as we have seen, had not except by implication condemned Penn's charter. Fletcher now produced, and in all likelihood devised for the occasion, a new and sweeping plea. Charles II., he said, could only alienate the rights of the Crown for his own life. Penn's grant, so far as it was political and not merely territorial, was he said at an end. Of the causes for the action of the Crown, the absence of the Proprietor was the least; there had been dangerous neglects and miscarriages; as for retaining the privileges granted by the Proprietor, 'the constitution of her Majesty's Government and that of Mr. Penn were in a direct opposition one to another.'

At the same time Fletcher at once came to close quarters with the Assembly on that ever-recurring battlefield, the need for public defence. The time was, he pointed out, one of special danger, since the French, exasperated by the recent loss of Martinique, would in all likelihood retaliate on the English colonies. Quakers though they might be,

Disputes between Fletcher and the Assembly.[3]

---

[1] Their petition is given by Proud, vol. i. p. 353.

[2] Fletcher's answer to the Assembly was given in writing. It is in Proud, vol. i. p. 355. It was prefaced by a speech reported in the Archives.

It was in the speech that he propounded the doctrine of the temporary nature of Penn's grant.

[3] For the whole of the dispute between Fletcher and the Assembly see the Records, vol. i. pp. 399-459.

they must, he said, keep soldiers and forts, just as they wall their gardens and keep watch-dogs. If any had tender consciences their contributions can be applied to civil purposes. Fletcher must have rated the intelligence of his opponents low if they could be satisfied with an arrangement whereby their own payments set other funds free for purposes which they condemned.

One passage in Fletcher's speech tends to confirm one of the worst charges made against him, that of conniving at piracy. An Act had been drafted in England, sent out to Fletcher, and adopted by the New York Assembly, to suppress that class of crime. Pirates were allowed a certain time within which to submit and give security for good behaviour. Fletcher recommended to the Assembly of Pennsylvania the passing of a like enactment, and suggested that the time of grace might be lengthened, with the comment 'pirates and privateers may become good men at last.'

One recommendation of Fletcher's deserves notice, as showing how schemes for bringing the whole body of colonies into closer union were in the air. He recommended to the Assembly a project for a postal service from Virginia to Boston.

In conclusion Fletcher told the Assembly that his time was precious, and that he hoped they would desist from all unnecessary debates.

The Assembly might be slow to perceive the strong constitutional ground on which they could take their stand, but the overbearing discourtesy of Fletcher could not fail to call out a spirit of resistance. In a dignified and temperate tone the Representatives pointed out that his charges of misgovernment and failure to administer justice were unfounded, and that in spite of the peace principles of many of the settlers the colony was exposed to no dangers from without.

A public man like Fletcher, whose corrupt practices

placed him at the mercy of private individuals, can hardly play the tyrant with consistency or success. Moreover his duties at New York kept him from giving much of his time to Pennsylvania, and his intermittent violence was no match for the steady obstinacy of his opponents.

One important advantage was gained by the Assembly. According to the original constitution as devised by Penn, the Assembly was to have no right of initiating legislation. But it seems to have been a singular and undesigned result of Fletcher's appointment that in this respect the Assembly actually gained by it. They apparently claimed and he admitted that they had the ordinary rights of a representative Assembly, and might therefore pass bills which were to be sent up to the Council for approval and amendment.

The Assembly, while prepared to fight Fletcher upon essentials, showed a somewhat grotesque anxiety to avoid giving offence on a mere matter of form. A resolution was passed voting certain moneys to Lloyd and Markham as Deputy-Governors of Pennsylvania and of the Territories respectively, and to Fletcher. In the resolution Fletcher's name appeared last. The Speaker of the Assembly, fearing that Fletcher would be offended, pointed out that in Holy Writ the name of the Baptist precedes that of Christ!

Their fears were apparently unfounded, since Fletcher professed himself indifferent on the point. But another phrase used by the Assembly did give offence. In a remonstrance addressed to Fletcher they referred to Penn's proprietary rights having been taken away because their Majesties were misinformed. Against this Fletcher protested, as 'very unmannerly.'

A more serious and substantial dispute arose over the whole question of legislation. The Assembly apologized for their lack of legislative and administrative skill on the ground that they had been 'put out of their old methods,' and they petitioned that the whole body of extant laws, a hundred and two in number, should be confirmed. To this Fletcher replied that he would consent to any laws not repugnant to the laws of England, but that he could not go blindfold and accept laws of which he only knew the titles. The point was one on which the colonial legislature was at variance within itself. This appeared at a conference between the Council and the Assembly. The former took the ground that laws passed by the colonial government required special and affirmative approval by the Crown. The Assembly contended that the absence of a specific veto was sufficient. The point was of some constitutional importance, as the systems differed in the directness and efficiency of the control vested in the Home Government. The course of the dispute is not very clear, but ultimately the laws came before Fletcher for approval, and the Assembly, according to sound constitutional precedent, made the granting of a supply dependent on the Governor's acceptance of their proposals.

Difficulty about legislation.

Gradually, by a process of compromise, of which the details are not recorded, the conflicting parties came together. The Assembly granted a subsidy of a penny in the pound, and Fletcher accepted some of the laws proposed. One recorded incident in the dispute throws a grotesque light on Fletcher's character. The legislature proposed to punish drunkenness, in the case of an official by deprivation, of an ordinary citizen by disfranchisement. Fletcher protested against this as unduly severe. 'It is hard for a false step in drinking a cup perhaps too much a man should be deprived of his birthright.' He added, with confidence hardly justified by facts, 'I will

Final agreement between Fletcher and the Assembly.

give you leave to banish me out of the government when you find me drunk.'

Next year Fletcher had to reopen that strife which formed so long and so weary a chapter in the history of Pennsylvania, and to reprove the Assembly for their indifference to the common defence of the colonies against the Indians. The Five Nations are going over to the French. Unless the natives on the frontier of Pennsylvania see that the English can and will fight, they will in self-defence do the same. The country above Albany is deserted. 'I pray God this leprosy may spread no further.' New Jersey has set a good example by contributing four hundred pounds and sixty men. If the principles of the Quaker settlers forbid war, they may at least help the distressed Indians on their frontier, feeding the hungry and clothing the naked.[1]

Disputes about defence of the colony.

Meanwhile the influence of Penn's friends at Court so far prevailed that the question of his restoration was opened. The law officers of the Crown were requested to report on the matter. They did so, and advised that the Crown had a right on a special emergency to grant a commission such as Fletcher's; when, however, the emergency ceased Penn's rights revived.[2]

Restoration of Penn.

The report was read by the Board of Trade. Penn was then called in. He undertook, if restored, to comply with the royal commands, and to provide for the support of government. Therefore his restoration was recommended by the Board to the Crown and carried through.[3]

This, however, did not carry with it the immediate supersession of Fletcher.

[1] Colonial State Papers, 1694, 2271.
[2] The statement of the case and the opinion upon it are among the Colonial State Papers, July 12, 1694.
[3] *Ib.* July 13, 1694

M M

In June 1695 the dispute between the Governor and the Assembly began again. Fletcher asked for eighty men as a contribution to a joint military force.[1] The Assembly pleaded the business of the harvest as an excuse for refusing to consider the matter. At this point Fletcher seems to have given up the contest as hopeless, and we hear no more of him in connexion with Pennsylvania.

Fletcher's interest in the colony ceases.

The strife, however, was carried on by Deputy-Governor Markham. The Assembly refused to make a grant of money except with an Act of Settlement, equivalent in its purpose to the Bill of Rights, appended. This Markham refused to accept as prejudicial to the Proprietor's interest. Neither party would yield and the Lieutenant-Governor dissolved the Assembly.

Dispute between the Assembly and Markham.[2]

The necessities of government, however, forced him to call another Assembly in the following year, and the strife began again. The dogged persistence of the Assembly prevailed, and the Act of Settlement was passed. This was a modification of the constitution of 1683. The tendency of the new instrument was wholly to strengthen the position of the electorate as against the Proprietor. The Assembly was to consist of four members from each county, elected in the usual manner, all at once, not, as heretofore, one-third at a time. The Council was also to be an elective body of two members from each county. By the constitution of 1683, it will be remembered, the Proprietor was to select an inner council, a real council as it might be called, consisting of one-third of the elective council. As nothing is said of such a provision we must suppose that it was now abrogated. The Council and the Assembly were both to be elected

Act of Settlement passed.[3]

---

[1] Records, vol. i. p. 480.   [2] Ib.
[3] The text of this is given by Proud in an appendix, vol. ii. p. 30.

annually. They were in fact two chambers, differing not in their composition, but only in the positions assigned to them. Either might initiate legislation. The Council, however, could only do so by way of suggestion to the Assembly. Speaking broadly, the Governor and Council were to be the chief administrative body, the Assembly the legislative. To avoid the necessity of oaths, forms of declaration were drawn up for the various public officials.

One change of form is a slight but significant illustration of the change from Quaker authority to the Anglican authority and back again. In the records till 1693 the months are indicated by numbers. Then they receive their conventional names, till 1701, when the use of numbers reappears.[1]

The close of the century shows a somewhat melancholy contrast between Penn the founder and the beneficent ruler of a Utopia free from the corruptions of the Old World and from the special dangers and temptations of the young communities around it, and Penn with limited and debateable powers over a community which was fast yielding to lowering influences and putting on moral and social habits not a whit better than those of the ordinary Englishman who had crossed the Atlantic. Within less than a year of his restoration we find Penn writing to the Council a strong protest against general laxity of life in the colony, and especially connivance with pirates and smugglers. The colonists, as Penn rather oddly put it, not only wink at pirates but embrace them. They violate the navigation laws, bringing goods from Holland and exporting their own produce to Scotland.

Penn's accusation of the colonists.[2]

---

[1] Records, vol. i. p. 380.
[2] Penn's letter and the reply of the colonists are in the Records, vol. i. p. 527.

A special committee of the Council was appointed
to deal with these charges. The existence of piracy
they denied. There might be smuggling. If
so it was due to the maladministration of the
revenue officers appointed by Randolph. They
admit, however, that the increase in the number of
ordinaries had brought with it laxity of morals.

The colonists deny the charge of piracy.

In the following year Penn revisited the colony.
His address to the Council shortly after his arrival
showed a characteristic tendency to take refuge in generalities. 'Away with all parties,
and look on yourself and what is good for the body
politic.'[2] A man who had enjoyed the opportunity of
observing political life for a quarter of a century might
have learnt that 'good' is a phrase patient of many interpretations, and that men embrace parties as an end to
what they believe to be good. That the departure of
Fletcher brought with it a certain restoration of Quaker
ascendancy may be inferred from the fact that the
numbers of the months now reappear instead of names.

Penn revisits the colony.[1]

Penn had not been in the colony long before he
found himself in pronounced opposition to the settlers
on what they deemed a fundamental article of
their common creed. A letter from the King
required from the settlers a payment of three
hundred and fifty pounds towards the fortification of New York. That a demand which
infringed the rights of self-taxation was unconstitutional, that one colony could not be expected to contribute money to be spent at the discretion of the
authorities in another colony, were pleas which would
have been wholly consonant with the political tradition
of the colonies. To protest against military expenditure

The Assembly refused to contribute to the fortifications of New York.[3]

[1] I cannot find any specific record of his arrival. But the Records
(vol. i. p. 506) show that on April 1, 1700, he was addressing the Council.
[2] Records, vol. i. p. 506.
[3] For this dispute see Proud, vol. i pp. 425 6.

of any sort would have been no more than consistent Quakerism demanded. The Assembly, however, took lower and less tenable ground, pleading their own poverty and the inaction of the neighbouring colonies.

Penn had reason to look with dread on anything which might bring the colony into conflict with the Crown. The mere territorial rights inherent in proprietorship which had just been restored to Penn might be secure. But, as we learn from a letter written by him to his son, there was reason to fear that the proprietary government would be dissolved and the colony brought into direct dependence on the Crown. To lose that would be, as Penn said, to lose everything that he valued. 'The land was but as the shell or ring, the government as the kernel or stone.'

<small>Penn's government in danger.</small>

The rights of the Crown, Penn pointed out, were fully secured as long as the King could veto the appointment of a Deputy-Governor. Proprietary governments had thriven better and more quickly than those dependent on the Crown. In support of this contention he cites the cases of New England and Rhode Island, neither of which ever had the semblance of a proprietary system. When one compares the fortunes of Maryland, Carolina and New Jersey with those of Virginia, Massachusetts and Connecticut, it is hard to say whether the general proposition or the selection of instance was the more daringly inaccurate.[1]

In February 1701 Penn announced to his colonists his intended departure. Statesmanlike regard for the public weal was in his case too strong for sectarian theories, and he sought to impress on the settlers the need for contributing to the common defence. The reply was a petition from the Assembly in twenty-one heads, all dealing

<small>Territorial dispute between Penn and the settlers.[2]</small>

---

[1] The letter is in the Archives, vol. vii. p. 11. It is dated 2.11.1700.

[2] For the whole of this dispute see Records, vol. ii. pp. 41–4.

with means for making the tenure of land by the colonists more secure. Of the main point urged by Penn, that of defence, it said nothing. When Penn became more urgent the Assembly answered that 'the country having been much straitened of late by the necessary payment of their debts and taxes, and as nothing appears what any of the other colonies who are equally concerned have done in the like demands on them, they must for the present desire to be excused.'

It is clear from the general tenour of the petition above referred to that the Proprietor and the colonists were becoming alienated by such grievances as always arise in the case of an absentee landholder. His expenditure in the past is forgotten. All that is remembered is the contrast between those whose labour is building up a fabric of prosperity and the man who contributes nothing and enjoys 'unearned increment.' The settlers asked that a large part of the Proprietor's lands should be treated as common, that rents should be fixed once for all irrespective of increase or value, and that quit-rents may be extinguished by a fixed payment. One clause in the petition suggests, though the matter is open to doubt, that the existing occupiers of land were asking to be protected not against the demands of the Proprietor, but against the original grantees from whom Penn had acquired his rights. Land, the petitioners say, had been granted as a free gift for the foundation of the city of Philadelphia. It is now 'clogged with divers rents and reservations contrary to the first design and grant.'

The tone of Penn is curt and businesslike, dealing with the petition article by article. It clearly shows a sense of estrangement and of irritation at what he not unjustly regarded as ingratitude.

This was not the only matter embittering the Proprietor's visit. At no small trouble and cost to himself he had united his original colony and the Delaware Territories in a single government.[1] Now the inhabitants of the Territories were calling out for a repeal of that Union. The main grievance specified was this: the Assembly met alternately at Philadelphia and Newcastle. The representatives of the upper colony were now trying to put the meetings at Newcastle on a lower footing by demanding that all laws passed there should be ratified at Philadelphia. Theoretically each Assembly consisted of the whole body of colonists. Practically, we may be sure that the difficulties of travelling must have given a decided advantage to the locality in which the Assembly met. The demand for ratification was practically one for giving the Territories a subordinate legislature.

Demand of Delaware for separation.

Penn pointed out to the settlers that to effect the union of the provinces had cost him over two thousand pounds; that the English Government in its recent administrative arrangements had dealt with Pennsylvania and the Territories as one colony, and that the demand for separation would certainly prejudice the colony with the English Government. The colonists showed that pertinacity which was their most fixed and abiding characteristic in public affairs, and affirmed their desire for separation. Penn's answer is so characteristic as to be worth quoting in full. 'Your union is what I desire; but your peace and accommodating each other is what I most expect from you; the reputation of it is something, the reality much more. And I desire you to remember and observe what I say; yield in circumstantials to preserve essentials, and being safe in one another you will always be so in esteem with me. Make me not sad now I am going to leave you; sure

[1] Records, vol. ii. p. 49.

it is for you as well as for your Friend and Proprietary and Governor, William Penn.'[1]

The vagueness and suavity, the inability to see that 'essentials' often need to be defined and guarded by 'circumstantials,' are thoroughly characteristic of Penn. So, too, is the underlying conviction that political benefits cease to be benefits when they are forced upon men against their will and judgement.

Nor did the inevitable sense of disappointment make Penn backward in gratifying the reasonable require- ments of the settlers. That another formal exposition of the constitution should have been needed, shows not so much the imperfection of the previous instruments as the impossibility of giving a definite and final form to the political life of a young and plastic community, with ever-changing conditions and ever-growing needs. In 1700 the colonists had surrendered their charter. In the following October a fresh charter was granted, setting forth, this time finally, the constitution of the colony. Neither in the act of surrender nor in the conditions of the new instrument does there seem to have been any difference of opinion between the Proprietor and the legislature. The right of all to religious toleration and freedom of worship was set forth more formally than in previous instruments. There was, however, no modification of any importance in the constitutional arrangements. The mode of election was left as it was, and the con- dition which required a majority of six-sevenths for any constitutional alteration was retained. Two im- portant clauses, however, were left open for subsequent change. The government and Assembly might increase the number of representatives, and the Territories might withdraw and have an Assembly of their own.

The new constitu- tion.[2]

[1] The letter is in Proud, vol. i. p. 442.
[2] The text of the charter of 1701 is given in Proud, vol. i. p. 443.

Almost simultaneously with this instrument, the Proprietor granted a charter incorporating Philadelphia as a city, with Mayor, Aldermen and Common Council, nominated in the first instance by the Proprietor, but thereafter to be a self-electing body.

Charter granted to Philadelphia.[1]

Penn departed, never to behold his colony again. His declining years were clouded. His mental faculties soon showed signs of failure; impoverished and discredited as he was, his benevolence could find no fitting sphere of action. His eldest son was wayward and shallow, wholly unfitted to be the legatee of Penn's beneficent schemes. From the philosophic ruler, the creator of an ideal commonwealth, Penn passes into an ordinary absentee landholder. Yet even in Penn's decline, that which, if we may not call greatness, we at least call magnanimity, still abides. In his days of energy and hopefulness he had consistently regarded himself as a trustee, administering his property conscientiously and generously, for the public good. It is not every deposed sovereign who can contentedly accept the post of an acquiescent and benevolent onlooker, but neither disappointment nor ingratitude could force Penn into an attitude unworthy of his past.

Penn finally departs.

About this time we find Penn involved in a dispute with Quarry, the judge of Admiralty cases in New York and Pennsylvania. According to Penn, Quarry was without legal training. Moreover, he was in two ways personally interested. Being himself largely concerned in trade, he could not deal with cases impartially. His salary consisted of a royalty of one-third on the duties received, which acted as a direct inducement to extortion.

Penn's dispute with Quarry.

Quarry's answer was, if not evasive, at least incomplete. His ignorance of law he practically admitted.

[1] The charter is in Proud, appendix vi. vol. ii. p. 45.

That he was paid by a royalty of a third he denies. He could not, he said, be a great trader because he was undersold by smugglers from Curesaw (*sic*) and Scotland.

He retorts on Penn by a charge of corruption. A Danish ship had brought in a cargo of prohibited commodities worth three thousand pounds. Penn, so Quarry avers, waited till the cargo had been landed, and the ship stripped of tackle, sails and all fitting, and then made a show of zeal by seizing the bare hulk.[1]

At the same time the Privy Council were addressing certain questions to Penn which showed, if not hostility, at least suspicion. Did all persons in a judicial position take an oath, or if not make an affirmation? Were all persons who were willing to take an oath permitted to do so?[2]

How completely Penn's last visit had brought with it a sense of failure may be inferred from the fact that in 1703 he offered to resign to the Crown that proprietorship for which a short while before he had battled so strenuously, and of whose value he had spoken so highly.[3]

The career of Hamilton, the Governor whom Penn had placed at the head of affairs when he left the colony, *Andrew Hamilton, Governor.* was in a little more than a year cut short by death. He did not, however, escape the experience, common to almost every Governor of Pennsylvania, of an unsuccessful attempt to induce the settlers to assist the neighbouring colonies in the task of defence.[4]

His death was followed by an interregnum of a year. During that time the two sections of the colony availed *An interregnum.* themselves of the right given them by the last charter and formed separate representative Assemblies.[5]

---

[1] Penn's complaint and Quarry's answer are among the Pennsylvania Papers in the Record Office. Pennsylvania, 559.
[2] *Ib.*   [3] *Ib.*   [4] Records, vol. ii. p. 79.
[5] Proud, vol. i. pp. 452–57.

Penn's wide experience of the world had not, if we may judge by his choice of subordinates, endowed him with the gift of insight into character. His appointment of Blackwell was far from fortunate, and he fared even worse in his selection of a successor to Hamilton. His choice fell on John Evans, a Welshman, without, as far as our records show, any experience of colonial life.

<small>Appointment of Evans as Governor.</small>

Evans's career as Governor was but one series of squabbles with the Assembly. At the very outset he made an unsuccessful attempt to induce the settlers to reverse the arrangement just arrived at for separation. Resistance came, we are told, not, as we would expect, from the weaker partner, but from the inhabitants of the upper province, who could no longer endure the fractiousness of their colleagues from the Territories.

One of the points of dispute between Evans and the Assembly was the standing question of military defence. Evans expected the Assembly to bear their share with the neighbouring colonies. That he should meet with refusal was a matter of course. He then made an acrimonious attack, accusing the settlers of gross ingratitude in raising unnecessary disputes, and in not raising money for the expenses of the government or the collective defence of the colonies.

<small>Dispute between Evans and the Assembly.[1]</small>

The answer of the Assembly was temperate in tone. It was unfair of Evans to argue as if the Proprietor had done everything and they nothing. Many of them had settled at considerable cost and with much effort. Evans replied with a general denunciation of the Assembly as disaffected.

At the same time there were other disputes touching the relations between the Assembly and the executive. The Governor claimed the right of pro-

[1] These disputes are all very fully set forth in the Archives of the colony.

roguing or dissolving the Assembly. The Representatives contended that the right was in them.[1] As a compromise, however, they were willing to limit any session to twenty days, unless specially extended by the Governor's permission, and to accept the further restriction that they might not meet again within three months. They also claimed and obtained the right to judge of their own qualifications and the validity of their own elections. Other disputes there were, all illustrating Evans's lack of judgement and tact. Wishing for a conference with the Assembly he insisted on meeting the whole body, in spite of their desire to be represented by a committee. In all likelihood both parties felt that a committee would be a more effective fighting body. He prosecuted a member for language used in the Assembly, and then followed up this breach of privilege by arbitrarily demanding his expulsion. On one occasion the speaker addressed the Governor sitting instead of standing, and this breach of etiquette was treated by Evans as a serious offence. When the Assembly demanded that judges should be removable at their pleasure Evans objected. His objection was no doubt in conformity with English political principles. But it was a shallow piece of sophistry to charge the Assembly with hindering justice by their refusal to give way. On that ground concession might as well have been demanded from the Governor.

Trifling and paltry though these disputes might be in themselves, they were far from unimportant in their consequences. For good or evil, they were part of the political education of the colony. Just at the time when it was taking definite shape as a body politic it was forced into certain tendencies of thought and conduct. A bent was given to the tree which grew with its growth, greatly influencing its character and deter-

[1] See Logan to Penn, 22.9.1704. Archives, vol. vii.

mining the part which it should play half a century later. Indeed, it is easy to see in these bickerings a foreshadowing of the later strife. The position of the judiciary was a burning question in the disputes which preceded independence. Moreover, the claim of the colonists to be exempt from all taxation save that imposed by their own Representatives, formed a part of the earlier dispute. The Assembly for the Territories, urged thereto it is said by Evans, imposed on all trading vessels not belonging to inhabitants of that district a duty of half a pound of gunpowder for every ton of freight, and the commander of the fort was ordered to fire on any vessel which refused to weigh anchor and submit to inspection. Evans's own private house was near Newcastle, and it is not unlikely that the dispute was embittered by a belief that he was acting as the supporter of the Territories.[1]

As so often in the later dispute, an alleged infraction of constitutional rights was met by open defiance.[2] A loaded vessel from Philadelphia ran under the guns of the fort and received a shot through her main-sail. French, the commander of the fort, then boarded her. While he was on board the owner of the vessel, who was himself navigating her, cut the painter of French's boat. Cornbury happened to be cruising about in Delaware Bay, and French was brought before him. It would be idle to speculate as to the motives which influenced such a man as Cornbury, in whose evil doing there was no touch of system or consistency. Acting apparently in his capacity of Vice-Admiral, he severely reprimanded French.

The opponents of the tax were not content with

[1] The fact of Evans having a plantation at Newcastle, and often residing there, is mentioned in the Records, vol. ii. p. 423.

[2] There is a very full and clear account of this in Proud, vol. i. pp. 471-5.

this measure of success. Hill, the owner of the vessel, petitioned the Assembly, and they, acting on the petition, drafted an address to the Governor. This document did not go into the abstract question of right. It took the ground that the settlers had under the charter a right to the free navigation of the river. At the same time the drafters of the protest at least suggested, if they did not explicitly assert, a claim to the right of self-taxation. 'How far they (the Representatives of the Territories) can be justified in making laws to raise money on the Queen's subjects in this government we intend shall be further considered hereafter.'

A like spirit shows itself in the answer which the Assembly gives to a manifesto drawn up by the Governor and Council. 'We cannot but observe how it borders upon an opinion that the privileges of the subject in the Plantations are merely dative and at the will of the Prince, which opinion had been formerly propagated in these parts though it had been theretofore as well as since exploded, and several authorities of law have been produced in this House to shew that the subjects coming into the Queen's Plantations abroad, have not the claim to their native English rights.' In that sentence we seem to hear a faint premonitory murmur of the storm which burst sixty years later.[1]

In February 1707, the Assembly extended its hostile action from the Governor to the Secretary, James Logan. He was both a political supporter and a personal friend of the Proprietor. The charges brought against Logan, and at least in large part admitted by him, show exactly that want of definite adhesion to sound political principles which was the besetting fault of Penn himself.

Attack by the Assembly on Logan.[2]

---

[1] Records, vol. ii. p. 293.
[2] For the impeachment of Logan see the Records, vol. ii.

Beside a general charge of illegal and arbitrary practices, six specific counts were preferred against Logan.

In drafting the commission for Evans, Logan had inserted two clauses contrary to the charter. One gave the Proprietor the right of veto; the other transferred the power of adjourning the Assembly from that body itself to the Governor. He had compelled tenants with a legal right to lands to take out patents for them; he had imposed illegal quit-rents, and when land had been granted in partnership he had apportioned it arbitrarily. He had combined in his own person the offices of Proprietor's Secretary and Surveyor-General, intended to act as a check on each other. He had concealed certain communications from the Crown. As a result the Assembly had sent home certain laws which were vetoed, but which with fuller knowledge they would have amended.

All these charges Logan admitted. To the last two he pleaded instructions received from certain members of the Assembly. In the other cases he defended himself on the ground that he had acted for the good of the colony, a plea quite in keeping with Penn's mode of thought.

The attack was frustrated by the Governor, who refused to admit the right of impeachment, regardless of the plea urged by the Assembly that against certain offences there was no other weapon.[1] Yet the vote of the Assembly was not a mere *brutum fulmen*. A formal vote of censure, even if followed by no penalty, acts as a restraint on the offender and a deterrent to others. It puts on record a formal and official opinion on a question of public policy.

Internal dissensions were not the only trouble under which the colony was suffering. In August 1708

[1] Records, vol. ii. p. 362.

Evans had to tell the Assembly that the rivers and capes of the colony were so beset with French vessels that navigation was impracticable.[1] The appeal was answered, as every such appeal was answered in the Assembly at Philadelphia for many a year to come. The Proprietor is the person who profits by the colony, and on him the burden of defence ought to fall. Evans pointed out that as a matter of fact the Proprietor was a loser by the colony. His plea was good in substance, but Evans according to his wont was needlessly prolix and needlessly contentious.

Further dispute between Governor and Assembly.

The question was complicated by a doubt as to the quarter in which naval authority was vested. Evans held that it was in Seymour, the Governor of Maryland, the Assembly that it was in Cornbury. There could hardly have been a stronger instance of the evil wrought by the absence of any effective central control acting within the different colonies.

Evans had a like conflict with the Assembly of the Territories sitting at Newcastle, and fared no better. When he called on them to make efforts for defence they raised technical points, questioning the authority of the Governor and inquiring what would be his position if war broke out.[2]

Dispute between Evans and the settlers at Newcastle.

The opponents of Evans were, however, but a bare majority, nine out of seventeen. After a division the defeated minority seceded.

There were rumours of danger more formidable to the general view of the settlers than the prospect of a French naval attack. French agents were intriguing among the Indians. During the summer of 1707, Evans thought it necessary to go himself into the Indian county, where he had a friendly interview with the Shawnees, Senecas, and

French intrigues with the Indians.

[1] Records, vol. ii. p. 414.   [2] Ib. pp. 362, 423.

others, and about the same time we find one Martin Chartier summoned to appear at Philadelphia and give an account of his dealings with the natives.[1]

In 1708 Penn superseded Evans. There is no evidence as to the special circumstances of his dismissal, but his endless disputes with the settlers present an ample explanation. His successor, Gookin, reached the colony in January 1709. There is nothing to show that he had any administrative experience to fit him for his post. His opening address to the Assembly was a vague exhortation to peace and goodwill, with a modest disclaimer of any knowledge of the constitution of the colony which he was sent to administer. His pacific counsels bore but little fruit. The Assembly, not satisfied with having got rid of Evans, drew up resolutions condemnatory of his conduct. In one of these his misdeeds were imputed to the influence of evil counsellors. The Council protested against this as a reflection on themselves, and the Assembly so far gave way as to explain that they only intended certain individuals, not the whole Council.

Gookin becomes Governor. His disputes with the Assembly.[2]

In the following June the ever-recurring difficulty about contributing to defence broke out again. Gookin asked for money for military purposes. The Assembly replied that their principles forbade such payments, but they would vote five hundred pounds for general purposes. Gookin represented that the authorities in England would be greatly dissatisfied with so meagre a contribution, and proposed a rate of fourpence, or at the outside of sixpence, in the pound. The Assembly stood firm and Gookin gave way.

Dispute about defence.[3]

[1] Records, vol. ii. pp. 385-90.
[2] *Ib.* p. 427. The Records are my authority for what follows.
[3] *Ib.* pp. 460, 482.

This dispute was speedily followed by a renewal of the attack on Logan. In a resolution passed by the Assembly in September 1709 he was denounced as an 'evil minister,' guilty of 'boundless insolence and scurrility,' and of 'attacking the Assembly with vile and wicked aspersions.' It is certain that there is nothing in Logan's extant letters to justify such charges.

The Assembly attacks Logan.[1]

His reply was temperate. He might, he says, answer specific charges, but those brought against him are 'an armament of general but scandalous calumnies.' For this reply the Assembly ordered Logan to be arrested. Gookin thereupon, abandoning his attitude of submission, ordered the High Sheriff to see that Logan was not molested.

In the following year the Assembly received a long and characteristic letter from the Proprietor.[2] He appeals to the settlers in temperate and often pathetic language against the ingratitude of their opposition. Their hostility to Logan is due to the fact that he has throughout studied the interests of the Proprietor. But nowhere in the letter does Penn fail to come to close quarters with the legal question, did the charter assign certain powers to the legislature or not?

Penn remonstrates with the settlers.

In 1710 a new Assembly came into being. Not a single member was re-elected.[3] This may have been in a measure due to some personal and temporary considerations of which the trace is lost. But it at least proves that the attacks on Penn and Logan did not represent the views of the majority of the settlers; and this is confirmed by the fact that at

Fresh Assembly elected.

---
[1] Records, vol. ii. p. 497.
[2] The letter is in Proud, vol. ii. p. 45.
[3] Proud states this, vol. ii. p. 53. His statement is confirmed by the Records.

the outset at least the relations of the new Assembly with both Gookin and Logan were harmonious.

Meanwhile troubles had been heaping themselves thick upon the Proprietor. It is clear from the letters which Penn received from Logan that his eldest son, Springett Penn, was giving trouble in the colony, partly by jealousy of the Proprietor's second family. 'I have had some difficulty to carry even between my duty to thee and my regard to him, but I hope I have not quite miscarried. . . . He has much good nature, wants not very good sense, but is unhappy by indiscretion.'[2]

<small>Penn's difficulties.[1]</small>

But of all Penn's troubles the worst probably were those which resulted from the gross dishonesty of his steward, Ford. So transparent and shameless were the devices whereby he swindled Penn that it is difficult not to think that he had acquired some hold over Penn, possibly by knowledge of political secrets. This view is confirmed when we read of his extracting a certain document from Penn 'by threats.' He falsified accounts. He held over money of Penn's which he had in hand, while he was actually at the same time meeting payments on Penn's behalf by advances from his own pocket at compound interest. Finally he induced Penn to mortgage to him his colonial property and then re-let it to Penn as his tenant, claiming at the same time that the mortgage carried with it a transfer of political rights.

Soon after this Ford died. Thereupon his widow and son claimed the property, and arrested Penn for an alleged debt of three thousand pounds.

At this stage Penn's friends seem to have inter-

---

[1] All these troubles which befell Penn are set forth in Mr. Shepherd's monograph above referred to.

[2] Logan to Penn, 22, ix. 1704. Pennsylvania Archives, vol. vii. p. 11.

vened. They arranged to pay off Ford's representatives, and to transfer the mortgage to certain friendly parties who would act as trustees for Penn.

In reality this necessity to mortgage may have been in one way a blessing in disguise. In 1717 the Earl of Sunderland petitioned to have the Territories assigned to him in quittance of a sum of money due to him from the Crown. His plea was that when the Duke of York assigned the Territories to Penn he himself had no legal right to the Territories. Moreover, the grant was charged with a condition that Penn should pay half his profits to the Crown, and that condition had not been fulfilled.

It was further set forth that Baltimore had in 1683 challenged Penn's right to the Territories. Apparently Sunderland's policy was to use Baltimore's claim as a means of overthrowing Penn's, and then argue that Baltimore's title had become null and void. The law officers of the Crown advised in the case. They reported that to cancel Penn's grant would be unfair to the mortgagees. He must, however, comply with the conditions of the grant and make over half the profits to the Crown.[1] Again Penn offered to make that very sacrifice against which he had before protested so strongly, and to arrange for the surrender of his colony to the Crown. That arrangement was prevented by a stroke of paralysis or apoplexy which left Penn incapacitated. It might have been well for Pennsylvania and for the whole body of American colonists if the surrender had taken place. The tenets and temper of the settlers would probably have made it impossible in any case for Pennsylvania to come into line and take her place effectively in a connected scheme for colonial defence against France.

[1] For the whole of this transaction see Colonial Papers, Pennsylvania 559, under the year 1717.

But the continuation of the proprietary government gave the settlers at once a motive and a weapon in their attitude of factious independence.

Penn died in 1718. During the later years of his life the prostration of his faculties had prevented him from taking any part in the affairs of the province. Henceforth the settlers could assert those claims of self-government without any show of personal ingratitude to their founder.

In 1715 strife again broke out. In February of that year the Assembly submitted to the Governor and Council certain bills for the establishment of a complete judicial system. These, as it would seem, were approved of and even desired by the Governor. But there was with them a bill for providing funds for the support of government by means of import duties. To this Gookin objected, pleading that the amount was inadequate, that there was no fixity about the duties, and that they would be unpopular with the general body of settlers. On these grounds Gookin refused his assent to the other bills till this one was amended. After some wrangling the Assembly accepted his view in part, increasing the duty and supplementing it by a land tax.

Dispute about taxation.[1]

The conflict was renewed the next year on different grounds. Some portion of Gookin's conduct was such as to make one believe that rumours of mental aberration were well founded.[3] He charged both Logan and the Mayor of Philadelphia, who was likewise the Speaker of the Assembly, with disaffection to the Crown. They had both, he said, wanted him to proclaim the Pretender. When

Further disputes between Gookin and the Assembly.[2]

---

[1] Records, vol. ii. p. 507.
[2] The Protest of the Assembly is given in full by Proud, vol. ii. pp. 74-93.
[3] This rumour is mentioned in the *Memorial History*, vol. v. p. 211.

the Assembly appointed a committee to inquire into this strange charge, Gookin refused to furnish them with any information. The committee reported that the charges were unfounded. They also retaliated against Gookin with a strange accusation. He had, they said, taken part with a notorious public criminal by granting a *nolle prosequi* in the case of one Lowder who had attempted to murder the Speaker.

This was followed by a somewhat curious and intricate dispute on a question of constitutional law. In the first year of the reign of George I. the law governing oaths and declarations was altered.

<small>Question about oaths.[1]</small>

The first Act on the subject which affected the Quaker colonies was that passed in 1696. This provided that while Quakers might for certain civil purposes substitute a declaration for an oath, yet that no Quaker or reputed Quaker might by virtue of this Act give evidence in a criminal case, serve on a jury, or hold any office or place of profit under the Crown.[2]

No exception was made in favour of the colonies. There seems, however, to have been an understanding that the last-named disqualification should not apply to an official appointed not by the Crown, but by a colonial Proprietor or Proprietors.

This Act was originally passed in 1696, to expire in 1704. In 1701, however, it was re-enacted, to be in force for a further period of eleven years from that date.[3]

In 1711 the Act was confirmed and amended by the added provision that a declaration made in the place of an oath must be supported by the oath of two witnesses who should swear that the person making the declaration was a Quaker.[4]

---

[1] Records, vol. ii. pp. 614-6.
[2] 7 and 8 Wm. III. c. 34.
[3] 13 Wm. III. c. 4.
[4] 10 Anne, c. ii.

In 1714 the statute of William III. was re-enacted.[1] The Act of Anne was not explicitly repealed, but the provisions of the new Act practically dispensed with the need for witnesses. The new Act further specified that so much of it as related to Quakers should be extended to Scotland and the colonies. In all likelihood this was only intended to apply to what one might call the beneficent clauses of the Act. It was, however, held that it also applied to the disqualifying clauses, and that under it no Quaker was eligible for office.

Hitherto the various changes in the laws were a matter of indifference to the Quakers in Pennsylvania. Now however a question arose, Did the colonies pass again under the operation of their own laws on the subject, or did the provision which extended the Act of Anne to the colonies operate so as to bring them under the new statute? To the settlers in Pennsylvania the question was one of great importance. Gookin took the view hostile to the claim of the settlers. This view was combated in a long and able protest issued by the Assembly.[2] Their pleading was at once dexterous and fair. They pointed out that in a community which had from the outset been essentially Quaker, the application of the Act would be a serious hindrance to the administration of justice.

They were also able to quote the authority of Hunter. He, with characteristic ingenuity in discovering a conciliatory interpretation, had ruled that although the Act said that no Quaker should be qualified, yet it did not prevent a Quaker from becoming qualified by some special indulgence. This assertion of the right of any colonial authority whether Governor or legislator to interpret an Act of Parliament might carry with it far-reaching and perilous consequences.

[1] 1 George I. 2, c. 6.
[2] Given in full by Proud, vol. ii. pp. 74-93.

The Assembly in their protest urged with reason that if Hunter adopted a lenient interpretation all the more should Gookin, who as Penn's deputy was under special obligations to consider the interests of Quakers.

They were also able in support of their view to quote the authority of the Chief Justice of New Jersey, and what was even a stronger point, an instruction issued by the King immediately after his accession to Hunter, as Governor of New Jersey. This provided that Quakers might be members of the Council or the Assembly, or hold any office of trust and profit, and might make a declaration instead of taking an oath.

Gookin seems to have accepted the plea of the colonists. In the following year he announced to the Assembly his impending departure and received a present of two hundred pounds, a fact which in itself raises a strong presumption of his surrender.

The disappearance of Penn from the field of colonial politics practically coincides with the accession of the House of Hanover. As in the case of the other colonies we may regard that as a convenient landmark, at which to alter our course and to take a more connected and comprehensive view of what was now a continuous territory, and potentially, though far from actually, an organic political body.

APPENDICES.

APPENDIX I. (p. 13).

THE following is the monument to Peter Heyn in the old church at Delft :—

Deo Opt. Max. Et Aeternae Memoriae
Sacrum, lugete, foederati Mortuum, quem praeclara in
Remp. Hanc merita non sinunt esse mortalem.
Petrus Heinius. Architalassus Brasiliae, mari
Mexicano, Lusitanis, Morinis, fatale nomen, hic jacet
cui fortitudo Mortem, Mors vitam dedit.
Delphorum Portu sub septentrione editus, natalis soli
Famam, Reportatis portu Matancae, ad Occidentem opimis
spoliis, gemino orbi intulit, parentum humilem sortem animi
magnitudine, et rerum gestarum Gloria transcendens, non
nasci semper Heroes docuit, sed audendo fieri, per inelucta-
-biles fortunae terra marique casus numinis favore eluctatus,
Indiam, Hispaniam, Flandriam, captivitatis suae mox
libertatis ac Victoriae testes habuit, sine temeritate intrepidus,
sine fastu magnanimus, disciplinae navalis tenax non
sine severitate, ut obsequii primum omnis patiens.
Sic imperii postmodum omnis capax.
Anno CIƆ. IƆC. XXIV. Praefecti vicem gerens, urbem
Salvatoris in Brasilia inter primos exscendens, Lusitanis
ereptvm ivit. A°. CIƆ. IƆC. XXVII. Classi praefectus
naves hostium sex et viginti, sub eiusdem urbis moenibus,
Stupendo facinore expugnavit, diripuit, exussit : alias in-
super tres, incredibili ausu, ad Maream insulam aggressus,
praemia Belli spectante hoste abduxit. A°. CIƆ. IƆC. XXVIII.
Classem navium viginti, auro, argento, mercibusque
pretiosissimis gravem, at Cube littora felici occursu offendens,

feliciore Marte superavit, et novus Argonauta, e nova
novi orbis Colchide, aureum Hispaniarum Regis vellus,
Principibus Europaeis formidabile, non in Graeciam sed
foederatorum terras, nullo hactenus exemplo, trans-
vexit et societati Occidentalis Indiae immensas
opes, Hispano inopiam, Patriae suae robur, sibi
Immortale decus paravit.
Tandem.
Maris Praefecturam quam foris meruerat, domi adeptus
dum navali praelio cum Morinis decernit, navium hostium-
que post cruentam pugnam victor, ipse machina maiore
ictus, fatalem metam, sine metu gloriose adivit.
Eius Famae virtutisque ergo,
Ex Ill. et praep. ordinum decreto rei maritimae praefecti
Senatores.
Mon. Hoc Pos.
Vixit Annos li Mens. VI. Dies XXIII.
TO · MEN · ΘANEIN · OYK · AIΣXPON · AΛΛ' · AIΣXPΩΣ · ΘANEIN

I am indebted for the text of this to Mr. G. A. Mounsey,
of the British Foreign Office.

APPENDICES II. AND III. (pp. 346 and 358).

I AM sorry to say that I mislaid my references for the statements made here. I had hoped to recover them in time to
place them in an Appendix, but failed to do so. I must
therefore ask my readers to take them on trust.

APPENDIX IV. (p. 375).

THESE special privileges are recorded in the New Jersey
Archives, vol. i. p. 88.

APPENDIX V. (p. 514).

THE authority for this statement is apparently Gabriel Thomas. His account of the matter is not very lucid. His words are: 'Now for these lots of land in city and country, and their first advancement since they were first laid out, which was within the compass of about twelve years, that which might have been bought for fifteen or eighteen shillings was sold for four score pounds in ready silver and some other lots that might have been the purchase of three pounds within the space of two years were sold for a hundred pounds a piece and I believe some land that lies near the city that sixteen years ago might have been purchased for six or eight pounds, the hundred acres cannot now be bought under a hundred and fifty or two hundred pounds.'

INDEX.

ADD

ADDERLY, Henry, 328
Adriaensen, Marvyn, 28
Albany, 145, 206, 230, 262-3, 292, 307-8, 314; name given, 136; changed to Willelmstadt, 176; charter of, 213; convention at, in 1689, 251; conference at, in 1693, 300; in 1694, 301
Algonquin Indians, 219
Allen, John, 180
Allerton, Isaac, 102
Alrichs, Jacob, 87-90
Alrichs, Peter, 176-7
Altona, Fort, 86
Amersfort, 44, 45, 46
Amsterdam, voyages from, 4
Amsterdam Company, 9
Amsterdam Fort, condition of, 123
Andros, 120, 187-9, 190-2, 197, 238, 240; dealings with New England, 193; replaces Dongan, 234; dealings with New Jersey, 380, 425-7; dispute with Philip Carteret, 392-6
Anne, Fort, 152
Annie's Hook, 101
Aquednek, 447
Archangel, the frigate, 271-5
Assize, Court of, on Long Island, 136
Atwood, Chief Justice in New York, 330

BALTIMORE, Lord, his patent, 106; his claim against Pennsylvania, 548
Bankes, John, 180
Barclay, John, 403

BUR

Barclay, of Ury, 403
Barillon, 228, 231
Barneveldt, his colonial policy, 6
Barre, De la, 222, 224-9
Bass, 431-3, 436-7, 441, 448-60, 466, 467, 472
Baxter, George, 102-3
Bayard, Colonel, 238, 244, 259, 260, 272, 276, 309-11, 315, 327-8, 334
Beets (or Bates), 5
Bellomont, 283 n., 312, 324, 392; Cornbury's charges against, 331; dealings with New Jersey, 431-3
Bergen, 367, 376, 447; church at, 53
Berkeley, Sir John, 114, 158, 168-9, 184-5, 366-7, 418; grant to, 293
Berry, John, 375
Beverswyck, 38; church at, 53
Bikker, Grant, 83
Birckes, 176
Blackwell, John, 516-20; his instructions, 516-7
Bogardus, Pastor, 52
Bonrepos, De, 231
Bowne, Andrew, 538
Brahe, Peter, 78
Brainford, 161
Breda, treaty of, 149, 158
Breuckelen, 37, 44-6; church at, 53
Bridlington, *see* Burlington.
Brockholls, Anthony, 198-200, 418
Brodhead, Daniel, 145-6
Brooke, Chidley, 271, 292-3
Bruyas, French missionary, 225
Budd, Thomas, 445
Burghership in New Mountains, Greater, Lesser, 48

BUR

Burlington, 386, 412, 441, 459, 462, 471
Burrows, Edward, 365
Byllinge, Edward, 185, 378, 391, 422, 426, 475

CADARAQUI, see Cataraqui
Cadillac, 305
Callières, De, 316-7
Campbell, Neil, 416
Cantwell, Edmund, Sheriff of Newcastle, 380, 386 n.
Carignan regiment, 152
Carr, John, 174, 190
Carr, Sir Robert, 130, 133-5
Carteret, Sir George, 114, 158-62, 168-9, 184-5, 210, 366, 367, 418; grant to, 293; death of, 391-2
Carteret, James, 169, 373, 393
Carteret, Philip, 160, 169, 368, 370, 374, 378, 379, 382, 418-9; attacked by Andros, 394-5
Carteret, Lady, 418-9
Cartwright, 125-30, 133
Casimir, Fort, 80, 82
Cataracouy, see Cataraqui.
Cataraqui, 305, 321
Cayenguirayo, Indian name for Fletcher, 302, 311
Cayugas, 153, 221-3, 305, 311, 318
Chamberlain, his scheme for a land bank, 445
Champigny, De, 229, 297 n.
Champlain, Lake, 152
Charter of Liberties in New York, 207
Chartier, Martin, 545
Chazy, De, 156
Chinese in Netherlands, 130
Christina, fort at, 74-7
Christina, Queen, 74-5
Church of England in New York, 215, 288
Clarendon, Lord, 216
Clayborne, sea-captain, 179
Cohansick, see Cohanzey
Cohanzey, 380, 441
Colbert, 151
Colden, Cadwallader, 283 n., 303
Coleman, Henry, 170
Collier, John, 380
Colve, Anthony, 176-80, 187-9
Conestago, 292

ERI

Connecticut, 110, 178-81, 184, 193, 211, 216, 254, 267, 292-5, 302, 308, 367
Corlaer, 224-5, 229
Cornbury, Lord, 283 n., 310, 321 331, 544, et passim; his Indian policy, 330; his misconduct, 336-342; in New Jersey, 448
Cortland, Van, 238, 241, 246, 259, 265, 272
Courcelles, De, 155, 239
Coventry, Sir William, 114
Coxe, Daniel, 426
Curtius, Alexander, 60
Cuyler, Henry, 243

DARIEN, 404, 413
Decanisora, 303
Decker, De, 132-3
De Lancey, 311
Delaware, 535; granted to Penn 497, 507
Dellius, Dr., 254, 309, 315
Denonville, 226, 228-9, 239, 303
De Vries, David, 20-2, 27, 51, 72
Dionondadies, 300, 304-5
Director in New Netherlands 19
Donck, Adrian von der, 100
Dongan, Thomas, 120, 202, 214, 223, 224, 227, 290, 320, 419, et passim; his anti-French policy, 216; is recalled, 234
Dort, Synod of, 177
Doughty, Francis, 100
Downing, George, 122
Dudley, Joseph, 276, 428
Duke's, Laws, 141
Dutch as colonists, 1
Dyer, William, 199

EASTHAMPTON 166, 167, 178, 205, 206
East India Company, Dutch, 7, 11; its monopoly of trade, 18
Eelkens, Jaques 21
Effingham, Lord, 223
Eight, Council of, 28
Elizabeth Town, 162, 176, 293, 367, 373, 375, 377
Elsenburg, 77
Enchuysen, voyages from, 4
Erie, Lake, 219, 225

INDEX.   559

Esopus, 133, 206
Evans, John, 537–45
Evertsen, Cornelis, 175

FENWICK, John, 185, 363, 378–81, 383, 386–7, 422, 475
Finns in New Jersey, 160
Five Nations, 151, 155, 219, 223, 224, 226, 228, 262, 295, 300–4, 308, 318, 330, 354; relations with New Netherlands, 67; make over their territory to the English, 321. *See also* Cayugas, Mohawks, Oneidas, Onondagas, Senecas
Fletcher, Colonel Benjamin, 289, *et passim*; appointed Governor of New York, 287; his instructions, 288; his ecclesiastical policy, 290; dealings with the Five Nations, 300; his misdeeds, 308–11; becomes Governor of Pennsylvania, 522; dispute with Penn, 523–4; at Philadelphia, 524; dispute with Assembly of Pennsylvania, 525–6
Fletcher of Saltoun, 403
Flushing, New York, 44, 101, 165
Ford, Penn's steward, 547
Fox, George, 365
Freehold, New Jersey, Scotch church at, 447
French and the Five Nations, 295–297; torture a Mohawk prisoner, 304
French, Philip, 334
Frontenac, Count, 218–20, 222, 225, 239, 260–2, 297, 300–3, 306–7; death of, 316
Frontenac, Fort, 225–8, 355

GARAKANTHIE, 221
Gilbert, Sir Humfrey, 5
Gookin, 545–52
Gordon, a politician in New Jersey, 455, 464
Gothenburg, New, 77
Gouverneur, Abraham, 314
Graham, James, Attorney-General in New York, 316, 392
Grande Gueule, 224–5
Grangula, *see* Grande Gueule
Gravesand, *see* Gravesend

Gravesend, Long Island, 36, 44, 101, 105; convention at, 129
Guildford, 193
Gustavus Adolphus, 71

HALL, Thomas, 102
Hamilton, Andrew, 416, 427, 430, 431, 436–8; Governor of Pennsylvania, 538; his death, 454
Hampton, John, 337
Hartford, disputes at, between Dutch and English, 99
Heathcote, Caleb, 311
Heemstede, 45, 101, 163, 165; convention at, 137
Hempstead, *see* Heemstede
Hester, ship, 432
Heyman, Albert, 147
Heyn, Peter, 12, 553
Hinoyossa, Alexander D', 90, 134, 135
Hopkins, Samuel, 173, 176, 376
Hudde, Andries, 79, 80
Hudson, Henry, 7
Hudson River, 8
Hues, Dr., 519
Huguenots in New Netherlands, 19; in New York, 209
Hunter, Colonel Robert, 283 *n.*, 345, 551–2, *et passim*; character of, 348; in New Jersey, 471–8
Huntington on Long Island, 166
Hurons, 154, 221, 222, 300
Hutchins, a tavern-keeper in New York, 328 *n.*
Hutchinson, Anne, 100

IBERVILLE, French admiral, 331
Indians in New Netherlands, 26; war with these, 29; legislation about, in New Jersey, 446; described by Penn, 509. *See* Five Nations, Algonquins, Hurons, &c.
Ingoldsby, Major Richard, 270, 276, 296, 469; arrival at New York, 271
Iroquois, *see* Five Nations

JAMAICA Bay, 125
Jamaica, Long Island, 165, 242 367; dispute at, 336

JAM

James Fort, 165
James II., *see* Duke of York
Jennings, Samuel, 422, 461, 462, 466
Jesuit missions, 295-6
Jews in New Netherlands, 19
Jogues, Father, 52, 93
Johnson, Thomas, 276
Johnstone, John, 415, 470
Joncaire, French missionary, 346
Jones, Sir William, 391
Juet, Robert, 7 *n.*

KEITH, George, 518-9
  Kieft, William, 22, *et passim*
Konigsmark, Count, 169

LABADISTS, 183
  La Chine, destruction of, 239
Lamberville, 228
La Salle, 216, 220
Laurie, Gawain, 378, 402-4, 409-411
Lawyers, Act against, in Pennsylvania, 514
Leisler, Jacob, 196, 314, 326, *et passim*; authorities for, 236; resists Ingoldsby, 272-5; submits, 276; his trial, *ib.*; sentenced to death, 278; executed, 282; effect of his rebellion, 283
Leisler, the younger, 326
Leonard, John, 438
Lewiston, 72
Livingstone, Robert, 229, 320, 325-327, 360
Lloyd, David, 516-9, 521, 527
Lodwick, Charles, 328 *n.*
Lodwyck, Colonel, 293-4
Logan, James, 542, 546-7
London, Bishop of, jurisdiction in New York, 288-9
Long Island, 206, 268; settlements on, 14; English settlements on, 242
Louis XIV., 228
Lovelace, Francis, 120, 164, 190, *et passim*
Lovelace, Lord, 343; in New Jersey, 469
Lovelace, Lady, 469
Lucas, Nicolas, 378
Lutherans in New Netherlands, 54
Luyck, 60

NEG

MAINTENON, Madame de, 263
  Manhattan, church at, 52
Manhattan Island, 9, 14
Manning, Captain John, 172-3, 189
Markham, William, 491, 503, 527-530
Martha's Vineyard, 206-7
Maryland, 22, 133; dispute with New Netherlands, 90, 107-8; raid from, on the Delaware, 170
Massachusetts, 179, 214, 216, 302
Matthews, Captain, 298
Mauritius River, 9
May, Jacobsen, 20
Mecklenburg, John of, 52
Mennonites, 92-5; attacked by Carr, 135
Meules, Intendant in Canada, 225
Michaelmas, 53
Michillimakinac, Indian fort at, 304
Middelburg, 44
Middletown, 307, 368, 370, 375, 401, 447, 554
Midwout, 44-6; church at, 53
Millborne, Jacob, 196, 275, 314; at Albany, 253-5; sentenced to death, 278; executed, 282
Millet, Father, a Jesuit, 260, 301, 307
Minuit, Peter, 20, 24, 70
M'Kemie, Francis, trial of, 337-9
Mohawks, 31, 151, 158, 221, 280, 297, 298, 301; dealings with the Dutch, 10
Mohicans, 26
Monseignat, official in Canada, 263
Montreal, 229
Moody, Lady Deborah, 36
Moore, Nicholas, 511
Morris, Lewis, 349, 435-8, 440, 447, 461, 465, 466

NANFAN, Colonel, 318, 324, 325, 334
Nantucket, 206-7
Nassau, Fort, on the Hudson, 9, 10, 14
Nassau, Fort, on the Delaware, 14, 74; seized by Marylanders, 21
Negro plot to burn New York, 358, 359
Negroes in New Netherlands, 61

NEL

Nelson, John, 290-2, 295
New Amstel, foundation of, 88; surrender to the English, 134; name changed to Newcastle, 136
New Amsterdam, variety of languages at, 19; becomes a city, 38; education in, 96; outward appearance of, 96; name changed to New York, 136
Newark, N.J., 367, 373, 375
Newcastle, 170, 499, 535
New Haven, 91, 111, 193, 367, 369
New Jersey, 159, 185, 210, 293-5, 302
New Jersey East, first constitution of, 407-11
New Netherlands, education in, 59; slavery in, 61; commerce of, 62; Anglicized, 98
New Rochelle, 101
Newtown, N.Y., 100, 105
New York Colony, ecclesiastical system in, 142, 195; religion in, 168; captured by the Dutch, 174; restored to England, 182; settlement of, after the Revolution, 285-7
New York City, name changed to Fort Orange, 176; incorporated, 210; charter of, 212
Nicholson, Francis, 238, 240, 246, 255-6, 271
Nicolls, Richard, 184-5, 190, 210, 293, 435, *et passim*; career and character, 120, 162-3; treatment of the Dutch, 144; Indian policy, 157
Nicolls, William, Councillor in New York, 272, 292, 340, 344.
Niewenhuysen, Van, 195
Nine, Council of, 35
Nottingham, Earl of, 268, 271
Noy, Peter de la, 275

OLIVER, Thomas, 423
Oneidas, 153, 221, 301
Onondagas, 224, 318
Onontio, 224, 225
Ontario, Lake, 226, 229
Orange County, New York, 314
Orange Fort, 14, 133; name changed to Albany, 136
Oswego, 321
Oxenstierna, 73

QUA

PALATINES, 360
Palmer, Captain, 230
Palmer, John, 418
Patrick, Captain, 100
Patroons, the, 16, 95
Pemaquid, 206
Penn, Springett, 548
Penn, William, 201, 283; abused by Leisler, 258; becomes a Proprietor in New Jersey, 378; remonstrates with Andros, 389-91; his character, 479-85; his form of government, 491-7; extension of his grant, 497; dealings with Indians, 503-4; dispute with Fletcher, 523-4; with the settlers, 533-6; with Quarry, 537-8; troubles of his latter years, 547; death of, 549
Pennsylvania, 292, 293, 308; grant of, 485; boundaries, 486; charter, 487-9; first Assembly in, 500; great body of laws, 501; second charter, 506-7; described by Penn, 509; constitutional changes in, 512-3; Indian alarm in, 515; piracy and smuggling, 531-2; third charter, 537
Perth Amboy, 411, 416, 431, 441, 444, 455, 459, 462, 471
Perth, Earl of, 402, 419
Philadelphia, foundation of, 502; growth of, 510, 514; incorporated as a city, 537
Philipse, Frederic, 238, 272
Pinhorne, William, 276
Piracy in Pennsylvania, 531-2
Piscataqua, 367, 370, 373, 375; Baptists at, 447
Piscataway, *see* Piscataqua
Popple, William, Secretary to Board of Trade, 356, 440, 510
Potherie, La, 304 *n*.
Prairie de la Madeleine, 267, 291, 355
Printz, John, 76, 82
Proud, history of Pennsylvania, 479

QUAKERISM as a power in politics, 364-6
Quakers in New Netherlands, 55-9; in New Jersey, 448; dispute about their right to hold office, 550-2

O O

INDEX.

QUA

Quarry, Colonel, 332, 455, 537-8
Queen's County, N.Y., 268

R EKENKAMMER, the, 32
Rensselaer, Nicolaus van, 195
Rensselaerwyck, 38, 206
Richardson, Samuel, 519
Riggs, John, 256
Rising, John, 81
Robinson, Sir Robert, 276
Rudyard, Thomas, 404
Ryswick, peace of, 308

S ALEM, N.J., 380, 386, 387, 459
Sandford, a Councillor in New Jersey, 473
Schaats, Dominie, 195
Schenectady, 154, 206, 230, 297, 307, 316; massacre at, 262, 280
Schute, Ewen, 83
Schuyler, John, 230, 267, 291, 295, 296, 301, 317
Schuyler, Peter, 254, 263, 325, 346, 347
Schuylkill, Swedish settlement on, 74
Scot, Euphemia, 415
Scot, George, of Pitlochie, 414-5
Scotch traders in New Netherlands, 19, 47
Scott, John, 112-5, 159
Senecas, 151-3, 221, 223, 305, 318
Seignelay, De, French colonial Minister, 226-9
Seymour, John, 544
Shackamaxon, 503
Shirley, Lord, 166
Shrewsbury, N.J., 367, 368, 370, 375, 401, 447, 554
Skene, John, 423
Slavery in New Netherlands, 61
Slechtenhart, Van, 38
Sloughter, Colonel, 285, 296; appointed Governor of New York, 270; his arrival delayed, 271; reaches New York, 275; his action as to Leisler's execution, 280-2, 287; death of, 287
Smit, Claus, 24
Smith, William, Chief Justice in New York, 316

VIE

Smith, William, of New York, the historian 238 *n*.
Smuggling in Pennsylvania, 531-2
Sonmans, agent in New Jersey, 456, 472
South Carolina, 332
Southampton, N.Y., 101, 166, 167, 178, 192
Southold, N.Y., 166, 178, 181, 192
Southwell, Sir Robert, 271 *n*.
Staten Island, 206, 210, 367, 417, 420, 455
Stuyvesant, Peter, appointed Director of New Netherlands, 33, *et passim*; his character, 33-4; dealings with Indians, 63-8; favours the English, 103; surrenders New Netherlands, 123-4
Sunderland, Earl of, 548
Swanendael, 15, 72
Swedes, 367-73; on the Delaware, attacked by Carr, 135; in New Jersey, 160
Swedish colonization, 68-72
Swedish colony destroyed by Stuyvesant, 83
Swedish Company, 73, 76
Sylvester, Nathaniel, 181

T ALBOT, Rev. John, 476
Talon, 151
Tatham, 428
Tawasentha, treaty of, 10
Territories, *see* Delaware
Tinicum, 77
Tracy, Marquis of, 152, 155, 156-7, 239
Trevor, Sir John, 294
Twelve, the, in New Netherlands, Twiller, Wouter Van, 20, 22

U NDERHILL, John, 29
Upland, 491
Usselinx, William, 5, 9, 20, 69-72
Utie, Colonel, 107
Utrecht, peace of, 354

V AUDREUIL, De, 342
Verhulst, William, 20
Vesey, a Jacobite, 476
Viele, Arnout, 224

WAA

WAALBOGHT, 15
   Waldenses in New Netherlands, 85
Wales, emigration from, to Pennsylvania, 498
Walloons in New Netherlands, 19
Weaver, Attorney-General in New York, 330
Werder, John, 192
West Chester, N.Y., 54, 100
Westminster, treaty of, 183
Whitehall, treaty of, 228
Willett, Thomas, 102
Willocks, a supporter of Hunter, 476

YOR

Wilmington, N.J., 74
Winthrop, John, Governor of Connecticut, 111, 125, 129
Winthrop, Fitz-John, 180, 266-8
Wodrow, 414
Woodbridge, 367, 372, 375
Wood Creek, expedition against, 345

YORK, Duke of, 215, 418, *et passim*; grant to, in 1664, 116; effects of his policy in New York, 285

www.ingramcontent.com/pod-product-compliance
Lightning Source LLC
Chambersburg PA
CBHW071712300426
44115CB00010B/1392